Intellectual Property, Entrepreneurship and Social Justice

ELGAR LAW AND ENTREPRENEURSHIP

Series Editors: Shubha Ghosh, *Vilas Associate and Professor of Law, Honorary Fellow and Associate Director, INSITE, University of Wisconsin School of Law* and Robin Paul Malloy, *E.I. White Chair and Distinguished Professor of Law and Director of the Center on Property, Citizenship and Social Entrepreneurism at Syracuse University, USA*

The primary goals of this series are two-fold. The first is to develop the theoretical foundation for law and entrepreneurship. As to this goal, central research questions involve but are not limited to developing an understanding of the various meanings of entrepreneurship. Although superficially associated with the creation of a profit-making business enterprise, the concept of entrepreneurship extends to any motivation and effort to create something new. What does it mean to create? In what sense is an enterprise or project new? Is creation a process or an instantaneous, unpredictable event? What are the channels of creativity and in what venues does it occur? Is creativity in art, science, and business a coherent whole or completely different exercises? These questions serve to define the contours of entrepreneurship and its relationship to law and legal institutions.

The second goal is to translate the theoretical understanding of law and entrepreneurship into concrete policy. At one level, this goal entails identifying key legal policy levers (taxation, property rights, competition policy, financial regulation, contract law) that structure and direct entrepreneurship. At a deeper level, the second goal mandates a detailed institutional analysis of successful and unsuccessful entrepreneurship activity. This deeper goal invites an inquiry into the definitions of success and its measures. These definitions and measures, in turn, provide a benchmark for accessing and defining implementable policies.

At its core, the Law and Entrepreneurship series examines the role of law and legal institutions in promoting and sustaining entrepreneurial activity.

Titles in the series include:

Creativity, Law and Entrepreneurship
Edited by Shubha Ghosh and Robin Paul Malloy

Entrepreneurship and Innovation in Evolving Economies
The Role of Law
Edited by Megan M. Carpenter

Comics Creativity and Law
Marc H. Greenberg

Intellectual Property, Entrepreneurship and Social Justice
From Swords to Ploughshares
Edited by Lateef Mtima

Intellectual Property, Entrepreneurship and Social Justice

From Swords to Ploughshares

Edited by
Lateef Mtima

Professor of Law, Howard University School of Law, USA

ELGAR LAW AND ENTREPRENEURSHIP

Cheltenham, UK • Northampton, MA, USA

© The Editor and Contributors Severally 2015

All rights reserved. No part of this publication may be reproduced, stored in a retrieval system or transmitted in any form or by any means, electronic, mechanical or photocopying, recording, or otherwise without the prior permission of the publisher.

Published by
Edward Elgar Publishing Limited
The Lypiatts
15 Lansdown Road
Cheltenham
Glos GL50 2JA
UK

Edward Elgar Publishing, Inc.
William Pratt House
9 Dewey Court
Northampton
Massachusetts 01060
USA

A catalogue record for this book
is available from the British Library

Library of Congress Control Number: 2014950970

This book is available electronically in the Elgaronline
Law subject collection
DOI 10.4337/9781783470259

ISBN 978 1 78347 024 2 (cased)
ISBN 978 1 78347 025 9 (eBook)

Typeset by Servis Filmsetting Ltd, Stockport, Cheshire
Printed and bound in Great Britain by T.J. International Ltd, Padstow

For Joseph and Primrose: the founts who inspire, the streams who replenish, and the rivers who guide.

Contents

List of contributors	ix
Acknowledgments	xvi
Prologue: A social activist's guide to intellectual property *Lateef Mtima*	xvii

1. An introduction to intellectual property social justice and entrepreneurship: Civil rights and economic empowerment for the 21st century 1
   Lateef Mtima

PART I ENTREPRENEURSHIP AND EMPOWERMENT

2. An entrepreneurship approach to achieving IP social justice 33
   John R. Whitman

3. Intellectual property as an essential 21st century business asset 64
   Valerie Rawlston Wilson

4. The colorblind marketplace? 76
   Shubha Ghosh

5. Public procurement's role in facilitating social justice, entrepreneurship and innovation in the global knowledge economy 95
   Danielle M. Conway

PART II EDUCATION AND ADVOCACY

6. Lawyers and innovation 119
   Rita S. Heimes

7. Intellectual property training and education for social justice 140
   Peter K. Yu

8. Intellectual property social justice in action: Public Interest Intellectual Property Advisors 163
   Michael Gollin, Pacyinz Lyfoung, Lateef Mtima and Connor McNulty

PART III ENGAGEMENT AND ACTIVISM

9. Worth more dead than alive: Join the NoCopyright Party and start killing copyrights for their own good — 191
   Ann McGeehan

10. I am my brother's keeper: How the crossroads of entrepreneurship, intellectual property and entertainment can be used to affect social justice — 209
    Loren E. Mulraine

11. Accentuate the positive, eliminate the negative: Intellectual property social justice and best practices for entrepreneurial economic development — 235
    Llewellyn Joseph Gibbons

PART IV COMMENCEMENT

12. From swords to ploughshares: Towards a unified theory of intellectual property social justice — 265
    Lateef Mtima

Index — 281

Contributors

Danielle M. Conway is the Michael J. Marks Distinguished Professor of Business Law and directs the University of Hawai'i Procurement Institute at the University of Hawai'i at Mānoa, William S. Richardson School of Law. She teaches in the areas of Intellectual Property Law; Licensing Intellectual Property; International Intellectual Property Law; Internet Law & Policy, and Government Contract Law. Named Outstanding Professor of the Year in 2003, and awarded the University of Hawai'i Regents' Medal for Excellence in Teaching in 2004, Professor Conway completed a 2006–07 Fulbright Senior Scholar post in Australia. In academic year 2007–08, Professor Conway held the Visiting E.K. Gubin Professor of Government Contract Law Chair at the George Washington University Law School; as well, she was selected as the 2008 Godfrey Visiting Scholar at the University of Maine School of Law. In 2008, Professor Conway was selected to hold a Chair-In-Law position at La Trobe University Faculty of Law & Management in Melbourne, Australia. She is an elected member of the American Law Institute, holds leadership positions in the American Bar Association's (ABA) Public Contract Law Section and State and Local Government Section, and is a member of the Plant Variety Protection Board. Professor Conway is the author or co-author of a treatise, books, book chapters, law review articles, and essays. She is Of Counsel at Alston, Hunt, Floyd & Ing in Honolulu, HI and is a Lieutenant Colonel in the U.S. Army Reserve.

Shubha Ghosh, Vilas Research Fellow and George Young Bascom Professor of Intellectual Property and Business Law, University of Wisconsin Law School, teaches and writes in the areas of IP, commercialization, and competition policy. One strand of his current research is on the emerging market for personalized medicine and the role of patents and social policy in shaping research, development, and marketing of personalized medicine products and services. He is the author of numerous articles, book chapters, and books, including Identity, Invention, and the Culture of Personalized Medicine Patenting (Cambridge 2012 [hardback], 2013 [paper]).

Llewellyn Joseph Gibbons is a Professor of Law at the University of Toledo College of Law. Professor Gibbons is actively involved with law reform issues and researching questions related to intellectual property and economic development. In 2013, he received the University of Toledo's Outstanding Research and Scholarship Award. He is an elected member of the American Law Institute (ALI) and a Fellow of the American Bar Foundation. In spring 2006 and again in spring 2007, Professor Gibbons was honored to be selected as a Fulbright Scholar. He was assigned to Zhongnan University of Economics and Law (ZUEL) in Wuhan China. Zhongnan University of Economics and Law is the home of the "national center" for study of intellectual property rights.

Michael Gollin, Venable, LLP, U.S.A., is a patent attorney who has pioneered intellectual property strategies that help clients put their ideas to work. He chairs the Life Sciences group, and has more than two decades' experience in intellectual property law and related areas including technology transfer, food, drug, and cosmetics law, and environmental law. He focuses on strategic counseling and IP monetization. He builds teams that prosecute patents and trademarks, negotiate intellectual property agreements, and litigate patent, trademark, copyright and trade secret cases. Mr. Gollin is an adjunct professor at Georgetown University's McDonough School of Business, where he created the Strategic Management of Intellectual Property course. He is also an adjunct professor at Franklin Pierce Center for Intellectual Property at the University of New Hampshire School of Law, where he teaches Global Intellectual Property Management. In 2002, he launched Public Interest Intellectual Property Advisors (PIIPA), a pro bono service for developing country clients, with Venable support.

Rita S. Heimes is Counsel at the New England-based law firm Verrill Dana, where she focuses her practice on intellectual property, information privacy and cyber security law. She recently served as Associate Dean for Academic Affairs, Clinical Professor of Law, and Director of the Center for Law + Innovation at the University of Maine School of Law, where she remains a Senior Fellow. Rita's scholarship focuses on issues of intellectual property, economic development, and legal education. She has a BA in Journalism with honors and highest distinction from the University of Iowa and a JD with honors from Drake University Law School. She lives in Portland, Maine with her husband and two children.

Pacyinz Lyfoung currently serves as the Program Director for Public Interest Intellectual Property Advisors (PIIPA). Coming from the Hmong American refugee community, she has a lifelong commitment to social justice work. In her career path, she has explored different approaches to building stronger communities from legal aid to state policy to philanthropy to environmental protection to community-based health care. After spending the first part of her career on addressing U.S. issues, she went back to school to get an LLM in Global Health Law and International Institutions, which gave her the opportunity to spend time in Geneva, Switzerland and train with multilateral organizations such as the World Health Organization. At PIIPA, she is pleased to promote the use of IP legal tools and strategies to support developing countries' sustainable economic development and enhancing livelihoods, focusing on global health, food security, technology transfer for climate change and traditional knowledge. Furthermore, serving as the Co-Chair for the IP Law Interest Group of the American Society of International Law and the Co-Lead of the Community of Practice on IP under the World Bank's Global Forum on Law, Justice and Development, she hopes to further promote IP as a social change and anti-poverty legal tool and strategy. She has experience organizing and speaking at global events sponsored by multilateral organizations, such as the World Bank and the U.N.

Ann McGeehan is General Counsel for the NoCopyright Party, U.S.A. The NoCopyright Party is an organization that is committed to euthanizing (or killing) copyrights for their own good. Ms. McGeehan's expertise includes strategic management and monetization of global intellectual property (IP) portfolios for public and private corporations. Ms. McGeehan is General Counsel for HR Pharmaceuticals, Inc., whose brand products have successfully been marketed since 1925. Under her leadership as General Counsel, HR has achieved Pre-Amendment Status for HR® Lubricating Jelly™, Kosher certification from the Orthodox Union, and ISO 9001:2008 and ISO 13485:2003 certified for the design and manufacturing of HR® Lubricating Jelly™. She is Adjunct Professor at Georgetown Law where she teaches Intellectual Property and Computer Software. Ms. McGeehan previously worked at top tier law firms including Covington & Burling and Pillsbury Winthrop. Ms. McGeehan's scope of work bridges the life sciences, telemedicine, data and information technology sectors. She has acted as lead counsel for software security, defense and pharmaceuticals companies with extensive IP portfolios. She was appointed first General Counsel of Novavax, Inc. (NASDAQ), a clinical-stage biopharmaceutical company creating novel vaccines and vaccine adjuvants to address a broad range of infectious diseases worldwide, where she helped to steward the company's management through a successful NDA. She has also served as chief intellectual property counsel for biotechnology and healthcare companies through her work overseas. In her commitment to our global community, Ms. McGeehan was President of the American Club of the Costa del Sol, dedicated to aiding

American expats. Ms. McGeehan is passionate about her work with children's causes. She is past President and CEO of the National Association for Children of Alcoholics (NACoA), the nation's oldest 501(c)(3) organization whose mission is to eliminate the adverse impact of alcohol and drug use on families and children, with over 140 Affiliate organizations nationwide. A graduate of the University of Pennsylvania, Ms. McGeehan received her Bachelor of Arts in the Honors Program. She completed a Post-Graduate Diploma in the History of Art from the Courtauld Institute of Art in London (Somerset House), a Master's Degree with High Honors in English Literature from the University of London (Kings College) and Juris Doctor from the American University Washington College of Law in the District of Columbia.

Connor McNulty. In addition to volunteering with PIIPA, Connor McNulty is an analyst who works on agriculture and energy issues. He graduated from the University of Illinois at Urbana-Champaign with honors in 2010 and received his Master's from Georgetown University in 2012. Connor has written and presented on technology and security matters, and lives in Arlington, Virginia.

Lateef Mtima is a Professor of Law at the Howard University School of Law. He is the Founder and Director of the Institute for Intellectual Property and Social Justice, an accredited Non-Governmental Organization Member of the World Intellectual Property Organization (WIPO). After graduating with honors from Amherst College, Professor Mtima received his JD degree from Harvard Law School, where he was the co-founder and later editor-in-chief of the *Harvard BlackLetter Journal*. He is admitted to the New York and Pennsylvania bars and has practiced intellectual property, bankruptcy, and commercial law, including a decade in private practice with the international law firm of Coudert Brothers. Professor Mtima has held the post of Distinguished Libra Visiting Scholar in Residence at the University of Maine School of Law, and has served as President of the Giles S. Rich Inn of Court for the United States Court of Appeals for the Federal Circuit and on the Advisory Council for the United States Court of Federal Claims, and was a founding member of the Editorial Board for the American Bar Association intellectual property periodical *Landslide*.

Loren E. Mulraine, is a Professor of Law at the Belmont University College of Law. He received his BA from the University of Maryland, College Park and his JD from Howard University School of Law. While at Howard, Professor Mulraine was a merit scholar, earned the Dean's Excellence Award in Government Contracts and served as lead articles editor of the

Howard Law Journal. He began his legal career as a government contracts attorney with the Federal Aviation Administration in Washington, D.C. before relocating to Nashville to practice entertainment law. His legal clients have included Grammy, Dove and Stellar award winners, gold, platinum and multi-platinum selling artists, producers and songwriters, as well as filmmakers, independent labels and management companies. Before joining the law faculty at Belmont, Professor Mulraine taught for 14 years at Middle Tennessee State University, most recently serving as the Chair of the Department of Recording Industry. He served two non-consecutive terms as interim Associate Dean of the College of Mass Communication at MTSU and has also taught at Oakwood University in Huntsville, Alabama. Professor Mulraine has significant experience as a songwriter and independent gospel artist with four solo recordings, several group projects, and session work which includes the Grammy award-winning Andrae' Crouch project, *Tribute: The Songs of Andrae' Crouch.* Professor Mulraine is a member of The Recording Academy, Gospel Music Association, American Bar Association, National Bar Association, MEIEA, Leadership Music, Leadership Middle Tennessee and the Black Entertainment and Sports Lawyers Association.

John R. Whitman, is Visiting Assistant Professor of Entrepreneurship and Leadership and Interim Director of the Innovation, Commercialization, and Entrepreneurship Lab (ICE Lab) at the College of Business Administration of The University of Alabama in Huntsville. In addition to teaching he is building the entrepreneurial ecosystem in Huntsville, serves on small company boards, mentors start-up CEOs, and judges and coaches students in business plan competitions. Prior to moving to Huntsville in 2013 he taught at Northeastern University, Babson College, and Harvard University in Massachusetts and at Georgetown University and American University in Washington, D.C. Before teaching, Dr. Whitman founded and sold an international software company, consulted to business school deans in assessment and evaluation, and developed international environmental programs.

In addition to creating online courses at the graduate level, he developed a wiki Curriculum on Cooperatives funded by Equal Exchange, conducted research on the cooperative model under contract with the U.S. Overseas Cooperative Development Council, and was a member of the Board of Directors of the Hoya Federal Credit Union. John has served on the U.S. Research Team for the Global Entrepreneurship Monitor, published peer-reviewed articles in *Nonprofit Management & Leadership*, authored book chapters in textbooks on the social economy, entrepreneurship, and intellectual property law, and co-authored a peer-reviewed book, *Understanding the Social Economy of the United States* (University of Toronto Press, forthcoming), and a book on *Delivering Satisfaction and Service Quality in Libraries* (American Library Association, 2001).

Valerie Rawlston Wilson, PhD, is director of the Economic Policy Institute's Program on Race, Ethnicity, and the Economy (PREE), a nationally recognized source for expert reports and policy analyses on the economic condition of America's people of color. Prior to joining EPI, she was an economist and vice president of research at the National Urban League Policy Institute in Washington, D.C., where she was responsible for planning and directing the Policy Institute's research agenda. She has written extensively on various issues impacting economic inequality in the United States – including employment and training, income and wealth disparities, access to higher education and social insurance – and has also appeared in print, television, and radio media. In 2010, through the State Department's Bureau of International Information Programs, she was selected to deliver the keynote address at an event on Minority Economic Empowerment at the Nobel Peace Center in Oslo, Norway. In 2011, Wilson served on a National Academies Panel on Measuring and Collecting Pay Information from U.S. Employers by Gender, Race, and National Origin. Dr. Wilson received her PhD in Economics from the University of North Carolina at Chapel Hill.

Peter K. Yu holds the Kern Family Chair in Intellectual Property Law and is the founding director of the Intellectual Property Law Center at Drake University Law School. He has served as Wenlan Scholar Chair Professor at Zhongnan University of Economics and Law in Wuhan, China and a visiting professor of law at the University of Haifa, the University of Hong Kong, the University of Strasbourg and Washington and Lee University. Before joining Drake University, he founded the nationally renowned Intellectual Property & Communications Law Program at Michigan State University, at which he held faculty appointments in law, communication arts and sciences, and Asian studies. Born and raised in Hong Kong, Professor Yu is a leading expert in international intellectual property and communications law. He also writes and lectures extensively on international trade, international and comparative law, and the transition of the legal systems in China and Hong Kong. A prolific scholar and an award-winning teacher, he is the author or editor of six books and more than 100 law review articles and book chapters. He serves as the general editor of *The WIPO Journal* published by the World Intellectual Property Organization (WIPO) and chairs the Committee on International Intellectual Property of the American Branch of the International Law Association. Professor Yu has spoken at events organized by WIPO, the International Telecommunication Union, the UN Conference on Trade and Development (UNCTAD), the UN Educational, Scientific and Cultural Organization (UNESCO), the Chinese, EU and US governments and at leading research institutions from around the world. His lectures and presentations have spanned more than 25 countries on six continents. He is a frequent commentator in the national and international media. His publications have appeared in Chinese and English and have been translated into Arabic, French, Hausa, Japanese, Persian, Portuguese, Spanish and Vietnamese.

Acknowledgments

It is through the support of many that this book has come to fruition. The Law and Entrepreneurship Series Editors Shubha Ghosh and Robin Paul Malloy believed in the unique contribution that this work could add to the intellectual property law, policy, and scholarly discourse. I also appreciate the support of the book's editing team at Edward Elgar Publishing, Aisha Bushby, Alison Hornbeck, David Fairclough, and Alan Sturmer. Colleagues Ryan Holte, Diedre Keller, and Greg Vetter, and the commentators at the Drake Intellectual Property Center 2014 Intellectual Property Scholars Roundtable and the First Annual IP Mosaic Conference at Marquette University Law School, all provided invaluable comments on various drafts, and my "colleagues-in-arms" Steven Jamar and John Whitman lent their unique insights to the project throughout.

The comments of my fellow members of the bar Matthew Bryan, Aishsa Cassis, Candice Cook, Kasara Davidson, Mia Grandpre, and Brittany Lee-Richardson provided professional resonance; Sara Chandler, Gena Thomas, and Anaek Johal provided critical research; and Public Interest Intellectual Property Advisors and the Institute for Intellectual Property and Social Justice provided institutional support. Finally, I would like to thank Elaine Griffith, Nadia Griffith, and Tameka Simmons for their unwavering faith and devoted spirits.

Prologue: A social activist's guide to intellectual property

Lateef Mtima

This book is about using intellectual property, the most valuable natural resource of the information age, to build economic and political empowerment. To gain control over your intellectual property – the products of your mind, talent, and cultural traditions – is to gain control over resources that can give you the leverage to do business in the national and global marketplace on a level playing field.

Although today we encounter the term almost everywhere, for most people, "intellectual property" is still an arcane and intimidating phrase. Many people, communities, and developing nations have highly valuable intellectual property, but because they do not understand what they have, or how to protect and exploit it, they do not enjoy the benefits their property could bring. Moreover, we should know from history that even if you possess the most valuable treasure in the world, if you do not understand what you have, someone who does will take it away from you.

The purpose of this "IP Primer" is to de-mystify intellectual property and provide a succinct and plain language explanation of the subject. It has been written for the lay person – from the small business owner to the social activist, from the artist to the clergyman, from the student to the politician – for anyone seeking economic or social or political advancement for themselves or for their community. The basic concepts and principles of intellectual property are relatively easy to understand, and will likely be surprising as you discover how much intellectual property you already own.

INTELLECTUAL PROPERTY (IN FIVE PAGES OR LESS . . .)

There are four types of intellectual property generally recognized in the global marketplace: patents, copyrights, trade secrets, and trademarks. Some countries recognize a fifth kind of intellectual property, referred to as the right of publicity.[1] Each type of intellectual property has specific characteristics, and in some cases, certain administrative steps must be followed in order to protect it.[2] Once the necessary requirements have been satisfied, the owner of intellectual property acquires certain legal rights, which differ depending upon the type of intellectual property involved. The specific characteristics, administrative steps, and accompanying legal rights for each type of intellectual property are briefly summarized.

Trade Secrets

Trade secrets are the oldest form of intellectual property, dating back at least 4,000 years. A trade secret is any secret, valuable information used in a business, which provides an actual or potential competitive advantage. This can include business information such as customer lists, marketing strategies, and financial information, but it can also include secret cooking recipes, home remedies, hair care techniques, manufacturing processes, and secret formulas (like Coca-Cola). Unlike some other kinds of intellectual property, there is no special legal registration process to follow to protect a trade secret – all that is needed is that the owner take proper measures to keep the information secret, such as filing it in locked drawers or "restricted access" areas, or requiring your employees and others to sign confidentiality and "non-competition" agreements.

The owner of a trade secret is protected from misappropriation of her secret by others. A trade secret is misappropriated when someone obtains it by dishonest means, such as by stealing a document, or where the owner disclosed the secret in exchange for a promise that it would be kept secret and the promisor breaks her promise. On the other hand, if the information is made public by the owner, even by mistake, it loses its status as a trade secret. To defend against an action for trade secret misappropriation, a defendant can argue that the information was already generally known or that she obtained the information through honest means, such as through

---

[1] Among the countries that recognize right of publicity or personality rights are the United States, Australia, Canada, Cyprus, Denmark, France, Germany, Greece, Guernsey, Hong Kong, Jamaica, People's Republic of China, and Spain. *See e.g.* M. Thomas McCarthy, *The Rights of Publicity and Privacy 1-2.1* (2nd edn, West Group 2002).

[2] For information on how to protect your intellectual property *see* Sue A. Purvis, "The Fundamentals of Intellectual Property for the Entrepreneur", accessed 10 October 2014 at http://www.uspto.gov/about/offices/ous/121115.pdf; *see also* World Intellectual Property Organization, accessed 10 October 2014 at http://www.wipo.int/about-ip/en/index.html#ip.

independent research or "reverse engineering" (that is, buying a product and then analyzing it to discover its ingredients or chemical composition).

Patents

Patents protect useful innovations, commonly referred to as inventions, such as machines, chemical compounds, articles of manufacture (such as a pair of shoes), and also methods or processes for performing tasks or manufacturing products. Inventions, including improvements upon pre-existing technologies, are eligible for patent protection if they are *useful*, *new*, and *"non-obvious"*. To qualify for a patent all three of these requirements must be met.

For an invention to be considered useful it simply has to do something, such as a machine that grinds a substance into powder, or a chemical compound that helps you to sleep. To determine whether an invention is also new and non-obvious, it is necessary to look at those inventions which already exist, which is referred to as the "prior art". If the invention is already present in the prior art then it is not new. If the invention is a variation upon something in the prior art, while it might be "new" in the sense that no one has done it before, it might be considered "obvious", and therefore not patentable.

For example, if someone invents a machine that grinds peppercorns into powder, that invention would be useful, and if that grinding method is not already in the prior art, it will also be new and non-obvious. Afterwards, if another person designs a peppercorn grinding machine which works on the same principles as the first, and just adds a set of smaller grinding gears to produce a more fine powder, the resulting machine would be useful and arguably even "new", but the addition of the gears would likely be considered "obvious", and consequently this later machine would not be patentable.

In order to obtain a patent the inventor must follow a formal procedure referred to as "patent prosecution", which involves the preparation of a detailed application which describes the invention, how to make and use it, and states which of its features are claimed to be inventive. The application is filed with the patent office with the appropriate fees and the invention is considered to be "patent pending". If the invention satisfies the legal requirements, the patent office issues a patent, which generally lasts for 20 years.[3] A patent prevents others from making, using, selling,

---

[3] Patent prosecution can be lengthy and expensive; for this and other reasons, some inventors choose instead to protect their inventions as trade secrets.

or importing the invention, and unauthorized engagement in any of these acts constitutes patent infringement. To defend against patent infringement litigation, defendants can argue that their conduct does not fall within the scope of the inventive claims of the patent, or that the patent office erred in issuing the patent in the first place, and thus the patent is invalid and unenforceable.

Copyrights

Copyright protects *original, creative* expression, such as a story, song, or a drawing, once it becomes "fixed in a tangible medium", meaning put on paper, canvass, or film, for example. Under the copyright law, a work is considered "original" so long as it has not been copied from someone else; consequently two authors who unknowingly produce the same work would each have an "original" expression. The requirement that the work be "creative" is not an assessment of artistic merit or quality; almost any personal choice of wording, sounds, colors, materials, etc. will reflect at least minimal creativity and will satisfy this requirement.

Literary, dramatic, musical, and other artistic material are all examples of copyrightable expressive works. Other kinds of expressive works, such as educational and instructive materials, including newspaper articles, sermons, gospels, textbooks, recipe books, instruction manuals, and even computer software programs (which are essentially instruction manuals written for computers) are also copyrightable. Just as artistic works express or describe aesthetic ideas, these other works express or describe factual concepts or information, and copyright protects all kinds of creative expression whatever the subject. Whether the work is artistic or informational, however, copyright protection extends only to the author's individual expression (that is, her specific sentences) and not to the underlying idea or factual information embodied within the work. Thus for example, in a copyrighted novel about gunfighters in the Old West, the copyright covers the author's specific wording but not the idea of gun-fighting in the Old West; others are free to write their own Old West stories, so long as they tell them in their own words.

Unlike patents, copyright protection arises upon fixation of the expression without the need for formal registration. However, certain administrative steps, such as registering the work with the copyright office, are required before a copyright can be enforced in court. Also unlike patents, copyright registration is easy and inexpensive – typically the applicant simply fills out a registration form which describes the work and submits it with a nominal registration fee. Copyright generally lasts for the life of the author plus 70 years.

A copyright provides the copyright holder with certain "exclusive rights", meaning that no one is permitted to engage in these uses of the work without the author's permission. These exclusive rights include the right to make a copy or distribute copies of the work; perform or display the work in public; or prepare a derivative version of the work (such as making a sequel, or making a collage which includes a copyrighted photograph). Engagement in any of the exclusive rights without permission constitutes copyright infringement. To defend against copyright infringement a defendant can argue that the work is not copyrightable (that is, not original or creative) or that her conduct does not constitute engagement in any of the exclusive rights. In certain countries, including the United States, a defendant can also argue that she is permitted to engage in the author's exclusive rights under legal doctrines such as "fair use" or "fair dealing", which permit unauthorized uses for important public purposes, such as academic or journalistic uses.

Trademarks

Trademarks are words, symbols, colors, phrases, designs, sounds or combinations of these which are used to identify the source of goods or services, and to distinguish the goods and services of one seller from those sold by others. A trademark conveys an expectation of a certain quality (or lack thereof) of the goods or services produced by that source. A good example is the brand burnt by a cowboy to mark the cattle from a particular ranch.

A source identifier must be "distinctive" in order to qualify as a trademark, meaning that it must serve to identify and distinguish the source, as opposed to describing the product. For example, the word "banana" would not be distinctive for selling bananas, because it describes the product as opposed to identifying its source, whereas "Chiquita" is distinctive for selling bananas, as in "Chiquita Bananas", which identifies bananas which are sold by the Chiquita Company. Trademark law recognizes the following spectrum of distinctiveness, from the most distinctive (which receives the strongest trademark protection) down to no distinctiveness (which receives no trademark protection): *inherently distinctive or fanciful* (for instance, "Kodak", a term that was made up to identify the product source) or *arbitrary* (for instance, "Apple" for selling computers); *suggestive* (for instance, "Grameen," which means rural, for banking services for impoverished villagers in Bangladesh); *descriptive* (for instance, "Daily News" for newspapers), and finally *generic*, which applies to terms that have no distinctiveness and cannot serve as a trademarks (i.e., "banana" for bananas, "chair" for chairs, etc.)

Similar to copyrights, while it is not necessary to register a trademark, registration provides several important, sometimes even critical rights. For example, the first to register is generally entitled to the trademark. Registration is undertaken by submitting the trademark and specifying the goods or services with which it is associated (for example, Coca-Cola for soft drinks). If there is no prior and confusingly similar mark, the registration is granted, which lasts 10 years, but can be renewed, in theory, forever.

A trademark owner can prevent others from using confusingly similar marks in connection with similar products (such as the case involving the "Mixed Chicks" hair products for women of color, which is discussed in the next chapter). Indeed, registering a brand name as trademarks can provide a valuable business asset to both start-ups and major corporations alike. The problem of counterfeit goods provides a good example: same mark, same product, but false source, such as the fake "Rolex" watches sold on many street corners; unwary consumers recognize the brand name and are deceived into believing that they are purchasing the genuine article. Another example would be using "Rohlex" or "Ralex" to sell watches, which would also likely confuse consumers into believing that they are buying Rolex watches. In a trademark infringement suit the key issue weighed by the court is whether it is likely that consumers will be confused if the defendant is allowed to use the same or a similar mark.

To defend against a trademark infringement claim a defendant can argue that her mark is not confusingly similar to that of the trademark owner. Owners of famous trademarks can also prevent others from "diluting" their marks, by using them on other goods, even if there is no confusion. For example, the use of "Toyota" to sell breakfast cereal might be prevented under the dilution right, even though no one would be confused into thinking that the auto manufacturer had manufactured the cereal.

Publicity Rights

The right of publicity protects an individual from the unauthorized commercial use of her name, likeness, or other recognizable attributes. Obvious examples include the use of a person's name or photograph on a product or in an advertisement, but the right also precludes more creative or complex uses, such as the unauthorized creation and use of a college athlete's "avatar" in a computer video game. Similar to trade secrets, no government registration process is required to protect or enforce the right of publicity. To defend against an action for infringement upon publicity rights, a defendant can argue that her activity does not refer to the plaintiff. A defendant can also argue that her conduct is protected by the First

Amendment, such as when the defendant refers to the plaintiff in a newspaper story or a novel. In these cases, the court will have to balance these competing rights, which can make the outcome very difficult to predict.

Entrepreneurial Exploitation

The owner of intellectual property can exploit her property commercially, by distributing it directly to the public – for example, through a business on the Internet. However, many inventors and artists, especially those in historically marginalized communities and many developing nations, lack the resources to undertake commercial production and distribution of their intellectual property. Consequently they typically enter into agreements with entities that have such resources, such as recording companies and pharmaceutical corporations. Usually the IP owner will license the right to produce and distribute her intellectual property in exchange for a fee, typically a royalty paid on each item sold. For example, the inventor of a drug who does not have her own laboratory and manufacturing plant can obtain a patent for her drug and then license the right to make, use or sell the drug to a pharmaceutical corporation, which will then produce and sell the drug to the public and pay royalties to the patent owner.

Intellectual property owners can exploit their rights for personal gain, to support a progressive social agenda, or both. With a basic understanding of intellectual property principles, you can start or expand a business, enter into licensing agreements, protect important cultural knowledge and traditions, and advance other important economic, social, and political goals. For example, intellectual property rights can determine whether low-income communities will have affordable access to educational materials, or whether people in a developing nation will have affordable access to drugs and medicines. As you read the chapters in this book, you will learn about the many ways in which intellectual property affects, and can be used to affect, the quality of life for individuals, communities, and even entire nations.[4]

---

[4] *See* Michael Golin, *Driving Innovation: Intellectual Property Strategies For a Dynamic World* (Cambridge University Press, New York 2008), 131–46; John Whitman, *Education for the Social Economy, Business With A Difference* (University of Toronto Press, Toronto 2012), 243–49, 251–56.

1. An introduction to intellectual property social justice and entrepreneurship: Civil rights and economic empowerment for the 21st century

Lateef Mtima

For those with access, the Internet is the worldwide means for sharing information, expressing ideas, and doing business – and an accepted fact of modern life. From national governments to neighborhood councils, from renowned universities to grade school tutors, from multi-national mega-corporations to web-based home businesses, the Internet is a means of global communication and commerce made manifest.

Given the Internet's present day significance and ubiquity, most people would be surprised to learn that in the Internet's early history, a single company had virtually sole control of the process through which individuals, organizations, and corporations could obtain a place on the Internet. In 1992, Network Solutions, Inc. was the sole bidder on a grant offered by the National Science Foundation for the development of a domain name registration service system for the Internet. Then as now, a domain name is the Internet address for one's web page or presence and is the means by which one enters and is located in cyberspace. As amazing as it seems, for years, a single company – Network Solutions – actually controlled a near monopoly on the gateway to the Internet.

And that company was the entrepreneurial brainchild of two African American men.

The story of Network Solutions[1] is one that depicts the uneasy

---

[1] *The History of Network Solutions*, accessed 10 October 2014 at http://www.ultimatehostingreview.com/learn/networksolutions.html; *A Brief History of NSF and the Internet*, accessed 10 October 2014 at http://www.nsf.gov/news/news_summ.jsp?cntn_id=103050; Kent D. Stuckey, *Internet and Online Law*, Sec. 7.07 (Law Journal Press, New York 2013); *Issues Litigated Against Internet*

relationship that persists between historically marginalized groups and communities and the intellectual property regime. On the one hand it is an inspiring story of how two African Americans, Emmit J. McHenry and Tyrone Grigsby, acted upon McHenry's almost augural appreciation for the importance and potential of the Internet and its prospective impact upon intellectual property rights and commodities to build one of the pioneering business entities of the information age. At the same time, however, it is also the all too familiar story of how African American innovators were unable to obtain sufficient financial backing and other support from within either the black or white communities to sustain their beachhead in the Information New World. In order to meet the company's financial needs, McHenry and Grigsby often found it necessary to rely upon their two white partners to act as "front men" to negotiate with banks for business loans and to attract investors to participate in the company.[2]

Although McHenry, Grigsby and their partners helmed Network Solutions for several years, the continuing challenge of financing its operations eventually forced them to sell the company. Whether theirs is ultimately a story of success, however, depends upon one's viewpoint. In 1995, Network Solutions was sold for $4.8 million, an impressive return for two black entrepreneurs at that time. On the other hand, five years later, the purchaser resold the company for $21 *billion*. Today, many of the domain name registration functions over which Network Solutions had an early monopoly are administered by the Internet Corporation for Assigned Names and Numbers (ICANN).[3]

More than anything else, the story of Network Solutions is a modern allegory that illustrates the need for historically marginalized groups and developing nations to construct a new, propitious and more equitable relationship with the intellectual property legal and economic system. In the global information society, such groups and nations must expand their priorities to include the development, protection and commercial exploitation of intellectual property if they are to succeed in their struggles for social,

---

Corporation for Assigned Names and Numbers, 32 A.L.R. Fed 2d 561 (2013). For a general explanation of domain names see *Umbro International, Inc., v. Canada, Inc.*, 1999 WL 117760 (Va. Cir. Ct.).

[2] Gina Henderson, "debacle.com", *Emerge*, p. 136, May 2000; Lauren deLisa Coleman, "Black Founder of Internet Domain Name Registry, Network Solutions, Reminisces on Racial Barriers in Tech Sector", *The Grio*, 28 June 2012, accessed 10 October 2014 at http://thegrio.com/2012/06/28/black-founders-of-internet-domain-registry-network-solutions-reminisce-on-racial-barriers-in-tech-sector/.

[3] http://www.icann.org/en/about/welcome (accessed 10 October 2014); *Coalition for ICANN Transparency, Inc. v. VeriSign, Inc.*, 611 F.3d 495, 500 (9th Cir. Cal. 2010).

political and economic empowerment. Moreover, their intellectual property efforts and endeavors should be focused toward the digital information technology context and the concomitant prospects for socio-economic uplift. Digital information technological development and exploitation of intellectual property output presents unprecedented opportunities for socio-economic advancement and independence.[4] If these opportunities are not timely and effectively seized, however, historically marginalized groups and developing nations will find themselves once again shackled into the bottom caste of the emerging global socio-economic order.[5]

While historically marginalized groups and developing nations are working to enhance their intellectual property portfolios and expertise, notably assisted by important efforts to increase Internet access and facility for those who remain unconnected, they must also take the lead in advocating for a doctrinal shift in the predominant intellectual property legal regimes and concomitant protection, exploitation and enforcement policies. Whereas most Western intellectual property regimes have been systemically deployed to abet and perpetuate the economic subjugation of historically marginalized groups and developing nations, in the global information society, intellectual property law and protection can and should be used to promote socio-economic development, parity and self-determination. Indeed, a fact rarely explored by intellectual property scholars or policy makers is that the intellectual property status and interests of historically marginalized groups in the developed world are more closely aligned with those of developing world communities than they are with the status and interests of their fellow developed world citizens. If Western intellectual property regimes are to remain relevant and viable in the post-colonial global community, the Western intellectual property perspective must be shifted away from the parallax view of intellectual property disenfranchisement and refocused toward the enlightened vantage point of intellectual property social justice.[6]

---

[4] *See e.g.* Derek Slater and Patricia Wruuck, *We Are All Content Creators Now: Measuring Creativity and Innovation in the Digital Economy*, The Global Innovation Index 2012, 163. ("If the Internet were a sector, it would be larger than agriculture and utilities in many economies today. From 2004 to 2009, the Internet contributed 15% to GDP growth in the United States of America (USA) and on average 21% in mature economies studied by McKinsey Global Institute.")

[5] Anthony G. Wilhelm, *Digital Nation: toward an Inclusive Information Society*, 59–61, 68–74 (MIT Press, Cambridge, MA 2004).

[6] *See* Lateef Mtima, "Symposium: Intellectual Property and Social Justice", 48 How. L.J. 571 (2005); Seema Sirohi, "This Squeaky Wheel Needs No Oil", *The Hindu*, accessed 10 October 2014 at http://www.thehindu.com/opinion/op-ed/this-squeaky-wheel-needs-no-oil/article4843669.ece.

The reorientation of intellectual property law toward principles of social justice, coupled with the stimulation of beneficent intellectual property socio-economic enterprise in historically marginalized communities and developing nations, will engender a paradigm shift in the prevailing intellectual property ideologies. Indeed, equitable opportunity to benefit from the intellectual property system means far more than mere access to intellectual property output; social justice in this context entails a comprehensive examination of and correction to the entire range of factors that explicitly or tacitly extend, rather than cure, the prolonged disabilities of centuries of racism. As traditions of imperialistic misappropriation and cultural piracy are supplanted by policies that promote equitable participation in the global intellectual property cornucopia, intellectual property protection will enter an unprecedented phase of ecumenical Intellectual Property Empowerment.[7]

A socio-philosophical shift toward Intellectual Property Empowerment would provide important benefits to all stakeholders in the global intellectual property system. Historically marginalized groups and developing nations will obviously benefit from increased intellectual property development, use and commercial exploitation activity. Finally in control of their indigenous knowledge, innovations and artistic creations, historically marginalized groups and developing nations will begin to reap the benefits from their intellectual property resources and output. Moreover, as equal stakeholders in the global intellectual property repository, they will also gain enhanced access to the expressive information, technological "know-how", pharmaceutical drugs and medicines and other advances developed by more established intellectual property rights holders, who would in turn be incentivized to barter for equitable intellectual property exchange and to collaborate in mutually beneficial intellectual property undertakings.

The benefits of Intellectual Property Empowerment to those currently vested in the prevailing intellectual property regimes will extend beyond

---

[7] Stephen R. Munzer, "Corrective Justice and Intellectual Property Rights in Traditional Knowledge", in Annabelle Lever (ed.), *New Frontiers in the Philosophy of Intellectual Property* (Cambridge University Press, Cambridge 2012), 58–87; Lateef Mtima, "What's Mine is Mine But What's Yours Is Ours: IP Imperialism, the Right of Publicity, and Intellectual Property Social Justice in the Digital Information Age", 15 SMU Sci. & Tech. L. Rev. 323, 332–6 (2012); Llewellyn Joseph Gibbons, "Do As I Say (Not As I Did): Putative Intellectual Property Lessons for Emerging Economies from the Not So Long Past of the Developed Nations", 64 SMU L. Rev. 923 (2011); Danielle Conway-Jones, "Safeguarding Hawaiian Traditional Knowledge and Cultural Heritage: Supporting the Right to Self-Determination and Preventing the Comodification of Culture", 48 How. L.J. 737, 745–6, 751–6 (2005).

access to the increased intellectual property output of historically marginalized groups and developing nations. Established rights holders will also enjoy enhanced respect for their own intellectual property rights and interests, as former "IP outsiders", having obtained a stake in the predominant intellectual property order, will become partners not only in intellectual property development and exchange but also in intellectual property education and anti-piracy initiatives. Under the rubric of Intellectual Property Empowerment, the developed powers can collaborate with historically marginalized groups and developing nations to establish a cohesive global intellectual property community.

This Introduction will present a theory of intellectual property social justice and posit how that theory might be delineated and tested by identifying an interrelationship between the American Civil Rights Movement and a proposed parallel movement for *Intellectual Property Empowerment* in the 21st century. It will further argue that a social action plan of grassroots intellectual property education and social entrepreneurship are critical components to the success of such a movement. The chapter will close with a challenge to implement and test the theoretical proposition through mobilized collaborative action, as outlined and presented in the subsequent chapters of this book.

ACHIEVING INTELLECTUAL PROPERTY EMPOWERMENT: SOCIAL JUSTICE CENTERED-LAW AND CIVIL RIGHTS ACTIVISM

The pursuit of Intellectual Property Empowerment is nothing if not a global challenge of the first order to rectify unjust legal and economic norms. Just as the acknowledgement of human equality was the singular social value that ultimately led to a coalition of otherwise disparate groups in the Civil Rights Era, a social justice theory of intellectual property can similarly provide a unifying concept built on the social value of equity. First, such a theory should embody prescriptive norms based on progenitorial principles such as those made manifest in positive law frameworks such as the Constitution or natural rights edicts. Second, the theory should encompass the entirety of the target society's political economy. Finally, the theory should lend itself to some form of empirical testing or other social confirmation. Accordingly, intellectual property social justice theory proposes that:

> The social utility objective that underlies protection for innovative and expressive output can only be achieved through legal norms that secure and enforce

intellectual property rights in a socio-economic system regulated to guarantee equal opportunity for productive IP participation to all.

Toward this end, a combination of normative legal action and concomitant social action is proposed.

Normative Legal Action

The first step toward achieving Intellectual Property Empowerment is promoting pervasive adherence to the obligations of social justice in the development, interpretation and enforcement of intellectual property law. For decades, many courts and governing bodies have simply failed to correct or curtail institutionalized intellectual property injustice. For example, in the United States, African Americans and other marginalized groups have been systemically deprived of the commercial revenues and public recognition due from their intellectual property achievements.[8] Even when confronted with uncontroverted evidence of intellectual property misappropriation and outright theft, courts have typically regarded these travesties as examples of the unwise or uneducated exercise of the freedom of contract, or "random" acts of race, gender or class exploitation, all beyond the purview of the intellectual property law.[9] Consequently American courts often fail to do equity or otherwise administer social justice, on the grounds that providing such redress would distort the structure and integrity of the intellectual property regime.

In the developing world, Western misappropriation of the traditional knowledge and cultural expressions ("TKE") of indigenous peoples is as widespread as the pillaging of their natural resources. While Western

---

[8] Patricia Carter Sluby, *The Inventive Spirit of African Americans* (Praeger, Westport 2004), 9–36; Melissa Harris-Perry, "The Harlem Shake", accessed 10 October 2014 at http://www.youtube.com/watch?v=mIgzzHOQWiA&feature=youtu.be; K.J. Greene, "'Copynorms,' Black Cultural Production, and the Debate Over African-American Reparations", 25 Cardozo Arts & Ent. L.J. 1179, 1183–9, 1196–9 (2008); Danielle M. Conway, "Intellectual Property: Implicit Bias and Gender Bias in Right of Publicity Cases and Intellectual Property Law Generally", in Justin D. Levinson and Robert J. Smith (eds), *Implicit Bias Across the Law* (Cambridge University Press, New York 2012), 179–82,; http://www.thenation.com/blog/173667/i-shattered-my-leg-ncaa-tournament-and-all-i-got-was-lousy-t-shirt?rel=facebook#, accessed 10 October 2014.

[9] *See e.g. Gee v. CBS,* 471 F. Supp. 600 (E.D. Pa 1979); *Brooks v. The Topps Company, Inc.*, 86 U.S.P.Q. 2d 1361 (S.D.N.Y. 2007) (ultimately unsuccessful lawsuits commenced to protect African American intellectual property rights and interests, brought by the heirs of Bessie Smith and Baseball Hall of Famer James Bell respectively).

intellectual property rights holders demand greater international protection for their own property rights, asserting them even in the face of health and education crises, many of these very same entities blithely ignore the rights and traditions of developing world communities, often relying upon Western precepts of intellectual property to justify their conduct.[10] Given their past and continuing experiences, it is not surprising that many historically marginalized groups and developing nations have little interest in participating in or respecting Western intellectual property regimes.

The recognition of the fundamental social justice tenets of equitable inclusion, access and empowerment in the promulgation, interpretation and enforcement of intellectual property law would dismantle this unfortunate status quo. Intellectual property imperialism and institutionalized chicanery would be rejected as contravening the social utility objectives which underlie intellectual property protection. Moreover, the recognition of intellectual property social justice would not only preserve the interests of historically marginalized and developing nation innovators and creators, it would incentivize their full participation in systemic intellectual property endeavor.[11]

Social Action

Equally important to the realization of Intellectual Property Empowerment is the adoption of a progressive intellectual property social action platform. Whereas the recognition of social justice obligations in intellectual property law will enhance protection for the rights and interests of historically marginalized groups and developing nations, a correlative social action strategy is necessary to provide intellectual property education

---

[10] *See e.g.* http://www.businessweek.com/articles/2013-10-24/africas-maasai-tribe-seek-royalties-for-commercial-use-of-their-name#p1, accessed 10 October 2014 (discussing unauthorized, commercial use of Maasai name and tribal indicia by multinational corporations). *See further*, Madahavi Sunder, *From Goods to A Good Life: Intellectual Property and Global Justice* (Yale University Press 2012), 2–3 (discussing Solomon Linda, the African composer of *The Lion Sleeps Tonight*, who died destitute while white American artists and entertainment conglomerates earned millions from the song). Indeed, many of these entities paradoxically assert that granting IP protection for TKE will shrink the public domain, which arguments not only beg the question, but are inconsistent with leading IP legal precedent. *See e.g. Golan v. Holder*, 132 S. Ct. 873 (2012).

[11] Lateef Mtima, Symposium, "Copyright Social Utility and Social Justice Interdependence: A Paradigm for Intellectual Property Empowerment and Digital Entrepreneurship", 112 W. Va. L. Rev. 97, 126–9, 141–7 (2009).

and to stimulate primordial intellectual property activity, particularly entrepreneurial intellectual property endeavor, within these communities. Through organized and entrepreneurial-minded "IP social activism", legal and entrepreneurial experts can collaborate with social activists and policy makers to open new avenues for economic empowerment, political self-determination and socio-cultural progress for communities and nations in need.

In constructing an Intellectual Property Empowerment social action platform, IP social activists might look to the American Civil Rights Movement, arguably the most effective socio-legal movement in modern history.[12] Whereas many of the social inequities of the Civil Rights Era were grounded in socially pernicious laws and public policies, in the information society, some of the most pressing social inequities and injustices are tied to the intellectual property legal and economic infrastructure. Inequitable access to information and knowledge and various technological and pharmaceutical innovations can all be linked in part to socially indifferent and exploitative intellectual property mores. Intellectual property is therefore the contemporary analogue to the social/legal equality agenda of the Civil Rights Era. The key intersection between the Civil Rights Movement and Intellectual Property Empowerment, however, is that Intellectual Property Empowerment provides a *Civil and Human Rights Economic Agenda for the 21st Century*, through which the unfinished economic business of the Civil Rights Movement can be pursued. Although the Civil Rights Movement achieved tremendous legal and social progress, it's the absence of a concrete economic agenda which left many historically marginalized groups and developing nations trapped in a state of economic subjugation and stagnation.[13] These strategic links between the Civil Rights Movement and Intellectual Property Empowerment compel a comparative assessment of the history, legal foundation and social action framework of the Civil Rights Movement, toward the implementation of Intellectual Property Empowerment as a socio-economic movement.

---

[12] *See e.g.* Tomiko Brown-Nagin, "Protest & Polarization: Law and Debate in America 2012: Does Protest Work?" 56 How. L.J. 721, 723–5, 730–3, 741–3 (2013).

[13] W. Sherman Rogers, *The African American Entrepreneur, Then and Now* (Praeger, Westport 2010), 3–14.

THE ANALYTICAL AND STRATEGIC INTERSECTIONS BETWEEN THE CIVIL RIGHTS MOVEMENT AND INTELLECTUAL PROPERTY EMPOWERMENT

Every American school child is taught how the passage of the Emancipation Proclamation freed African Americans from chattel slavery. The realities of the century of African American dehumanization that followed, however, are not as widely discussed.[14]

For a brief time after the end of the Civil War, African Americans enjoyed a period of legal equality in America. Blacks were generally permitted to begin their lives as "freedmen", pursuing education and practicing trades, exercising the right to vote and even holding important public offices.[15] However, as a result of a controversial presidential election in 1876, the constitutional rights of African Americans were sacrificed as the political price of resolving the electoral dispute. Southern democrats agreed to withdraw their objections to the election results in exchange for the end of federal involvement in the South's ongoing Reconstruction.[16] Consequently Southern states were permitted to re-institute laws and policies mandating racial segregation, while private citizens formed terrorist organizations to quell black resistance, all without fear of federal intervention. African Americans were once again prevented from obtaining education, pursuing economic autonomy and exercising the right to vote. Even the basic human rights to be protected from murder, rape, unjust imprisonment and forced labor were denied them.[17]

Although the evisceration of the constitutional amendments which granted African Americans full citizenship had commenced in the legislative sphere, the death knell to black legal and civil rights was sounded when racially discriminatory laws and policies were given constitutional imprimatur by the United States Supreme Court. In *Plessy*

---

[14] *See* Lerone Bennett, Jr., *Before the Mayflower* (5th edn, Penguin Books, 1984), 255–96; Robert Weisbrot, *Freedom Bound: A History of America's Civil Rights Movement* (W.W. Norton & Co., New York 1990), 3–13.

[15] Bennett, note 14 above, 214–54.

[16] John Sibley Butler, *Entrepreneurship and Self Help Among Black Americans* (State University of New York Press, Albany 1991), 63–4; Rogers, note 13 above, 50–1.

[17] Joanne Grant, *Black Protest: History, Documents, and Analyses, 1619 to The Present* (Fawcett Publications, Robbinsdale 1968), 175–9; Genna Rae McNeil, *Groundwork: Charles Hamilton Houston and the Struggle for Civil Rights* (University of Pennsylvania Press, Philadelphia 1983), 5–7.

v. Ferguson,[18] the Supreme Court ruled that state laws which mandated "separate but equal" public accommodations for whites and blacks did not impose any "badge of servitude" upon blacks, nor did they designate blacks as inferior merely by "distinguishing" them from whites. Thus the legal and social subjugation of blacks was effectively held to be constitutionally permissible. For decades thereafter, African Americans endured the stigma of "Jim Crow"[19] racial discrimination, until an effective legal challenge to *Plessy* could be formulated and advanced through the courts.

Charles Hamilton Houston: The Legal Architect of the Civil Rights Movement

Beginning in the 1930s, Charles Hamilton Houston, the progenitor of Howard Law School,[20] devised an Equal Protection-centered assault on *Plessy*, which on its face did not challenge America's system of legal apartheid but rather, sought to *enforce* it.[21] The genius of Houston's strategy was its practicality: one of the key reasons that Jim Crow "worked" was the fact that whereas governmental authorities pervasively enforced its directive of *separation*, no efforts were made to comply with its corollary mandate of *equality*. Thus Jim Crow in practice actually violated the terms of *Plessy*, which held that the constitutional price for racial segregation was the provision of "equivalents" for blacks. If governmental authorities were required to in fact provide blacks with equivalent institutional facilities and opportunities, however, the tab for Jim Crow would prove to be a bill they simply could not afford. Houston therefore reasoned that if the states were actually required to establish equal albeit separate institutions for blacks, allowing blacks full access to white institutions would be their only viable recourse.

Throughout a period that stretched over 20 years, Houston and his disciple Thurgood Marshall worked with the NAACP and other black organizations to pursue Houston's legal strategy in a series of cases in state and federal courts, and ultimately before the United States Supreme

---

[18] 163 U.S. 537 (1896). In *Plessy* an African American citizen brought suit against the state of Louisiana, arguing that the state law that required him to give up his seat on a public train and move to a "colored section" violated his constitutional rights under the Thirteenth and Fourteenth Amendments.
[19] Bennet, note 14 above, 255–9.
[20] McNeil, note 17 above, 69–85.
[21] McNeil, note 17 above, 115–17, 129–39, 150–1; Rawn James, Jr., *Root and Branch: Charles Hamilton Houston, Thurgood Marshall, and the Struggle to End Segregation* (Bloomsbury Press, New York 2010), 65–8, 73–4.

Court. Beginning with *Murray v. Maryland*[22] in 1935 and *Missouri ex. rel. Gaines v. Canada*[23] in 1936, Houston carefully mounted a constitutional challenge to racial segregation in public education, arguing that state law schools that denied admission to black applicants violated their constitutional rights because the states had not established any alternative black law schools which these applicants could attend.[24] Ironically in *Murray*, Houston and Marshall were actually able to assure the state trial court that a decision in favor of the plaintiff would be consistent with existing legal precedent and indeed, was required by *Plessy*.

Houston's litigation campaign reached its apotheosis in the landmark case of *Brown v. Board of Education*.[25] Up until then, Houston's legal victories hacked away at Jim Crow segregation by demonstrating that it was a socio-legal institution unconstitutional in practice; in *Brown*, Marshall argued to the United States Supreme Court that Jim Crow was *inherently* unconstitutional, in that legally enforced isolation of a minority group by society's majority bestows an indelible social and psychological stigma upon that minority group.[26] More than a half century after its infamous decision in *Plessy*, the Supreme Court accepted these arguments, and directed that the policy of separate but equal be abolished from public education and that public schools be racially integrated "with all deliberate speed". The meticulous erosion of Jim Crow which began in *Murray* and *Gaines* had achieved its tactical metamorphosis with the Court's overruling of *Plessy*, and *Brown* marked the beginning of the affirmative dismantling of apartheid in American law and public policy.

Beyond the Courts: The Civil Rights Social Action Platform

While Houston's legal theories provided the litigation framework for the Civil Rights Movement, he and the other architects of the Movement understood that the eradication of *de jure* racial discrimination alone would not provide full legal and social equality for blacks in America.[27] Because racial discrimination against blacks was a legally sanctioned public policy, the initial focus was necessarily directed toward changing the law. But Jim Crow was more than just a statute on the books: racial

---

[22] 169 Md. 478 (1936).
[23] 305 U.S. 337 (1938).
[24] James, note 21 above, 68–74; 117–18.
[25] 347 U.S. 483 (1954).
[26] Weisbrot, note 14 above, 11; Grant, note 17 above, 253.
[27] Juan Williams, *Eyes on the Prize: America's Civil Rights Years 1954–1965* (Penguin Books 1987), 60, 122–61; McNeil, note 17 above, 170–1.

animus and discrimination toward blacks was the way of life in America, and thus the initiative for racial justice would begin with black political and social leaders who helped African Americans to aspire and organize toward the full legal and civil franchise.

In the post-Reconstruction era, various political and social leaders came to prominence within the black community, each propagating a different school of thought on redressing the plight of African Americans. Most prominent was Booker T. Washington, the founder of Tuskegee Institute, who advocated that blacks should eschew political agitation and instead focus their attentions on pursuing whatever economic and other opportunities Jim Crow left available to them, and thereby advance themselves in ways such that whites would come to see for themselves that racial discrimination against blacks was a disservice to the nation.[28] At the beginning of the 20th century, W.E.B. Du Bois emerged as the leading proponent for full equality for blacks, directly challenging Washington's policies of socio-political conciliation.[29] Du Bois urged African Americans to press for immediate legal and social equality and reasoned that educated blacks, a "Talented Tenth", would be able to lead the community in undertaking the rights and privileges of full citizenship. Throughout the 1920s and 1930s, Marcus Garvey in turn provided a counterweight to Du Bois. The first internationally prominent black leader to spread an uncompromising message of black racial pride, Garvey argued that blacks in the New World needed first to shed the racial inferiority complex foisted upon them through slavery and reinforced under Jim Crow, and thereafter repatriate to Africa and build their own independent nation.[30]

As conditions worsened for African Americans and the federal government repeatedly reneged on its promises to protect their civil and human rights, it became increasingly difficult for many blacks to accept Washington's philosophy of patient acquiescence. Moreover, while Du Bois and Garvey each struck emotional chords with their uncompromising rejection of white supremacy, many African Americans had difficulty envisioning a life outside of America, and thus Du Bois' philosophy of full equality "at home" ultimately gained prominence.

---

[28] Booker T. Washington, *Up from Slavery* (Doubleday Page, New York 1901), 105–15.

[29] Manning Marable, *Black Leadership* (Columbia University Press, New York 1998), 41–6; Bennett, note 14 above, 330–3.

[30] Marcus Garvey, *Philosophies and Opinions of Marcus Garvey* (Amy Jacques-Garvey (ed.)) (Atheneum 1923), 17–18, 26, 47, 52–4, 68–72; Grant, note 17 above, 179; McNeil, note 17 above 8–9. Indeed, some African Americans did emigrate to the Pepper Coast of Africa and subsequently founded the Republic of Liberia.

In 1909, Du Bois joined a group of prominent white liberals and black activists in organizing the National Association for the Advancement of Colored People,[31] its formation instigated by the infamous Springfield, Illinois race riot of 1908.[32] Much the same as how Houston meticulously established the legal precedent that would culminate in *Brown*, for decades the NAACP explored various social protest stratagems through which to construct a social action platform for African American civil rights. Long before Rosa Parks refused to give up her seat on a public bus in 1955, the NAACP had been confronted with occasions whereupon black passengers were jailed for refusing to relinquish their seats to whites.[33] The NAACP saw in Parks, however, a lodestar which could arouse blacks and perhaps even induce sympathy from whites.[34] An NAACP secretary and Youth Council adviser, the demure, bespectacled seamstress seemed the perfect symbol of quiet but righteous resistance to an unjust regime. The ensuing Montgomery Bus Boycott would not only lead to the desegregation of public transportation in Montgomery, Alabama, it would ultimately ignite a nationwide grassroots movement of student lunch counter sit-ins, a tactic originated by the Congress of Racial Equality in the 1940s, which in turn would prod the established civil rights leadership toward a more aggressive campaign of civil disobedience.[35]

The Montgomery Bus Boycott would also serve as the watershed moment at which Dr. Martin Luther King would come to national prominence, and wherein he and activist James Lawson would infuse the philosophy of passive non-violent resistance into the Movement's civil protest strategy.[36] Dr. King understood that it was vital that the burgeoning movement for racial equality evoke the moral empathy of the American

---

[31] Previously in 1905, Du Bois and the activist/journalist Monroe Trotter organized the Niagara Movement, the functional predecessor to the NAACP and the first major social activist organization dedicated to the cause of African American legal and social equality, so named to reflect "the mighty current of change" it was intended to bring about. *See* Grant, note 17 above, 206–14; Manning Marable note 29 above, 42; McNeil, note 17 above, 86–7; Bennett, note 14 above, 333–6; http://en.wikipedia.org/wiki/Niagara_Movement, accessed 10 October 2014.

[32] Bennett, note 14 Jr., 337–9.

[33] Williams, note 27 above, 60–63, 70.

[34] Williams, note 27 above, 66; Grant, note 17 above, 251–2, 276–80.

[35] Sara Bullard, *Free At Last: A History of the Civil Rights Movement and Those Who Died in the Struggle* (Oxford University Press, New York 1993), 16–29; Weisbrot, note 14 above, 13–14; Grant, note 17 above 255; Williams, note 27 above, 126–32, 140–2.

[36] Williams, note 27 above, 76, 79, 122–5; Weisbrot, note 14 above 15–18.

people, and under his leadership, peaceful protestors endured the savage assaults of racist mobs, tacitly supported by complicit authorities and officials, and the raw ugliness of American racial animus was revealed to a horrified and now largely sympathetic nation.[37]

INTELLECTUAL PROPERTY EMPOWERMENT AS CIVIL AND HUMAN RIGHTS IN THE 21ST CENTURY

Problems of social inequity or injustice can arise from any number of causes and are not always directly attributable to flaws or gaps in the law. Economic upheavals, outmoded social mores and even beneficial but unregulated technological advance can result in social developments inimical to the public good.[38] However, when the law is in fact the direct cause of a pernicious social condition, the modality of redress is necessarily diandrous. Effective reform requires remedial change in the law, which must then be reinforced with positive social action, such as ameliorating public attitudes and awareness, restructuring institutional priorities and adopting detersive legislation and policies.[39]

The Civil Rights Movement is the modern exemplar of efficacious law-centered social action. When Charles Houston became the NAACP's Special Counsel in 1935, his legal theories gave the NAACP's civil rights agenda an articulable legal strategy. The relationship between Charles Houston's legal strategies and the NAACP's social action campaigns was therefore strategically symbiotic: public social action helped to raise awareness of the plight of African Americans under Jim Crow and to create a more receptive environment for civil rights litigation and legal

---

[37] Williams, note 27 above 133, 138–9, 148–52; Bullard, note 35 above, 22–35.

[38] Hannibal Travis, "Cyberspace As a Product of Public-Private Censorship", in Hannibal Travis (ed.), *Cyberspace Law* (Routledge, New York 2013), 1; Allen S. Hammond, "Symposium Bridging the Digital Divide in the Information Age: The Digital Divide in the New Millennium", 20 Cardozo Arts & Ent. L.J. 135, 141–5 (2002); Nicholas W. Allard, "Digital Divide: Myth, Reality, Responsibility", 24 Hastings Comm. & Ent. L.J. 449, 451–53, 458–65 (2002). ("In some parts of [Kentucky and the Ohio River Valley] a 'lap top' is where the kitty cat sleeps. A 'mouse' lives in the barn. 'Click' is what you do with your gun, and 'double click' is what you do when you are really serious.")

[39] Richard L. Abel, "Law Without Politics: Legal Aid Under Advanced Capitalism", 32 UCLA L. Rev. 474, 576–9, 600–2 (1985); *see generally* David M. Trubek, "Symposium: Back to the Future: The Short, Happy Life of the Law and Society Movement", 18 Fla. St. U.L. Rev. 4 (1990).

reform; the ensuing litigation victories brought credibility to the public campaigns and inspiration to the civil rights rank and file; this in turn led to an evolution of civil rights activist stratagems into a nationwide movement for positive legislative and social reform.[40]

The Civil Rights Movement is thus the issue and tactical forebear to Intellectual Property Empowerment. In the strategic tradition of the Civil Rights Movement, the Intellectual Property Empowerment agenda calls for progressive change in the application of intellectual property law to be combined with commensurate action in the socio-economic sector. Accordingly, the achievement of Intellectual Property Empowerment requires (i) an articulable legal theory and (ii) a compatible social action platform.

The Legal Theory of Intellectual Property Empowerment: Intellectual Property Social Justice

In formulating a litigation strategy to dismantle legalized segregation, Charles Houston devised a legal theory that not only targeted a practical weakness in the Jim Crow socio-legal infrastructure but was also rooted in the Constitution. Similarly, the legal theory of intellectual property social justice also finds its beginnings in a constitutional edict. In the United States, the Constitution expressly authorizes Congress to provide for intellectual property protection as a means by which to "promote the progress of the arts and sciences".[41] The importance of this protection to the Framers of the Constitution cannot be overstated, given that it appears not in the Bill of Rights or subsequent Amendments, but in the very first Article of the Constitution. Moreover, the articulated social utility function of such protection is to stimulate intellectual property production, dissemination and re-ignition inuring to the greatest societal good. Thus, the constitutional scheme is dependent upon the broadest possible participation: the nation's cultural and technological advancement requires the creative and inventive contributions of all of her citizens.

Notwithstanding the constitutional directive, intellectual property exclusion, inequity and injustice have a long history in America. From the age of chattel slavery and throughout the era of Jim Crow and beyond, African Americans and other marginalized groups have been robbed of the credit for and economic fruits of many of their intellectual property achievements. Slaves, being property themselves, could not

---

[40] Brown-Nagin, note 12 above, 722–6.
[41] U.S. Constitution, Article I, Section 8.

hold patents as a matter of law.⁴² From Bessie Smith to Elijah McCoy to Henrietta Lacks, the artistic revelations, technological inventions, scientific contributions and entrepreneurial innovations of African Americans have been systematically misappropriated or undermined by majority enterprises and individuals who enjoy the advantages of racial and financial capital.⁴³

The recent case of Mixed Chicks, LLC provides an illustrative example. As bi-racial women, Mixed Chicks co-founders Wendy Levi and Kim Etheredge were well aware of the lack of hair care product options for bi-racial women of color. Beginning in 2003, Levi and Etheredge worked with a chemist to develop a line of hair care products, which they then sold to salons and beauty supply chains across the country. Eventually Sally Beauty Supply, LLC, the world's largest retailer of professional beauty supplies, approached Levi and Etheredge with an offer to distribute their products, which Levi and Etheredge declined. Thereafter, Sally Beauty introduced a line of hair care products for bi-racial women called "Mixed Silk", utilizing product textures, scents, packaging and marketing (including an Internet search engine that directed searches for "Mixed Chicks" to "Mixed Silk") that so closely resembled the Mixed Chicks product line that many Mixed Chicks customers were confused into thinking that "Mixed Silk" was simply a less expensive product line being offered by Mixed Chicks.⁴⁴

Unlike many intellectual property start-up entrepreneurs, particularly those in marginalized communities, Levi and Etheredge had access to the resources needed to pursue intellectual property litigation against Sally Beauty. In a rare dispensation of intellectual property social justice, the

---

⁴² Patricia Carter Sluby, note 8 above, 10–15; 30–36.

⁴³ Van Smith, "Wonder Woman: The Life, Death, and Life After Death of Henrietta Lacks, Unwitting Heroine of Modern Medical Science", City Paper, 17 April 2002, accessed 10 October 2014 at http://www2.citypaper.com/news/story.asp?id=3426&p=2; Kia Makarechi, "Robin Thicke Sues Marvin Gaye's Family To Protect 'Blurred Lines'", accessed 10 October 2014 at www.huffingtonpost.com/2013/08/16/Robin-Thicke-Sues-Marvin-Gaye's-Family-To-Protect-'Blurred Lines'_n_3767108.html; K.J. Greene, "Copyright, Culture & Black Music: A Legacy of Unequal Protection", 21 Hastings Comm. & Ent. L.J. 339, 340–1 (1999); Keith Aoki, "Distributive and Syncretic Motives in Intellectual Property Law (With Special Reference to Coercion, Agency and Development)", 40 U.C. Davis L. Rev. 717, 722–4, 738–48, 755–68 (2007); Butler, note 16 above, 48–62.

⁴⁴ Lisa Shuchman, "Mixed Chicks Gets $8.5M Jury Award for Infringing Mixed-Race Hair Products", accessed 10 October 2014 at http://interval-recognized.blogspot.com/2012/12/the-multiracial-advocacy-blog-mixed.html; 35 Trials Digest 16th 13, 2012 WL 8963677 (C.D.Cal.).

court permitted the case to reach the jury, which returned a verdict for Mixed Chicks.[45]

Unfortunately the Mixed Chicks outcome is atypical. More often than not, marginalized innovators and artists lack the information and financial resources to protect their rights and interests, and thus rather than incentivizing intellectual property endeavor in these communities, the intellectual property system in practice discourages it. Accordingly, the relationship between intellectual property social utility and intellectual property social justice is interdependent and symbiotic. To assure the greatest possible "progress of the arts and sciences", the intellectual property law must be formulated, interpreted and enforced such that all Americans enjoy equal incentives and opportunities to contribute to the national intellectual property storehouse.[46]

The social justice theory of intellectual property law acknowledges socially equitable inclusion, access and empowerment as fundamental objectives of intellectual property protection. Socially equitable access to books, inventions and other artistic and innovative works and accomplishments, irrespective of wealth, class, race, or gender status, ensures that the widest possible audience of minds and hearts will find the inspiration to conceive, express and invent. Socially just application and enforcement of intellectual property rights protects the interests of marginalized and developing world creators and inventors and preserves their incentives not only to produce but also to disseminate intellectual property output. Socially balanced exploitation of intellectual property product equalizes health and education standards, promotes civic and entrepreneurial endeavor and fosters universal respect for the intellectual property regime.[47]

---

[45] This victory is reminiscent of Granville T. Woods' successful defense of his intellectual property rights against the machinations of Thomas Edison a century before. *See* Butler, note 16 above, 61–2; http://web.mit.edu/invent/iow/woods.html, accessed 10 October 2014.

[46] Institution for Intellectual Property and Social Justice Enforcement Comments on IP Enforcement by the Federal Government, accessed 10 October 2014 at http://infojustice.org/wp-content/uploads/2012/08/IIPSJ.pdf; Rita Heimes, "Trademarks, Identity and Justice", 11 John Marshall Rev. of Intell. Prop. L. 133, 145–55 (2011).

[47] Steven D. Jamar and Lateef Mtima, "A Social Justice Perspective on Intellectual Property, Innovation, and Entrepreneurship", in Megan M. Carpenter (ed.), *Entrepreneurship and Innovation, Evolving Economies* (Edward Elgar, Cheltenham, UK and Northampton, MA, USA 2012), 89–101; Cristian Timmermann, "Life Sciences, Intellectual Property Regimes and Global Justice", 18–34, accessed 10 October 2014 at http://www.academia.edu/4963224/_2013_Life_Sciences_Intellectual_Property_Regimes_and_Global_Justice; Shubha Ghosh, *Identity, Invention, and the Culture of Personalized*

IP social justice-conscious lawyers can deploy the Houston strategy by identifying and litigating appropriate intellectual property disputes to build a body of IP social justice precedents and jurisprudence. Indeed, some courts have begun to render social justice-minded decisions that protect the intellectual property rights of historically marginalized rights holders. Recently federal courts have ruled that video game purveyors that create avatars of college athletes without their permission violate the athletes' intellectual property rights. Cognizant of a system wherein colleges and universities, coaches and television networks earn billions off the talent and skill of student athletes, many of whom hail from inner city communities and rural towns and all of whom are prohibited by collegiate competition rules from profiting from their athletic exploits, courts are becoming increasingly intolerant of industry practices that deprive historical marginalized and other student athletes of their fair share of the intellectual property bounty.[48]

Courts have also begun to acknowledge the intellectual property law's social justice obligations beyond those of remedial justice and to otherwise inform their assessments of the law's social utility function.[49] Recently a federal court held that an initiative by a group of universities to make digital scans of books in their libraries, so as to render them accessible to the blind and amenable to digital scholarly research, is a fair use, citing, among other things, "the unprecedented ability of print-disabled individuals to have an equal opportunity to compete with their sighted peers".[50]

Medicine Patenting, 179–84, 194 (Cambridge University Press, New York 2012); Sunder, note 10 above, 173–99.

[48] *Hart v. Elec. Arts, Inc.*, 717 F.3d 141(3d Cir. 2013); *In re NCAA Student-Athlete Name & Likeness Licensing Litigation*, No. 10-15387, 2013 WL 3928293, (9th Cir. 31 July 2013); *see* Rev. Jesse Jackson, "Big Money for College Sports, Nothing for Players", accessed 10 October 2014 at http://www.suntimes.com/news/jackson/26549238-452/big-money-for-college-sports-nothing-for-players.html#.U5OgGE0U_IU.

[49] *The Authors Guild vs. Google, Inc.*, 770 F. Supp. 2d 666, 679 (S.D.N.Y. 2011), *citing* Lateef Mtima and Steven D. Jamar, "Fulfilling the Copyright Social Justice Promise: Digitizing Textual Information", 55 N.Y.L. Sch. L. Rev. 77, 79–80 (2010); Sean Flynn, "Human Rights and Access to Medicines Cases" (27 April 2013), accessed 10 October 2014 at infojustice.org/archives/29409.

[50] *The Authors Guild, Inc. v. HathiTrust*, 902 F. Supp. 2d 445 (S.D.N.Y. 2012), affirmed, 2014 U.S. App. LEXIS 10803; *see also* William Patry, How to Fix Copyright, 10 (Oxford University Press 2011) "[T]he inability of the blind and other visually impaired people to have access to printed…copies of books should be the copyright civil rights issue of our time. In the wealthiest countries, only some 5 percent of published books are made accessible in formats the visually impaired can use; this figure drops to less than 1 percent in poorer countries. Copyright laws are the principal reason for this scandal."

Similarly, another federal court has held that the Google Books Project, which undertook digital scans of books in several university libraries in order to enhance public access to, scholarly research in, and archival preservation of these books, is also a fair use.[51]

Consideration for intellectual property social justice has also begun to impact judicial determinations in the developing world. Recently, India's Intellectual Property Appellate Board affirmed a decision by the India Patent Office to allow a local manufacturer to produce a generic version of the patented cancer drug Nexavar, in order to make the drug available to the public at an affordable price.[52] Similarly, the India Supreme Court rejected a challenge to the production of inexpensive generic versions of the cancer drug Glivec, and further held that an application to patent a "newer version" of the drug was essentially an attempt to extend the term of the expiring Glivec patent.[53] These decisions reflect an evolving judicial sensitivity to the relationship between prevailing intellectual property precepts and the failure to address various health crises and other socio-economic problems which persist in the developing world.[54]

---

[51] *The Authors Guild, Inc. v. Google, Inc.*, 05 CV813 6 (DC) (S.D.N.Y. 2013). These decisions herald a continuing evolution of judicial application of fair use, from the groundbreaking theories of "aesthetic transformation" formulated by Judge Pierre Leval, to Internet indexing as "functional transformation", to what might arguably be characterized as "social justice transformation", which would include uses essential to promoting cultural preservation, diversity, and parity in the digital information age. See Lateef Mtima, "The Promise of Information Justice", in Travis (ed.) *Cyberspace Law*, note 38 above, 69. For an excellent analysis of the contemporary judicial approach to fair use, *see* Patricia Aufderheide and Peter Jaszi, *Reclaiming Fair Use* (University of Chicago Press, Chicago 2011), 80–93.

[52] *Cancer Drug Ruling Seen As Victory for the Poor*, accessed 10 October 2014 at http://www.stuff.co.nz/business/world/8386127/Cancer-drug-ruling-seen-as-victory-for-poor; *India Board Rules Against Bayer in Cancer Drug Patent Case*, accessed 10 October 2014 at http://www.reuters.com/article/2013/03/04/us-india-bayer-idUSBRE9230LC20130304.

[53] Amy Kapczynski, "Engineered in India – Patent 2.0", *The New England Journal of Medicine*, 8 August 2013, accessed 10 October 2014 at http://www.nejm.org/doi/full/10.1056/NEJMp1304400; *Human Rights Win as Big Pharma 'Novartis' Loses Patent Case*, accessed 10 October 2014 at https://www.commondreams.org/headline/2013/04/01-3.

[54] One of the most important examples of IP social justice progress is the recent adoption of the Marrakesh Treaty to Facilitate Access to Published Works by Visually Impaired Persons and Persons with Print Disabilities on 28 June 2013, signed by 51 countries. *See The 2013 Marrakesh Treaty: Providing Access to Copyrighted Works for the Blind and Print Disabled*, accessed 10 October 2014 at http://www.pijip.org/events/marrakesh/; *From Book Famine to Book Banquet:*

Intellectual property social justice theory further conceptualizes equitable participation in intellectual property production and consumption as a civil and human right.[55] By employing Houston's strategy, intellectual property attorneys can promote and enhance judicial recognition of the law's social justice obligations.[56] Promulgated in concert with a progressive social action platform, intellectual property social justice implements positive Intellectual Property Empowerment.

The Intellectual Property Empowerment Social Action Platform: Embracing Entrepreneurship

> When people are suffering ... they don't want rhetoric and processes which seem to go slowly ... they want direct participation. They want to be able to say, 'What I'm doing here gives me power and is going to help us *change this business*.'[57]

While a social justice-centered interpretation of the intellectual property law will redress certain injustices and social problems which plague historically marginalized and developing communities, the impact on their economic advancement will be limited unless they also produce and protect intellectual property which they can exploit. Just as the carefully constructed campaign of mobilizing strategies, including public marches, sit-ins and other acts of civil protest provided inspiration, direction and opportunity for ordinary individuals to move the frontline of the Civil Rights Movement from the courts to the streets, a campaign of Intellectual

---

Ghana Gets Ready for Ratification, accessed 10 October 2014 at http://www.eifl.net/news/book-famine-book-banquet-ghana-gets-ready. Intellectual property social justice thus transcends notions of redistributive justice or particular theoretical bases (that is, positive law or natural rights) for IP protection. *See further* Chapters 8, 11, and 12.

[55] *See e.g.* Steven D. Jamar, "Symposium: The Global Impact and Implementation of Human Rights Norm: A Social Justice Perspective on the Role of Copyright in Realizing International Human Rights", 25 Pac. McGeorge Global Bus. & Dev. L.J. 289, 290–7 (2012); Laurence R. Helfer, "Toward a Human Rights Framework for Intellectual Property", 40 U.C. Davis L. Rev. 971, 976–82, 1015–20 (2007); Margaret Chon, "Intellectual Property and the Development Divide", 27 Cardozo L. Rev. 2821, 2823–9, 2876–8, 2885–97, 2909–12 (2006); Julie E. Cohen, "Creativity and Culture in Copyright Theory", 40 U.C. Davis L. Rev. 1151, 1197–8 (2007). *See* Chapters 6, 8, and 12.

[56] Lateef Mtima, "The Promise of Information Justice", in Travis (ed.) *Cyberspace Law*, note 38 above, 57–8, 70.

[57] James Lawson, social activist and Dr. King's advisor on non-violent protest, quoted in Williams, note 27 above, 123 (emphasis added); Weisbrot, note 14 above, 21.

Property Empowerment similarly requires appropriate mobilizing strategies to promote communal intellectual property awareness, education and grassroots engagement "to help us change this business".

The proposition that development and exploitation of intellectual property will promote socio-economic empowerment can seem somewhat abstract to the average person. To capture attention, spark imagination and motivate action, Intellectual Property Empowerment objectives must be concretely aligned with the socio-economic perspectives and priorities of the target community. The Civil Rights protest movement gave voice to decades of frustration with Jim Crow oppression and provided people with the means to directly challenge that system. Intellectual property-oriented social action should be similarly directed toward the frustrations with (i) the perennial lack of individual economic opportunities and (ii) the historic and ongoing misappropriation of marginalized community and developing nation TKE and IP output, and presented as an avenue toward personal economic autonomy and communal socio-economic empowerment.

Principles and strategies of entrepreneurship provide an accessible and pragmatic structure for intellectual property-oriented social action in underserved communities and developing nations. In the tradition of teaching the hungry to fish, the entrepreneur offers a romantic and enticing image of self-empowerment in hostile terrain.[58] This is one reason why there is a long tradition of immigrant socio-economic upward mobility through "middleman" entrepreneurship and other engagement in "undesirable" but essential enterprise, as evident in the experiences of some European Jews, East African Asians, Japanese Americans and South African Indians, among others.[59] Even African Americans, who were denied most of the opportunities for "middleman" entrepreneurial socio-economic mobility enjoyed by America's voluntary immigrants, have a long tradition of entrepreneurial enterprise.[60] Thus entrepreneurship is a familiar and proven empowerment path for many marginalized individuals and communities.

---

[58] David E. Pozen, "We Are All Entrepreneurs Now", 43 Wake Forest L. Rev. 283, 285–7 (2012); Eric J. Gouvin, "Of Small Businesses and Entrepreneurs: Toward a Public Policy that Supports New Venture Formation, Entrepreneurship and Innovation", in Megan M. Carpenter (ed.), *Entrepreneurship and Innovation in Evolving Economies* (Edward Elgar, Cheltenham, UK and Northampton, MA, USA 2012), 27–9, 37–8.

[59] Butler, note 16 above, 1–33.

[60] Rogers, note 13 above, xviii–xx, 27–38, 59–63, 84; Butler, note 16 above 68–78, 143–64, 224–5; Patricia Carter Sluby, *The Entrepreneurial Spirit of African American Inventors* (Praeger, Westport 2011), 23–66.

Moreover, entrepreneurial solutions are particularly well-suited to addressing some of the special socio-economic problems with which many historically marginalized communities and developing nations currently grapple. Affordable access to knowledge and pharmaceutical drugs, empowering vocational training and conquering endemic diseases such as sickle cell anemia all require innovative but affordable, cost-effective solutions.[61] Thus, entrepreneurially-focused intellectual property activity can be responsive to many imminent marginalized community and developing nation socio-economic needs.

By definition, entrepreneurial intellectual property endeavor involves the development and commercial exploitation of new intellectual property or at least the innovative commercial application of pre-existing intellectual property.[62] Intellectual Property Empowerment, however, does not promote intellectual property commercial enterprise for its own sake: the primary goal is communal socio-economic progress and empowerment. Consequently it is important to identify entrepreneurial theories or mechanisms that are most consistent with this overarching social objective and to contextualize them in the larger civil and human rights discourse.

Intellectual Property Empowerment and Social Entrepreneurship: A Civil Rights Historical Perspective

We have seen how Civil Rights legal theory can inform Intellectual Property Empowerment legal theory. Similarly, the history and structure of the Civil Rights social action strategy can help to shape the Intellectual Property Empowerment social action platform. Certain aspects of the African American socio-economic struggle are particularly resonant with the intellectual property socio-economic empowerment agenda. Intellectual property injustice conflates cultural misappropriation and economic subjugation,[63] presenting a socio-economic landscape similar to that which made economic progress an aspect of the political agendas of

---

[61] *See* Carpenter (ed.), *Entrepreneurship and Innovation in Evolving Economies*, note 58 above; Banji Oyelaran-Oyeyinka and Padmashree Gehl Sampath, *Latecomer Development: Innovation and Knowledge for Economic Growth* (Routledge, New York 2010).

[62] William D. Bygrave, "The Entrepreneurial Process", 49–56, in William Bygrave and Andrew Zacharakis (eds), *Entrepreneurship* (2nd edn, John Wiley & Sons, Chichester, 2011); Oyelaran-Oyeyinka and Sampath, note 61 above 7–10; Michael Golin, *Driving Innovation: Intellectual Property Strategies For a Dynamic World* (Cambridge University Press, New York 2008), 11–21.

[63] Otha Richard Sullivan, *African American Inventors* (John Wiley & Sons, Hoboken 1998); Greene, note 8 above, 1183–9, 1196–9.

all of the major black leaders.[64] Economic advancement held the utmost priority for Booker T. Washington, and for Marcus Garvey its importance was second only to black racial pride.[65] And while legal and social equality took precedence for W.E.B. Du Bois, economic justice was certainly an important component of his political agenda.[66]

A key element of Du Bois' vision for African American uplift was his concept of a civically capable and socially sanguine "Talented Tenth" leadership caste,[67] who Du Bois reasoned would helm African American progress, including the community's economic advancement. In terms of entrepreneurial classification, Du Bois' "Talented Tenth Economic Uplift" is perhaps best considered as a model of "classic" entrepreneurship. Classic "creator/destroyer" entrepreneurship is generally defined in terms of individual innovation and risk taking in business enterprise that introduces new products, services or practices and ultimately revolutionizes the market place by displacing predecessors in the market.[68] In a similar fashion, Talented Tenth Economic Uplift anticipates a measure of unprecedented economic endeavor in the majority marketplace by a select group of African Americans, displacing segregated enterprise and eventually contributing to the socio-economic transformation of the African American community and the American marketplace as a whole.

Evaluating African American economic progress during and since the

---

[64] Brown-Nagin, note 12 above, 728–30; Gavin Wright, *Sharing the Prize: The Economics of the Civil Rights Revolution in the American South* (Harvard University Press, Cambridge, MA 2013), 10–15. African American economic empowerment ideology therefore transcends mere economic progress, and like Intellectual Property Empowerment, its scope encompasses political autonomy and cultural dignity.

[65] Washington, note 28 above 106–7; Garvey, note 30 above, 48, 56.

[66] *See e.g.* W.E.B. Du Bois, 14(4) *The Crisis*, 163–6 (1917); Wright, note 64 above, 224–5; Grant, note 17 above, 206–9. In addition to backing Charles Houston's litigation strategies to desegregate public education, the NAACP also supported Houston's litigation against railroad labor unions, which forced blacks out of the industry to placate their southern white membership. Houston would successfully argue before the United States Supreme Court that by virtue of their exclusive collective bargaining rights, the unions owed a fiduciary obligation to represent the interests of all their trade members, including blacks. *See* James, note 21 above, 166–73; McNeil, note 17 above, 156–8, 168–71.

[67] Harry T. Edwards, "The Journey from Brown v. Board of Education to Grutter v. Bollinger", 102 Mich. L. Rev. 944, 949–50 (2004); Kevin Brown and Jeannine Bell, "Symposium: The School Desegregation Cases and the Uncertain Future of Racial Equality: Demise of the Talented Tenth: Affirmative Action and the Increasing Underrepresentation of Ascendant Blacks at Selective Higher Educational Institutions", 69 Ohio St. L.J. 1229, 1239–42 (2008).

[68] Pozen, note 58 above, 287–93; Gouvin, note 58 above, 30–1.

Civil Rights era, it seems fair to say that Talented Tenth Economic Uplift has not resulted in pervasive economic progress for the African American community. There are various factors to which this might be attributed. First, many pre-integration black business ventures were undertaken principally to address unmet African American needs in rigidly segregated markets, and thus were only "low" or "quasi-entrepreneurial" in nature. Although "lone wolf" risk takers would identify and service unmet needs, they could typically do so without employing innovative products, services or mercantile practices; the restrictions of segregation necessitated only the provision of "black alternatives", such as black barbers and undertakers. Once these markets proved profitable, however, majority business entities, particularly in the post-segregation era, could easily displace or absorb black operators. Thus, while some pioneering individuals initially did well, often there was little permanent, community-wide economic advancement.[69]

When black entrepreneurs did innovate, their "uneasy relationship" with the intellectual property regime often permitted non-blacks to misappropriate their innovations. Unlike Granville T. Woods or Mixed Chicks, most black entrepreneurs lacked the resources to procure and protect their intellectual property rights, thus non-black competitors could offer "knock-offs" of black innovations and otherwise usurp the markets that blacks actually created. Consequently, even when blacks engaged in classic "creator/destroyer" entrepreneurial activity, neither the individual entrepreneur nor the African American community was able to capture or retain the full economic benefits.[70] Moreover, "creator/destroyer" displacement of segregated black enterprise did not always lead to substitute opportunities in the majority marketplace, which resulted in a net loss to the post-integration community.

Finally, it should be understood that the first order of Talented Tenth Economic Uplift is not economic advancement in the ordinary sense, but rather, support for Du Boisian socio-legal equality. Accordingly, social advancement goals such as underwriting college and professional educations for family members was often prioritized over business reinvestment or expansion, and without subsequent application of the acquired professional skills to the family enterprise. The history of the Imperial Broom Company, a five-generation African American business which

---

[69] Benjamin Means, "A Lens for Law and Entrepreneurship", 6 Ohio St. Entrepreneurial Bus. L. J. 1, 9, 13 (2010–11); Gavin Wright, 223–5, 227.

[70] Butler, note 16 above, 203–4, 217–23; Rogers, note 13 above, 84–90, 95–98; Wright, note 64 above, 223–8.

began operation in 1900, is a typical example. A rare African American "middleman" enterprise which successfully serviced mainstream markets, the business would ultimately underwrite professional degrees for three generations of family descendants. However, after more than a century of continuous and profitable operation, the company has all but closed its doors, in part due to a lack of family members whose professional careers are compatible with undertaking management of the company.[71]

From one perspective, Imperial Broom represents a successful application of Talented Tenth Economic Uplift.[72] For Du Bois, African American social equality was paramount and the expansion of the black professional class and its diffusion into mainstream society was a central objective of his agenda. In the post-Civil Rights/information society, however, "pure" economic progress has moved to a higher position on the list of priorities, not only for African Americans but for many marginalized communities and developing nations. Consequently the pursuit of Intellectual Property Empowerment and similar objectives warrant alternative entrepreneurial strategies and goals.

In contrast to W.E.B. Du Bois, Booker T. Washington not only placed the highest priority on black economic advancement, but he also advocated for entrepreneurship and business development as an egalitarian path that all blacks could pursue. Even under "anything-*but*-equal" Jim Crow, every African American could "cast down her bucket" and gather up the meager opportunities available to her. Washington argued that while whites might shun blacks *socially*, they would do business with blacks in circumscribed fields, and as blacks excelled in permissible areas of endeavor, the social barriers between the races would eventually give way.[73]

From an entrepreneurial perspective, Washington's "Equality through Economics" philosophy might best be understood as a form of "social" entrepreneurship. Social entrepreneurship is distinguished from classic entrepreneurship by virtue of the social entrepreneur's driving motivation: the achievement of some objective of social change or progress through

---

[71] Elizabeth Cogar, 'Sweeping Questions', *Style Weekly*, 5 January 2005, accessed 10 October 2014 at http://www.styleweekly.com/richmond/sweeping-questions/Content?oid=1379833; Notable Henricoans Database, accessed 10 October 2014 at http://events.henricolibrary.org/nhdb/.

[72] Wright, note 64 above, 234–5.

[73] Washington, note 28 above, 106–7, 114–15; Rogers, note 13 above, 81–4. Although Marcus Garvey shared Washington's emphasis on economic empowerment, his overarching strategy advocated repatriation to Africa, and thus was ultimately parallel to the Civil Rights Movement.

entrepreneurial endeavor.⁷⁴ While the social entrepreneur certainly seeks monetary profit in her business pursuits, such returns are not the end-goal of the enterprise but are considered the means by which to achieve her social agenda.

Washington's Equality through Economics ("ETE") philosophy can be considered as social entrepreneurship for several reasons. First, the principal goal is not monetary profit but *social change through business endeavor*: through successful business enterprise, blacks could attain a respected place in society. Indeed, the amount of profit is not particularly important. Even if she only makes enough to live on, the black entrepreneur or business person gains a measure of autonomy while at the same time demonstrating her valuable function in society. Moreover, Washington's ETE ideology tends to subordinate individual aspirations and preferences in favor of communal social progress. Indeed, much of the Talented Tenth distaste for Washington's philosophy stemmed from his willingness to accept the relegation of blacks to menial crafts and trades, irrespective of the more sophisticated vocational appetites and aptitudes of many educated blacks. In many ways, Equality through Economics bespeaks more of a plan for the social elevation of African Americans, than of a capitalist agenda for individual wealth enhancement.⁷⁵

In light of the legal and social gains achieved through the Civil Rights Movement, an application of ETE social entrepreneurship presents a viable social action platform for African American and other Intellectual Property Empowerment initiatives. First, the need to prioritize economic development should be self-evident. While the struggle for black legal and social equality has not been won completely and should not be abandoned, changed circumstances and opportunities warrant a new emphasis on economic justice. By employing intellectual property protection to promote communal economic advancement, the African American community takes full socio-economic advantage of its most valuable resource: its creative and inventive capability.

Second, the ETE social entrepreneurship approach is consistent with cooperative enterprise, which is essential to Intellectual Property

---

⁷⁴ John Whitman, "Social Entrepreneurship: An Overview", 563–6, in Bygrave and Zacharakis (eds), *Entrepreneurship*; Roger Spear, *Social Entrepreneurship: A Comparative Perspective, Businesses With A Difference*, 202–4 (University of Toronto Press, Toronto 2012); Pozen, note 58 above, 294–8.

⁷⁵ Washington, note 28 above, 114–15; Butler, note 16 above, 151–2; Wright, note 64 above, 225–6, 234; Danielle M. Conway, "Promoting Indigenous Innovation, Enterprise, and Entrepreneurship Through the Licensing of Article 31 Indigenous Assets and Resources", 64 SMU L. Rev. 1095, 1096–8, 1101–3 (2011).

Empowerment.⁷⁶ Intellectual property development, protection and commercial exploitation can sometimes be prohibitively expensive. Whereas copyright registration can be had for a nominal $35 fee, pursuing even a relatively simple patent application can cost tens of thousands of dollars.⁷⁷ Many African American inventors, artists and entrepreneurs simply lack the resources to pursue "lone-wolf" intellectual property entrepreneurship. Those who insist on "going it alone" often end up watching their ideas die on the vine, or desperate to avoid such an outcome, they sell out their interest for a fraction of its worth after having rejected more equitable, communal cooperative opportunities. Ironically, many of those who more readily agree to cooperative ventures actually have the resources to pursue their projects independently, but they recognize that equitable communal cooperation not only spreads the risk, it can also *economically empower the community as a whole*.

Finally, ETE social entrepreneurship would promote enterprise that targets pressing intellectual property-related needs in the African American community.⁷⁸ Whether or not addressing the community's access to knowledge and affordable medicines deficiencies presents the most lucrative business opportunities, the mandate of Intellectual Property Empowerment is not indiscriminate wealth maximization, but rather, communal socio-economic progress.⁷⁹ Indeed, where the African American intellectual property owner's pecuniary objectives conflict with this goal, social entrepreneurship resolves the conflict in favor of her community.

---

⁷⁶ Henderson, note 2 above, 140–2; Roger Spear, note 74 above, 210–11; Pozen, note 58 above, 331.

⁷⁷ http://www.copyright.gov/docs/fees.html; http://www.uspto.gov/web/offices/ac/qs/ope/fee010114.htm, accessed 10 October 2014.

⁷⁸ *See* Victoria F. Phillips, "Symposium, Commodification, Intellectual Property and the Quilters of Gee's Bend", 15 Am. U. J. Gender Soc. Pol'y & L. 359, 363–70 (2007) (discussing a highly successful communal social entrepreneurship business through which local women sell indigenous culture quilts). I have asked entrepreneurship and entertainment law experts to explore ideas for similar enterprises, including low-cost online community IP education programs staffed by pro bono attorneys, IP litigation support for marginalized clients provided on a quasi-contingency/royalty assignment basis, and tax shelter/trust and estate advice provided in conjunction with IP social justice trust and foundation formation. Some applications of these proposals are discussed in Chapter 10.

⁷⁹ Whitman, note 74 above, 566–70.

Applying ETE Social Entrepreneurship to Other IP Empowerment Contexts

Although there is no "one size fits all" approach to Intellectual Property Empowerment, ETE social entrepreneurship can be adapted to a variety of Intellectual Property Empowerment contexts. For example the Grameen Bank, which provides "solidarity loans" to groups of impoverished villagers in India, might be considered an exercise in ETE social entrepreneurship. Grameen lending effectively addresses imminent socio-economic deficiencies by investing in underutilized human capital, by extending loans which are "collateralized" by communal collaboration: the members of each borrower group undertake collective responsibility to ensure that each member repays her individual loan.[80] By assessing the pertinent socio-political history, cultural traditions and economic conditions and priorities of the subject community, ETE social entrepreneurship can be similarly applied to a wide variety of intellectual property-related socio-economic problems.

IMPLEMENTING INTELLECTUAL PROPERTY EMPOWERMENT: ENGAGING COLLABORATIVE ACTION

Intellectual Property Empowerment is intended as a socio-economic movement comprised of (i) intellectual property social justice legal theory, which is based on the principle that the social utility objectives underlying IP protection can only be achieved through legal norms that assure socially equitable IP participation for all; and (ii) a social action plan centered around social entrepreneurship, and which requires incentivized "IP social activists", equipped with a command of basic intellectual property principles.

Intellectual Property Empowerment is an adaptable social action tool. It can be implemented as a linear, grassroots organizational strategy in principal stages of (i) intellectual property social justice theory dissemination/community IP education; (ii) identification of and devising solutions for communal/development IP social priorities, deficiencies and long-term goals; and (iii) redressing systemic IP social deficiency through law and policy initiatives. Alternatively, Intellectual Property Empowerment can be implemented through modular and targeted application, the topic/chapter

---

[80] http://en.wikipedia.org/wiki/Grameen Bank, accessed 10 October 2014.

arrangement of this book being one such example. Consistent with the collaborative nature of Intellectual Property Empowerment, IP social activist scholars, theorists and experts from a variety of fields herein consider the theory of intellectual property social justice and assess aspects or problems of IP Empowerment. Through *Entrepreneurship and Empowerment*, IP social activists apply the tools of social entrepreneurship to specific as well as systemic IP social deficiencies; through *Education and Advocacy*, IP social activists illustrate how communities and nations can be assisted with and empowered to undertake IP social reform; and through *Engagement and Activism*, IP social activists explore how IP social justice theory can be used to harmonize IP protection with broader social needs and development goals.

Collectively the contributors to this work provide a framework for the reorientation of prevailing intellectual property perspectives toward a more inclusive and cohesive global IP system. Our purpose is to inspire as much as it is to inform; if this volume sparks ideas and ignites action, the foundation for Intellectual Property Empowerment will have been laid.

PART I

Entrepreneurship and empowerment

2. An entrepreneurship approach to achieving IP social justice
John R. Whitman

That we accept the world as it is does not in any sense weaken our desire to change it into what we believe it should be – it is necessary to begin where the world is if we are going to change it to what we think it should be. That means working in the system.

Saul D. Alinsky, *Rules for Radicals* (1989/1971, p. xix)

For the United States to survive and continue its economic leadership in the world, we must see entrepreneurship as our central comparative advantage. Nothing else can give us the necessary leverage.

Carl Schramm, President of the Kauffman Foundation, quoted in *Start-Up Nation* (Senor and Singer, 2009, p. 19)

Money (That's What I Want).

Barrett Strong, 1959

INTRODUCTION

The aim of this chapter is to describe how entrepreneurship, properly understood, can provide a strategy and a mode of action to advance social justice by changing intellectual property practices and laws consistent with the theory proposed in the introductory chapter. As Alinsky suggests in the opening quotation, the key is to grasp how entrepreneurship works within a system of social institutions consisting of norms and rules that must be understood for needed social change to occur, if it can occur at all. A conceptual framework and a menu of strategies for change are offered to facilitate this understanding.

To some, principally in business schools, the idea of entrepreneurship is restricted to the classical Schumpeterian business entrepreneur, but as we will see below, acting entrepreneurially is spreading to other domains, including nonprofit organizations (Dees, Emerson and Economy, 2001), philanthropy (Van Slyke and Newman, 2006), education (Hess, 2008) and policy (Hart, 2003b), to achieve innovative and effective outcomes.

Conventional usage of the term "entrepreneur" implies an individual; however, collective undertakings have been described in terms of the "entrepreneurial state" (Eisinger, 1988) and "community-based enterprise", in which "a community [acts] corporately as both entrepreneur and enterprise" (Paredo and Chrisman, 2004). This chapter encourages the reader, whether engaging individually or collectively, to think about how to act entrepreneurially in a number of alternative roles in order to achieve IP social justice. This chapter does not, however, address contested views of property itself in the literature concerning economic liberty, creativity and justice, but it should be acknowledged that the debate involving individual versus collective ownership merits further consideration elsewhere (Adam MacLeod, personal correspondence, 20 December 2013).

Why entrepreneurship? Entrepreneurship in times of economic growth has resulted in new business formation, new product and service creation and many new jobs, all of which in turn grow the economy and contribute to tax revenues, better neighborhoods and lower crime. According to popular belief in the West, capitalism, the prevailing economic system in liberal democracies, has over time produced an unprecedented quality of life for more people than ever.[1] The entrepreneur is celebrated as the capitalist hero who innovates higher quality and lower costs for innumerable consumer products and services that make life easier and more rewarding for citizens, and that generate profits more efficiently for businesses. Indeed, the persuasive magic of this narrative is such that by promoting free markets that unencumber entrepreneurs with regulations and "red tape", politicians have themselves achieved great power, security and popular legitimacy.[2]

Sooner or later, entrepreneurship had to follow administration, management and leadership to become a core attribute of professional agency and a distinct research topic in graduate business schools, as well as a focus of public policy, in countries competing in the global economy. Indeed, President Obama announced his Startup America initiative in

---

[1] A more nuanced analysis compellingly shows that there are many "recipes" for economic success, depending more on policy practices and institutional development than any single, monolithic economic ideology (Rodrik, 2007).

[2] The image of the totemic individual, heroic entrepreneur, is more mythological than a realistic description of how entrepreneurs are fortunately embedded in and opportunistically exploit a vast infrastructure of social investments, including their own formal education, an intellectual property system, and a legal system to enforce their property rights. Popular misconceptions of individual entitlements and free markets, both of which ignore government and social investments, have been compellingly debunked (Alperovitz and Daly, 2008; Block and Keller, 2011; Lazonick, 1993/1991), but the myths endure.

January 2010, declaring, "Entrepreneurs embody the promise of America: the idea that if you have a good idea and are willing to work hard and see it through, you can succeed in this country. And in fulfilling this promise, entrepreneurs also play a critical role in expanding our economy and creating jobs".[3] The Startup America initiative has launched a nationwide flurry of communities engaged in building "entrepreneurial ecosystems" to harness the creative individual agency and ingenuity that is latent everywhere to increase economic and social well-being (Feld, 2012).[4]

Yet entrepreneurial performance in times of economic decline and stagnation has been mixed. According to the Business Employment Dynamics data of the Bureau of Labor Statistics, the number of establishments less than one year old has plummeted from a high of 667,341 in 2005 to 505,473 in 2010, the lowest point since data collection began in 1994, and jobs created by these firms have fallen from 4.1 million in 1994 to 2.5 million in 2010 (http://data.bls.gov/cgi-bin/print.pl/bdm/entrepreneurship/entrepreneurship.htm, accessed 10 October 2014). Nevertheless, there is a difference between main street entrepreneurship and high-tech entrepreneurship, including the information and communications technology (ICT) segment, and, according to the Kauffman Foundation (Hathaway, 2013), "high-tech companies play an outsized role in job creation. High-tech businesses start lean but grow rapidly in the early years, and their job creation is so robust that it offsets job losses from early-stage business failures".

Overall, entrepreneurship has been emerging as a respected, mainstream professional discipline. Business schools now vie for top standing based on ratings of their entrepreneurship faculty, curricula and extra-curricular activities.[5] Entrepreneurship is also taking a place in the economic development policy discourse (Eisinger, 1988; Hart, 2003a; Naudé, 2011; Stam and van Stel, 2009) as well as in schools of law. One legal scholar, who provides an excellent overview of entrepreneurship for lawyers, declares, "We are all entrepreneurs now" (Pozen, 2008), a stance echoed by Phil Weiser, dean of the Colorado University Law School (Feld, 2012, p. 124):

> For students at the Law School and across campus, we are emphasizing a basic point: you are all entrepreneurs now. Whether or not they join a startup or a

---

[3] Source: http://www.whitehouse.gov/economy/business/startup-america, accessed 10 October 2014.

[4] See also the Kauffman Foundation's initiative, One Million Cups (http://www.1millioncups.com/, accessed 10 October 2014).

[5] See, for example, http://grad-schools.usnews.rankingsandreviews.com/best-graduate-schools/top-business-schools/entrepreneurship-rankings, accessed 10 October 2014.

large company, the reality is that all students should think of themselves as entrepreneurs.

The inception of modern entrepreneurship is often linked to the era of the Industrial Revolution, and the first use of the term "entrepreneur" and descriptions of entrepreneurial characteristics appear in the economic writings of Richard Cantillon (1775) and Jean-Baptiste Say (1803). But the activity can precede the term, and a compendium of scholarly accounts of the history of entrepreneurship linking it to economic growth (Landes, Mokyr and Baumol, 2010) indicates that entrepreneurship may have emerged at the time of transitioning from traditional gift exchange between persons and bulk trade at market prices, described as the shift "from 'anthropological' to 'economic' exchange and production" (Hudson, 2010, p. 10). In this compendium, Baumol and Strom present a definition of an "*entrepreneur* as anyone who undertakes some economic activity on her own initiative on the basis of alert observation of an opportunity to enhance her wealth, power, or prestige" (Baumol and Strom, 2010, p. 530). They then distinguish between *replicative* entrepreneurs, who essentially duplicate the activities of existing firms and *innovative* entrepreneurs, who "offer new products, use new production processes, enter new markets, or adopt new forms of organization" (p. 531).

Entrepreneurs may further be divided into *productive* or *unproductive* entrepreneurs. *Innovative unproductive entrepreneurs* pursue novel approaches to "rent-seeking, criminal, and other unproductive or even socially-damaging activities", such as taking bribes or engaging in lawsuits for monetary rewards, or, we might add, exploiting for their own benefit the IP creations of others. Much of history features such entrepreneurs grabbing riches for themselves rather than creating wealth for all. By contrast, *innovative productive entrepreneurs* are the drivers of wealth creation, particularly in the industrial and post-industrial eras. Yet a critical assessment of these two categories might blur the lines, especially in the earlier industrial era before government regulations imposed constraints on the exploitative practices of otherwise productive entrepreneurs including John D. Rockefeller and Andrew Carnegie.

This brief account does not do the compendium justice, but its conclusions can be summarized by noting the contribution of economist Douglass North, who "has long-emphasized, it is the institutions of society that arguably have served to reallocate entrepreneurial activity to a considerable extent from rent-seeking and military violence to innovation and production" (p. 535), and in particular, the following institutions are mentioned as key to this process: the patent system; antitrust law; bankruptcy protection; and the banking system. "The evolution of this rule of law", Baumol and Strom note, "in fact, was perhaps the most important contribution to the flourishing of productive entrepreneurship and the birth of capitalism" (p. 535). The compendium closes by asking how such institutions arise, and suggests that they often emerge by historical accident (Baumol and Strom, 2010).

From an historical perspective, entrepreneurship as a business practice originated in an economic sphere in which the characteristics of the entrepreneur – in essence, individual agency – describe thought and behavior relevant to profit-seeking activities in the market. Yet more recently, such characteristics have been generalized to describe entrepreneurial thought and behavior taking place in other, non-market venues, such as civil society, policy, international relations and religion, to achieve social and/or environmental, rather than economic goals. Thus some now speak of social entrepreneurs, policy entrepreneurs, norm entrepreneurs and moral entrepreneurs (Pozen, 2008). To repeat to a broader audience Pozen's declaration above, "We are all entrepreneurs now", and it is in the spirit of this more inclusive sense that readers are encouraged to be entrepreneurs in seeking IP social justice.

In short, "why entrepreneurship?" is perhaps best answered by the increasing historical and geographic evidence that individual agency, when allowed and encouraged to take the initiative to meet human needs and wants without depending on corporate, governmental or divine action, can be extraordinarily productive and effective. It only makes sense to learn from entrepreneurial thinking and behavior and to promote such a process to address a broad range of social needs, within and beyond the market.

Without taking ideological issue with either capitalism or entrepreneurship, it is worth noting that not everyone in a capitalist society necessarily benefits from the social arrangements in even the most advanced liberal democracies, and some may be harmed. This chapter is particularly concerned with those typically left behind, exploited or overlooked in the capitalist bounty, and considers how, working *entrepreneurially* within the capitalist system, social justice may yet prevail for historically disadvantaged populations. Richard Florida, who has written about the rise of the Creative Class and the emergence of the Creative Economy, calls for cultivating creativity among disadvantaged populations, to which it should be added, *and* protecting their intellectual property (Florida, 2012/2011, p. 10):

> I strongly believe that the key to improving the lot of underpaid, underemployed, and disadvantaged people lies not in social welfare programs or low-end make-work jobs, nor in somehow bringing back the factory jobs of the

past, but rather in tapping their innate creativity, paying them appropriately for it, and integrating them fully into the Creative Economy.[6]

In this chapter, having already sketched out the historical context of entrepreneurship, I will next:

- distinguish *classical* business entrepreneurship from *social* entrepreneurship;
- further refine the roles and qualities of the entrepreneur;
- note the impulse to change the status quo; and
- delineate the steps in the entrepreneurial process.

Subsequently, I will introduce concepts for applying an entrepreneurial approach:

- a model of social change;
- specific strategies to achieve social change;
- the *theory of change* model as a planning tool; and
- possible obstacles and unintended consequences.

These latter considerations can be used as a roadmap to guide the entrepreneurial actors whose roles are defined below. Before closing I address several considerations for the future, and finally I conclude by recapping the chapter.

Key consideration: The operative term in this chapter is "entrepreneur", and as such, the focus here is on the agency of an individual, one who independently takes action necessary to effect change. However, it is important to include in the discussion the possibility of collective entrepreneurship, that is, a group acting entrepreneurially together as a means to achieve a common goal.[7] While graduate schools of business and law focus on the *investor-owned firm* (IOF) as the principal (one would think only) model of business organization, in fact, capitalist economies allow several other models of business organization to flourish, including *non-profit organizations*, which in the United States prohibit individual accrual of assets, and *cooperatives*, in which individual members own, control and benefit from the organization (Whitman, 2012). Cooperatives, and in particular

---

[6] Certainly this line of thinking is reminiscent of Amartya Sen's exploration of cultivating human capabilities in *Development as Freedom* (Sen, 1999).

[7] Moreover, recent literature on entrepreneurship is beginning to acknowledge that entrepreneurs do not act alone, but depend on forming effective teams that bring together complementary skills (Aulet, 2013).

worker-owned cooperatives, exemplify the concept of collective entrepreneurship (Zeuli and Cropp, 2004/1980; Zeuli and Radel, 2005). The reader is encouraged to consider such cooperatives as well as nonprofit organizations, where feasible and desirable, as a means to achieve IP social justice, and not to assume that the IOF is the only available organizational form.

1. DISTINGUISHING CLASSICAL AND SOCIAL ENTREPRENEURSHIP

Classical business entrepreneurship has been practiced for centuries if not millennia. The first appropriation of the term "entrepreneurship" for other than classical entrepreneurship perhaps began with the contemporary field of "social entrepreneurship", which is relatively recent and its research agenda is still nascent (Mair, Robinson and Hockerts, 2006; Martin and Osberg, 2007, Spring). As in business entrepreneurship, the activity called social entrepreneurship most certainly predates the term. Bill Drayton, founder of Ashoka, is usually credited with launching attention to contemporary social entrepreneurship starting in 1978 (Bornstein, 2004); Gregory Dees may be the first to offer a social entrepreneurship course in a U.S. business school (Harvard) in the late 1990s (Dees, 2008); Muhammad Yunus donned the laurel as the first Nobel Prize for Peace-winning social entrepreneur, sharing the award in 2006 with the Grameen Bank, which he founded following a research project begun in 1976 (Yunus, 2007); and President Obama may be the first to invoke social entrepreneurship as a global policy opportunity in his 2009 Cairo speech: "And I will host a Summit on Entrepreneurship this year to identify how we can deepen ties between business leaders, foundations and social entrepreneurs in the United States and Muslim communities around the world" (Obama, 2009, 4 June).

Just as classical business entrepreneurship evokes an enterprising individual taking responsibility to help him or herself achieve economic rewards through innovation, social entrepreneurship conjures up a spirit of proud independence and self-reliance that would warm the heart of anyone loathe to provide public or governmental assistance to help those in need. As recounted by Pozen, George W. Bush was particularly fond of social entrepreneurship as a means to address social problems, declaring, "That's one of my favorite words, think about it: social entrepreneurship" (Pozen, 2008, p. 299, n. 267). Yet if social entrepreneurship is targeted to meeting social needs not otherwise being met by the market or the government, which suggests market and government failure, should a high incidence of social entrepreneurship in a society be considered a good or a bad thing?

Both classical and social entrepreneurship, of course, entail acting entrepreneurially, but the difference is that in classical entrepreneurship the effort typically produces a *financial* reward (profit), while in social entrepreneurship, the principal goal is to achieve a *social* benefit, not a financial reward. While this distinction may appear clear cut, it has failed to resolve a variety of contested and obfuscating definitions of social entrepreneurship, most emphasizing the creation of *social value*, others concerned with solving *social problems*, and some requiring *social change*, specifically systemic change, to achieve a social benefit (Whitman, 2010; Zahra, Gedajlovic, Neubaum and Shulman, 2009). It is not our goal to settle this debate, but for the pragmatic purposes of this chapter, which is to provide a practical conceptual framework for taking an entrepreneurial approach to achieving IP social justice, we will employ the following working definitions of classical business and social entrepreneurship, inspired by widely quoted definitions for entrepreneurship (Austin, Stevenson and Wei-Skillern, 2006) and social entrepreneurship (Dees, 2001/1998):

> *Classical business entrepreneurship* is the impulse to overcome all barriers to convert innovation to practice in the market.
>
> *Social entrepreneurship* is the impulse to overcome all barriers to convert innovation to practice in order to achieve social change.

Key consideration: Note in both cases the term, "impulse". An initial consideration for the reader concerns exactly what goal to be achieved motivates the entrepreneur(s), and whether it can be secured by existing rules or whether some impediment must be changed in order to achieve success. Among possible goals might be:

(a) to secure intellectual property protection and exploitation for one's self;
(b) to secure the same for another, either an individual or a class of aspiring IP owners; or,
(c) to protect the interests of people or the environment facing potential harm from the consequences of IP registration and/or enforcement by others.

Whatever the case, the immediate concern is whether the desired goal is readily achievable. If the goal is not readily in reach, its barriers must be ascertained and the process of devising a strategy to overcome such barriers must be deliberated.

2. REFINING THE ROLES AND QUALITIES OF THE ENTREPRENEUR

The approach offered here discerns five types of roles that actors can play to achieve intellectual property (IP) social justice goals addressed in the Introduction to this chapter.

- First: The *IP Creator* – the author or artist, the inventive scientist or engineer, the imaginative child or practical-minded homemaker, indeed, anyone who conceives and develops an innovation worthy of protection for its monetary potential in the market is at the center of the stage, for our principal concern is that this individual's rights are understood, protected and appropriately represented.
- Second: The *IP Business Entrepreneur* – the business savvy agent who seeks to exploit the value of IP through the market is crucial to the story, for without such an entrepreneur the IP would languish. It is important to recognize that the IP Creator could also act as the IP Business Entrepreneur, directly taking his or her own IP to the market. More often, the IP Creator works with an independent IP Business Entrepreneur to monetize the innovation. For example, the author disseminates work through a publisher, or a musician through a record label. Sadly, as the case study at the end of this chapter recounts, there are too many cases of IP Business Entrepreneurs who appropriate IP from its creators and fail to provide them proper, if any, monetary compensation or even credit.

    The classical business entrepreneur is described by Schumpeter as one who starts a new business or production process or introduces such innovations to new areas (Schumpeter, 2008/1934). It is this business entrepreneur who, as Carl Schramm declares in the second quotation above, is central to the comparative advantage essential to the United States in the global economy. But as is argued in this chapter, an even broader range of actors than business entrepreneurs will provide a far greater, more effective and socially just comparative advantage.
- Third: The *IP Lawyer* – the legally trained individual who plays a facilitating role to inform and guide the IP Creator can play a crucial and entrepreneurial role to overcome social justice barriers to expand opportunities for emerging creators to protect their IP and be appropriately compensated for it.
- Fourth: The *IP Policymaker or Activist* – the individual who seeks to create policy or to change policy can effectively advance IP social justice. Policymakers and activists will be crucial to ensuring that

all aspiring IP creators have equal access to and resources for IP protection.
- Fifth: The *IP Educator* – the individual who uses the conceptual tools described here for educational or training purposes in formal or informal settings can play a key role to inform, inspire and mobilize promising creators, business entrepreneurs, lawyers, policymakers, activists and members of privileged groups and the general public (Goodman, 2001), beginning with understanding how and why IP creators serve the common wealth and should be protected and compensated accordingly.

With these five roles identified, the challenge becomes how to think and act entrepreneurially, as a way to empower human agency, in playing any of these roles, or indeed, playing more than one such role, to achieve social justice – that ideal of a society in which everyone has access to the capabilities that allow them to reach their full, desired potential (Sen, 1999). Collectively, any or all such actors engaging in entrepreneurial thought or behavior will be referred to as *IP Entrepreneurs*.

Key consideration: The reader may determine which of the above roles is most suitable to the interest at hand: creator, business entrepreneur, lawyer, policymaker/activist or educator. The reader may then proceed, focusing on how entrepreneurship pertains to the selected role.

The opportunity afforded by the framework constructed here is that all five types of actors can deliberate and behave in entrepreneurial ways to achieve their respective goals. As entrepreneurs driven to overcome barriers in order to achieve innovation, such players may choose one of two approaches as defined above: *Classical Entrepreneur*, who operates by exchanging goods or services for financial reward in the market, or *Social Entrepreneur*, who may operate in the market for financial purposes secondary to achieving social change, but may be more effective by operating in other institutional venues, such as in a legal or regulatory environment, educational setting or media channel.

All entrepreneurs begin with identifying an *opportunity*: "The process starts with opportunity, not money, strategy, networks, team, or the business plan" (Timmons and Spinelli, 2009, p. 110). The entrepreneurial opportunity in IP is not the creative output alone, but the demand for it, which exists or can be created. The social entrepreneurial opportunity is recognition of a gap between existing social arrangements and what they ought to be. Closing this gap is the social change that constitutes the goal of the social entrepreneur. In both cases, the entrepreneurial venture will also require *resources* and usually a *team* to complement needed skills. In Classical Entrepreneurship, the team typically requires at least three capacities, no more than two of which are likely to be found in a single individual: product/service knowledge, marketing skill and financial skill: what Sirolli refers to as the Trinity of Management (Sirolli, 2012; Whitman, 2013).

All social entrepreneurs exhibit the following essential characteristics (some of which may also apply to classical entrepreneurs):

- *Vision*: The social entrepreneur sees opportunity – desirable possibilities and outcomes – that others may not. The social entrepreneur is not satisfied with the status quo, but is driven to achieve his or her vision and to change the status quo in order to achieve this vision.
- *Motivation*: The standard economic model describing the rational person employs the function of *incentives* to influence behavior. Incentives are typically financial rewards, such as income or wealth. However, the model described here posits that entrepreneurs are not driven by such incentives, but are deeply *intrinsically motivated* to achieve their aims, so much so that they may actually forego or delay even attractive external incentives in order to pursue their vision.
- *Innovation*: The entrepreneur is an innovator, either creating something new or transforming an existing thing or process in a new way, or introducing it to a new area. The social entrepreneur innovates to achieve his or her vision.
- *Activation*: There are no armchair social entrepreneurs; action is required to achieve the envisioned change.
- *Change*: Changing the status quo is the intentional consequence of all the above entrepreneurial characteristics; and achieving the desired change is the acid test of success. Social entrepreneurs effect social change. But failed entrepreneurs are no less entrepreneurial for the effort, and indeed, failures are learning opportunities. A record of past failure is no certain indication that an entrepreneur cannot succeed in the future, and may even help the entrepreneur achieve subsequent success.

The entrepreneur concerned with IP social justice begins by identifying an opportunity in the form of a market or government failure or a normative failure concerning intellectual property and then must be sufficiently incentivized or motivated to correct this failure. For example, an IP social justice gap might exist where IP Creators in a historically marginalized community are unfamiliar with IP protection and thus fail to take the steps necessary to protect their rights and consequently are deprived of revenue generated from their innovations. The IP Entrepreneur might see this gap as an opportunity to provide IP information and support on a for-profit (classical) or nonprofit (social) basis.

Key considerations: The reader must first identify an entrepreneurial opportunity, and may then decide whether to operate through the market or through other, non-market venues to address this opportunity. The reader may also reflect on whether he or she seeks conventional compensation or is intrinsically motivated to pursue social change. The above checklist can be consulted to determine whether the reader's selected role is socially entrepreneurial in nature.

3. THE IMPULSE TO CHANGE THE STATUS QUO

Of all the above entrepreneurial characteristics, perhaps the most crucial to success is motivation. Entrepreneurship is a very difficult undertaking,[8] and while financial or non-monetary rewards may provide incentives, the degree of effort to overcome barriers can require a deeply internalized motivation to persevere.[9]

Where does this motivation come from? My proposition is that the individual is guided by deeply internalized social values[10] that impel the entrepreneur to take action to realize those values, providing the impulse in the definitions above. For the subsistence level, necessity-driven entrepreneur that characterizes millions of souls in poor economies, daily survival is a powerful motivator, animated by needs at the very base of Maslow's hierarchy (Maslow, 1943). For others, the urge to create something new that does not exist in the status quo can be the spark. For still others, a disturbing dissonance with the injustice of the status quo may be sufficient to take action, and this is the hallmark motivation of the social entrepreneur. Yet Albert Cho reminds us to be circumspect of the values claims of the social entrepreneur: "When entrepreneurs organize their actions around values they have identified as 'social,' they have already made demanding epistemological and political claims about their ability and entitlement to articulate what lies in the public's interest" (Cho, 2006, p. 42). Actors advocating for social justice losers – even in cases where

---

[8] The special opportunities, conditions, and challenges facing women entrepreneurs is the subject of the Diana Project; see http://www.dianaproject.org/, accessed 10 October 2014.

[9] The role of entrepreneurial motivation is more extensively explored by Bird (Bird, 1989).

[10] The literature on values and their influence on behavior is addressed in the following works: Rokeach, 1973; Schwartz, 2012; Whitman, 2008, 2009.

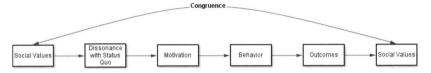

Figure 2.1 Logic model of entrepreneurial motivation

vulnerable populations welcome such advocacy – might well consider the consequences of change for status quo winners and be prepared to justify what is in the public's interest.

The relevant social values guide the behavior of the entrepreneur to seek the desired outcomes, which, when achieved, convey his or her preferred social values and satisfy and resolve the entrepreneur's impulse. Thus, social values (which, for some, may be survival, for others purely monetary or instrumental, for others still, purely emotional or expressive) are the basis for behavior and for allocating resources, such as time and money, and may explain the ultimate rewards for the effort. Figure 2.1 illustrates the chain of successive factors that compel the entrepreneur to action to achieve the outcomes that will satisfy his or her need to change the status quo.

With reference to the entrepreneurial actors described above, the IP Creator is typically intrinsically motivated to create. The IP Entrepreneur is also intrinsically motivated at the outset to be creative and to seek rewards from his or her innovations. The IP Lawyer and IP Policymaker/Activist may need to deliberate as to the relative contribution of internalized motivation or incentive structure required to compel them to action, for they typically act on behalf of others (usually clients or constituents), not for themselves. If a lawyer or policymaker is sufficiently disturbed by an IP injustice, the magnitude of the financial incentive may not be as material as the internalized commitment to right the wrong – to resolve the dissonance with the status quo. Once the motivation is in place, the entrepreneur then envisions a preferred change (innovation) in the status quo and takes action to achieve it.

Once motivated, natural entrepreneurs instinctively follow their noses. It is worth noting that many of the most successful innovation-driven, productive classical entrepreneurs of all time never completed higher education: Andrew Carnegie, John D. Rockefeller, Sr., Henry Ford, Thomas Edison, Walt Disney, Ray Kroc, Richard Branson, Bill Gates, Steve Jobs, Steve Wozniak, Michael Dell, John Mackey, Mark Zuckerberg and many more. However, the success of such innovators has not gone unstudied, and we are now able to draw some preliminary insights from the evidence that can be used to guide the thought and action of prospective entrepreneurs in training.

Key consideration: The reader may reflect on what moves him or her to take on the work ahead. Is it, for example, the incentive of payment offered by a client? Or does the motivation derive from an internalized urge to right a wrong? And how strong is that impulse? Will it sustain the level of commitment required to overcome all barriers to achieve success?

A special note is reserved here for IP Educators, particularly educators teaching in graduate business schools and law schools. Courses in entrepreneurship and social entrepreneurship are indeed taught in many business schools. Students interested in entrepreneurship are likely motivated by profit, and those intrinsically motivated by profit self-select to learn the requisite skills in business schools. "But", asks Gregory Dees (Dees and Anderson, 2003),

> does it make sense to blend the profit motive with a social objective? Adam Smith was skeptical. In concluding one of his most famous passages about the "invisible hand", Smith (1776) makes the following observation about business people, "I have never known much good done by those who affected to trade for the public good. It is an affection, indeed, not very common among merchants, and very few words need be employed in dissuading them from it (p. 478)." Even those who do not share Smith's skepticism must admit that successful examples are rare and the risks of conflict between pursuing profit and serving a social objective are significant.

Social entrepreneurship taught in a way that emphasizes *social change*, rather than making a profit, may not resonate well among students who pay a significant tuition fee or accumulate serious debt to attend business schools, though there may well be exceptions among those who are open to non-financial intrinsic motivation. Aaron Wildavsky, writing about the challenges of teaching in a school of public policy, posed the question (Wildavsky, 1987/1979, p. xxxiii), "Why does one go to a school of public policy? It cannot be because he thinks everything is just wonderful the way it is; if so, he would go to a school of business. Our students are change-oriented." By contrast, law students, particularly those who sign up for elective public policy clinics, may be among the most intrinsically motivated to effect needed social change, and may also be responsive to a social entrepreneurship approach.

4. STEPS IN THE ENTREPRENEURIAL PROCESS

Business schools have traditionally taught a linear, sequential approach to starting a business, reflected in the logic model in Figure 2.2 below

Figure 2.2   Steps in the entrepreneurial process

(Whitman, 2011). The entrepreneur identifies an opportunity; prepares a business plan; forms the appropriate organization, usually an investor owned company in the case of for-profit intentions, but it could as well be a cooperative or non-profit organization; raises needed financial resources and assembles a team of fellow workers; and they then get to work. The venture is monitored and evaluated as to its objectives along the way and eventually, if the firm has not already been acquired and reaches a growth limit to its resources, the decision is made to "go to scale".

At some point the firm may face the opportunity to be acquired by, or merge with, another company, or, if a privately held firm, to solicit public capital investment through an initial public offering. The owners of the firm may also decide to sustain operations without a further growth or harvest objective as a type of "lifestyle" business, or perhaps to wind down operations and cease to exist as an entity. In the case of a closely held company owned by an aging founder, there may be the option to pass ownership and control to a son, daughter or other family member, or to sell the enterprise to employees through an employee stock ownership plan or to convert it to a cooperative, owned and controlled by the employees. Yet another option may be to franchise the business.[11]

In a study of 27 serial entrepreneurs, Sarasvathy found that they typically do not prepare business plans (Sarasvathy, 2008). She describes a more organic process, which she calls *effectuation*, in contrast to the linear, predictive process implicit in the logic model above. Effectuation is essentially driven by three factors: Who you are, what you know and whom you know; or intellectual capital, human capital and social capital (p. xiii). Drawing on their own capacities and knowledge, entrepreneurs begin pursuing an opportunity and readily engage others, who add their own capacities and knowledge, so that the original idea may evolve sometimes quite rapidly into something different from, but more viable than the original concept. Entrepreneurs try to avoid or reduce risk as much as possible, and invest only what they deem would be an acceptable loss.

---

[11]   Two popular textbooks for business students on the campus of Babson College, well known for its entrepreneurship curriculum, are *Entrepreneurship* (Bygrave and Zacharakis, 2011) and *New Venture Creation* (Timmons and Spinelli, 2009).

Whether a strategic or organic approach is considered, most agree that the discipline involved in preparing a business plan allows the entrepreneur to anticipate possible threats and opportunities, and thus prepares the entrepreneur for such eventualities (for guidance in preparing business plans, see, for example, Abrams, 2010). Moreover, in the case of needing financial investors or loans, a business plan will almost certainly be required by any institutional source of funds. Finally, it behooves the entrepreneur to anticipate his or her desired ultimate goal for the venture, for if a transfer of ownership is ever contemplated it will be imperative to be able to prove that the firm's assets, including its intellectual property, are owned by the firm and are beyond claim by anyone else. This point was poignantly brought home to many software entrepreneurs in the movie, *The Social Network*, in which a software programmer working for a couple of IP Creators who failed to protect their IP through an employment contract, took off to start his own competing venture: Facebook. Therefore, in the business planning process, it makes sense to start with the desired end goal, and then work backwards to determine the elements of the plan, including securing IP ownership, to achieve that goal.[12]

5. APPLYING AN ENTREPRENEURSHIP APPROACH

As noted above, there are two, distinct entrepreneurial motivations, one primarily financial, to secure a monetary return for one's efforts, the other primarily social, to effect a change in the status quo to achieve a social goal. As we read in Chapter 1, it is reasonable to view Booker T. Washington's program of Equality Through Economics as an agenda for social entrepreneurship. In this context, classical entrepreneurship is prescribed for Blacks as the road to yield monetary rewards, but Washington's own primary aim is social: to raise the social and economic status of Blacks and, in a larger scope, any marginalized population, through economic achievement. And indeed, this logic is not essentially distinct from that of many champions of business who see financial enterprise as the road to personal and social betterment, a point exemplified by Peter Brooke in his global campaign to spread a culture of venture capital as a path to economic and social development (Brooke, 2009).

---

[12] Backward planning and forward execution is a common approach in a variety of fields, including law and policy making (Neumann, 1990) and curriculum design (Wiggins and McTighe, 2005)

Classical entrepreneurship is amply addressed in many contemporary business textbooks, and we strongly encourage further study of such entrepreneurship for those keen to secure the financial rewards by taking IP to the market. As noted above, entrepreneurship is a difficult path, and the IP Creator who wishes to be entrepreneurial or the IP Entrepreneur exploiting his or her own IP or that of another is well advised to consult one or more texts (e.g., Bygrave and Zacharakis, 2011; Scarborough, 2012; Timmons and Spinelli, 2009) and to take an entrepreneurship course, such as FastTrac, created by the Kauffman Foundation (http://fasttrac.org/, accessed 10 October 2014).

Whether one decides to pursue IP social justice through classical or social entrepreneurial activity, one kind of IP entrepreneurship that warrants special consideration is that of high-tech entrepreneurship. As there is a qualitative difference between general entrepreneurship in small and medium sized enterprises found up and down Main Street and high-tech, high-growth entrepreneurship largely consisting of STEM (science, technology, engineering, mathematics) experts (Aulet and Murray, 2013; Hathaway, 2013), it is important to seek the relevant training and advice specific to each type. Those with high-tech innovations are advised to consult with an accountant or lawyer experienced in high-tech business, angel investors (see http://www.angelcapitalassociation.org/, accessed 10 October 2014), or venture capitalists (see http://www.nvca.org/, accessed 10 October 2014) in their areas. Such professionals may have direct access to qualified and experienced technology entrepreneurs familiar with the relevant technology markets. Those employed by a university should consult the university's resources for marketing and licensing assistance.[13]

As discussed in Part 1 of this Chapter, social justice can be pursued by classical or social entrepreneurs; however, the objectives of IP social justice are more directly connected to social entrepreneurship that emphasizes social change over monetary profit. Accordingly, the balance of this chapter turns to social entrepreneurship with the specific aim of changing the status quo to achieve IP social justice. The framework described below provides a roadmap for an entrepreneurship approach to achieving IP social justice. The first step in this roadmap is to consider the analytical *Model of Social Change*.

---

[13] See, for example, the MIT Technology Licensing Office (http://web.mit.edu/tlo/www/) and the Office of Technology Commercialization at the University of Alabama in Huntsville (http://www.uah.edu/otc), both accessed 10 October 2014.

A Model of Social Change

While the definition of the classical business entrepreneur places such work in the market, the operative term in the definition of social entrepreneurship is *social change*. The market as a venue for the exchange of goods and services is fairly well understood, but what does social change mean, and how is it achieved?

Social change takes different forms, both in terms of type and venue. As to type, social change may be *systemic* or *local*, and it is crucial when speaking of systemic change to define the system that pertains; otherwise, the "systemic" qualifier has no reference.

The theory of institutional change proposed by Douglass North, winner of the Nobel Prize in Economics in 1993 (North, 2005/1990), attempts to explain both historic and contemporary social change. North defines two generic types of change: *Normative Change*, in which social norms and behaviors are changed, and *Codified Change*, in which written laws, regulations and rules are changed. North postulates that institutions (education, government, law, the market and so on) in all societies operate according to certain "rules of the game", and that such rules are of these two types. All social change can be explained by these rules or changes made to these rules, which constitute the codified laws and regulations of a society and the actual, normative behavior of the population (which of course may deviate from the codified rules).

It stands to reason that if you can change behaviors (for example, practices) to achieve social justice (Normative Change), there may be no need for a law or regulatory instrument and an associated enforcement mechanism. However, in some cases, it may be necessary to pass a law – a sanctioned code (Codified Change), which even alone may be inadequate to achieve the intended behavioral change. Consider, for example, the 14th Constitutional Amendment ratified in 1865, which notwithstanding its nominal status as the law of the land was followed by a bloody and disgraceful Jim Crow era that ultimately ended 99 years later by the 24th Amendment explicitly granting Congress enforcement power for related legislation. Yet there is no doubt that the values and norms of racism yet persist to influence behavior in some quarters.

With reference to venue, normative rules and codified rules may be considered at the national or societal level, and describe a society as a whole. But it is also clear that normative and codified rules can be introduced or changed within specific social institutions (such as education, law and the market) and even within specific organizations within those institutions (such as schools, courts and banks). Thus, in addition to the *type* of change, the *venue* of change is also a key consideration (see Table 2.1).

Table 2.1 Model of social change

		Type of Change	
		Normative change through informal, behavioral rules: social values, norms	Codified change through formal, written rules: constitution, laws, regulations
Venue	Higher Level (Societal or Institutional)	Education, socialization processes	National laws, regulations
	Lower Level (Community or Organizational)	Local civil society, interpersonal relations	Local laws, company policies

Using this analytical framework, the IP Entrepreneur can determine the type of change (Normative or Codified) and venue of change (Higher Level or Lower Level) needed to change the status quo.

Strategies for Social Change

The second step in the roadmap for social change is to select specific, actionable strategies for social change within the four quadrants of the Model above:

1. *Education*, which takes many forms, has traditionally been employed as a strategy to inculcate norms and values that guide social behavior.
2. *Law* has similarly traditionally been the strategy for effecting sanctioned codes and rules for enforcement.
3. *Charity* has been from pre-Biblical times a means to palliate the condition of the poor, disaster victims and other distressed individuals and populations.
4. *Market Exchange* has a similarly ancient history as the institution for value exchange in a defined physical or virtual venue.
5. *Grassroots Mobilization* strategically organizes resources at the community level to effect social change.
6. *Movements* mobilize resources at the national level to effect social change.
7. *Advocacy* is a strategy in which the rights of marginalized populations are represented by advocates, often legally trained activists.
8. *Capacity Building* is a strategy that creates new resources, technology or knowledge to support social change.

9. *Innovation* is a strategy to create new resources (capacity building) to achieve social change.
10. *Funding* is a strategy to support any of the prior strategies to effect progressive social change.

Reflecting on the elements of the Model of Social Change and the strategies listed above should reveal a rather broad range of options available to the social entrepreneur for achieving desired social change. These strategies can be selected, sequenced or combined to achieve normative or codified social change in higher or lower level social venues.

Key consideration: The reader may ponder for a moment whether and how specialized schools of graduate level education, including law, business, education and social work (or similar schools) are more or less oriented toward specific strategies for social change listed above, and are thus examples of education as a strategy to effect (or impede) change in their respective social institutions.

To demonstrate and test this framework, apply it first to a brief examination of certain historical arrangements: The first slaves in continental North America arrived from Africa to Jamestown, Virginia, then a British colony, in 1619. Thus began an era spanning 244 years, or 12 generations, during which slaves could not own property, including their own ideas, which like their labor were appropriated by their masters; and they could not participate in the making of policies that affected them. How was this regime defined by the laws of the time? How were these laws followed, or in some cases defied, by the norms and values of individuals at the time? How might a social entrepreneur of the 17th century use the Model of Social Change to reveal actionable strategies for achieving social change?

Market Exchange might offer the possibility of purchasing slaves in order to then grant them freedom. Or, slaves could be granted at least some compensation for their ideas as an incentive to share their innovations with their owners, or pay for their entrepreneurial management of their owner's business, both of which cases are documented practices in the antebellum period (Walker, 2009). Charitable Change might deliver temporary care to ameliorate certain conditions of slavery. Education might suggest a program to enlighten slave owners to change how they treat their slaves.

The Law as a strategy, unlike all the other strategies, provides the opportunity to eradicate slavery through the law, and one could argue that President Lincoln, like Booker T. Washington, was thinking and acting like a social entrepreneur when he proposed the Emancipation Declaration, an innovative device meant to create social change to improve the well-being of those in slavery.

The third step in the roadmap for change following an analysis of options is to create a *theory of change* to explain a plan of action.

Theory of Change

Entrepreneurs are traditionally taught to write a business plan when preparing to undertake a new venture. Social entrepreneurs may write a similar type of plan that may include a section on how to finance, sustain and evaluate the endeavor. But the social entrepreneur's plan is principally concerned with working through how a social mission will be achieved, and this in most cases does not involve a financial analysis. Instead, it involves an examination of how resources will be mobilized to effect the desired social change. One methodological tool commonly requested by philanthropic foundations that fund social engineers is called a *Logic Model* (Kellogg Foundation, 2004). In this model, one lays out a causal chain, beginning with financial, human and other resources and ending with the social outcomes generated by applying these resources (see, for example, Figure 2.2 above). The logic model is a useful tool to describe the logical connection between elements of the proposed plan of action. However, it is descriptive, and does nothing to explain *why* a desired outcome will necessarily result from the proposed resources and actions.

The *Theory of Change* model attempts to explain the connections underlying the logic model (Eilinghoff, 2005). Equipped with the conceptual tools that constitute a framework for an entrepreneurial approach to IP social justice, follow these steps to construct a theory of change as a plan to achieve your goal:

1. Determine the desired goal (that is, to protect ownership and reap financial reward for IP in a market exchange, or to effect social change to achieve IP social justice).
2. Decide, based on who you are (your values, motivation, training, knowledge, resources and so on) whether your inclination is to be a Classical Entrepreneur or a Social Entrepreneur in order to achieve the above goal.
3. Work backwards to identify the elements that must be in place to achieve that goal.
4. Explain *why* each such element is a necessary condition at each stage of the plan.
5. Determine the resources required to undertake the plan. At this stage you will likely discuss your plan with those you know and, to the extent they become engaged, they may influence the goal and direction of the plan and its need for resources.

6. Solicit and mobilize the resources needed (such resources could include, for example, government funding, user fees, philanthropic grants, individual donations, corporate sponsorship and voluntary assistance).
7. Execute the plan and modify it, as conditions require.

While the above steps appear linear and logical, they embed Sarasvathy's recipe of who you are, whom you know and what you know, and they also embed feedback loops for dynamic change based on the influence of others and the conditions that unfold with execution. But just as entrepreneurship is hard, social entrepreneurship is not without its own challenges, and the fourth step in the roadmap for change is to be mindful of potential *obstacles to change*.

Resistance, Inertia, Hegemony

Systemic social change is hardly ever achieved without resistance. Some resistance will be overt and deliberate; other resistance will come from the inertia of tradition and a reluctance to rock the boat. As observed by community organizer Saul Alinsky, "All societies discourage and penalize ideas and writings that threaten the ruling status quo" (Alinksy, 1989/1971, p. 7). And as Frederick Douglass famously admonished in a letter to an abolitionist associate, 1849/1857 (Douglass, 1994/1845/1855/1893):

> Let me give you a word on the philosophy of reform. The whole history of the progress of human liberty shows that all concessions yet made to her august claims have been born of earnest struggle. . . . If there is no struggle there is no progress. . . . This struggle may be a moral one; or it may be a physical one; or it may be both moral and physical; but it must be a struggle. Power concedes nothing without a demand. It never did and it never will. Find out what people will submit to, and you have found the exact amount of injustice and wrong which will be imposed upon them; and these will continue until they are resisted with either words or blows, or with both. The limits of tyrants are prescribed by the endurance of those whom they oppress.

Confrontation is one form of overt resistance. More subtle than confrontation and often completely unnoticed is a deeply seated form of resistance or inertia that political economy theorist Antonio Gramsci called "hegemony" (Gramsci, 2003). All societies have evolved ways of transmitting their preferred culture from generation to generation through the family and other social institutions. What is imparted tends to preserve traditional social arrangements and convey pride in such arrangements among all citizens. The result is that social change takes place slowly and incrementally, rarely precipitated by revolution (North, 2005/1990).

According to Stephen Brookfield, "One of the theorists of hegemony, Antonio Gramsci, points out that because people learn hegemonic values, ideas, and practices, and because schools and other cultural institutions play a major role in presenting these ideas as the natural order of things, hegemony must always be understood as an educational phenomenon" (Brookfield, 2005, p. 13). Thus hegemony has attracted the attention of a number of critical scholars and activists of adult education, including Stephen Brookfield (Brookfield, 1987, 2000), Moses Coady (Coady, 1959), Paolo Freire (Freire, 1970), Miles Horton (Horton, Bell, Freire, Gaventa and Peters, 1990), Jack Mezirow (Mezirow, 1995) and Michael Welton (Welton, 1995). As Brookfield explains (2005, p. 93), "Hegemony is the process by which we learn to embrace enthusiastically a system of beliefs and practices that end up harming us and working to support the interests of others who have power over us. [Cornel] West (1982) describes a hegemonic culture as 'a culture successful in persuading people to "consent" to their oppression and exploitation' (p. 119). Hegemony describes the way we learn to love our servitude".

It is unsurprising, therefore, that schools in capitalist American would be unlikely places to challenge capitalism (Bowles and Gintis, 1976). It should be similarly unsurprising that philanthropic foundations created by riches accrued through capitalism might be reluctant to fund a strategy to mobilize an alternative, more just economic system (Roelofs, 2003). The challenge, then, is to discern how education and philanthropy, though traditionally unmoved to initiate IP social justice, can be employed to achieve IP social justice. It is incumbent on social entrepreneurs and the readers of this book to understand how the world is, see how the world ought to be, and execute effective strategies for change.

As suggested by Paolo Freire in his classic, *Pedagogy of the Oppressed* (1970), one educational strategy for change to achieve IP social justice might be to raise the consciousness of those whose talents are being exploited by the system to become aware of their rights, their exploitation and their options for protecting and benefiting from what is rightfully theirs. While some populations may appear to be apathetic to their situation – beaten down, passive and without hope – their awakening to an understanding of oppression may kindle a spark of hope and a renewed motivation to secure their rights. The social entrepreneur who facilitates this awakening thus helps others help themselves.

The final step in the roadmap is to be aware that *unintended consequences* may ensue, and to try to anticipate such consequences as a reality check of possible outcomes.

Unintended Consequences

While positive unintended consequences would be a felicitous surprise, "the road to hell is paved with good intentions" sums up the untoward effect of unintended consequences brought about by well-meaning social engineers. Could the same apply to creators of IP? Innovators are understandably enthusiastic about their discoveries, inventions and enterprises. Mindful consideration of social justice consequences by IP Creators and/or their advocates should include the possible downside effects on unsuspecting populations. Of course, any productive tool may be used as a weapon, which is not in itself necessarily a reason to withhold creation or production of the tool, though in some cases regulation may be wise.

An interesting historical but ambiguous case in point for reflection is the invention of the cotton gin. Inventive credit is conventionally given to Eli Whitney, a White sojourner to the South, who, after observing the painstaking process of cleaning cotton bolls, designed and fabricated the now famous gin that does so automatically, immensely increasing the productivity of processing cotton. Some contemporary revisionists propose that Blacks in slavery actually invented the cotton gin and have unjustly been denied credit. Perhaps more likely, Whitney may have listened to their comments as they cleaned the bolls and have been inspired by such talk. But if slaves had, in fact, conceived a device that would leverage their productivity, would they be so sanguine to encourage its utility? In retrospect, it is clear that the cotton gin was instrumental in prolonging the institution of slavery for decades (Rivoli, 2009). Without more definitive evidence, it is hard to claim either that Black slaves were ingenious inventors denied the justice of credit for their creation, or that they were presciently wise in trying to keep their genius under wraps by anticipating its self-defeating consequences. Walker, to her credit, reports that on this matter the jury is still out (Walker, 2009).

Thus one is cautioned to "be careful what you ask for". The pursuit of IP social justice can create blowback, as in the case of a hypothetical effort to enhance protection for certain marginalized creators by facilitating their own channeling of their IP through high bandwidth digital media could unintentionally reduce access to their creations by other members of the marginalized community who may not have access to such digital media. Mindful social entrepreneurship demands consideration of such tensions and possible tradeoffs among competing interests in order to navigate a progressive and viable path to social change.[14]

---

[14] Accordingly, although IP Social Entrepreneurship favors communal over competing individual interests, the ramifications of such decisions must be assessed

6. CASE STUDY: BARRETT STRONG

Barrett Strong's quotation opening this chapter is the name of a song he composed and partially authored in 1959: "Money (That's What I Want)". The song was published by Motown Records, founded by Berry Gordy, Jr., who was also Mr. Strong's personal manager, and became the recording label's first national hit.[15] Mr. Strong was credited as the songwriter on the original registration with the United States Copyright Office, but his name was removed three years later; reinstated on the copyright renewal date in 1987, and then crossed out the next year. Mr. Strong has never received any of the millions of dollars of royalties generated by the song, recorded and performed over the years by such megastars as the Beatles and Rolling Stones.

According to Mr. Gordy's lawyers, Mr. Strong, who learned of his name's removal in 2010 on the copyright registration, never asserted his claim. According to *The New York Times* (Rohter, 2013),

> "For 50 years, I had no idea about any of this", Mr. Strong, 72, said in an interview here, in which he acknowledged his lack of business acumen. "It was hidden from me. So how do they expect me to have acted to protect myself? It's crazy and unfair."
>
> "I wasn't getting any statements, so I started asking not too long after the record came out", he recalled. "You couldn't ask too many questions back then, because they'd say: 'You're being a bad boy. You're getting smart.' But I kept inquiring, and Mr. Gordy told me, 'Don't worry about statements and things, you'll make your money on the road.' On the road to what?"

Because the Copyright Office is not required to notify copyright holders of any changes to registrations, it is up to such holders to monitor potential alterations, a limitation "that record and music publishing companies have not hesitated to exploit" (Rohter, 2013).

Now living in a retirement home and recovering from a stroke, Strong needs money to pay his bills more than ever. But there is another consideration beyond compensation that touches the roots of a person's identity and dignity, as recounted by *The New York Times* (Rohter, 2013):

> "Songs outlive people", he said, with a mixture of sadness, resignation and anger. "The real reason Motown worked was the publishing. The records were

---

on a case-by-case basis. For a discussion of the consideration of unintended consequences in the development context, see Chapter 8 herein.

[15] This case is drawn from a *New York Times* article by Larry Rohter (Rohter, 2013).

just a vehicle to get the songs out there to the public. The real money is in the publishing, and if you have publishing, then hang on to it. That's what it's all about. If you give it away, you're giving away your life, your legacy. Once you're gone, those songs will still be playing."

Key considerations: To glean the lessons from this contemporary case of IP social justice, first identify the various past and prospective roles of IP Creator, IP Entrepreneur, IP Lawyer, IP Policymaker/Activist and IP Educator. Next consult the analytical Model of Social Change and while you consider alternative strategies for change, cast your analysis of the case in light of different perspectives on the type of problem at hand: Is this a problem of legal ownership; or of bureaucratic (Copyright Office) procedure? Is it a problem of affording access to justice; or of a lack of awareness and access to information? Is the problem still relevant for songwriters; for other authors; or for other creative professions? Of course, multiple problems may pertain. Deliberate and discuss what role you would play to remediate injustice in the case, whether your role would be as a Classical Entrepreneur or Social Entrepreneur, and whether your outcome would involve Charitable Change, Market Change (Exchange), Normative Change and/or Codified Change. Finally, prepare a plan of action based on a theory of change and execute it. You are now on your way to applying an entrepreneurship approach to achieving intellectual property social justice goals.[16]

7. CONSIDERATIONS FOR THE FUTURE

How a framework to pursue an entrepreneurial approach to achieving intellectual property social justice through changes in practice and the law will evolve will be influenced by, among other factors, the rapid pace of change in the emergence of new intellectual property opportunities – particularly through new technologies, the development of new channels for applying innovation to practice, the increasingly multi-jurisdictional claims on incipient innovations, the laws and amendments that impinge on intellectual property across pertinent jurisdictions, the challenges and clarifications of ethical and moral dimensions of such innovations, and, of course, new knowledge.

---

[16] Accordingly in Chapter 5 the Barrett Strong case is revisited as an IP social justice challenge, in connection with which proposals for (i) the application of IP social justice legal strategies and (ii) entrepreneurial empowerment mechanisms are explored.

These are all non-trivial factors that demand ongoing attention and discussion, such as in forums organized by the Institute for Intellectual Property Social Justice and conducted at various venues including at Howard University. As the quest for IP social justice becomes increasingly compelling on a national and worldwide basis, it would not be surprising to see similar forums emerge in other nations and subsequent international and global meetings on the topic.

8. CONCLUSION

This chapter has presented a conceptual framework for how to apply an entrepreneurial approach to achieving intellectual property social justice, based on a consideration of the history and characteristics of entrepreneurship and key factors that allow entrepreneurship, particularly social entrepreneurship to achieve social change. Because the task necessarily crosses several contested fields – entrepreneurship, intellectual property and social justice – the approach takes liberties in making pragmatic choices in defining terms and choosing from relevant conceptual models to propose a framework that may be empirically tested by practitioners, including the readers of this book.

Any such framework is, of course, subject to future change, evermore likely in a rapidly evolving world. Whether or not the proposed framework withstands the tests of utility, the hope is that the considerations presented here will at least constructively advance the discourse and inspire readers to activate the legal and social change needed to test the intellectual property social justice theory proposed in the Introduction to create a more just world.

ACKNOWLEDGEMENTS

I would like to thank Kikuyu Daniels, Chad Emerson, Louise A. Howells, Benjamin Leff, Adam MacLeod, Jack Quarter and Jessica Seney for reading and commenting on formative versions of this chapter.

REFERENCES

Abrams, R. (2010). *Successful Business Plan: Secrets and Strategies* (5th edn). Palo Alto: The Planning Shop.

Alinksy, S. D. (1989/1971). *Rules for Radicals: A Practical Primer for Realistic Radicals.* New York: Vintage Books.

Alperovitz, G. and L. Daly (2008). *Unjust Deserts: How the Rich are Taking Over Our Common Inheritance*. New York: The New Press.

Aulet, B. (2013). *Disciplined Entrepreneurship: 24 Steps to a Successful Startup*. Hoboken: John Wiley & Sons, Inc.

Aulet, B. and F. Murray (2013). *A Tale of two Entrepreneurs: Understanding Differences in the Types of Entrepreneurship in the Economy* (p. 9). Kansas City: Ewing Marion Kauffman Foundation.

Austin, J., H. Stevenson and J. Wei-Skillern (2006). "Social or commercial entrepreneurship: Same, different, or both?" *Entrepreneurship: Theory and Practice*, 30(1), 1–22.

Baumol, W. J. and R. J. Strom (2010). "'Useful knowledge' of entrepreneurship: Some implications of the history", in D. S. Landes, J. Mokyr and W. J. Baumol (eds), *The Invention of Enterprise: Entrepreneurship from Ancient Mesopotamia to Modern Times* (pp. 527–541). Princeton: Princeton University Press.

Bird, B. J. (1989). *Entrepreneurial Behavior*. Glenview, IL: Scott, Foresman and Company.

Block, F. and M. R. Keller (eds) (2011). *State of Innovation: The U.S. Government's Role in technology Development*. Boulder: Paradigm Publishers.

Bornstein, D. (2004). *How to Change the World: Social Entrepreneurs and the Power of New Ideas*. New York: Oxford University Press.

Bowles, S. and H. Gintis (1976). *Schooling in Capitalist America: Educational Reform and the Contradictions of Economic Life*. New York: Basic Books.

Brooke, P. A. (2009). *A Vision for Venture Capital: Realizing the Promise of Global Venture Capital and Private Equity*. Boston: New Ventures Press.

Brookfield, S. D. (1987). *Developing Critical Thinkers: Challenging Adults to Explore Alternative Ways of Thinking and Acting*. San Francisco: Jossey-Bass Publishers.

Brookfield, S. D. (2000). "Transformative learning as ideology critique", in J. Mezirow (ed.), *Learning as Transformation: Critical Perspectives on a Theory of Progress* (pp. 125–148). San Francisco: Jossey-Bass Publishers.

Brookfield, S. D. (2005). *The Power of Critical Theory: Liberating Adult Learning and Teaching*. San Francisco: Jossey-Bass Publishers.

Bygrave, W. and A. Zacharakis (2011). *Entrepreneurship* (2nd edn). Hoboken: John Wiley & Sons, Inc.

Cho, A. H. (2006). "Politics, values and social entrepreneurship: A critical appraisal", in J. Mair, J. Robinson and K. Hockerts (eds), *Social Entrepreneurship* (pp. 34–56). New York: Palgrave Macmillan.

Coady, R. M. M. (1959). *My Story*. Antigonish, Nova Scotia: St. Francis Xavier University.

Dees, J. G. (2001/1998). "The meaning of social entrepreneurship". Accessed 10 October 2014 at http://www.caseatduke.org/documents/dees_sedef.pdf

Dees, J. G. (2008). "The joys and challenges of teaching social entrepreneurship", in D. D. Brock (ed.), *Social Entrepreneurship: Teaching Resources Handbook*. Arlington, VA: Ashoka.

Dees, J. G. and B. B. Anderson (2003). "For-profit social ventures", in M. L. Kourilsky and W. B. Walstad (eds), *Social Entrepreneurship*. Senate Hall Academic Publishing.

Dees, J. G., J. Emerson and P. Economy (eds) (2001). *Enterprising Nonprofits: A Toolkit for Social Entrepreneurs*. New York: John Wiley & Sons, Inc.

Douglass, F. (1994/1845/1855/1893). *Autobiographies: Narrative of the Life of Frederick Douglass, an American Slave, My Bondage and My Freedom, Life and Times of Frederick Douglass*. New York: Literary Classics of the United States, Inc.

Eilinghoff, D. (2005). "Theory of change tool", in D. Eilinghoff (ed.), *Rethinking Philanthropic Effectiveness: Lessons from an International Network of Foundation Experts* (pp. 68–73). Gütersloh: Bertelsmann Foundation.

Eisinger, P. K. (1988). *The Rise of the Entrepreneurial State: State and Local Economic Development Policy in the United States*. Madison: University of Wisconsin Press.

Feld, B. (2012). *Startup Communities: Building an Entrepreneurial Ecosystem in your City*. Hoboken: John Wiley & Sons, Inc.

Florida, R. (2012/2011). *The Rise of the Creative Class, Revisited*. New York: Basic Books.

Freire, P. (1970). *Pedagogy of the Oppressed*. New York: Continuum.

Goodman, D. J. (2001). *Promoting Diversity and Social Justice: Educating People from Privileged Groups*. Thousand Oaks, CA: Sage Publications, Inc.

Gramsci, A. (2003). *Selections from the Prison Notebooks*. New York: International Publishers.

Hart, D. M. (2003a). "Entrepreneurship policy: What it is and where it came from", in D. M. Hart (ed.), *The Emergence of Entrepreneurship Policy: Governance, Start-ups, and Growth in the U.S. Knowledge Economy* (pp. 3–19). Cambridge: Cambridge University Press.

Hart, D. M. (ed.) (2003b). *The Emergence of Entrepreneurship Policy: Governance, Start-ups, and Growth in the U.S. Knowledge Economy*. Cambridge: Cambridge University Press.

Hathaway, I. (2013). *Tech Starts: High-Technology Business Formation and Job Creation in the United States* (p. 31). Kansas City: Ewing Marion Kauffman Foundation.

Hess, F. M. (ed.) (2008). *The Future of Educational Entrepreneurship: Possibilities for School Reform*. Cambridge: Harvard Education Press.

Horton, M., B. Bell, P. Freire, J. Gaventa and J. M. Peters (1990). *We Make The Road by Walking: Conversations on Education and Social Change*. Philadelphia: Temple University Press.

Hudson, M. (2010). "Entrepreneurs: from the near eastern takeoff to the Roman collapse", in D. S. Landes, J. Mokyr and W. J. Baumol (eds), *The Invention of Enterprise: Entrepreneurship from Ancient Mesopotamia to Modern Times* (pp. 8–39). Princeton: Princeton University Press.

Kellogg Foundation. (2004). *W. K. Kellogg Foundation Logic Model Development Guide*. Battle Creek, MI: W. K. Kellogg Foundation.

Landes, D. S., J. Mokyr and W. J. Baumol (eds) (2010). *The Invention of Enterprise: Entrepreneurship from Ancient Mesopotamia to Modern Times*. Princeton: Princeton University Press.

Lazonick, W. (1993/1991). *Business Organization and the Myth of the Market Economy*. Cambridge: Cambridge University Press.

Mair, J., J. Robinson and K. Hockerts (eds) (2006). *Social Entrepreneurship*. Basingstoke: Palgrave Macmillan.

Martin, R. L. and S. Osberg (2007, Spring). "Social entrepreneurship: The case for definition". *Stanford Social Innovation Review*, 5(2).

Maslow, A. H. (1943). "A theory of human motivation". *Psychological Review,* 50(4), 370–396.
Mezirow, J. (1995). "Transformation theory of adult learning", in M. R. Welton (ed.), *In Defense of the Lifeworld: Critical Perspectives on Adult Learning* (pp. 39–70). Albany: State University of New York Press.
Naudé, W. (ed.) (2011). *Entrepreneurship and Economic Development.* New York: Palgrave Macmillan.
Neumann, R. (1990). "On strategy". *Fordham Law Review,* 59(3), 299–346.
North, D. C. (2005/1990). *Institutions, Institutional Change and Economic Performance.* New York: Cambridge University Press.
Obama, B. (2009, 4 June). "Cairo speech: Remarks by the President on a new beginning". Cairo University, Cairo, Egypt.
Paredo, A. M. and J. J. Chrisman (2004). "Toward a theory of community-based enterprise". *Academy of Management Review* (9 September).
Pozen, D. E. (2008). "We are all entrepreneurs now". *Wake Forest Law Review,* 43, 283–340.
Rivoli, P. (2009). *The Travels of a T-shirt in the Global Economy* (2nd edn). Hoboken: John Wiley & Sons, Inc.
Rodrik, D. (2007). *One Economics Many Recipes: Globalization, Institutions, and Economic Growth.* Princeton: Princeton University Press.
Roelofs, J. (2003). *Foundations and Public Policy.* Albany: State University of New York Press.
Rohter, L. (2013). "For a classic Motown song about money, credit is what he wants". *The New York Times,* 31 August. Accessed 10 October 2014 at http://www.nytimes.com/2013/09/01/arts/music/for-a-classic-motown-song-about-money-credit-is-what-he-wants.html?hp
Rokeach, M. (1973). *The Nature of Human Values.* New York: The Free Press.
Sarasvathy, S. D. (2008). *Effectuation: Elements of Entrepreneurial Expertise.* Cheltenham: Edward Elgar.
Scarborough, N. M. (2012). *Effective Small Business Management: An Entrepreneurial Approach.* Boston: Prentice Hall.
Schumpeter, J. A. (2008/1934). *The Theory of Economic Development: An Inquiry into Profits, Capital, Credit, Interest, and the Business Cycle.* New Brunswick: Transaction Publishers.
Schwartz, S. H. (2012). "An overview of the Schwartz Theory of Basic Values". *Online Readings in Psychology and Culture, Unit 2,* 2(1).
Sen, A. (1999). *Development as Freedom.* New York: Knopf.
Senor, D. and S. Singer (2009). *Start-Up Nation: The Story of Israel's Economic Miracle.* New York: Grand Central Publishing.
Sirolli, E. (2012). *How to Start a Business and Ignite Your Life: A Simple Guide to Combining Business Wisdom with Passion.* Garden City Park, NY: Square One Publishers.
Stam, E. and A. van Stel (2009). Types of Entrepreneurship and Economic Growth (p. 16): United Nations University World Institute for Development Economics Research.
Timmons, J. A. and S. Spinelli (2009). *New Venture Creation: Entrepreneurship for the 21st Century* (8th edn). Boston: McGraw Hill.
Van Slyke, D. M. and H. K. Newman (2006). "Venture philanthropy and social entrepreneurship in community redevelopment". *Nonprofit Management & Leadership,* 16(3), 345–368.

Walker, J. E. K. (2009). *The History of Black Business in America: Capitalism, Race, Entrepreneurship, Volume I to 1865* (2nd edn). Chapel Hill: University of North Carolina Press.

Welton, M. R. (ed.). (1995). *In Defense of the Lifeworld: Critical Perspectives on Adult Learning*. Albany: State University of New York Press.

Whitman, J. R. (2008). "Evaluating philanthropic foundations according to their social values". *Nonprofit Management & Leadership, 18*(4), 417–434.

Whitman, J. R. (2009). "Measuring social values in philanthropic foundations". *Nonprofit Management & Leadership, 19*(3), 305–325.

Whitman, J. R. (2010). *The Social Entrepreneurship Model: Past, Present, and Future*. Paper presented at the Worcester Polytechnic Institute Venture Forum, Worcester, MA.

Whitman, J. R. (2011). "Social entrepreneurship", in W. Bygrave and A. Zacharakis (eds), *Entrepreneurship* (2nd edn, pp. 563–595). New York: John Wiley & Sons.

Whitman, J. R. (2012). "Education for the social economy", in L. Mook, J. Quarter and S. Ryan (eds), *Business with a Difference: Balancing the Social and Economic* (pp. 243–266). Toronto: University of Toronto Press.

Whitman, J. R. (2013). "Enterprise facilitation: Local economic development and the challenge of going mainstream". Available 10 October 2014 at http://surveytools.com/styled-4/index.html

Wiggins, G. and J. McTighe (2005). *Understanding by Design* (2nd edn). Alexandria, VA: Association for Supervision and Curriculum Development.

Wildavsky, A. (1987/1979). *Speaking Truth to Power: The Art and Craft of Policy Analysis*. New Brunswick: Transaction Publishers.

Yunus, M. (2007). *Creating a World Without Poverty: Social Business and the Future of Capitalism*. New York: Public Affairs.

Zahra, S. A., E. Gedajlovic, D. O. Neubaum and J. M. Shulman (2009). "A typology of social entrepreneurs: Motives, search processes and ethical challenges". *Journal of Business Venturing, 24*(5), 519–534.

Zeuli, K. A. and R. Cropp (2004/1980). *Cooperatives: Principles and Practices in the 21st Century ('the Schaars book')*. Madison: University of Wisconsin-Extension.

Zeuli, K. A. and J. Radel (2005). "Cooperatives as a community development strategy: Linking theory and practice". *Journal of Regional Analysis and Policy, 35*(1), 43–54.

3. Intellectual property as an essential 21st century business asset

Valerie Rawlston Wilson

In Chapter 1 of this book, the social justice theory of intellectual property law was introduced as one that "acknowledges socially equitable inclusion, access, and empowerment as fundamental objectives of intellectual property protection".[1] Further, it was suggested that this theory should be operationalized through the construction of a social action platform, ideally modeled after the American Civil Rights Movement, and "similarly directed toward the frustrations with (i) the perennial lack of individual economic opportunities and (ii) the historic and ongoing misappropriation of inner-city urban and other indigenous culture and knowledge, and presented as an avenue toward personal economic autonomy and communal socio-economic empowerment".

In 2013, as the United States of America marked the 50th anniversary of the historic 1963 March on Washington for Jobs and Freedom, a watershed moment for the Civil Rights Movement, we were led to reflect both on the victories won through that movement and the challenges that still remain. In fact, in the 50 years since the March on Washington, the three-pronged strategy of the Civil Rights Movement – legal action, social activism and individual empowerment – has effectively improved access to educational and employment opportunities that have raised the standard of living for many of those who have been historically marginalized, including countless African Americans. Since 1963, the percentage of blacks with a college degree has increased five-fold while the percentage

---

[1] Steven D. Jamar and Lateef Mtima, "A Social Justice Perspective on Intellectual Property, Innovation, and Entrepreneurship", in Megan M. Carpenter (ed.), *Entrepreneurship and Innovation in Evolving Economies*, 89–101 (Edward Elgar, Cheltenham, UK and Northampton, MA, USA 2012); Madahavi Sunder, *From Goods to A Good Life, Intellectual Property and Global Justice* (Yale University Press, New Haven 2012).

of blacks living in poverty has fallen by nearly half.[2] Fifty years later, the nation also bears witness to some very public manifestations of Dr. Martin Luther King Jr.'s dream of equality – namely, President Barack Obama, twice elected as the nation's first African American president; Eric Holder, the first African American Attorney General of the United States of America; and Nancy Pelosi, the first female (former) Speaker of the House of Representatives.

Yet, despite the progress that has been made in the educational, social and political and arenas, large economic disparities persist along racial lines. Fifty years after the historic March on Washington, African Americans remain nearly twice as likely to be unemployed as whites. Median household income for African Americans is only 60 per cent of that of whites.[3] The average African American household holds only six cents for every dollar of wealth held by the average white household, and over one-third of African American households have zero or negative net worth compared to 14 per cent of white households.[4]

The fact that such stubborn and persistent economic inequalities remain in a post-Jim Crow, though far from post-racial, America calls for a more targeted and strategic focus on economic empowerment and economic justice as a primary objective of the modern day civil rights movement. This means learning to engage new weapons in fighting freshly nuanced, but all too familiar battles. It also means finding new ways to advance the economic empowerment agenda along the rails of America's constantly evolving service and information sectors. This is where we find potential intersection between the modern day civil rights and intellectual property social justice movements.

Building wealth by establishing ownership of tangible assets, such as property or business enterprises, has long been central to the quest for economic empowerment of African Americans and other marginalized communities. But, the information age has sparked a renewed growth in entrepreneurship as technology helps to eliminate many of the non-financial barriers to business formation and expansion. For African Americans, this growth has also been driven by necessity as long-standing employment disparities persist.

In this modern economic era, the significance of securing ownership

---

[2] Valerie R. Wilson, "Introduction to the 2013 Equality Index" in *State of Black America 2013, Redeem the Dream: Jobs Rebuild America* (National Urban League, New York 2013), 13.

[3] Ibid.

[4] United States Census Bureau, Survey of Income and Program Participation, 2010.

rights to intellectual property has been elevated as well. Intellectual property is defined by Mirriam-Webster's dictionary as *property* (as an idea, invention, or process) that derives from the work of the mind or intellect. Though intellectual property, as defined above, is less tangible than either property or a business, it derives its tangible value as an asset from its potential for commercialization. What this means in a rapidly evolving information economy, where the term innovation is commonly associated with new opportunities for economic growth and prosperity, is that an intellectual property rights agenda is critical in driving a 21st century agenda for economic empowerment through innovation and entrepreneurship.

This chapter explores the premise behind intellectual property rights as a valuable 21st century business asset by examining trends in intellectual property ownership and exploitation among new start-ups during the last decade. Specifically, I examine patterns in firm outcomes, including firm survival and revenue growth, across different industries as well as for different racial and ethnic groups.

AFRICAN AMERICAN BUSINESS OWNERSHIP IN THE 21ST CENTURY

In order to frame this analysis of the value of IP rights as an important 21st century business asset, specifically for African-American and other minority-owned businesses, it is important to first provide an overview of the current landscape of minority-owned business enterprises. According to the most recently available Survey of Business Owners (SBO),[5] the total number of U.S. businesses increased by 17.9 per cent between 2002 and 2007 while the number of all minority-owned businesses increased by 45.5 per cent, from 4 million to 5.8 million. The number of African-American businesses rose 60.5 per cent over this five-year period, totaling 1.9 million in 2007. Of these, only 106,566 were employer firms, meaning that the business had employees other than the owner. African-American-owned employer firms created approximately 167,000 new jobs from 2002 to 2007. In 2007, black-owned businesses generated a total of $137.5 billion in revenues, but the vast majority (93 per cent) had revenues of less than $100,000 and only one per cent had revenues over $1 million.[6] Relative to

---

[5] Survey of Business Owners is conducted by the Census Bureau every five years. It provides the most comprehensive look at business ownership in the U.S.

[6] Valerie R. Wilson, et al., *State of Urban Business 2011: Metro Areas that Lead the Way* (New York: National Urban League 2011), 10.

similarly sized white-owned firms, the average black-owned firm with 1 to 4 employees generated 66 per cent of the amount of revenues generated by the average white-owned firm of the same size, but the average black-owned firm with 500 or more employees generated only 28 per cent of the amount of revenues generated by a similarly sized white-owned firm.[7]

The above statistics make a critical point that the biggest weakness in black entrepreneurship in the U.S. is not failing to create businesses. Rather, the greatest challenges lie in growing businesses to the point where they are able to generate levels of employment and revenue that are comparable to similarly situated white-owned businesses.[8] In an innovation-driven economy, protection and proper management of intellectual property is part of the strategy for growing businesses whose owners have ideas, inventions or processes with potential for commercialization. Next, I explore the prevalence of intellectual property rights among a group of recent business start-ups.

INTELLECTUAL PROPERTY OWNERSHIP BY NEW BUSINESS OWNERS

Consistent with the move toward a more information-driven economy, making the case for and plotting a path toward a modern economic empowerment agenda that incorporates the role of IP requires a thorough analysis of the dynamics involved in the creative, legal and commercial processes. The Kauffman Firm Survey (KFS) is a panel study of 4,928 businesses founded in 2004 and tracked over the early years of operation (currently through 2011). The survey focuses on the nature of new business formation activity; the characteristics of the strategy (including use of IP), offerings, and employment patterns of new businesses; the nature of the financial and organizational arrangements of these businesses; and the characteristics of their founders. This sample of business start-ups is used to explore patterns in IP ownership, firm survival and business revenue.

One-fifth of all new business owners in the KFS sample owned some form of intellectual property when they founded their business in 2004 and the most commonly held form of IP was a trademark.[9] A trademark is the

---

[7] Ibid, 11.
[8] Ibid, 11.
[9] The United States Patent and Trademark Office defines a trademark as "a word, phrase, symbol or design, or a combination of words, phrases, symbols or designs, that identifies and distinguishes the source of the goods of one party from those of others".

best way for a business to establish and protect its brand name, making it an important asset for new businesses seeking to build a recognizable brand and capture market share.

The KFS sample indicates that rates of IP ownership varied across different racial and ethnic groups. For example, 23.2 per cent of business owners who identified their race as "other" (than white, black, Asian or Hispanic) own some form of IP, followed by 21.9 per cent of Asian business owners, 19.8 per cent of Hispanic business owners, 19.6 per cent of white business owners and 18.9 per cent of black business owners. In fact, those who identified as "other" had the highest rates of ownership across all types of intellectual property, including patents (5.4 per cent), copyrights (12.5 per cent) and trademarks (14.4 per cent). In absolute numbers, white business owners far outnumbered all other racial and ethnic groups as IP holders of any kind. Seventy per cent of all IP holders were white, 8.7 per cent were African American, 6 per cent were Hispanic, 4.9 per cent were Asian and 2.5 per cent were of some other race.

Among IP holding firms, white business owners were also the most likely to have multiple IP holdings. On average, white business owners held twice as many patents and copyrights as the average non-white business owner. One factor that might account for this difference is lack of equal access to capital. For minority business start-ups, who already face more obstacles than whites in securing financial capital,[10] the high cost associated with intellectual property development, protection, and commercial exploitation, particularly for patent applications, can be even more cost prohibitive.

One solution to overcoming these cost barriers might be taking on equity partners to help with financing. Among all the start-ups participating in the Kauffman Firm Survey, businesses with multiple owners were most common among firms for which the primary owner[11] identified his/her race as "other" or Asian. However, for the group of IP holding firms, businesses with a white primary owner were more likely than non-white IP holding firms to have multiple owners. However, very few firms were jointly owned by people of different races. Less than half a per cent of start-ups for which the primary owner was not black had black equity

---

[10] Robert W. Fairlie, Alicia M. Robb and David T. Robinson. *Patterns of Financing: A Comparison between White- and African-American Young Firms* (Kauffman Foundation, Kansas City 2009).

[11] The primary owner is defined as the owner with the largest equity share in the company. In cases where equity was shared equally, the primary owner was identified as the one who reported working the most hours. These indicators further support the adoption of communal ETE social entrepreneurship strategies to achieve IP Empowerment goals. *See* Chapter 1.

partners and less than two per cent of white primary business owners shared ownership with non-whites.

In addition to differences in IP ownership by race of the primary business owner, IP ownership also varied quite a bit across industries, as did the form of IP held by new firm owners in different industries. Overall, firms in the professional, scientific and technical (PST) services or retail trade industries were most likely to hold some form of intellectual property rights when they founded the business (19.6 per cent and 15.4 per cent, respectively). For firms in these industries, copyrights were the most common form of IP held. However, patent holders were most commonly found in the manufacturing (24.6 per cent) or PST services (21.9 per cent) industries. Patent holders were also commonly identified as high tech firms (18.3 per cent), representing either "technology employers" or "technology generators" within the PST Services, Manufacturing or Information industries. Trademark holders were most commonly doing business in the PST services (16.5 per cent) or retail trade (15.0 per cent) sectors.

Firms in the PST services industry have such high rates of IP ownership because businesses in this industry are typically engaged in more technologically creative or innovative endeavors. The PST services industry covers a wide range of service-based businesses including legal, accounting, architectural and engineering, specialized design (including graphic and interior design), computer systems design and related services, management, scientific and technical consulting, scientific research and development, advertising and public relations.[12]

A subset of business owners in the KFS sample, referred to as innovators, included those who reported that they founded their business around a new or customized product or service. Over 25 per cent of firms surveyed in KFS identified themselves as "innovative" start-ups, and 6.5 per cent of these firms were founded by African American owners.[13] Over 40 per cent of all innovators reported that they owned some form of intellectual property when they founded the business – twice the rate of IP ownership among all new firms.[14]

---

[12] Industry designations are based on the Census Bureau's North American Industry Classification System (NAICS). All full listing of all sub-industries included under THE professional, scientific and technical services category are available at http://www.census.gov/cgi-bin/sssd/naics/naicsrch?chart_code=54&search=2012%20NAICS%20Search (accessed 13 October 2014).

[13] Sonali K. Shah, Sheryl Winston Smith and E. J. Reedy, *Who Are User Entrepreneurs? Findings on Innovation, Founder Characteristics, and Firm Characteristics* (Kauffman Foundation, Kansas City 2012), 9.

[14] The group of innovator firms should more accurately be referred to as surviving innovator firms because the question about founding the business around

SURVIVAL RATES, MERGERS AND ACQUISITIONS OF NEW BUSINESSES

The KFS survival rates for newly formed businesses from 2004 through 2010 shed light on the fact that black-owned start-ups face greater difficulty than other groups when it comes to staying in business. Forty-eight per cent of new black-owned businesses in the sample were still in business in 2010, compared to 55 per cent of all new firms. The survival rate for all minority businesses was about 50 per cent and the survival rate for white-owned businesses was 56 per cent.

Comparing start-ups that owned IP at founding to those that did not, I find that on average, IP owners were more likely to stay in business longer than those who did not. Fifty-six per cent of those with IP rights at founding were still in operation six years after founding, compared to 54 per cent of non-IP holders – a difference of two percentage points. *For minority-owned start-ups, the difference was more notable. Six-year survival rates for all minority-owned businesses with IP rights at founding was seven percentage points higher than for minority-owned businesses without IP rights at founding.* The difference for African American business owners was three percentage points, and for whites it was two percentage points.

Looking specifically at the industries for which IP rights were most common, the relative advantage in business longevity for founding IP holders over those without IP was greatest for those in the PST services sector. Sixty-six per cent of businesses with IP in this sector were still in operation after six years compared to 59 per cent of those without IP – a difference of seven percentage points. In the retail sector the difference was four percentage points. However, IP owners in the manufacturing sector were actually less likely to still be in operation six years after founding than those without IP. This difference may be associated with the higher risks and costs faced by those actually manufacturing a new product to introduce to the market. Overall, the highest rates of survival were among high tech firm owners. Specifically, 71 per cent of high tech firm owners with IP reached the six-year mark, compared to only 62 per cent of high tech firm owners without IP. These numbers suggest that access to capital and the development and exploitation of intellectual property assets can factor into entrepreneurial success in the modern information economy.

The above mentioned survival rates include only businesses that remain

---

a new or customized product or service was only added to the survey in 2009. Therefore, innovative firms founded in 2004, but no longer in business by 2009, are missing from this group.

in operation under their original ownership, but another potentially positive outcome for a new business owner might be merger or acquisition. Launching a business and then selling it for a profit has been an important factor in the history of black entrepreneurship and when undertaken with proper knowledge and information, can be a beneficial economic empowerment strategy.

Six per cent of all new start-ups in the KFS merged with or were acquired by other firms within the first six years of operation. On average, black-owned firms were less likely to merge or be acquired than other firms – 3.4 per cent of black-owned firms compared to 6.8 per cent of all minority firms and 6.1 per cent of white-owned firms. However, black-owned IP-holding firms (4.9 per cent) merged or were acquired by other firms at nearly the same rates as white-owned IP-holding firms (5.1 per cent). Five and a half per cent of all IP-holding firms owned by non-whites merged with or were acquired by other firms within the first six years of operation.

Finally, at the business sector level, high tech firm owners with IP rights (8.2 per cent) were more than twice as likely as those without IP rights (3.3 per cent) to merge or be acquired. Differences within each of the other industries highlighted in this chapter were much less pronounced.

REVENUE AND LICENSING ACTIVITIES OF NEW BUSINESS OWNERS

One of the biggest determinants of whether a new business is able to remain in operation is the ability to generate revenues significant enough to cover expenses and ultimately make a profit. In 2004, the first year of operation, over one-third of all firms in the KFS sample earned no revenue. By 2010, only 11.1 per cent of surviving firms reported no revenue, but 43.3 per cent of surviving firms earned over $100,000 in revenue and 10.9 per cent earned over $1 million.

Next, I consider how IP ownership contributes to new businesses reaching the important milestone of $100,000 or more in revenue. The share of surviving firms in the KFS sample with revenue over $100,000 peaked at 43.3 per cent in 2009 (five years after founding), so I will focus on surviving firm revenues in year five.

More than half (54.3 per cent) of surviving IP-owning firms exceeded $100,000 in revenue in year five, compared to 41.6 per cent of surviving firms without IP. Even after controlling for the effects of other factors, such as type of business (product, service or both), business industry, previous business experience, education and race of the owner, IP-owning firms were still ten percentage points more likely than non IP-owners to have revenue over $100,000. This suggests that IP ownership has a positive effect on revenue generation for new businesses.

As was noted earlier in this chapter, according to the Census Bureau's Survey of Business Owners, the vast majority of black-owned businesses earn revenue of less than $100,000 per year. The analysis of firm mergers and acquisitions in the previous section, however, highlighted how IP ownership was associated with a narrowing of the gap between the proportion of black-owned and white-owned firms that either merged or were acquired within the first six years of operation. Next, we examine whether IP ownership has a similar effect on closing racial differences in revenue generation among new firms.

On average, 23 per cent of all surviving black-owned firms in the KFS sample had revenue over $100,000 in 2009, compared to 44 per cent of all white-owned firms. In other words, white-owned firms were nearly twice as likely as black-owned firms to reach this milestone after five years. Comparing the average black-owned firm with IP to the average white-owned IP holding firm, I find that the share of firms with revenue over $100,000 was 44 per cent for black-owned firms and 54 per cent for white-owned firms. Thus, IP ownership not only increased the likelihood of black-owned firms reaching the $100,000 mark, but it also narrowed the difference between white and black firms by about half. After accounting for the effects of IP ownership along with other firm and owner characteristics (that is, type of business, previous business experience and education), black-owned IP-holding firms were just five percentage points less likely than white-owned IP-holding firms to have revenue over $100,000. Again, these results suggest that IP-owning firms have certain advantages in generating revenue, and that this is particularly beneficial for black-owned firms.

Given that the nature and scale of businesses can vary considerably across industries, we next examine how revenues of IP-holding firms differ from those of non IP-holding firms within select industries identified as having relatively high rates of IP ownership. Among those industries – manufacturing, retail and PST services – IP ownership only had a significant impact on revenue in the PST services industry and for high tech businesses. On average, over half (53.3 per cent) of IP-owning firms in the PST services industry had revenue over $100,000 in year five, compared to about one-third (35.6 per cent) of firms in this industry without IP rights. Among high tech businesses, 65.6 per cent of IP holding firms earned revenue over $100,000 compared to 48.5 per cent of firms without IP rights.

One of the ways in which IP holders can capitalize on their intellectual property is through licensing agreements. Already, my analysis has shown that IP-owning firms were about 30 per cent more likely to exceed $100,000 in revenue by year five than firms without IP. Next, I further examine differences between IP holding firms that license their IP to others and those that do not.

For the group of start-ups in the KFS, licensing seemed to have more of an effect on differences in revenue between licensing and non-licensing firms in the early stages of a business. While only 20 per cent of all IP-holding firms earned more than $100,000 the first year in business, more one-third (36 per cent) of new firm owners that licensed their IP to others earned more than $100,000 in revenue. The following year, 36.5 per cent of all IP-holding firms exceeded $100,000 in revenue, compared to over half (52.4 per cent) of licensing firms.

At the industry level, licensing revenue was most significant in the manufacturing and PST services industries. Interestingly, although IP ownership did not significantly increase a manufacturing firm's overall chances of exceeding $100,000 in revenue, among IP holding firms in this industry, those who licensed their IP to others were more than twice as likely to reach this milestone in year one than those who did not license IP to others. The likelihood of exceeding $100,000 in revenue was 2.5 higher for firms in the PST services industry that licensed their IP, and 2.3 times higher among high tech businesses.

SUMMARY OF FINDINGS

Two-thirds of firm owners in the Kauffman Firm Survey that were still in operation six years after the business was founded reported that they believed owning intellectual property gave them a major competitive advantage. This chapter offers some empirical evidence of the value of intellectual property as an important business asset for 21st century businesses.

All else equal, IP-owning firms were still ten percentage points more likely than non IP-owners to have revenue over $100,000 by their fifth year in business. IP ownership was especially important to revenue generation for firms in the PST services industry and for high tech businesses. On average, IP-owning firms in the PST services industry were 1.5 times more likely to have revenue over $100,000 in year five than firms in this industry without IP rights. Among high tech businesses, IP holding firms were 1.4 times more likely to earn revenue over $100,000 than high tech firms without IP rights.

The choice by firm owners to license intellectual property provided an additional boost to their ability to exceed $100,000 in revenue. While only

20 per cent of all IP-holding firms earned more than $100,000 the first year in business, more one-third (36 per cent) of new firm owners that licensed their IP to others earned more than $100,000 in revenue, and this increased to 52.4 per cent of licensing firms in the second year. Licensing was particularly important in the PST services industry and among high tech businesses where licensing firms were 2.5 times and 2.3 times more likely to exceed $100,000 in revenue, respectively, than other IP holding firms that did not license.

In the introduction to this chapter, we identified revenue generation over $100,000 as a major challenge facing black-owned businesses as a whole. However, this analysis has demonstrated how effective IP ownership can be in helping new business owners to reach this milestone. On average, white-owned firms were nearly twice as likely as black-owned firms to reach this milestone after five years. However, IP ownership not only increased the likelihood of black-owned firms reaching the $100,000 mark, but it also narrowed the difference between white and black firms by about half – 44 per cent for black-owned firms and 54 per cent for white-owned firms had revenue over $100,000 in year five. After accounting for the effects of IP ownership along with other firm and owner characteristics (that is, type of business, previous business experience and education), black-owned IP-holding firms were just five percentage points less likely than white-owned IP-holding firms to have revenue over $100,000.

In terms of firm survival, IP ownership again proved to yield the greatest returns for businesses in the PST services industry and for high tech businesses. Sixty-six per cent of businesses with IP in this sector were still in operation after six years compared to 59 per cent of those without IP – a difference of seven percentage points. Overall, the highest rates of survival were among high tech firm owners – 71 per cent of high tech firm owners with IP reached the six-year mark, compared to only 62 per cent of high tech firm owners without IP.

While, even for African-American IP owners, business longevity remains a challenge – survival rates for IP owners versus those without IP differed by only three percentage points (50.7 per cent and 47.5 per cent, respectively) – the chances of selling a business (and hopefully for a significant profit) are increased for African American IP owners. On average, 3.4 per cent of black-owned firms merged with other firms or were acquired within six years, compared to 6.1 per cent of white-owned firms. However, black-owned IP-holding firms (4.9 per cent) merged or were acquired by other firms at nearly the same rates as white-owned IP-holding firms (5.1 per cent).

CONCLUSION

As we work to advance an intellectual property rights agenda that is closely aligned with achieving economic empowerment through innovation and entrepreneurship for African Americans and other marginalized groups, there are a number of recommendations that can be gleaned from this analysis. First, given the economic benefits of intellectual property ownership, particularly for new black-owned business start-ups, we must continue to encourage and nurture the intellectual curiosity and entrepreneurial spirit of future innovators. This is something that must begin in early childhood and continue through adulthood. This not only includes much needed investments in STEM education, but might also take the form of grants that will allow people to take time from work to develop a new idea or product. Programs, such as "hackathons" and "pitch competitions" also offer much needed practical experience in collaborating with others on a project or selling an idea to potential investors. All of these opportunities must be specifically advertised and targeted toward underrepresented minorities in order to be most effective at bridging access and information gaps.

Second, we must increase access to the resources that are critical to protecting intellectual property once it is created, including financial, human and social capital. This involves marshaling diverse resources, such a legal professionals, business advisors, and a range of financing options, to creatively address some of the barriers faced by minority business owners.

Finally, though a good start, this analysis is not perfect. Expanding the body of research on the effect of intellectual property ownership on business outcomes requires the availability of current, detailed, reliable data on businesses, their owners and their ability to capitalize on IP rights. Better data availability would allow for more complete models of revenue generation and firm survival, including the ability to distinguish between the effects of different types of intellectual property – information that would be useful as new business owners consider their options for protecting intellectual property and the costs and benefits associated with each. Also, there must be more data on the process leading up to innovation. This would allow us to evaluate the experiences of those who have not yet reached the point of securing intellectual property rights, but would also give us more information on the characteristics of IP owners. It is reasonable to assume that IP owners possess certain traits and experiences that not only make them more likely to develop and protect their intellectual property, but also influence other business decisions that affect revenue growth and the survival of their firms (including licensing).

4. The colorblind marketplace?
Shubha Ghosh

"Our Constitution is color blind",[1] Justice Harlan famously exhorted in his dissent to the Supreme Court's opinion upholding state policies of separate but equal facilities for whites and nonwhites in *Plessy v. Ferguson*. Over the nearly century and half since, color blindness has evolved into a constitutional principle undermining state actions that seek to segregate and differentiate among persons based on racial characteristics. Blindness to color has expanded to gender equality and a disregard to other inherent characteristics by the state in its distribution of benefits and imposition of burdens.

The colorblind principle, however, has come under scrutiny by legal scholars and policymakers as it serves to block progressive policies designed to integrate public institutions and promote racial and cultural diversity.[2] Some scholars have gone further to claim that colorblindness serves to enforce racial hierarchies with white culture, or even the white race, being the norm and color as a mark of difference.[3] Defenders of colorblindness, on the other hand, claim that any mention of race is itself racist, including any accusation of racism. There is a vertiginous circularity to a strong adherence to the colorblind principle, especially when used to block any government policies that seek to remedy past discrimination.

Central to the controversies over colorblindness is the value of diversity.[4] Affirmative action policies, particularly in the area of school admissions, may have justification in the promotion of diversity. To the extent that goals of diversity align with those of pluralism of perspectives, diversity is consistent with colorblindness. Tensions arise, however, with

---

[1] 16 Sup. Ct 1138, 1146 (1896).
[2] See, e.g., Ian Haney Lopez, *Dog Whistle Politics: How Coded Racial Appeals Have Reinvented Racism & Wrecked the Middle Class* (Oxford University Press, New York 2014), 77.
[3] Ibid, 90.
[4] See *Parents Involved in Community Schools v. Seattle School District No. 1*, 127 S. Ct. 2738 (2007).

the troubling assumption that social and cultural perspectives map onto racial, ethnic, or gender difference. Colorblindness arises once again to resolve this tension by emphasizing that differences in perspectives reflect individual differences that are in turn the product of individual experiences and associations with certain group characteristics, whether defined in terms of race, ethnicity, gender, religion or sexual orientation. Diversity is about individuals, not about balkanized groups.

The world of separate but equal was one of segregated public places. Schools were separate as were churches and public accommodations. Correspondingly, markets were also segregated with different products and services provided for white and non-white customers. Integration since the overruling of Plessy in *Brown v. Board of Education*[5] has moved towards creating pluralistic public places marked by a diversity of individual backgrounds and perspectives. Consequently, markets also ceased to be separate with access to products and services not divided based on racial or other characteristics. The result seems to be a colorblind marketplace.

Readers should be familiar with the argument that the only color that matters in the marketplace is the color of money.[6] Any attempt to treat customers or sellers differently based on racial or other animus would be self-destructive. Pursuit of economic gain trumps bigotry in the marketplace with the result that the marketplace would truly be colorblind. Countering this argument is that the pursuit of status might lead to unequal outcomes based on race, gender or other characteristics. If a customer or supplier is not ostensibly a bigot, but status is associated with social indicia, like type of clothing, the neighborhood one lives in or particular forms of comportment, then the pursuit of status by a customer or a supplier may lead to unequal outcomes that reflect social and historical differences based on race or other characteristic. In other words, the marketplace may not be colorblind at all even if there is a general attitudinal change in society against racial animus and discrimination. The pursuit of personal gain, especially when understood in terms of status and not pure profit maximization, may reflect or even exacerbate racial and other forms of segmentation.

While the Constitution may be colorblind, social institutions like the marketplace may not be. At one level, this situation is not paradoxical.

---

[5] 74 S. Ct. 686 (1954).
[6] See Amartya Sen, "Foreword", in Albert Hirschman, *The Passions and the Interests: Political Arguments for Capitalism Before Its Triumph* (Princeton University Press, Princeton 1997), x.

The Constitution limits government action, except for the Thirteenth Amendment which prohibits all forms of slavery. The marketplace is the realm of private action with Constitutional limits coming into place on government involvement in the market. However, Justice Harlan's famous phrase is not a statement solely about what the Constitution means. Instead, Justice Harlan was stating a moral principle, one that would prohibit any form of social segregation or market segmentation stemming from decision making that was racially minded. Under this view, if our Constitution is colorblind, so must be all our institutions, whether labelled private or public.

The last proposition, if it is accepted, leads us to the vexing question of what colorblindness means, especially when pluralism is seen as a virtue. Particularly troubling is the meaning of a colorblind marketplace. One meaning is that the marketplace and its actors are neutral with respect to race. But this neutrality may often be illusory if the market is a means to pursue status, which in turn reflects social segmentation. Another meaning is that the marketplace reflects a plurality of interests. If anyone, regardless of race, has the opportunity to enter the marketplace and compete, then effectively the market is colorblind even if outcomes may reflect social segmentation. This view of the colorblind marketplace is equally vexing. If market outcomes result in homogeneity and the expression in the form of products and services reflecting the majority aggregating their dollars, then markets may respect pluralism as an input, but not as a result or output. Is a homogeneous social landscape one that is colorblind, or just a mask for the dominant group? Or put another way, is equality of opportunity enough for a colorblind marketplace?

The issues set forth are critical in my mind for how we understand social entrepreneurship. If the current mantra is that anyone can be an entrepreneur, how should we respond to outcomes that seem to suggest that some groups succeed more systematically than others? In other words, is it sufficient to have equal opportunity for entrepreneurship? Furthermore, if we desire more than equal opportunity, how do we promote a plural marketplace, one that responds to and reflects a plurality of interests and supports a diversity in products and services? This chapter addresses these questions through one example of entrepreneurship that attempted to respond to a market need based on a colormindful strategy. The failure of that example addresses many of the questions about markets and colorblindness presented in this introduction.

CASE STUDY OF NITROMED AND BIDIL

Nitromed began in a university laboratory.[7] Dr. Jay Cohn, a research scientist at The University of Minnesota Medical Center, undertook a study of medical data from the Veteran's Administration (VA) to identify the use of nitrous oxide in treatment of hypertension and heart disease in the early 1980s. The focus of Dr. Cohn's research was the use of a compound called BiDil, which was a combination of hydralazine and isosorbide dinitrate. The chemical compound BiDil was a vascular dilator to combat heart failure which was found to be more effective than ACE inhibitors, an alternative method for treatment. Dr. Cohn published his findings from the Veteran Administration studies in 1986 and applied for a patent a year later. The patent issued in 1989. This patent was the first one covering BiDil and was not limited by race. Dr. Cohn applied for trademark on BiDil in 1992 and began negotiations with MedCo Research Inc., a North Carolina company, to manufacture and market BiDil at around the same time. In 1995, Dr. Cohn transferred its trademark and patent associated with BiDil to MedCo., which began clinical testing of BiDil for bioequivalence with the use of hydrazaline and isosorbate dinitrate separately. In 1996, MedCo completed its clinical trials and applied for approval from the Food and Drug Administration. However, because of problems identified in Dr. Cohn's VA studies, the FDA denied approval for marketing BiDil. As a result of the denial, MedCo decided not to pursue the marketing of BiDil and let all intellectual property rights revert back to Dr. Cohn. At this point, Nitromed enters the narrative.

Nitromed was formed in 1992 by two research scientists from Harvard Medical School and Brigham and Woman's Hospital. Its primary goal was to investigate and identify medical uses of nitrous oxide therapy. The founders' focus in the early to mid-1990s was the development of treatments for erectile dysfunction, the subject of one of its first patents. The introduction and success of Viagra by Pfizer in 1995, however, caused Nitromed to seek out other applications. In 1999, Nitromed obtained intellectual property rights and a new drug application (NDA) from Dr. Cohn who had resumed research on BiDil after the FDA rejection. What motivated Nitromed's interest were published studies by Dr. Cohn, who had found a more refined application for BiDil therapy.

In response to the FDA rejection of the BiDil application in 1997, Dr.

---

[7] The background presented below is distilled from Jonathan Kahn, "Patenting Race", 24(11) *Nature Biotechnology* 1349 (2006) and the description in the 2002 and 2004 patents.

Cohn revisited his VA studies. Pursuing growing interest in race specific treatments for disease, Dr. Cohn focused on the oversample of African-Americans in the original VA studies. His review of the VA data from 1997 to 1998 helped Dr. Cohn to identify a drug therapy specific to the African-American population. Dr. Cohn's studies were timely in many ways. In 1997, Congress passed the FDA Modernization Act, asking the Secretary of Health and Human Studies to develop guidelines for the appropriate inclusion of race and gender in clinical trials. Health care scholars and advocates called public attention to diseases and demographic groups ignored by medical researchers. Given this climate and the shared focus on nitrous oxide therapies, a relationship between Nitromed and Dr. Cohn was predictable.

Based on Dr. Cohn's success in identifying a drug therapy specific to treating African Americans, Nitromed agreed to fund Dr. Cohn's clinical trials for a race specific use of BiDil to address the needs within the African-American community for effective treatment of hypertension. In 2001, Nitromed obtained over 30 million dollars of venture capital funding to support the clinical trials in a collaboration with the Association of Black Cardiologists. In 2002, Nitromed obtained the first patent on a race specific use of BiDil and shortly thereafter Nitromed went public with a proposed market cap of $ 305 million. The path was paved for marketing the new therapy with the grant of second patent (as a continuation of the 2002 patent) issued in 2004 and the FDA approval of race specific uses of BiDil in 2005. Nitromed's stock price quadrupled after the patent issuance in 2004 from about five dollars to a level of 20 dollars per share. Despite this initial spate of good news, Nitromed confronted resistance from medical providers who were reluctant to prescribe the drug. Therapies were developed that were able to work around Nitromed's patent with similar effectiveness. Consequently, Nitromed's stock price fell to between two and three dollars a share in 2007, where it has stayed until the time of this writing.

Despite criticism of the race specific drug, Nitromed's patents were never challenged. At the same time, Nitromed never attempted to enforce its patent against competitors. While patents on a human genetic sequence, such as one associated with such intimate diseases as breast and ovarian cancers, raised the specter of ownership of a human being and the denial of access to life saving therapies, an invention aimed specifically at the African-American population was a response to neglected diseases and treatments. Nonetheless, the Nitromed patent illustrates controversies over patenting of treatments that were personalized along racial lines. A look at how a race specific patent is issued provides a telling story of patent strategies in the area of personalized medicine.

The pursuit of a patent starts with the filing of a patent application, which is reviewed by a patent examiner in the United States Patent and Trademark Office, or other appropriate national patent office, in a process called patent prosecution. The examiner often finds reasons under the Patent Act to reject the application, and the applicant responds to these rejections. The process is a matter of give and take and involves strategic decision making on the part of the applicant. The pursuit of the patent on BiDil provides a good example of this dynamic. There are two patents on the chemical composition for BiDil, one issued in 2002 with 54 claims[8] and one in 2004, from a continuation application, with 84 claims.[9] The race specific claims are the same for the two patents, and therefore by the rules against double patenting, the claims in the patent issued in 2002 would be effective.[10] The abstracts for both patents use identical language in describing the composition:

> The present invention provides methods or [sic] treating and preventing mortality associated with heart failure in an African-American patient with hypertension and improving oxygen consumption, quality of life and exercise tolerance by administering a therapeutically effective amount of at least one is isorbinate dinitrate and isorbinate mononitrate.[11]

The first claim echoes this race specific aspect of the invention through the following language: "A method of reducing mortality associated with heart failure in a black patient in need thereof comprising administering to the black patient hydralizine...in an amount about 30 milligrams per day to about 300 milligrams per day and isosorbinate dinitrate in an amount of about 20 milligrams per day to about 200 milligrams per day."[12]

A challenging question is why the claim is limited to a "black patient".[13] The written description presents the clinical trials administered to test the efficacy and the safety of the chemical composition. According to the description, "the placebo group mortality...did not differ between white and black patients...The inventors unexpectedly discovered that black patients exhibited a significant survival benefit...from treatment with the

---

[8] U.S. Patent No. 6465463 (issued 15 Oct. 2002).
[9] U.S. Patent No. 6784177 (issued 31 Aug. 2004).
[10] Double patenting is not allowed under 35 USC § 101, which states that "a" patent shall issue to an inventor whose application meets the requirements of patentability. See *Miller v. Eagle Manufacturing Co.*, 151 U.S. 186 (1894) (establishing rule against double patenting).
[11] See note 8 above.
[12] Idem.
[13] Idem.

combination of hydralazine and isosorbide dinitrate".[14] The inventors speculate on why there is this observed difference in response between black and white patients. They cite literature showing that black patients are less responsive to ACE inhibitors than white patients and this difference in turn reflects a less active rennin-angiotensin system among black patients.[15] Although the inventors could not identify the source of the difference, the statistical difference uncovered in the clinical trials was the basis for the racially limited claim.

The racial limitations reflect another important dimension to the development of the invention. Both the 2002 and the 2004 patents cite a 1989 patent issued to one of the inventors for a "Method of Reducing Mortality associated with Congestive Heart Failure Using Hydralizine and Isosorbide Dinitrate".[16] The patent expired in 2003.[17] It is instructive to read the first claim of the 1989 patent and compare it with the more recent ones:

> A method of reducing the incidence of mortality associated with chronic congestive heart failure in a patient with impaired cardiac function and concomitant reduced exercise tolerance, comprising the oral administration to said patient in need of the same of a combination of (a) between about 75 and about 300 milligrams of hydralazine, or a pharmaceutically acceptable acid addition salt thereof, per day, and (b) between about 40 and about 160 milligrams of isosorbide dinitrate, per day.[18]

The two obvious differences between the 1989 claim and the 2002/2004 claim are the differences in dosages and the absence of any racial limitations. A consideration of these two differences illustrates three points about the role of racial categories in patent law.

The first point is that the 1989 patent would allow the patent owner to prevent uses of the chemical composition on any patient, without regard to race or other characteristic. Perhaps the broad applicability of the invention reflects an assumption that a pharmaceutical invention, or more broadly any invention, can be used by all members of the population absent some evidence, such as the clinical trials documents in the 2002/2004 written descriptions, that the invention empirically is suitable for only one group.[19] Whether this assertion is true, I will argue in the next section, rests on the normative foundations of patent law. But if it is true,

---

[14] Ibid.
[15] Idem.
[16] U.S. Patent No. 4868179 (issued 19 September 1989).
[17] Ibid. The patent term at the time of the issuance of this patent was 14 years from the date of issuance.
[18] Idem.
[19] See note 7 above at 1350.

the conclusion suggests a baseline rule of race neutrality in patent law with the inventor being permitted to draw racial lines if there is some empirical basis to support the limitation. Since the inventor could not explain the racial disparity in the 2002/2004 patent, the racial imitation arguably need not be explained and can be supported by statistical disparities.

The second point is the role of race specific studies in support of the claimed invention. It is telling that the 1989 written description does not disclose any racial disparities or racial differentiation in clinical trials while the 2002/2004 trials do. This difference may reflect a heightened sensitivity to racial differences in the incidence and treatment of diseases that has arisen in the 13-year period. While the National Institute of Health did implement guidelines for race specific clinical trials and funding incentives for research in previously underserved populations and diseases in the Nineties,[20] these incentives may have been less important for private, commercial researchers working for industry, such as the inventors of the chemical composition in the BIDIL patent. A more likely explanation is that the inventors were seeking to find some additional commercial exploitation of the invention and discovered the strategy of targeting the invention to a racially defined market.[21] Hence, the clinical trials demonstrated how the chemical composition could be tailored to a racial enclave of the market based on differential efficacy.

Building on the ways in which race seemingly entered into the experimentation on and marketing of a chemical composition, I turn to the third, and most crucial, point that follows from a comparison of the two patents. The second invention builds on the first invention by identification of different dosage levels and of different efficacy for a racially defined group. The question is why these two together, or separately, would be sufficient to warrant a second patent on the chemical composition. By itself, discovering

---

[20] In 1994, the National Institute of Health issued the National Institutes of Health Guidelines on the Inclusion of Woman and Minorities as Subjects in Clinical Research, which outlined "a wide range of new responsibilities for clinical researchers funded by the NIH and for institutional review boards". Under these Guidelines, "all NIH-funded clinical research must now include representative numbers of women and members of racial or ethnic minority groups". Charles Weijer and Robert A. Crouch, "Why Should We Include Women and Minorities in Randomized control Trials?" in Ezekiel J. Emanuel et al. (eds), *Ethical And Regulatory Aspects Of Clinical Research: Readings And Commentary* (Johns Hopkins University Press, Baltimore 2003), 171–2.

[21] See note 7 above at 1351; Michael D. Ruel, "Using Race in Clinical Research To Develop Tailored Medications: Is The FDA Encouraging Discrimination or Eliminating Traditional Disparities in Health Care for African Americans?", 27 *Journal of Legal Medicine*, 225, 227–9 (2006).

a different dosage level of a chemical compound would not be enough to satisfy the non-obviousness requirements of patentability, unless there was some "unexpected result" from what was in the prior art.[22] The racial limitation, however, is more problematic. If the inventor in fact discovered a new or different chemical composition that worked solely for a discrete group, there may be an argument that she has found something new and non-obvious in light of the prior art.[23] The problem is determining why this distinction occurs as an empirical matter in a way that would warrant generalization from a few clinical trials. Demonstrating that the chemical composition was found not to work on some groups in some cases does not warrant a claim, either as a matter of logic or of patentability, for the use of the exclusive use of the chemical composition in all cases.

Even if this logical gap could be resolved, there is still the question of whether modifying an invention for a specifically defined group meets the non-obviousness requirement. The racial tailoring of the 1989 invention also explains the non-obviousness of the 2002/2004 invention. On 5 December 2001, the patent examiner rejected the race-specific claims in the application supporting the 2002 patent for being obvious in light of the 1989 patent.[24] The patent applicant responded on 6 May 2002, arguing that there was nothing in the 1989 patent that would "disclose or suggest" the race-specific claims.[25] In addition, the applicant argued that the efficacy in the African-American population was an "unexpected result" which supported a conclusion of non-obviousness.[26] The patent examiner accepted this argument, and in an office action on 18 May 2002, concluded that the claims were non-obviousness in light of the unexpected result.[27]

---

[22] See, e.g., *Ortho-McNeil Pharmaceuticals v. Kali Laboratories, Inc.*, 482 F.Supp. 2d 478 (D.N.J. 2007) (change in dosage level not sufficient for non-obviousness), citing *Merck & Co. v. Bocraft Labs, Inc.*, 874 F.2d 804, 805–806 (Fed. Cir. 1989) (changes in conditions for using invention, such as temperature or concentration, not enough to establish non-obviousness unless there is some unexpected result); *Pfizer, Inc. v. Apotex, Inc.*, 480 F.3d 1348 (Fed. Cir. 2007) (altering chemical formulation not enough to show non-obviousness).

[23] See *Takeda Chemical Industries, Ltd. v. Alphapham Pty., Ltd.*, 2007 WL 1839698 (Fed. Cir. 2007) (discussing the issue of patentability of species claims over genus claims in the prior art and proposes allowing such claims if there is evidence of unexpected results).

[24] Memorandum from Raymond Henley, Jr. Primary Examiner, to Edward D. Grieff, Registration No. 38,898 (5 December 2001) (on file with author).

[25] Memorandum from Edward D. Grieff, Registration No. 38,898 to Raymond Henley, Jr., Primary Examiner (6 May 2002) (on file with author).

[26] Ibid.

[27] Memorandum from Raymond Henley, Jr. Primary Examiner, to Edward D. Grieff, Registration No. 38,898 (18 May 2002) (on file with author).

This exchange illustrates, in part, the application of the "teach, suggest, motivate" test (TSM) to the legal question of non-obviousness. Under TSM, an invention is non-obvious if a disclosure in the prior art taught, suggested or motivated the elements that makes the invention different from those disclosed in the prior art. In other words, a party challenging the patentability of an invention on non-obviousness grounds must show what in the prior art taught, suggested or motivated the invention. If the party fails to produce such a teaching, suggestion or motivation, he has not met the burden to show obviousness. In the case of the 2002 patent, the applicant asserted that the patent examiner failed to meet the TSM test and furthermore pointed to the unexpected result, a secondary consideration to support the conclusion that the invention was non-obvious.

There might be a question as to whether the racially tailored invention would be found non-obvious in light of the United States Supreme Court's 2007 decision in *KSR v. Teleflex*.[28] In this decision, the Court cautioned against a mechanical application of TSM and acknowledged that common sense of the person having ordinary skill in the art can serve to distinguish obvious from non-obvious inventions. Under this "common sense" approach, a patent examiner could look at Nitromed's application for a treatment aimed at African-Americans and ask whether someone skilled in medical treatment of hypertension would view Nitromed's invention as common knowledge regardless of whether the prior art would have suggested such a treatment. Dr. Cohn's investigations show that conventional treatment of hypertension was less effective in African-American populations. Furthermore, identifying more effective treatments for African-Americans suffering from hypertension had not been the object of research. Consequently, Nitromed's treatment likely would have been found nonobvious even under the more stringent test announced by the Court in *Teleflex*.

Pharmaceutical inventions examined under the *Teleflex* standard have often failed to meet the non-obviousness requirement if the inventor has simply changed the dosage level to increase effectiveness or changed the delivery method from pill to capsule. Examiners have found these changes to be common-sensical to someone with knowledge in the field. As a policy matter, these changes were deemed as attempts to extend the life of the patent without improving or altering the original pharmaceutical patent issued in 1989 and that expired in 2003. Dr. Cohn's patent could also be seen as an attempt to alter the original treatment for hypertension by altering the underlying chemical composition. The innovation, however,

---

[28] 550 U.S. 398 (2007).

is finding a new dosage that more effectively treats a subpopulation. As pointed out in the previous paragraph that may be sufficient to meet the requirements of patentability. While other changes to inventions covered by expiring pharmaceutical patents raised policy concerns of extending the life of a patent without any substantial new benefit, Dr. Cohn's modifications arguably did add benefit by serving the needs of an ignored population. The policy question raised by the BiDiL patent is whether innovation targeted at particular groups characterized by a racial category should be encouraged.

GENERAL LESSONS FOR SOCIAL ENTREPRENEURSHIP AND MARKET THEORY

The Fourteenth Amendment of the United States Constitution assures the equal protection of the laws. At the minimum, equal protection requires that persons be treated the same under the law. The government shall not make distinctions among persons in the enactment and application of its laws. One may think that the Fourteenth Amendment has no relevance to personalized medicine since the government is not acting. Personalized medicine is the domain of private researchers and companies. But the relevant question is whether government is violating the Fourteenth Amendment in granting race-based patents like the one issued to Nitromed. Posing the question broader, one may ask whether the government might run afoul of the Fourteenth Amendment when it grants a patent that distinguishes among persons using any category, including genetic ones.

Even with the requisite government action, there is still the question of whether the Fourteenth Amendment is even relevant to personalized medicine. Equal protection means that Group A and Group B be treated equally. The Equal Protection Clause places limits on the government from allowing, for example, Group A, but not Group B, to have a particular benefit, such as schooling or participation in an election. To take another example, the Fourteenth Amendment limits the government from giving a vaccine against a disease to Group A and not to Group B. But what if Group B does not suffer from the disease that the vaccine prevents? Arguably, Group B is not being denied a benefit that Group A has.

As an example of this normative quandary consider the patent for the chemical composition that constitute BiDil. The claim restricts use of the composition for treatment of hypertension in "black patients". Suppose a medical practitioner administers the composition to a patient without the authorization of Nitromed, the company to whom the patent is assigned.

If the medical practitioner is sued for patent infringement, the court will have to determine whether the patient who received the drug was black. If the patient is black, then there has been infringement of the patent. If the patient is not black, then Nitromed would argue that the racial identity of the patient is equivalent to "black" in order to succeed on its legal claim for patent infringement under the doctrine of equivalents.[29] In this hypothetical law suit, the court would have to construe the racial identity of the patient in order to determine patent infringement, much as courts had to construe the racial identity of defendants to see if there had been a violation of the myriad restrictions on activity under Jim Crow laws.

But the analogy to the Jim Crow laws is in many ways a misguided one in the context of determining the infringement of a race specific patent claim. Under Jim Crow laws, legal entitlements were allocated based on the race with the intention of stigmatizing members of the designated inferior race. In the BiDil context, there is no intention to stigmatize.[30] Instead, the goal is to provide incentives for the development of pharmaceutical products that benefit neglected racial or ethnic groups. While it is true that a court, in enforcing Nitromed's patent, can enjoin unauthorized users from administering the drug to a black patient but cannot enjoin the administration of the same drug to a non-black patient, the distinction is arguably not based on invidious discrimination. Instead, the analogy is more closely made to the review of affirmative action programs, which

---

[29] Under the doctrine of equivalents, the patent owner can sue a party who has used, made, sold, or offered to sell an invention that does not literally fall within the language of the patent claims. The general test is that the defendant's infringement accomplished the same function through the same way to reach the same result as every element of the claim. See *Warner-Jenkinson Co. v. Hilton Davis Chemical Co.*, 520 U.S. 17 (1997).

[30] The BiDil patent and the push for personalized medicine more broadly are examples of "liberal eugenics", in contrast with the racist or nativist use of eugenics in the 19th and early part of the 20th centuries. Liberal eugenics involves genetic selection or genetic manipulation for the purposes of enhancing individual or even group attributes. See Nicholas Agar, *Liberal Eugenics: In Defense of Human Enhancement* (Wiley-Blackwell, New York 2004), 5 (contrasting liberal use of eugenics with the totalitarian and racist uses under the Nazi regime); Michael J. Sandel, *The Case against Perfection: Ethics in the Age of Genetic Engineering* (Belknap Press, Cambridge 2007), 75–83 (contrasting liberal eugenics with the "old eugenics" and "free-market eugenics"). For an early, and simplistic, attempt to deal with the ethical and constitutional issues raised by biotechnology, see John B. Attanasio, "The Constitutionality of Regulating Human Genetic Engineering: Where Procreative Liberty and Equal Opportunity Collide", 53 U. Chi. L. Rev. 1274 (1986) (formulating the issues in terms of a broad tension between liberty and equality).

deny certain benefits to particular races in favor of others. As with affirmative action programs, the legality of racial categories in patent claims may rest on a compelling state interest, analogous to the diversity rationale recognized in the *Grutter* decision.[31]

Designation of racial categories as either stigmatizing or beneficial is only one of many potential problems raised by racial categories in patents. The infringement example assumed that the granting of the injunction by the court based on consideration of race constituted state action. The implicit assumption is that the patent infringement case involving a racially specific claim would be analogous to the enforcement of a racially restricted covenant as in *Shelley v. Kraemer*[32] or the allowance of peremptory challenges based on race as in *Batson v. Kentucky*.[33] If patent rights, like contractual rights, are private rights,[34] the superficial conclusion would be that state action does not arise. But in the infringement example, the court is seeking to exclude a party based on the consideration of race analogous to the injunction of sale of real property or to the exclusion of a juror based on race. The black patient is in the same position as an African-American purchaser or real property in *Shelley* or the potential African-American juror being stricken from the pool. In all three instances, the court is complicit in the act of private party seeking to deny a benefit based on race. Therefore, even if a patent is a species of private property, the existence of state action is not tenuous.[35]

---

[31] *Grutter v. Bollinger*, 539 U.S. 306, 326 (2003).
[32] *Shelley v. Kraemer*, 334 U.S. 1, 20 (1948).
[33] *Batson v. Kentucky*, 476 U.S. 79 (1986).
[34] For an analysis of patents as a set of contractual rights, see Shubha Ghosh, "Patents and the Regulatory State: Rethinking the Patent Bargain Metaphor After Eldred", 19 Berkeley Tech. L. J. 1315 (2004). See also Jay P. Kesan and Mark Banik, "Patents as Incomplete Contracts: Aligning Incentives for R&D Investment With Incentives to Disclose Prior Art", 2 Wash. U.J.L. & Pol'y 23 (2000); Vincenzo Denicolo and Luigi Alberto Franzoni, "The Contract Theory of Patents", 23 Int'l Rev. L. & Econ. 365 (2000).
[35] Arguably, the use of racial categories in the granting of a patent would constitute constitutional state action under *Burton v. Wilmington Parking Authority*, 365 U.S. 715, 81 S.Ct. 856, 6 L.Ed. 2d 45 (1961) (finding state action when private discriminatory conduct was "intertwined" with the state). But see *Moose Lodge No. 107 v. Irvis*, 407 U.S. 163 (1972) (granting of liquor license did not sufficiently implicate the state in private discriminatory behavior to create constitutional state action). The Court's analysis in *Shelley v. Kraemer* has been questioned, but the case offers an important analogy for discussing the role of constitutional state action in patent law since the public entity is quite clearly creating private rights. For a discussion of the controversy over the *Shelley* decision, see Mark D. Rosen, "Was *Shelley v. Kraemer* Incorrectly Decided? Some New Answers",

However, the existence of state action in the recognition of racial categories in patent law can readily be seen once patents are recognized as private property rights granted by the state.[36] In the case of BiDil, a patent examiner, an agent of the state, reviewed the patent application and the available prior art to determine that the use of the chemical compound as limited to black patients is a protected right owned by the patent applicant and secured by the state. Race, therefore, was a factor in the determination by the state to grant the right of exclusion secured through patent law. In this context, however, the consideration of race is different from the use of racial categories in affirmative action programs,[37] in the grant of voting rights,[38] or in the selection of employees,[39] where the racial identity of persons being denied a benefit by the state is key to the decision. In the case of BiDil, the racial identity of the patent applicant or inventor is irrelevant to the decision.[40] Instead, the state is making the decision to grant a right to a specific individual in order to benefit a racially identified group.

When state action is understood in this way, there are three possible responses. One is to conclude that this use of racial categories is different from the stigmatizing uses that arise in conventional racially discriminatory state action because the state is not directly targeting certain groups and therefore is not problematic. The second is to conclude that the state is internalizing and reinforcing private animus and discriminatory attitudes and therefore the state action is suspect. The third is to conclude that the state's consideration of race can be beneficial if it corrects differences that have been created through the use of racial categories. This third approach

---

95 Cal. L. Rev. 451, 473 (2007) (justifying the decision in *Shelley* under the Thirteenth Amendment which does not require state action). For a current discussion of the distinction between state action and private action, see Mark Tushnet, "State Action, Social Welfare Rights, and the Judicial Role: Some Comparative Observations", 3 Chi. J. Int'l L. 435 (2002) (analyzing the place of state action in the social democratic state); Cass R. Sunstein, "State Action Is Always Present", 3 Chi. J. Int'l L. 465 (2002) (arguing that state action also exists in the classic liberal state although the state assumes a different set of affirmative obligations).

[36] See *Webber v. State of Virginia*, 103 U.S. 344 (1880) (Congress' power to grant patents); *James v. Campbell*, 104 U.S. 356 (1881) (Congress' power to define patent rights and make use of patents).

[37] See *Parents Involved in Community Schools v. Seattle School District No. 1 et al.*, 551 U.S. 71 (2007).

[38] See *Baker v. Carr*, 369 U.S. 186 (1962).

[39] See *Wygant v. Jackson Board of Education*, 476 U.S. 267 (1986).

[40] For a discussion of racial restrictions on patenting that were imposed in the 19th century, see J.S. Butler, *Entrepreneurship And Self-Help Among African Americans: A Reconsideration Of Race And Economics* (SUNY Press, Albany 1991), 55.

is the most problematic because it suggests that there are certain uses of racial categories that may be beneficial, creating the difficult task of distinguishing between beneficial and harmful uses of racial categories. As I elaborate in the rest of this section, distinguishing among these positions requires coordinating the normative goals of patent law with those of the use of racial categories by the state.

Colorblindness is the hallmark of liberal theories of race.[41] But there are shades of colorblindness. At the ideal level, proponents of liberal theories aspire to a world in which decisions about the allocation of market resources and the distribution of political power are made without any consideration of race. What this means in practice is that such decisions are made on the merits of the situation and the character of the individual participants. A less idealistic view would recognize that power often, perhaps always, plays some role in the functioning of markets and of politics, but the exercise of economic and political power needs to be absent of racial considerations. Colorblindness does not, however, mean social homogenization of either skin tones or culture. Most liberal theorists of race would celebrate a healthy pluralism, the clichéd melting pot.[42] But such diversity in the public realm is a reflection of individual group identity rather than subordination of or discrimination against groups. There is, however, a sense that once racial difference is understood as irrelevant to individual decision making in any context, racial difference will go away to be replaced with a mutual respect for individual autonomy and self-creation.

Liberal theories of race retreat from the principle of colorblindness in many instances. In defining the cultural sphere, race can arise as a healthy and much needed ingredient to the promotion of a vibrant and healthy workforce and marketplace.[43] Race may also be an element in remedies

---

[41] See Andrew Kull, *The Color-Blind Constitution* (Harvard University Press, Cambridge 1992) (exploring the implications of Justice Harlan's dissent in *Plessy v. Ferguson*); John A. Powell, "The Colorblind Multiracial Dilemma: Racial Categories Reconsidered", 31 U.S.F. L. Rev. 789 (1997); Jerry Kang, "Cyber-Race", 113 Harv. L. Rev. 1130, 1154–60 (1999).

[42] See Peter H. Schuck, "The Perceived Values of Diversity, Then and Now", 22 Cardozo L. Rev. 1915, 1927–8 (2001).

[43] Judge Alex Kozinski illustrated this point vividly when he described an affirmative action plan in Seattle designed to racially integrate elementary schools as giving "the American melting pot a healthy stir without benefiting or burdening any particular group". *Parents Involved in Community v. Seattle School*, 426 F.3d 1162, 1196 (9th Cir. 2005) (Judge Kozinski's concurrence to majority opinion upholding the plan). The United States Supreme Court reversed the decision, with Chief Justice Roberts asserting the color blind position: "The way to stop

for past discrimination and continuing obstacles that are historical relics from less liberal times.[44] Therefore, in the affirmative action debate, race can be a factor to be considered in some public decision making but only in a narrowly tailored remedial fashion to correct for specifically identified instances of past group discrimination.[45] Furthermore, race can be used sometimes in the university admissions context to promote the goals of diversity, specifically in public service professions such as law.[46] Race, however, is a constitutional suspect class and only very narrow policy justifications can support its use.[47]

Economist Glenn Loury has written about the complexities posed for liberal theories of race by the principle of colorblindness.[48] In the 1980s, Professor Loury was a staunch conservative with respect to race, advocating a strict colorblind position that mandated self-help and the avoidance of the culture of victimhood.[49] Recently, Professor Loury has made an about-face for pragmatic reasons and has espoused a critique of strict colorblindness. In his *The Anatomy of Racial Inequality* (2002), given as the W.E.B. Du Bois Lecture at Harvard in 2000, Professor Loury posits three axioms: (1) race is socially constructed; (2) race is not an essentialist category, but a social artifact; and (3) as a socially constructed category, race has resulted in the creation of stigma and prejudicial attitudes harmful to racialized groups.[50] In addition to these axioms, Professor Loury identifies three contexts in which racial categories are used: (a) policy implementation; (b) policy evaluation; and (c) civic construction of a nation's shared purpose and common fate.[51] He argues that colorblindness is appropriate only for public decision making in the third forum, but not in the first

---

discrimination on the basis of race is to stop discriminating on the basis of race". *Parents Involved in Community*, note 14 above, 82.

[44] See *Adarand Constructors, Inc. v. Pena*, 515 U.S. 200, 253–5 (1995) (adopting strict scrutiny for use of racial classifications by Federal government and remedying past discrimination may serve as a compelling interest if narrowly tailored).

[45] See *Grutter*, note 31 above, 328–32; *Gratz v. Bollinger*, 539 U.S. 244 (2003).

[46] See *Grutter*, note 31 above. See *Johnson v. California*, 543 U.S. 499, 505 (2005) (affirming strict scrutiny standard for state use of racial category).

[47] See *Johnson v. California*, 543 U.S. 499, 505 (2005) (affirming strict scrutiny standard for state use of racial category).

[48] Glenn C. Loury, *The Anatomy of Racial Inequality* 8–11 (Harvard University Press, Cambridge, MA 2002).

[49] Professor Loury's early conservative position was stated in Glenn C. Loury, "A New American Dilemma", 31 December 1984. An about face can be seen in the article, Glenn C. Loury, "How to Mend Affirmative Action", 127 *The Public Interest* 33–43 (1997).

[50] Loury, note 48 above at 5.

[51] Idem at 148–9.

two.[52] Specifically, racial categories should not be considered in the broad mandate of an open and inclusive society but should be considered in the areas of policy implementation and policy evaluation in order to reach the goal of an open and inclusive society.[53]

Professor Loury presents a pragmatic approach to colorblindness, one that acknowledges the failure of a strict colorblind position to combat continuing stereotypes and animus based on race. The approach almost, but not quite, echoes the critical theory position presented below: almost, because of the emphasis on the recognition that race continues to be debilitating; not quite, because of the appeal to assimilation. Liberal theories of race falter around the principle of assimilation.[54] On the one hand, assimilation supports the goal of inclusion and leads to fairness and equality of opportunity. On the other hand, assimilation can deny difference by mandating that individuals comport their distinctiveness and cultural affiliations to the will of the majority. Pragmatic turns appeal to concepts like diversity or pluralism or phrases like "rainbow republicanism" to accommodate difference to the colorblind principle.[55] Such accommodation leads to charges of balkanization and fragmentation of public spaces and the call for a return to strict colorblindness.[56] Professor Loury's approach attempts to recognize the use of racial categories as an instrument to reach certain policy goals while retaining an open, inclusive civic sphere demarcated along assimilationist lines.

The connections between race and wealth maximization, between race and markets, and between race and culture can be understood against the liberal goal of assimilation. Under the colorblind principle, in both the strict and pragmatic forms, race should be irrelevant to the goals of wealth maximization and therefore needs to be expunged as a category. More pragmatic forms, however, would recognize that racial animus and the persistence of past discrimination requires consideration of race in the implementation of particular policies, such as admissions or the award of other public benefits. Therefore, the intersection of wealth maximization

---

[52] Idem at 150–2.
[53] Idem at 153.
[54] See, e.g., Ian F. Haney Lopez, "'A Nation of Minorities': Race, Ethnicity, and Reactionary Colorblindness", 59 Stan. L. Rev. 985, 993 (2007).
[55] See Kathleen Sullivan, "Comment: Rainbow Republicanism", 97 Yale L. J. 1713, 1716 (1988) (arguing against a civic republican view of social pluralism in favor of a structure of private voluntary associations that are independent from the purview of the state).
[56] See Lopez, note 54 above, 996.

and colorblindness would support the use of racial categories to reach the goals of corrective justice to remedy past harms.

Liberal theories of race would find little room for racial categories in the market sphere. In such an arena, willing buyers and willing sellers should coordinate solely in order to engage in voluntary, mutual enhancing transactions. While liberal theorists would not deny that the specter of race can appear in the market sphere, the animus arising from race can be cured through proper implementation of race conscious policies in the public sphere through anti-discrimination laws or through race conscious policies in providing benefits, such as education. When racial pluralism arises in the market arena, for example, through the development of enclave or ethnic markets, within which members of certain racially or ethnically defined groups trade with each other, racial categories are a useful tool to promote diversity and cultural pluralism in the marketplace.[57] Such appeal to "rainbow commercialism" would support the use of racial categories as brands, or trademarks, much like the use of colors as a trademark upon the showing of secondary meaning, through which sellers and buyers can signal to each other their willingness to engage in beneficial trades.[58] Racial signals of this sort serve to invite inclusion rather than impose exclusion. As a result, the civic sphere, which includes the market, is enriched.

Finally, when liberal theories of race connect racial categories with culture, the result is the promotion of diversity.[59] The appeal to diversity does not arise from a rejection of the colorblindness principle, but as a necessary complement to the goal of assimilation. If the difficult truth is that it is illiberal to abolish difference, whether racial or otherwise, while moving towards the goal of assimilation and inclusiveness, then difference is accommodated by creating a zone within the civic sphere in which difference can flourish but not intrude into the workings of politics or the market. This sphere of cultural diversity is one in which racial categories

---

[57] See, e.g., Lan Cao, "The Diaspora of Ethnic Economies: Beyond the Pale?" 44 Wm. & Mary L. Rev. 1521, 1530 (2003) (although not using the term "rainbow commercialism", illustrating the point through an analysis of ethnic enclaves and markets in major global cities). For a striking example of this phenomenon, see American Multicultural Marketing, accessed 13 October 2014 at http://american-multicultural.com.

[58] See Susan Scafidi, *Who Owns Culture?: Appropriation And Authenticity In American Law* (Rutgers University Press, New Jersey 2005), 151 (proposing trademark like protection for culture identities in commodified public spaces).

[59] See Will Kymlicka, *Multicultural Citizenship: A Liberal Theory of Minority Rights* (Oxford University Press, Oxford 1995), 23–31; Amartya Sen, *Identity And Violence: The Illusion Of Destiny* (W.W. Norton & Co., New York 2006), 149–52.

can be tolerated, even encouraged, as individuals can play out their racial or ethnic identities through celebration of festivals and displays of costumes and customs. The cultural sphere provides an escape hatch from the color-blind realm that allows markets and politics to function in a seemingly neutral manner. Differences are recognized with the understanding that they be put aside in the boardroom and the political arena.

CONCLUSION: TOWARDS AN INCLUSIVE MARKETPLACE

With better scientific understanding of the human genome has come the market for personalized medicine. Entrepreneurs rush to fill the marketplace with medical diagnostic and therapeutic products targeted to particular genetic sequences correlated with racial and ethnic groups. Sometimes these products are not based on genetic evidence but on clinical trial data mined according to self-identified identity categories. Whether such tailoring of medicine is the future of pharmaceuticals and medical kits indicates the future, or is a mere fad, is left to be seen. What seems to be clear is that human genomics and data mining provide a new way to market medical products and health care delivery. Is such entrepreneurship desirable from a social perspective? This Chapter has presented reasons for skepticism and possible policy responses.

The lessons from personalized medicine extend to social entrepreneurship more broadly. If social entrepreneurship seeks to benefit previously ignored needs in society and in the marketplace, then a colorblind marketplace may be troubling. Colorblindness may be a mask for majoritarianism and a reaction to desirable goals of pluralism and diversity. At the same time a color conscious marketplace may lead to too narrow a focus on the needs to be met in the marketplace. Such is the lesson from Nitromed and BiDil. A color conscious marketplace is one that is inclusive with the goal of expanding access. The problem is one of short-term profits and expediency. Social entrepreneurship should develop to counter narrow self-interest.

5. Public procurement's role in facilitating social justice, entrepreneurship and innovation in the global knowledge economy

Danielle M. Conway

I. INTRODUCTION

The field of public procurement is not always celebrated, yet it is ever-present in a globalizing society. United States public procurement – inclusive of Federal, state, and local governments – has garnered significant interest among key players in global procurement markets. Recent interest is driven largely by the potential for United States procurement markets to contribute to the expansion of the existing global procurement market. While all too difficult to project accurately, it is reasonably conceivable that among the 50 states, six territories and 87,525 local governments comprising the United States,[1] state and local procurement spending may be roughly valued at approximately $1.5 trillion[2] annually for the purchase of goods, supplies, equipment, services

---

[1] *See* Clifford P. McCue, Kirk W. Buffington and Aaron D. Howell, "The Fraud/Red-Tape Dilemma in Public Procurement: A Study of U.S. State and Local Governments," in Louise Knight et al. (eds), *Public Procurement: International Cases and Commentary* (Routledge, Abingdon 2007).

[2] In some countries, public sector expenditure may comprise 30 to 50% of gross national product (GNP). *See* "Government Procurement in FTAs: An Examination of the Issues" accessed 27 October 2014 at www.twnside.org.sg/title2/resurgence/182-183/Cover05.doc (copy on file with author); *see also* McCue et al., note 1 above (reporting that state and local governments are spending, conservatively, 25% to 40% of every tax dollar on purchased materials and supplies); *see also* Matthew Potoski, "State and local government procurement and the Winter Commission", 68 Pub. Admin. Rev. 58 (Dec. 2008).

and construction.[3] In 2011 alone, total federal procurement spending reached $537 billion.[4]

As globalization and normalization of laws take higher precedence in developed and developing societies, efficacious laws, rules, and regulations are necessary to support the strong public policy of fostering honest competition to assure prudent and economical use of public monies and to facilitate the acquisition of high quality goods and services at the lowest possible cost. The objectives of a system of good public procurement, in addition to the protection of taxpayers and the public treasury by obtaining the best work at the lowest possible price or cost, is to guard against favoritism, improvidence, extravagance, fraud and corruption in the awarding of public contracts. Inasmuch as good public procurement and its underlying laws are intended for the benefit of the taxpayers, and not to help enrich the corporate bidders and their interests, a public procurement system and its governing laws are to be construed and administered so as to accomplish such purpose fairly and reasonably with sole reference to the public interest.

Government procurement policies can be further shaped, however, to attain social benefits beyond securing the best bargains for the public procurement dollar. Federal, state, and local governments can also direct public procurement resources toward the achievement of intellectual property social justice and economic empowerment in the 21st century global market place. In compliance with the mandate that governments promote fair and open competition in the procurement process, procurement laws and policies should promote the inclusion of heretofore marginalized and underserved communities in intellectual property procurement, as a means by which to explore and exhaust all available sources for satisfying government needs for innovative intellectual property deliverables. Sound procurement policy requires identification of a strong pool of contractors willing and capable of meeting the government's minimum needs as well as government officials, particularly contracting officers and other personnel, who are obligated to serve in a trust relationship to guard and ensure the proper expenditure of taxpayer dollars. Infusing Intellectual Property

---

[3] *See* Danielle M. Conway, *State and Local Government Procurement* (ABA, Chicago 2012), xiii. The unprecedented growth of USA state and local procurement markets can be attributed largely to the federal government's policies shifting program responsibility more and more to the states, a trend that seems to be accelerating, rather than stabilizing.

[4] *See* GAO Report, Strategic Sourcing: Improved and Expanded Use Could Save Billions in Annual Procurement Costs, GAO-12-919 (2012) accessed 27 October 2014 at http://www.gao.gov/assets/650/648644.pdf.

Empowerment into the government procurement agenda symbiotically expands and diversifies the procurement vendor pool while promoting entrepreneurship and innovation in marginalized communities, all toward the greater public good.

II. THE SOCIO-ECONOMIC IMPACT OF GOVERNMENT PROCUREMENT

The upward trend in procurement spending at all levels of government has major implications for international trade as well as for domestic economic development. Legislators are becoming more aware that the upward trend in their procurement spending is attracting the attention of foreign governments and multinational contractors. The spotlight on public procurement has never been brighter and as a result governments are proceeding with caution as they consider how to respond to international obligations under legal instruments such as the Government Procurement Agreement (GPA) and other bilateral free trade agreements (FTAs). In addition to considering how to respond to the internationalization of historically insular procurement markets, all levels of government are reassessing social, economic, and political policies, in light of the ever-present foundational principles of competition, transparency, and integrity.

The speed of globalization, particularly in the innovation sector, the dismal and lingering economic climate and the upward trend in procurement spending have caused Federal, state, and local governments to attempt to transform procurement policies and infrastructures to meet the challenges of greater expectations for meeting government minimum needs with enhanced scrutiny on the expenditure of public resources while continuing to promote the important objectives of competition, transparency, and integrity. It is no surprise that contemporary governments' minimum needs are consistently pointed in the direction of the acquisition or use of innovation, technology, and access to intellectual property. By virtue of these innovation requirements, public procurement has become, more than ever before, a complex and sophisticated effort. This new environment in which innovation, technology, and intellectual property are the primary deliverables requires equally sophisticated and transformative procurement processes that continue to promote the additional important objectives of a well-functioning public procurement system – wealth distribution, risk management, best value, and efficiency.

The United States government and, at various times, state and local governments historically have been actively involved in creating inclusive, wealth distribution opportunities for small businesses through the establishment of important and unique social, economic, and political goals and objectives, often referred to as collateral policies. Collateral policies in large measure have been successful because governments are willing to use their purchasing power to direct desired outcomes. And why not? Enhanced small business participation in public procurement by virtue of investment in government processes that promote small business inclusion in governments' contractor industrial bases while also promoting small business' ability to compete and to win government contracts should be a universal effort by governments at all levels. In particular, efforts at capacity building within the small business sector are critical to emerging rapid growth industries, such as innovation, research and development, technology, and intellectual property. These futures fields are the engines of economic policy and growth and it makes sense from a wealth distribution, efficiency, and risk management perspective to build capacity so as to create competitive pools of service providers that can harness dual-use technologies, reap reasonable commercial returns, and serve the needs of taxpayers.

Collateral policies, however, are inherently controversial; some commentators have gone farther by stating that government promotion of collateral policies is anathema to the most fundamental principle of public procurement – competition. Politically speaking, using the term "collateral policies" instead of the more apt term "social justice" illuminates the act of manipulating the rhetoric to downplay the extent to which many governments recognize their unique responsibility to intercede where societal dysfunction continues to foster discrimination in employment, opportunity, the obtaining of credit, and the development of business relationships. Whether called collateral policies or social justice, few have had the courage to express the power of public procurement to ameliorate discrimination and its harmful effects on markets, institutions, segments of society, and competition. Those who recognize the relationship between public procurement and wealth distribution, equality, and social progress face opprobrious criticism. Government itself faces routine opposition to its use of the power of its purse to achieve social justice; politically speaking, however, government remains largely undeterred in its social justice efforts because public procurement, while an executive function, is primarily controlled by the legislative branch of government,[5] itself comprised of democratically elected officials responsible to constituents who have come

---

[5] Lewis J. Baker, "Procurement Disputes at the State and Local Level: A Hodgepodge of Remedies", 25 Pub. Cont. L.J. 265 (1996).

to expect that the government act in furtherance of progress. Just how governments act to achieve progress through public procurement can be described as a strategic use of procurement.

The expanding role of strategic public procurement requires a simultaneous initiative to reform and transform the laws and best practices in the formation and administration of public contracts. Procurement law facilitates the proper functioning of a public procurement system. Laws governing the formation and administration of public contracts exist to support the strong public policy of fostering honest competition to assure prudent and economical use of public monies and to facilitate the acquisition of high quality goods and services at the lowest possible price/cost.

These objectives are furthered when procurement law and policy incorporates an intellectual property social justice and empowerment perspective. Procurement policies that actively promote participation from marginalized and underserved communities enhance the talent pool for innovative and entrepreneurial business enterprise. Socially strategic public procurement provides minority and marginalized entrepreneurs with opportunities to develop and implement their own unique ideas for innovative products, services, and methods for doing business. Moreover, economically challenged communities are able to blaze new pathways to prosperity while the nation as whole benefits from the resulting contributions to its intellectual property storehouse and the fortification of its global competitive edge. In sum, pursuing IP Empowerment through strategic public procurement is simply good business judgment.

The purpose of this chapter is to explore just how governments can utilize public procurement policies and procurement laws to promote IP Empowerment in response to ever increasing government minimum needs for innovation, technology, and intellectual property deliverables. As well, this chapter attempts to address the requirement that governments balance fair and open competition with policies promoting social justice in order to develop and optimize acquisition plans that promote entrepreneurship and innovation for the benefit of marginalized and underserved communities and toward the greater public good.

III. PUBLIC PROCUREMENT AND THE POWER OF THE PURSE

As the largest purchaser of goods and services in the world, buying just about every category of commodity and service available, the United States government and its state and local governments carry extraordinary weight in the marketplace. Spending almost $2 trillion dollars annually, the United States has, in contemporary times, strategically used its concentrated spending power, "the power of the purse", in reasonably bounded efforts to impact and drive public policy to achieve social goals and objectives. Whatever the method, when state and local governments use their purchasing power in the marketplace, arguably they are acting akin to a private enterprise and, consequently, they are able to exercise the right to favor one supplier over another.

With spending power comes obligation and responsibility. Federal, state, and local governments must perform their procurement functions in an era of hyper-vigilance in the form of oversight. Spending power, coupled with the millennium's first recession, has resulted in severe scrutiny of government procurement practices, in the form of stringent reporting requirements, high standards of accountability and unprecedented calls for near-absolute transparency.[6] This heightened level of oversight, while adding complexity to the public procurement process, ensures that there are appropriate limits on the use of the government's acquired power.[7]

Yet it must be understood that appropriate limits on the use of a government's acquired power, by virtue of its position as a market actor spending procurement dollars, is not antithetical to the government's use of strategic public procurement to drive public policy that ensures equitable access to procurement markets. As well, governments have a rational basis to use purchasing power to facilitate the diversification of the government's industrial contractor base in order to promote wealth distribution and employment opportunities to disenfranchised populations. One study has found that "increasing the opportunities for more economic agents, particularly small and medium-sized enterprises (SMEs) to engage in the delivery of goods and services can result in improved outcomes for the alleviation of poverty and [inequality]."[8]

---

[6] *See* Danielle M. Conway, "Emerging Trends in International, Federal, and State and Local Government Procurement in an Era of Global Economic Stimulus Funding," 32 U. Haw. L. Rev. 1, 4 (2009).

[7] *See* J. Christopher McCrudden, *Buying Social Justice: Equality, Government Procurement, & Legal Change* (Oxford University Press, Oxford 2007), 2 (defining the power of the purse as "the use of government funds, usually raised through taxation, to achieve social goals[,]" and explaining that governments combine the "power of the purse" with the regulatory function, a sometimes controversial practice, "because the conditions on which grants . . . are given involve a balancing of considerations: supporting what is good, whilst not supporting what is considered objectionable").

[8] *See* Raymond Mark Kirton, "Gender, Trade and Public Procurement Policy: Kenya, India, Australia, Jamaica", accessed 27 October 2014 at http://the

IV. STRATEGIC PUBLIC PROCUREMENT IN FURTHERANCE OF SOCIAL JUSTICE

A. Desiderata

The common mandate for government procurement is to timely meet user minimum needs with the delivery of best value products or services, while ensuring the highest standards of integrity in order to maintain the public's trust and fulfilling state and local government public policy objectives. A government hopes to meet its needs by using the least resources necessary while also projecting its long-term needs to ensure the availability of suppliers capable of meeting those needs. In satisfying short as well as long-term needs, a government builds a public procurement system to attract suppliers now and for the future. In order to maintain the level of available suppliers, a government must foster an environment that is attractive for these suppliers to do business. A government is not only responsible to potential suppliers but is equally, if not more so, accountable to the public, specifically the taxpayer. Thus, in order for a government to meet the obligations to suppliers, the public, and the taxpayer, it must establish a public procurement system that promotes public trust. In promoting public trust, three principles emerge – transparency, integrity, and competition.[9]

Transparency can be described as a means or method of employing procedures and practices that ensures that government business is conducted in an open and impartial manner.

Integrity refers to the adherence to exemplary standards of conduct in the government's procurement of goods, services, and construction. Integrity requires that government business be conducted in a manner above reproach with complete impartiality and the absence of favoritism.

Finally, competition is the underlying principle of a well-functioning procurement system. Borrowing from the private sector, the promotion of competition ensures that a buyer will receive the best value in terms of price, quality and contract terms and conditions. The government seeks the same benefits by fostering competition in public procurement.

There are myriad goals that support or enforce the three principles of transparency, integrity and competition. These goals include efficiency,

---

commonwealth.org/sites/default/files/news-items/documents/Gender, Trade and Public Procurement Policy.pdf.

[9] *See* Steven L. Schooner, "Desiderata: Objectives for a System of Government Contract Law," 11 Pub. Proc. L. Rev. 103, 104 (2002); *see generally* Conway, note 3 above.

best value, customer satisfaction, wealth distribution, risk avoidance, and uniformity. All of the goals are critically important to the procurement process, but any one may be more important than another depending on a government's particular goals and objectives. For example, small business concerns may be much more keen on laws and regulations that focus on wealth distribution as opposed to risk avoidance. Small businesses may be concerned that they must have a place within the industrial contractor base, and they should not fall victim to a procurement system that has traditionally favored large businesses on the ground that these entities are more competitive and more efficient. Arguments can be made that including more small businesses in the industrial contractor base will help to satisfy long-term competition policies by ensuring that enough contractors with integrity have experience to supply goods, services, or construction to the government in future procurements.

Others might find that uniformity is a paramount goal of the procurement process. If all agencies use the same or similar procurement processes or methods or follow the same laws, rules, and procedures, then efficiency can be achieved. Specifically, government instrumentalities and contractors alike throughout the system could rely on the same rules, thus allowing transactions to become more routine while transitions between agencies could be made much more smoothly.

The larger picture is this – a vision and an objective for Federal, state, or local procurement is required before acquiescing to various, possibly unrelated procurement activities. Just as a vision and an objective are necessary before adopting a procurement code, an understanding of that code is necessary before challenging the code or acquiescing to historical application of a procurement process. Policy makers and procurement professionals recognize that procurement law and best practices must be updated frequently because the public procurement environment changes rapidly. But what will guide the changes of any public procurement system are the three stalwart principles of transparency, integrity and competition. These are the guides for understanding the purpose and goals of any public procurement system.

B.   Preferences, Subcontracting Incentives, and Set-Asides

Small businesses are generally viewed as a primary source of economic progress, especially in challenging economic times. Small businesses drive job-creation and long-term growth. Recognizing this, Federal, state, and local governments have historically attempted to implement regulatory frameworks on two fronts to capitalize on the critical role that small businesses play in the economy: (1) governments have to develop policies and best practices that address barriers to entry facing small businesses; and (2) governments recognize the need to promote small business access to entrepreneurship skills.[10]

Preferences, subcontracting incentives, and set-asides advance important social goals pursued at all levels of government. Government efforts to advance these social goals may range from the support of a certain industry that will employ citizens to mandatory purchasing programs to promote sustainable development. Whatever the method, when governments use their purchasing power in the marketplace, arguably they are acting akin to a private enterprise and, consequently, they are able to exercise the right to favor one supplier over another. Implementing social and economic goals through the acquisition process can conflict with the government's primary policy of achieving full and open competition and, in the short-term, may increase the total cost of procurement, but government's more important obligation to all of its constituents is to weigh and balance all of the relevant factors comprising a well-functioning public procurement system and make policy choices that promote fairness and equality throughout all of society.

Proponents of social and economic policies argue that aiding small businesses and small, disadvantaged businesses helps to reduce unemployment, pollution, and energy loss, while also broadening the base of government suppliers, ultimately increasing competition for federal contracts in the long term. Opponents of social and economic policies argue that aiding small and small, disadvantaged businesses increases prices, excludes competitors offering potentially lower prices, increases the government's administrative costs, increases the potential for contractor defaults, sours relations with potential contractors, and slows the formation phase of the procurement process. The tensions are real, but so are the inequalities that persist due in large measure to a society that sanctioned slavery, institutional racism, and racial discrimination.

Thus, many of the social justice goals linked to public procurement

---

[10] Three statutes are implicated directly by the Federal government's desire to achieve social goals above the primary goal to conduct procurements to attain fair prices and terms. These statutes are the Competition in Contracting Act of 1984 (CICA), 41 U.S.C. § 3301 (formerly 41 U.S.C. § 253), the Federal Acquisition Streamlining Act of 1994 (FASA), 41 U.S.C. § 4103 (formerly 41 U.S.C. § 253h), and the Small Business Act, 15 U.S.C. § 637. These statutes are in some measure implemented by the Federal Acquisition Regulation (FAR) Part 19 and FAR Part 52, Contract Clause. *See* Danielle Conway-Jones [Danielle M. Conway], "Research and Development Deliverables under Government Contracts, Grants, Cooperative Agreements and CRADAs: University Roles, Government Responsibilities and Contractor Rights", 9 Comp. L. Rev. & Tech. J. 181, 192 (2004).

are largely the result of a uniquely American experience with slavery, racial and ethnic subordination, and the lingering present effects of institutional racial discrimination. In contemporary times, governments use their purchasing power to attempt to correct injustices that have been visited upon certain groups in American society and that will continue to plague our society and its marketplace absent necessary government intervention.

To be clear, social justice policies of this nature are not meant to replicate discrimination against historically privileged segments of American society; instead these social justice policies are meant to respond to an American tradition that cultivated disadvantage, disenfranchisement, and exclusion from business opportunities against certain segments of society and have resulted in poverty, instability, and displacement against these groups and peoples.

Accordingly, it is the policy of the U.S. government to provide maximum practicable opportunities in its acquisitions to small business, veteran-owned small business, service-disabled veteran-owned small business, Historically Underutilized Business Zone (HUBZone) small business, small disadvantaged business, and women-owned small business concerns. Small business concerns must also have the maximum practicable opportunity to participate as subcontractors in the contracts awarded by any executive agency, consistent with efficient contract performance.

C. Structural Changes to a Government's Industrial Contractor Base – The Intellectual Property Illustration

Structural changes in organizations, in markets, and in industries occur when entities, conditions, or actors undergo a change in operation, inputs and/or outputs and function. Structural change impacts growth and the growth process. Structural change can result from shock, as illustrated by financial crises or global power shifts, or from adoption of major disruptive technologies, as illustrated by driverless air and ground vehicles or cloud computing. When structural change occurs, public procurement policies and processes must also change in order to respond to government requirements. The impact of structural change on public procurement policy and best practices is best exemplified by the U.S. government response to the rise in significance of intellectual property to the competitive positions of dual-use contractor-developers and the increased need for private sector driven research and development in the mid-20th century.

Prior to the 1960s, the Federal government and very large contractors like AT&T and Bell Laboratories drove the train of research and development and innovation.[11] This model of innovation was extremely centralized and top down in terms of innovative direction. The types of research and development that received attention were those areas that specifically interested the Federal government and its close-knit list of large contractors. Thus, to accomplish technological and innovative research, a company had to be willing to submit to the centralized regime.

Under the historical centralized system of innovation, the Federal government often insisted upon taking commercial rights to inventions developed during the performance of government contracts.[12] In return for contract performance, contractors received royalty-free, non-exclusive licenses to inventions.[13] In a time when large contractors received the benefit of a monopoly environment by virtue of an exclusive business relationship with the Federal government, such assignments of title to inventions were not repulsive because new entrants and competitors were essentially excluded from the innovation sector of the procurement marketplace. Historically, the Federal government allowed its respective executive agencies to determine when the allocation of rights or title to inventions had to inure to the government and usually these determinations varied depending on the needs of the acquiring agency.[14] While most agencies, including the Department of Defense, allowed title to remain in contractors, these agencies reserved for themselves irrevocable, non-exclusive, non-transferable and royalty-free licenses to practice the inventions for the benefit of the government.[15] In the late 1960s and early 1970s, the government's policy on patent rights came under severe attack by private industry. In various studies, the government was seen as a detractor to the full commercialization of inventions for the benefit of the American economy.[16] Observers concluded that the government

---

[11] *See generally* Lawrence Lessig, *The Future of Ideas: The Fate of the Commons in a Connected World* (Vintage Books, New York 2001).

[12] *See* Danielle Conway-Jones [Danielle M. Conway], note 10 above.

[13] *See* Office of the Under Secretary of Defense for Acquisition, Technology and Logistics, "Intellectual Property: Navigating through Commercial Waters – Issues and Solutions when Negotiating Intellectual Property with Commercial Companies", Appendix E, History p. E-1 (Ver. 1.1) (15 October 2001), accessed 27 October at http://www.acq.osd.mil/dpap/Docs/intelprop.pdf.

[14] Diane M. Sidebottom, "Intellectual Property in Federal Government Contracts: The Past, The Present, and One Possible Future", 33 Pub. Cont. L.J. 63, 67 (Fall 2003).

[15] *See* Office of the Under Secretary of Defense, note 13 above.

[16] *See* Jack E. Kerrigan and Christopher J. Brasco, "The Technology Transfer Revolution: Legislative History and Future Proposals", 31 Pub. Cont. L.J. 277, 279 (Winter 2002).

was either not developing technologies or not funding such development in a proper fashion.[17] Likewise, private industry refused to develop technologies in which there would be no control over the commercialization of applied research and development.[18] Government and congressional studies indicated that the government's research and acquisition policies were incompatible with the development and commercialization of innovative technologies.[19] The determination of incompatibility is a clear example of structural change. As evidence of this incompatibility, one need only look at the Federal government's posture with respect to ownership of inventions as compared to industry's posture. Prior to the passage of the Bayh-Dole Act of 1980, various statutes and regulations concerning patents established the government's right to take title to federally funded patents and patentable inventions developed during the performance of government contracts.[20] In addition, the government retained the right to distribute the information resulting from these federally funded projects to the general public.[21] The government premised its right to release information from these federally funded patents on the theory that taxpayer dollars paid for the research and its outcomes and, therefore, the results should inure to the general public.[22] Thus, patents from these sponsored projects were freely published or provided to anyone requesting access to the materials for unrestricted purposes.[23]

Contractors during this time period were competing without the benefit of government sponsored or approved monopolies as this was the era of free market competition. Accordingly, free and open access to patents developed during the performance of government contracts presented insurmountable problems to private industry. Contractors wanted to retain the benefits of commercial applications of new technologies for themselves and any economic benefits that flowed from their research. The thought that the government would give away freely what seemed proprietary convinced contractors, especially small businesses, universities,

---

[17] *See ibid.*
[18] *See ibid.*
[19] *See* Office of Technology Assessment, *Federal Technology Transfer and the Human Genome Project*, 21 (September 1995), accessed 27 October 2014 at http://ota.fas.org/reports/9526.pdf (finding that "[f]or industry, exclusivity is particularly important, and the prior dicta that federal inventions were required to be nonexclusive posed a barrier to commercialization of federal funded research results").
[20] *See* Office of the Under Secretary of Defense, note 13 above.
[21] *Ibid.*
[22] *Ibid.*
[23] *Ibid.*

and research centers not to develop potentially commercially viable technologies for the government.[24]

In response to critical observations and reports about the dysfunctional nature of government use and deployment of technology to the market, Congress enacted crucial legislation to balance government and industry interests in developing and commercializing new technologies.[25] Congress enacted a series of laws to promote technology transfer and to provide technology transfer mechanisms and incentives.[26] The intent of these laws is to encourage partnerships in the use of resources and in the development of dual-use technologies. Three legislative initiatives inspired the decentralization of the research and development industry – The Stevenson-Wydler Technology Innovation Act of 1980;[27] the Bayh-Dole Act of 1980;[28] and the Federal Technology Transfer Act of 1986.[29] With these three pieces of legislation, Congress began its trek to enhance private sector development and application of results from federally funded research previously ongoing at universities, research institutions, and federal laboratory facilities.

V. STRATEGIC PUBLIC PROCUREMENT AND THE PROMOTION OF IP SOCIAL ENTREPRENEURSHIP (INCLUSION OF SMALL, DISADVANTAGED BUSINESS IN PROCUREMENT MARKETS)

As the public procurement function is perceived more and more as an instrument of strategic social reform, politicians and policy makers are routinely called upon to work alongside strategic procurement personnel to achieve targeted positive results in furtherance of inclusion and equality in procurement markets. The pursuit and achievement of IP Empowerment is a social objective that fits squarely within these social policy goals. The strategic use of public procurement is best illustrated by

---

[24] *Ibid.*
[25] *Ibid.*
[26] *Ibid.*
[27] Stevenson-Wydler Technology Innovation Act of 1980, 15 U.S.C.A. § 3701 (West 2014).
[28] Bayh-Dole Act of 1980, Pub. L. No. 96-517, 94 Stat. 3015 (1980) (codified at 35 U.S.C. §§ 200-211, 301-307 (1994)).
[29] Federal Technology Transfer Act of 1986, Pub. L. No. 99-502, 100 Stat. 1785 (codified as amended in scattered sections of 15 U.S.C.).

the successes and failures of the social justice policies supporting small, disadvantaged businesses.

A. Wealth Distribution, Entrepreneurship, and the 8(a) Business Development Program

The primary program in the Federal government designed to assist small disadvantaged businesses is commonly referred to as the 8(a) program. The program derives its name from Section 8(a) of the Small Business Act, a statute creating the U.S. Small Business Administration (SBA) whose function is to "aid, counsel, assist, and protect, the interests of small business concerns". Section 8(a) authorizes the SBA to enter into contracts with other federal agencies. The SBA then subcontracts with eligible small disadvantaged businesses (SDBs). To qualify as an 8(a) contractor, the firm must be owned and controlled by a socially and economically disadvantaged person(s). Specifically, the regulations require 51 per cent ownership and control by one or more individuals who are both socially and economically disadvantaged.[30] Socially disadvantaged individuals are those who have been subjected to racial or ethnic prejudice or cultural bias within American society because of their identities as members of groups and without regard to their individual qualities. The social disadvantage must stem from circumstances beyond their control.

B. Obstacles to Entrepreneurship: The Lingering Controversy Over The Small Disadvantaged Business Certification Program

The Department of Defense (DoD) implemented the 1207 Program in 1987. Other federal agencies copied the structure of the program to achieve percentage goals for awarding prime contracts to socially and economically disadvantaged businesses.[31] Under DoD's "rule of two" set-aside program, contracting officers were required to restrict competition in an acquisition for participation exclusively by small disadvantaged businesses (a) when a reasonable expectation existed that there would be offers received from at least two responsible SDBs, (b) who would offer the goods or service requested at a price that did not exceed 10 per cent of the fair market value.[32] The effect of the 1207 program was to increase the

---

[30] *See* 13 C.F.R. § 124.103(a) (2011); *see also Software Sys. Assoc. v. Saiki*, No. 92-1776 (D.D.C. 24 June 1993).
[31] *See* 48 C.F.R. § 19.000 (2014).
[32] *See Adarand Constructors, Inc. v. Pena*, 515 U.S. 200 (1995).

award of DoD procurements performed by SDBs from 1.9 per cent to a goal of at least 10 per cent.[33]

In *Adarand*, a non-disadvantaged contractor initiated litigation in 1990 after it was denied a subcontract on a federal lands highway project. In 1992, the district court held that the programs at issue were constitutional, and in 1994 the United States Court of Appeals for the Tenth Circuit affirmed that decision.[34] The Supreme Court in *Adarand* did not rule on the constitutionality of the 1207 program or other similar programs; rather, the decision dealt with the level of scrutiny to review race-conscious federal affirmative action programs, like DoD's rule of two, SBA's 8(d) presumptions of social and economic disadvantage, and the Department of Transportation's Subcontracting Compensation Clause. In a 7-2 decision the Supreme Court in *Adarand* held that federal government programs that rely on "race-based" classifications must (a) serve a compelling government interest, and (b) must be narrowly tailored to further that interest.

The Supreme Court sent the case back to the lower courts, directing them to apply the strict scrutiny standard and then determine whether the programs were narrowly tailored to further a compelling governmental interest. The remand of the case by the Supreme Court did not end the litigation, and the case continued to move through the federal courts.

In its most recent petition for *writ of certiorari*, Adarand Constructors asserted that it was not challenging any part of DOT's state and local procurement program. Instead, it claimed to be challenging only the statutes and regulations that pertained to DOT's direct procurement of highway construction on federal lands. But the statutes and regulations relating to direct procurement were quite different from the statutes and regulations reviewed by the Tenth Circuit.

The Supreme Court, mindful that it is a court of final review and not first review, declined to reach the merits of Adarand Constructor's most recent challenge. Adarand Constructors pointed out that its case presented questions of fundamental national importance calling for final resolution by the Supreme Court. The Supreme Court held, however, that the importance of an issue should not distort the principles that control the exercise of jurisdiction. To the contrary, "by adhering scrupulously to the customary limitations on the Supreme Court's discretion regardless

---

[33] *See* Danielle Conway-Jones [Danielle M. Conway] and Christopher Leon Jones, Jr., "Department of Defense Procurement Practices after *Adarand*: What Lies Ahead for the Largest Purchaser of Goods and Services and Its Base of Small Disadvantaged Business Contractors", 39 How. L.J. 391 (1995).

[34] *See Adarand Constructors, Inc. v. Pena*, 965 F. Supp. 1556 (D. Colo. 1997).

of the significance of the underlying issue, it promotes respect ... for the adjudicatory process".[35] For the foregoing reasons, the Supreme Court dismissed as improvidently granted the petition for *writ of certiorari*.

After significant political struggles and much back and forth debate, civilian agencies have passively allowed SDB regulations permitting SDB set-asides, according to specific situations and standards, to expire. Unlike allowing expiration of the program, the DoD annually actively suspends its SDB program based upon the rule of two and the granting of price preferences.

Although the less than dispositive result in *Adarand* has left palpable uncertainty with respect to government diversity set-aside policies, the fact remains that the Supreme Court has not held such policies to be unconstitutional and has only ruled that they are subject to strict scrutiny. Accordingly, where such policies serve a compelling social interest, they should survive (and indeed be supported by) *Adarand*. The breadth and scope of government procurement needs and resources, coupled with the beneficial impact of procurement supplier diversity upon the nation's innovation and entrepreneurial interests would appear to constitute compelling interests consistent with the *Adarand* mandate. Consequently an IP Empowerment procurement agenda is both socially progressive and legally sustainable.

VI. ACHIEVING INTELLECTUAL PROPERTY SOCIAL JUSTICE AND FACILITATING ENTREPRENEURSHIP IN THE INNOVATION INDUSTRY

The United States government is keenly aware that it must look to the private commercial sector, including small businesses, for leadership in technology innovation. To ensure that technology innovation retains the characteristics of dual use, the Federal government must be in a position to partner with the private commercial sector as well as universities to make sure that its needs are considered during the research and development process.

There are also other government policies that affect advanced development indirectly. The Federal government affects the levels of advanced technology investment in certain areas by both creating incentives for private firms to invest and in supporting advanced technology in key

---

[35] *Adams v. Robertson*, 520 U.S. 83, 92, n. 6 (1997).

areas where private participation is inadequate.³⁶ The Federal government's policies for protecting intellectual property are major engines in promoting innovation. Similarly, the Department of Defense's revised outlook on intellectual property protection for contract deliverables and research and development also stimulate to some degree dual use innovations.³⁷ Finally, the Federal government's ability to open markets overseas impacts on American firms' willingness and ability to invest in research and development.³⁸ Thus, the role of the Federal government as well as the Department of Defense in the facilitation of increased research and development is at the policy level to ensure an attractive legislative and regulatory climate for large and small business investment in innovation and advanced technologies.

One example of the Federal government's stake in promoting entrepreneurship and small business inclusion while also promoting competition can be gleaned from the government's desire to innovate in the federal information technology industry. In meeting its innovation needs, the government must do more with less, which invariably requires the government to have access to more suppliers, not less. In responding to its information technology needs, the government is faced with the fact that the "market will be driven by two major forces – pressure to cut federal IT budgets without losing efficiency and the implementation of new technologies". The current Administration has started an overhaul of the entire Federal IT organization, betting on new technologies, "rent, not buy" principles, and open source.³⁹ The technology segments like business intelligence, cloud computing, eDiscovery, GIS and geospatial, non-relational database management systems, Smart Grid, Service Oriented Architecture (SOA), unified communications, and virtualization will see double digit growth in the period 2013–2018. The total annual U.S. Federal IT market will surpass $93 billion by 2018.⁴⁰ This means that small businesses, particularly nimble, entrepreneurially skilled ones, may be able to meet government IT needs in relatively greater proportion than large businesses. To take full advantage of the opportunities offered by small business, the government must ramp up its efforts to build and sustain frameworks that

---

[36] *See* W. Bruce Shirk, "Technology Transfer and Technology Reinvestment – A Comparison of Two Statutory Frameworks", 41 Fed. B. News & J. 64 (Jan. 1994).
[37] *See* Lessig, note 11 above.
[38] *Ibid*.
[39] *See* Market Research Media, US Federal IT Market Forecast 2013–2018, accessed 27 October 2014 at http://www.marketresearchmedia.com/?p=193.
[40] *See ibid*.

Figure 5.1   U.S. Federal IT market 2013–2018

will ensure small business inclusion in the contractor industrial base at significantly greater rates for the near future.

State and local governments also impact the innovation and advanced technology industry. As market actors with massive purchasing power of their own, state and local governments have considerable potential to encourage and drive market innovation. As program responsibilities shift from the Federal government to state and local governments, the latter entities are expected to promote new initiatives and to keep pace with the rate of technology development in the commercial marketplace. Accordingly, state and local governments are being obliged to innovate by encouraging the creation of markets for new technologies, products, and services.

In order to fulfill this obligation, state and local governments are being asked to use their large procurement budgets to seek out innovative solutions to existing and projected agency needs. In pursuing new solutions for existing and projected needs, state and local governments can spur demand for both new and prototype technologies, products, and services. In this respect, state and local governments are serving as "launch customers" in three distinct scenarios:

- driving research and development for currently unavailable technologies;
- serving as beta purchasers of prototype technologies; and/or
- becoming users of available technologies that have yet to achieve market penetration.[41]

In each of these scenarios, state and local governments are trading the certainty of conventional purchasing for the risks associated with the adoption of new solutions.

Some critics of the government and its involvement in creating markets for new technology, products, and services rely upon hackneyed arguments to address the issue whether government procurement should be used in such a way.[42] These arguments focus on whether such government conduct is truly an appropriate function, the degree to which the government incurs excessive costs associated with the implementation of social justice policies that often do not yield an adequate return on investment, or the potential for government efforts to fail to stimulate the creation of private markets or to spur demand for certain products. More relevant concerns, however, relate to the innovation-implementation chasm. The concern is that government in its strategic procurement efforts may be looking for new, game-changing innovation rather than implementing new technologies, products, and services that are already available but that are kept from the market because of the price-gap between new solutions and conventional solutions, the latter being cheaper on the large scale.[43] Reframing the issue demonstrates the significant role that public procurement plays in creating a market or demand for new technologies, products, and services.

---

[41] Danielle M. Conway, "Sustainable Procurement Policies and Practices at the State and Local Government Level", in Hirokawa and Salkin, (eds), *Legal Strategies for Greening Local Government* (ABA, Chicago 2012); *see also* Jeffrey Harris et al., "Energy-Efficient Purchasing by State and Local Government: Triggering a Landslide Down the Slippery Slope to Market Transformation", accessed 27 October 2013 at http://www.eceee.org/library/conference_proceedings/ACEEE_buildings/2004/Panel_6/p6_16/paper.

[42] *See* Jennifer McCadney, "The Green Society? Leveraging the Government's Buying Powers to Create Markets for Recycled Products", 29 Pub. Con. L.J. 135, 149–52 (1999).

[43] *See* Christian Parenti, "*The Big Green Buy*", accessed 27 October 2014 at http://www.thenation.com/article/37528/big-green-buy#axzz2f0YWpueF.

A. Targeted Support for IP Empowerment in the Innovation Industry

The Federal government has a long history of partnering with the private sector to develop innovations and technology. In 1802, Thomas Jefferson on behalf of the government placed the first order for the domestic refining of saltpeter, an ingredient in gunpowder, with a new Delaware manufacturing company called E.I. du Pont. On or about 9 September 1908, at Fort Myer, Virginia, Orville Wright flew the first Wright plane made under a $25,000 government contract with the U.S. Army Signal Corps for 62 minutes, completing 57 circles at an altitude of 36.6 meters. Government contracts have also led to the development of items as diverse as Superglue, Tang, and the Internet.

With these successes, the Federal government was viewed as the leader in developing industries around innovation. Thus, in the first half of the 20th century, the U.S. government was the single largest source of funding for research and development.[44] During this period, the government conducted extensive research and development in its own laboratories and in government-owned laboratories run by contractors.[45] The government oversight agency, the General Accounting Office (renamed the Government Accountability Office under the George W. Bush administration), estimated that government laboratories spent $16.225 billion in fiscal year 1990 alone.

As this history illustrates, strategic procurement not only assures efficient expenditure of public funds, but also the beneficial investment in the nation's greatest resource: its human capital. These policies can and should be pursued in the cause of IP Empowerment, to harvest the greatest innovation bounty to the nation's benefit.

B. Embracing IP Empowerment and Other Social Justice Considerations in the Public Procurement of Innovation

Strategic public procurement that expressly addresses and integrates social justice policies throughout acquisition planning, formation, and

---

[44] Jack E. Kerrigan and Christopher J. Brasco, "The Technology Transfer Revolution: Legislative History and Future Proposals", 31 Pub. Cont. L.J. 277, 279 (2002) (citing James V. Lacy et al., "Technology Transfer Laws Governing Federally Funded Research and Development", 19 Pepp. L. Rev. 1, 3 (1991)).

[45] Ralph C. Nash and John Cibinic, "Transfer of Technology From the Government to the Private Sector: Can It Be Effectively Accomplished?", 6 No. 7 Nash & Cibinic Rep. 40 (1992); *see also* Danielle Conway-Jones [Danielle M. Conway], note 10, above.

administration of public contracts is central to a government's requirement to manage and distribute scarce resources fairly, transparently, equally, and with integrity. In essence, using public procurement to increase marginalized community, minority group, and small business participation in the creation of new markets and in the production of demand for new technologies, especially those that exist but have yet to reach acceptance in the market, promotes social justice as well as demonstrates government leadership in achieving fairness and equality.

Moreover, structuring procurement policy so as to promote Intellectual Property Empowerment and other social justice goals can provide important benefits to the nation's intellectual property infrastructure. Strategic procurement can be used to promote and support intellectual property oriented incubator enterprise in underserved and marginalized communities and nurture intellectual property and entrepreneurial talent. Incentivized to focus their efforts toward intellectual property, innovation, and entrepreneurial endeavor, these communities can explore unprecedented opportunities for economic advancement and independence and thereby ameliorate their economic conditions and lessen and ultimately extinguish their dependence on government social welfare support programs. With enhanced intellectual property portfolios and expertise, marginalized communities and developing nations will become active stakeholders in the intellectual property regime and will collaborate with established rights holders in developing additional IP output, promoting intellectual property education and anti-piracy initiatives, and stimulating further innovation for the ultimate public good.

Thus, to drive competition, entrepreneurship, and innovation, governments should be encouraged to: engage in market research to identify industry capacity within marginalized community and small business sectors to supply new technologies, products, and services; engage in acquisition planning to establish performance-based specifications[46] that do not restrict innovation or disadvantage small businesses and local

---

[46] A performance based specification describes the function or performance to be achieved rather than specifying the exact product or service that will meet the government's need. Performance-based specifications allows the market to suggest the best way in which an agency may meet its need, without being technically prescriptive. Performance-based specifications describe the required results and provide criteria for verifying whether or not these results have been met. Performance-based requirements do not state the methods for achieving the required results. *See* Ned H. Criscimagna, "Performance Based Requirements", accessed 27 October 2014 at http://www.theriac.org/DeskReference/viewDocument.php?id=207.

suppliers of new, innovative solutions; commercialize new technologies, products, and services that have yet to penetrate the market; support and maintain lines of communication with small business suppliers to stay abreast of innovations in new technologies, products and services; encourage a culture and philosophy of small business entrepreneurship through meaningful partnerships between governments, large businesses, and small businesses; and collaborate with industry to stimulate a market for new technologies, products, and services. Exercising leadership in creating markets for new technologies, products, and services is consistent with the view that the public procurement function is a vital tool to effect strategic social reform in the quest for a more perfect society.

VII. CONCLUSION

There are many roles to play in the innovation industry for the 21st century. Innovation depends on industry players performing these roles under optimal circumstances. The government has the role of setting policy, promoting leadership in innovation, and providing the means and the mechanisms to accomplish research and development at the basic, applied, and advanced research levels of science and technology. A significant role for the government is to train its agencies, departments, and personnel about supporting innovation efforts through correct identification and uses of contractual vehicles to form lasting and productive relationships with, among others, small businesses to guarantee inclusion in the industrial contractor base and to widen and deepen the pool of current and potential competitive suppliers. Likewise, the government has the power to motivate financial industry and large contractors to provide resources and access to capital to small businesses. In turn, small business and entrepreneurs must seek out opportunities to collaborate with government and large businesses to build capacity and competitiveness. Incorporating intellectual property, social justice, and economic empowerment principles into strategic procurement policies furthers these objectives and strengthens the nation's competitive position in the global marketplace.

PART II

Education and advocacy

6. Lawyers and innovation
Rita S. Heimes

INTRODUCTION

The United States is a nation of vast inequality. Only the most fortunate have access to elite schools and high-paying jobs. Americans in middle and lower economic categories are struggling and falling further behind. Their incomes are stagnating, their educational opportunities are limited, infant mortality rates and teenage pregnancies are higher, literacy rates are lower, and they are more likely to live in single-parent homes.[1] The potential prosperity of American children is more dependent on their parents' success than in most other developed countries.[2] If these social trends and conditions are permitted to persist, the burden of unproductive and unfulfilled groups and communities will inevitably diminish our nation's ability to compete in the global economy and otherwise undermine our position as the leader of the democratic capitalist world.

It behooves us as a nation, therefore, to help low income and underprivileged citizens become economically self-sufficient and successful. Just as the emergence of the industrial society presented new opportunities for class migration and equalization, the information society also offers novel means by which to close social gaps and inequities, not only to the benefit of those most directly affected but for the benefit of the nation as a whole.

One proven means for socio-economic advancement of underprivileged groups and communities is entrepreneurship, including businesses founded on innovation. Today's entrepreneur – defined as "an agitator who mixes things up by introducing new information into a complacent market"[3] – can

---

[1] Eduardo Porter, "Inequality in America: The Data is Sobering", *New York Times*, 30 July 2013.
[2] Ibid.
[3] D. Gordon Smith and Dariam M. Ibrahim, "Law and Entrepreneurial Opportunities", 98 Cornell L. Rev. 1533, 1541–2 (2013) (citing Jonathan T. Eckhardt and Scott A. Shane, "Opportunities and Entrepreneurship", 29 J. Mgmt. 333, 341 (2003)).

come from any background and take advantage of the information economy's potential low barrier to entry.

Lawyers can play a key role in closing the income gap by helping individuals and communities gain access to property rights and business deals that will advance their economic goals and lead to greater prosperity. Scholars have shown that well-designed legal institutions foster economic development and innovation. Intellectual property (IP) laws, financial markets, robust property and contract laws, and a fair and accessible judiciary encourage strong economies based on creativity, invention and entrepreneurship. But few scholars have analyzed lawyers' duties and opportunities to promote and facilitate innovation and intellectual property ownership, particularly among individuals who generally lack access to sophisticated legal services and complex legal institutions.

This chapter explores how lawyers can help the poor and marginalized individuals of countries like the United States – with its strong IP regime and enforcement system – to reach their personal expressive and inventive potential through access to intellectual property education, property acquisition, rights enforcement and contractual negotiation. Legal assistance for inventors and creators is a crucial way for attorneys to use their unique professional skills to foster and nurture an innovative society.

Part I addresses the role of law and legal institutions – principally intellectual property and contract law – in economic development, and discusses ways in which lawyers and legal advice advance economic development goals. Part II explores arguments related to social justice and human rights as enhanced by intellectual property laws and IP lawyers. Part III addresses professionalism obligations and highlights various programs designed to help underprivileged persons gain access to empowering legal systems. The chapter recommends that governments, lawyers and law schools work to provide affordable IP and business law services to less fortunate Americans in pursuit of economic equality and social justice.

I. LAW, ECONOMIC DEVELOPMENT AND INNOVATION

A fundamental premise of this chapter is that entrepreneurship is one mechanism for personal empowerment. Those who assist poor, underprivileged and/or marginalized people and groups with their business development efforts are performing a social justice function. This premise is probed more critically in Part II, but for now it is useful to assume that empowering individuals and groups with economic opportunity through entrepreneurship and property acquisition fulfills a social justice function.

What are the necessary legal and public support structures for an entrepreneurial society? How can legal regimes, government policy and ultimately lawyers themselves foster personal and small-group efforts for economic gain through business development and ownership?

One ingredient is a strong intellectual property rights regime with neutral application to all participants regardless of race, income or social status. Another is a reliable and enforceable contract law regime that allows for complexity, flexibility and creativity. Entrepreneurship policy tags along with these fundamental systems by encouraging business development through broad-based support systems without attempting to choose winners in advance. All components fail, however, without highly-skilled legal talent accessible to marginalized individuals and groups seeking to enter the start-up business environment.

A. Intellectual Property Rights

To paraphrase Robert Cooter, a community's wealth will come from the "productivity of its citizens" which in turn depends upon "resources, technology and organization".[4] One valuable resource in an innovation economy is information. As private information held initially by an inventor or creator becomes public information through competition, that inventor loses control of the information and potentially the chance at wealth.[5]

Property law is one foundation of economic cooperation that helps individuals and communities experience economic growth. Property principles allow those who generate wealth to keep most of it, which motivates people to make their own wealth rather than take it from others.[6] The rights to exclude that define property principles as "inextricably linked to the creation of entrepreneurial opportunities" because without them entrepreneurs may not explore new ideas and opportunities for fear of immediate appropriation by others.[7] The United States has highly developed private property rights regimes, including rights in intellectual property – patents, copyrights and trademarks. These laws form a foundation for even poor and marginalized communities to begin to develop wealth

---

[4] Robert Cooter, "An Escape from Poverty: Developing Productive Organizations", 12 Sw. J. L. & Trade Am. 181, 183 (2006).
[5] Ibid.
[6] Ibid, 186.
[7] Smith and Ibrahim, note 4 above, 1554 (citations omitted).

and opportunity, provided systems are in place to help them gain access to and protect these rights.

Patent law provides inventors with the right to exclude others from making, using, selling or importing for sale the invention as claimed in the issued patent.[8] For the entrepreneur, patents are important to provide property interests and competitive advantage when the enterprise involves development and sale of novel products and processes, such as machinery, chemical compositions and information technologies.[9] Copyright law is appropriate for businesses that profit from original works of expression, including music, art, film, sculpture, literature and software.[10] Trademark law applies to the words, symbols and devices used to identify and distinguish products and services from those sold by others.[11] All of these forms of intellectual property law are important to business development, and are thus crucial to any broad-based, national-level economic development strategy.

In the United States, patent and copyright laws have a common origin in Article I, Section 8, Clause 8 of the Constitution, which provides:

> Congress shall have the Power . . . to promote the Progress of Science and useful Arts, by securing for limited Times to Authors and Inventors the exclusive Right to their respective Writings and Discoveries.[12]

Underlying this provision of the Constitution and the intellectual property laws based upon it are utilitarian notions that humans require incentives to innovate and create, and that creation and innovation are beneficial to society as a whole.[13] Property incentives are necessary to encourage, if not invention and creativity in the first instance, at least their disclosure to the public. For fear that disclosure will involve immediate and inexpensive copying by others, undercutting the creator's market and preventing him from recouping his investment, a creator may never bring to light something novel, useful, entertaining, thought-provoking or otherwise contributing to society.[14] Patent and copyright law allow a

---

[8] 35 U.S.C. § 271(a).
[9] 35 U.S.C. § 101.
[10] 17 U.S.C. § 102(a).
[11] 15 U.S.C. § 1127.
[12] U.S. Const. art. I, § 8, cl. 8.
[13] *See* Jonathan M. Barnett, "Do patents matter? Empirical evidence on the incentive thesis", in Robert E. Litan (ed.) *Handbook on Law, Innovation and Growth* (Edward Elgar, Cheltenham, UK and Northampton, MA, USA 2011), 178.
[14] *See, e.g.*, James Boyle, *Shamans, Software & Spleens* (Harvard University Press, Cambridge, MA 1996), Preface, xi. ("In market terms, information has

creator to recover damages from one who copies without authorization, and thereby encourage creation, disclosure and commercialization of science and art.

Many scholars have raised concerns that IP rights (so-called "IPRs" and particularly patent and copyright law) encourage exclusivity, which in turn restricts supply, which results in higher prices and thus causes wealth transfer from consumers to producers.[15] Because poor people tend to be consumers, strong national IP laws are presumably detrimental to their interests. In the realm of development economics, for instance, scholars like Margaret Chon contend that adopting a strong IPR regime on the "assumption that pure wealth or utility-maximization" are appropriate measures of social welfare is short-sighted and fails to promote balanced wealth distribution across society.[16]

These theories are worthy of exploration and indeed may bear on whether a developing nation should adopt a strong IPR regime in the first instance. But the United States already has such a regime, and this chapter considers how to assist poor and marginalized Americans within the existing IPR structure. Recent empirical research, moreover, indicates that intellectual property rights "have direct and significant effects on stimulating productive economic activity".[17] Patents, for example, are used to promote innovations in multiple industries, to secure financing, obtain licensing revenue, provide competitive advantage and negotiation leverage, and even to enhance a firm's reputation.[18]

Properly construed and applied, copyright law can also enhance economic opportunities not merely by protecting existing creative works but also by encouraging new ones. For poor and marginalized members of society, and especially for those without access to technical tools and materials for invention, copyright law can provide property rights and accompanying licensing/revenue opportunities at little cost to the creator. With many exceptions, the creative and expressive industries can have low financial barriers to entry. Copyright registration is easily completed with

---

significant 'public good' qualities; it is often expensive to create or generate but cheap to copy. Economic theory tells us that 'public goods' will be underproduced because there will be too little incentive to create them.")

[15] Jonathan D. Putnam and Andrew B. Tepperman, "Intellectual property rights and economic progress: a review of the literature", in Robert E. Litan (ed.), *Handbook on Law, Innovation and Growth* (Edward Elgar, Cheltenham, UK and Northampton, MA, USA 2011), 112 (hereafter "Putnam and Tepperman").

[16] Margaret Chon, "Intellectual Property and the Development Divide", 27 Cardozo L. Rev. 2821, 2831–2 (2006). *See also* Chapter 8 herein.

[17] Putnam and Tepperman, 113.

[18] Ibid, 122.

little more than $35 and an Internet connection.¹⁹ Thus, copyright law provides a form of property interest accessible to even those of limited means. Copyright's generous fair use and compulsory licensing provisions, moreover, allow follow-on creators to learn and adapt from others and thus encourage additional creation.²⁰

Trademarks, born of common and not constitutional law, do not share the lofty ideals of copyright and patent law.²¹ Yet even trademarks can serve important economic empowerment functions. Like copyrights, trademarks cost little to acquire (they are protected under common law with no need for formal registration) and provide a property interest that can enhance reputation and provide competitive advantage.²² By definition a trademark exists only when associated with goods or services and thus evidence of trademark ownership is a sure sign of economic activity.²³

Intellectual property lawyers are crucial components to any community seeking to foster entrepreneurship. Because understanding the IP regime is a first step to maximizing its value, entrepreneurs need access to intellectual property lawyers who can explain IPRs and how they apply to a

---

¹⁹ See www.copyright.gov/eco (accessed 13 October 2014).

²⁰ For a thorough discussion of copyright's role in economic progress and social justice see Lateef Mtima, "Copyright Social Utility and Social Justice Interdependence: A Paradigm for Intellectual Property Empower and Digital Entrepreneurship", 112 W. Va. L.R. 97 (2009).

²¹ See, e.g., William A. Landes and Richard A. Posner, *The Economic Structure of Intellectual Property Law* (Harvard University Press, Cambridge, MA 2003), 172 (hereafter "Landes and Posner").

²² Trademarks can be protected as property rights under the common law without registration if they are distinctive of and used commercially on goods or services. The federal Lanham Act provides for litigation in federal court provided the marks are used in interstate commerce. See 15 USC 1125(a). Unfair competition principles also support trademark owners seeking to prevent others from passing off counterfeit goods or confusing consumers as to the goods' origin. To register a trademark with the United States Patent and Trademark Office (USPTO), one completes an electronic form through the Trademark Electronic Application System (TEAS), see www.uspto.gov/trademarks (accessed 13 October 2014). The TEAS process is designed to be fairly simple and user-friendly; while legal advice is always recommended, it is not required that an applicant appoint counsel. Fees range from $275 to $325 for a single classification of goods or services, with an additional $100 fee required if the application files under Section 2(b) of the Lanham Act indicating an "intent to use" the mark in commerce rather than current, actual use. See 15 U.S.C. § 1051(a) (actual use) and 15 U.S.C. § 1051(b) (bona fide intention to use).

²³ See Rita S. Heimes, "Trademarks, Identity and Justice", 11 John Marshall Rev. Intell. Prop. L. 133, 138 (2011).

new venture. Once a creator understands these property regimes, he needs assistance to avoid infringing others' rights and to acquire rights of his own. Again, skilled lawyers specializing in IP law should be available at affordable rates to assist entrepreneurs who do not have – but who seek – economic advantages and opportunities.

B. Entrepreneurship Policies

An entrepreneur may drop out of college, leave employment with one firm full of knowledge and a new idea, join with partners after business school, or even transition from being a full-time parent into business ownership. There are no fixed qualifications for entrepreneurial ventures, other than "novelty and dynamism"[24] and strong personal drive to succeed.

Government policies and legal systems can help create an environment welcoming and supportive of entrepreneurial activity. The macroeconomic reasons for such policies are well known: Entrepreneurship is "the fundamental engine that sets and keeps the capitalist engine in motion by creating new goods, inventing new methods of production, devising new business models, and opening new markets".[25] It behooves society, therefore, to generate and support infrastructure that encourages entrepreneurship among all members of society.

What can governments do? First, their policies should not only be neutral to race, social, and economic background, they should also be neutral to technology sector. In other words, governments should not try to pick industry "winners" in advance.[26] Second, programs designed to educate new market entrants, including independent inventors and creators seeking to commercialize their crafts, have been shown to have a positive impact on economic activity and ultimately entrepreneurial success. These programs provide information and even individualized advice on intellectual property law, financing strategies, accounting and marketing.[27] Such programs can be targeted to low-income communities and located in places that are convenient and familiar to the people who live

---

[24] David M. Hart, "Entrepreneurship Policy: What It Is and Where It Came From", in David M. Hart (ed.) *The Emergence of Entrepreneurship Policy, Governance, Start-Ups and Growth in the U.S. Knowledge Economy* (Cambridge University Press, New York 2003), 6.

[25] Ibid, 3 (quotation omitted).

[26] *See* Josh Lerner, *Boulevard of Broken Dreams*, 132 (Princeton University Press, New Jersey 2012) ("how can the typical government leader identify good prospects in a compressed time period with limited information?").

[27] *See* ibid, 99–100; *see also* Chapter 9 herein.

in those communities. Instead of holding a seminar in a distant location – such as a government building, university classroom, or high-tech business incubator setting – classes on marketing and finance can be located at churches, community centers, public libraries, and local schools.

Government programs to fund new ventures have also been successful under certain conditions. Because access to capital is a major barrier to the vast majority of new businesses, a publicly-funded program designed to invest in promising ventures can kick-start an entrepreneurial business that may otherwise never get off the ground. Such programs should not be hand-outs, however, free from accountability and mutual investment. Instead, government-backed financing programs that require matching funds and "skin in the game" have been shown to be the most effective.[28] Ventures that operate primarily if not exclusively on government funding are also to be discouraged; a funding program should require proof of a strategy that can show private returns (either angel investment, venture capital, bank financing or commercial success) rather than a strategy to rely on additional public support as the enterprise's long-term financial foundation.[29]

Finally, innovative enterprises need access to deals and deal lawyers. Whether the entrepreneur is a musician seeking publishing and promotion opportunities, a programmer trying to get crowd funding for a new mobile app, a mom who came up with a clever gadget to perform a task more efficiently, or an employee whose new idea could be the foundation for a new firm, contracts of varying degrees of complexity will invariably determine each step of the entrepreneurial venture.

C. Private Ordering

A well-ordered society, in which individuals and groups are encouraged to be self-reliant, assume risks, grow an enterprise, and become economically successful – in short, one in which entrepreneurship is encouraged – ideally has a legal system recognizing the enforceability of contracts and property rights, and a judicial system capable of fairly resolving disputes.

Contracts allow parties to trust each other in a deal. They facilitate sharing of information, resources, business opportunities and property

---

[28] *See* ibid, 132. Cf. the highly successful Grameen Bank and its program of "solidarity lending" to impoverished villagers in India, which employs a system of borrower group collective responsibility to ensure that each group member repays her individual loan, *see* http://en.wikipedia.org/wiki/Grameen_Bank (accessed 13 October 2014).
[29] *See* Lerner, *Boulevard of Broken Dreams*, 141.

rights. Through contract law, people are enabled "to commit to doing what they say" allowing sufficient trust that people will "work together, even though money is at stake".[30]

Product development and distribution agreements can be complex. A new venture seeking financial resources to begin operation will likely have some form of contract – a promise to perform – between the entrepreneur and the financier.[31] Because the United States legal system has a highly developed understanding of contract law, there is no need to create the system here as one would in a less developed country.

More importantly, the history and stability of transactional lawyering in the United States has generated an informally defined but powerful legal regime of its own, namely, a world of legal structures, relationships, and forms set forth in private ordering arrangements. The "deal, corporate, transactional, technology, or business lawyers" who create, negotiate and perpetuate these structures and relationships are crucial to promoting innovation and entrepreneurship.[32] Skilled attorneys understand the short- and long-term consequences of the various clauses in a contract, and can help define not just the basic terms of sale, license or acquisition but as well the parties' relationship over time. Deal lawyers add value to entrepreneurial ventures through understanding judicial interpretations of standard contract language and by being willing to create new business models and arrangements.[33]

An economically disadvantaged entrepreneur unsophisticated in matters of finance, intellectual property, licensing and business formation, requires access to a seasoned transactional lawyer. This is all the more important if networks of influence and opportunity are closed to the entrepreneur due to racial or cultural bias. Represented by an attorney with experience in business entity formation, finance and licensing, an innovator can approach business opportunities with confidence and may have access to deals unavailable to him acting alone. In addition, legal representation can help an entrepreneur avoid costly early missteps such as failure

---

[30] Robert Cooter, "Doing What You Say: Contracts and Economic Development", 59 Ala. L. Rev. 1107, 1109 (2008).
[31] *See* Lerner, *Boulevard of Broken Dreams*, 94 (discussing the "importance of the ability of entrepreneurs and investors to enter into complex contracts" such as preferred stock agreements "where different outcomes can result if the company's progress varies").
[32] Sean O'Connor, "Controlling the means of innovation", in Robert Litan (ed.), *Handbook on Law, Innovation and Growth* (Edward Elgar, Cheltenham, UK and Northampton, MA, USA 2011), 276.
[33] Ibid, 278; see also Chapters 7 and 9 herein.

to incorporate correctly, violation of securities regulations, untimely or ill advised disclosure of proprietary information that jeopardizes intellectual property rights, violation of confidentiality or non-compete agreements, and multiple other traps for the unwary.

In sum, the basic ingredients of a society encouraging and supporting economic activity among poor people include intellectual property laws and the ability to enforce them; economic development policies including technology-neutral government financing that requires matching or other "skin in the game"; and skilled deal lawyers available and willing to help low-income clients reach their business goals. The next section explores why such systems are grounded in and supportive of social justice norms.

II. ENTREPRENEURSHIP AND SOCIAL JUSTICE

A. Improving Human Capabilities

According to a study conducted by the United States Patent and Trademark Office (USPTO), minority-owned businesses are ten times less likely to seek patents and four times less likely to file for trademark registration than their non-minority counterparts. In other words, minority groups may be systematically excluded from the U.S. innovation system through lack of awareness or lack of resources to seek access to such systems.[34] IPRs in and of themselves are race-neutral. This suggests that policies should be adopted and systems put in place to encourage minorities to take advantage of IP regimes and other entrepreneurship programs. In short, minorities and other marginalized groups should be supported in their capacity to innovate.

As Amartya Sen explained, pursuit of wealth can be akin to freedom. Assisting individuals and groups with developing their own capabilities fulfills the aims of social justice. Wealth and income are desirable not for their own sake, but because they provide means to achieve substantive freedoms – "to lead the kind of lives we have reason to value".[35]

Development policies should thus work toward the goal of enhancing freedom of actions and decisions. This includes creating opportunities for people to generate wealth. Through providing infrastructure to help

---

[34] *See* Remarks of Undersecretary of Commerce and USPTO Director David Kappos to the 2010 National Minority Enterprise Development Conference (accessed 14 October 2014 at http://www.uspto.gov/news/speeches/2010/Kappos_National_Minority_Enterprise.jsp); *see also* Chapter 10 herein.

[35] Amartya Sen, *Development as Freedom* (Knopf, New York 1999), 14.

people develop their own capabilities, development policies can increase the freedom of individuals and their communities to develop their social and economic lives.

> [F]reedom is not only the basis of the evaluation of success and failure, but it is also a principal determinant of individual initiative and social effectiveness. Greater freedom enhances the ability of people to help themselves and also to influence the world, and these matters are central to the process of development.[36]

Sen's philosophies expand the definition of poverty beyond income and financial status to lack of capabilities.[37] This allows legal service providers to include people of varying degrees of education and income provided they lack the capacity to fully participate in the entrepreneurial economy. In the case of African-Americans and other minority communities in the United States where generations may have routinely been denied access to educational and employment opportunities, there could be a community-wide lack of capacity with regard to legal services and in particular lack of access to complex business and transactional expertise. A sound development policy with social and distributive justice goals will address this capacity gap through providing legal services in IP acquisition and business transactions, and as well by training more attorneys from those communities to become "deal lawyers" themselves.

B. Intellectual Property and Human Rights

Intellectual property rights are property interests created and defined by public law.[38] The State causes them to exist through statute, and thus as well can limit them, force them to be licensed, or take them away.[39] As such, intellectual property rights differ fundamentally from human rights, which are "enduring, fundamental, inalienable and universal entitlements".[40] Human rights advocates have raised concerns that strong IPR regimes can undermine traditional values. They can encourage

---

[36] Ibid, 18.
[37] Ibid, 20.
[38] Patent and copyright law, at least, are creatures of statute. Trademarks are recognized under common law, although also defined and enforced through the federal Lanham Act.
[39] (Laurence R. Hefler, "Toward a Human Rights Framework for Intellectual Property", 40 U.C. Davis L. Rev. 971, 992–3 (2007)) (quoting U.N. Subcommission on IPRs and Human Rights).
[40] Ibid (internal quotations omitted).

selfish behavior in a community traditionally accustomed to sharing and group behavior. They can also be used to deny the poor access to useful knowledge or medicines.[41]

Human rights advocates also recognize, however, the role of IPRs in building the capabilities of individuals and communities. Copyright law and sui generis laws that protect author's rights and traditional knowledge can "safeguard the personal link between authors and their creations and between peoples, communities, or other groups and their collective cultural heritage" and "protect basic material interests which are necessary to enable authors to enjoy an adequate standard of living".[42]

Trademark law can also be deployed to promote individual and community rights.[43] In particular, a close cousin of trademark law known as "geographic indications" (GIs) is a growing form of trademark-like protection for communities. Sometimes called "the poor people's intellectual property rights,"[44] GIs work well to promote the goods of artisans, farmers, craftsman and related creators whose reputation for quality is intertwined with geography (for example "Rocquefort" cheese).[45] As a form of trademark protection, GIs can be used by historically poor or disempowered groups to generate a unique brand that may lift all boats through a common identifier.

Individuals can be empowered through trademarks as well. An artist who through hard work and creativity becomes well known for her music, for example, may develop her own personal name into a trademark. The law of publicity rights and trademarks will serve to protect unauthorized exploitation of her likeness and identity.[46] By properly deploying the right

---

[41] Conflicts between the Agreement on Trade Related Aspects of Intellectual Property (TRIPS agreement) and social and cultural development concerns "cut across a wide swath of legal terrain, including: (1) the transfer of technology to developing countries; (2) the consequences for the right to food of plant breeders' rights and patents for genetically modified organisms; (3) biopiracy; (4) the protection of the culture of indigenous communities; and (5) the impact on the right to health of legal restrictions on access to patented pharmaceuticals." (Helfer, note 40 above, 985). *See* Part III of this chapter.

[42] Ibid, 995–6.

[43] *See generally* Heimes, note 24 above.

[44] Madhavi Sunder, "IP³", 59 Stan. L. Rev. 257 (2006).

[45] Ibid; *see also* Chapter 7 herein.

[46] *See, e.g.* Heimes, note 24 at 155–7. *See also* Roberta Rosenthal Kwall, "The Right of Publicity vs. The First Amendment: A Property and Liability Rule Analysis", 70 Ind. L. J. 47, 55–56 (1994) ("whatever the means through which an individual's persona comes to have value, that value should be attributable to the persona of the publicity plaintiff who has a right to participate in decisions about how her persona is utilized by others.").

legal structures and remedies, she can reap the reward of her notoriety and success and avoid letting others control her persona.[47]

An individual's trademark rights must of course be balanced against fundamental human rights and societal interests such as freedom of expression. These interests can conflict when trademarks are used in speech without the trademark owner's blessing.[48] Much of what is created today draws upon yesterday's creations. Popular culture, music, advertising and entertainment take cues, references and inspiration from each other, and a broad enforcement of trademark and publicity rights would certainly shrink the public domain.[49]

Patent law may be the most difficult to defend on the basis of individual rights and freedom. There is a general assumption among scholars that patents are more likely to be used against society than in its favor, and that preventing patent abuse is a higher calling than promoting individual autonomy, capabilities and economic potential.[50] Patents are still regarded as appropriate rewards for inventions, necessary to incentivize innovation, and useful for encouraging invention disclosure. But the system adopted to manage patent activity is, in the United States anyway, frequently described as unfair if not broken.[51]

---

[47] Steven D. Jamar and Lateef Mtima, "The Centrality of Social Justice for an Academic Intellectual Property Institute", 64 SMU L. Rev. 1127, 1144–45 (2011) ("Resourceful ingenuity and creativity exercised under challenging conditions often spur the development, refinement, and stylization of personal attributes and individual innovations, which sometimes engender enormous popular culture interest and concomitant commercial potential. However, institutionalized barriers to information, financial capital, and legal support often preclude commercial exploitation by marginalized innovators, while facilitating exploitation by majority enterprises and concerns. By invoking publicity rights . . . socially equitable and progressive policies can be pursued and achieved through strategic invocation and application of right of publicity law and doctrine.").

[48] *See, e.g. White v. Samsung*, 989 F.2d 1512, 1513 (9th Cir. 1993) (Kozinski, J., dissenting from the order rejecting the suggestion for rehearing *en banc*) ("Private property, including intellectual property, is essential to our way of life . . . But reducing too much to private property can be bad medicine . . . Culture, like science and technology, grows by accretion, each new creator building on the works of those who came before. Overprotection stifles the very creative forces it's supposed to nurture.")

[49] David Dante Troutt, "A Portrait of the Trademark as a Black Man: Intellectual Property, Commodification, and Redescription", 38 U.C. Davis L. Rev. 1141, 1192 (2005) ("Together with an increasingly lax concern for preserving First Amendment freedoms, courts have allowed intellectual property law to become an enabler of increased propertization for no consistent reason.").

[50] Hefler, note 40 above, 996.

[51] Adam B. Jaffe and Josh Lerner, *Innovation and its Discontents: How Our*

The patent system works well when the person who is the first to invent a novel, useful and non-obvious product or process is the one awarded the patent.[52] Among the changes to the patent system in the past three decades, however, has been an expansion of patent-holders' rights that has made patents easier to acquire and enforce. Patent filings have skyrocketed and patent quality has declined.[53] Patent litigation ballooned in the 1990s, creating a business culture that both craves and fears patents. The U.S. patent system is thus "a distraction from innovation rather than a source of incentive".[54]

In an effort to harmonize U.S. law with that of other nations, and reform the patent office, in 2011 Congress passed the Leahy-Smith America Invents Act ("AIA") which came into effect in March 2013.[55] The statute provides, among other things, a new system whereby the first inventor to file for a patent wins the patent rights (as opposed to the prior first-to-invent rule).[56] A first-to-file system favors inventors with resources who can hire attorneys to quickly submit applications to the U.S. Patent Office. It puts small businesses and solo inventors at a disadvantage.[57]

The policy battles on behalf of individual inventors are lost for

---

Broken Patent System is Endangering Innovation and Progress and What to Do About It (Princeton University Press, New Jersey 2004), 2–3.

[52] Ibid, 8.
[53] Ibid, 10–11.
[54] Ibid, 13.
[55] Leahy-Smith America Invents Act, Pub. L. No. 112-29, 125 Stat. 284 (2011).
[56] *See* 35 U.S.C. 102(a). For an explanation of the law and legislative history, *see* Joe Matal, "A Guide to the Legislative History of the America Invents Act: Part I of II", 21 Fed. Cir. B.J. 435, 453 (2011–2012) ((1) a patent's filing date is objective and simple to determine, whereas an invention date "is often uncertain, and, when disputed, typically requires corroborating evidence as part of an adjudication"; (2) the first-to-file system would avoid the expense and burden of interference proceedings and eliminate the need for inventors to maintain recording and document-retention systems; and (3) because many U.S. inventors and companies file for patent protection in foreign countries (which all use the first-to-file system), they "are forced [by the United States' maintenance of the first-to-invent system] to follow and comply with two different filing systems.").
[57] *See, e.g.,* Eugene Sisman, "Protecting the Incentive to Disclose for Small Inventors in the Wake of Patent Reform", 35 T. Jefferson L. Rev. 77, 79–80 (2012) ("While a large company may have the money to prosecute a patent application for every possible invention it conceives, such aggressive and expensive prosecution may not be economically feasible for a small company. Thus, while the AIA is mostly benign streamlining legislation, it poses a significant risk for small companies and solo inventors previously relying on the protections of the first-to-invent system.").

now. When it comes to helping poor and marginalized individuals and communities gain economic opportunities under an IP regime that strongly favors rights holders, the remedy is access to these regimes on as fair a footing as possible. It is not possible to replicate the legal services available to persons and businesses of financial means and privilege. But, as explored in the next section, private practice attorneys and law school clinics should make every reasonable effort to include service to economically disadvantaged and historically disenfranchised business owners among their professional and societal obligations.

III. SERVICE AND PROFESSIONALISM

A. Pro Bono Obligations

Early in my career as a law school clinician, we approached a major law firm in Boston to assist us with patent matters that exceeded our expertise. Our contact there informed us that the firm's pro bono standards did not apply to persons or businesses who were seeking commercial endeavors, such as acquiring intellectual property rights or otherwise engaging in for-profit business activity. She agreed to take on the clinic as a client because we were a non-profit, but could not represent our inventor- and entrepreneur-clients themselves. Other IP attorneys have refused to provide pro bono IP for fear of conflicts with their existing clients, a particular problem in patent law where helping one client obtain a patent can inadvertently exclude a future one from the same opportunity.

Lawyers are professionals who have long had a duty to use their skills and bar licenses to help poor and underrepresented people gain access to the legal and judicial system. In law schools, most of which are accredited by the American Bar Association, law students are encouraged (and in some cases required) to perform pro bono representation as part of their new professional duties. Complying with ABA standards, law schools urge aspiring lawyers to "understand the law as a public profession" which compels them to help those in need without charge.[58]

After they pass a bar exam, lawyers are committed to ethical standards often adopting or mirroring the Model Rules of Professional Conduct, which provide that lawyers shall "devote professional time and resources and civic influence to ensure equal access to our system of justice for all

---

[58] Am. Bar Association Standards and Rules of Procedure for Approval of Law Schools viii (2010).

those who because of economic or social barriers cannot afford or secure adequate legal counsel".[59]

Former Undersecretary of Commerce and Director of the U.S. Patent & Trademark Office David Kappos declared that the "economic security of this country and its minority communities continues to depend on its ability to innovate" and just as importantly its citizens' ability to acquire IP.[60] Under his leadership, the USPTO began several initiatives to help make the patent and trademark registration system more accessible to individuals of limited means and encouraged lawyers to provide pro bono patent representation.[61]

By offering free or low-cost IP legal services to poor and underserved people and communities, attorneys help to level the playing field of economic opportunity. They also can prevent the misuse of hard-earned money by steering inventors and entrepreneurs away from costly investments that have a low likelihood of return. Even short of taking on clients in trademark, copyright, and patent matters, attorneys can contribute to social welfare by volunteering their time to teach communities about IPRs and the IP legal system. As IP literacy rises, infringement should decline and economic activity increase. Struggling individuals may become fee-paying clients who employ their neighbors and contribute to the economic health and stability of their communities.

Pro bono services should not be limited to IP advice and acquisition, moreover. Lawyers specializing in complex commercial transactions should engage as well in helping employees spin off their own firms; inventors license their patents; musicians sign recording deals; filmmakers obtain proper publicity and copyright releases; local brewers comply with labeling laws; crowd-funded app developers comply with securities laws; and with many other important transactions that drive a modern small enterprise.

Litigation is also a crucial area for helping the struggling entrepreneur, particularly when she receives a "cease and desist" letter from another

---

[59] Model Rules of Professional Conduct pmbl, para 6.

[60] David Kappos, Under Secretary of Commerce for Intell. Prop. and Dir. of the U.S. Pat. & Trademark Office, "Remarks as Prepared for the 2010 National Minority Enterprise Development Week Conference" (26 August 2010) accessed 14 October 2014 at http://www.uspto.gov/news/speeches/2010/Kappos_National_Minority_Enterprise.jsp.

[61] See e.g. Press Release, Patterson Thuente IP, "Minnesota to Pioneer Pro Bono Patents", 1 (11 February 2011), accessed 14 October 2014 at http://www.ptslaw.com/news/Pro_Bono.pdf. See Chapter 7 herein for a discussion on IP lawyer pro bono initiatives in the development context.

and more established IP owner. Because the U.S. has a well-developed civil justice system, contracts and property rights are enforceable which lays the groundwork for economic development activity.[62] Such systems can be abused by large players against small ones, however, particularly as the cost of litigations climbs. Poor people need lawyers to help them gain access to and prevent being bullied by others using the civil litigation system.

B. Legal Education

If lawyers as professionals serve social justice functions, it follows that the social justice must be central to the missions and functions of the law schools that train them.[63]

Legal scholars should continue to explore the fundamental questions about intellectual property rights and their impact on developing economies, as well as on individuals living within fully developed economies like that of the United States. Law professors should also continue to impress upon aspiring attorneys the importance of serving underprivileged individuals and communities, including advising them about intellectual property law or assisting with business transactions. And law schools should continue to offer clinics – which traditionally have provided live-client training to students while giving low-income people access to justice and legal institutions – specializing in intellectual property and business development advice.

Law school clinical education advances social justice ideals as follows:

> First, ... through the provision of services and pursuit of legal and social reform on behalf of clients and community groups lacking meaningful access to societies' institutions of justice and power. ... Second, ... by exposing law students to an ethos of public service or pro bono responsibility in order to expand access to justice through law graduates' pursuit of pro bono activities or public service careers. ... Finally ... by facilitating transformative experiential opportunities for exploring the meaning of justice and developing a personal sense of justice, through exposure to the impact of the legal system on subordinated persons and groups and through the deconstruction of power and privilege in the law.[64]

---

[62] *See, e.g.* Robert Cooter, note 5 above, 187 (describing how poor countries may have strong property and contract laws "on the books" but will struggle with economic development because of inadequate legal systems for people to enforce these rights).

[63] *See* Jamar and Mtima, note 48 above, 1132.

[64] *See* Jon Dubin, "Clinical Design for Social Justice Imperatives", 51 SMU L. Rev. 1461, 1475–6 (1998) (legal aid clinics have "the double purpose of legal aid

When law school clinics engage in IP and entrepreneurship service for economically disadvantaged and marginalized people and communities, they serve a dual function of helping people with empowerment and self-reliance, and training lawyers who will provide necessary private ordering services to the entrepreneurial economy fostered by the clinic.[65]

Many law schools have answered this call. For example, the University of Maine School of Law has an intellectual property clinic that serves independent inventors with patent questions, entrepreneurs seeking trademark advice and registration, artists with copyright questions, and offers myriad other intellectual property licensing and pre-litigation counseling. Maine Law is one of 28 law schools participating in the USPTO's Law School Clinic Certification Pilot program through which law students are invited to submit patent and trademark applications on behalf of clients and under the supervision of clinical professors.[66]

Another exemplary law school IP clinic is housed in the Intellectual Property Institute of William Mitchell College of Law. The program allows students to work with clients on patent and trademark cases, and the faculty engage in studies and reports on issues like trademark litigation

---

to the poor as a public service and legal education by the clinical method") (quotations omitted).

[65] Ibid, 1464.

[66] *See* http://www.uspto.gov/ip/boards/oed/practitioner/agents/law_school_pilot.jsp (accessed 14 October 2014). The other law schools are: American University, Washington College of Law (trademarks); Arizona State University College of Law (patents and trademarks); California Western School of Law (trademarks); Case Western Reserve University School of Law (patents); Fordham University School of Law (patents and trademarks); Howard University School of Law (trademarks); Michigan State University School of Law (trademarks); North Carolina Central University School of law (patents and trademarks); Rutgers Law School – Newark (trademarks); South Texas College of Law (trademarks); The George Washington University School of Law (trademarks); The John Marshall School of Law (patents); Thomas Jefferson School of Law (patents and trademarks); University of Akron School of Law (trademarks); University of Colorado School of Law (patents); University of Connecticut School of Law (patents and trademarks); University of Maryland School of Law (patents and trademarks); University of New Hampshire School of Law (trademarks); University of Notre Dame School of Law (patents and trademarks); University of Puerto Rico School of Law (patents and trademarks); University of Richmond School of Law (trademarks); University of San Francisco School of Law (trademarks); University of Washington School of Law (patents and trademarks); Vanderbilt Law School (trademarks); Wayne State University Law School (patents); West Virginia University School of Law (trademarks); William Mitchell College of Law (patents and trademarks).

and trademark bullying.[67] William Mitchell's program is also novel in its integration with the local patent bar, which has worked closely with the pro bono legal services entity of Minnesota – Legal Corps – to offer pro bono patent services to inventors. The IP clinic takes referrals from the program to provide provisional patent application assistance to eligible clients.[68]

Law schools must take yet another crucial step to expand access to IP and entrepreneurship legal counseling in pursuit of social justice. They must continue to train attorneys who will live in and work closely with communities that have traditionally lacked access to legal counsel for economic, cultural or other reasons. As persons from those communities become lawyers themselves, they have the opportunity to lift their families to a new economic strata, to serve their neighbors with business and IP advice, and possibly to help their children succeed as well.

One law school has answered these calls on every level: Howard Law School in Washington, D.C. With an overall social justice mission as a school, a history of training African American lawyers, a program conducted by the Institute for Intellectual Property and Social Justice[69] to conduct research and outreach on IP social justice issues, and now a clinical practicum to work with needy individuals and communities, Howard Law exemplifies a commitment to IP social justice that many law schools should emulate.[70]

C. Duties of Care

Law school clinics or other public service legal agencies traditionally seek to contribute to social welfare rather than undermine it. Academic scholars specializing in intellectual property law have made numerous compelling cases against strong IP policies on the national level. They demonstrate how patent-friendly legal systems can drive up the costs of and prevent access to medicine and genetic testing. They note that copyright law can be used to deprive communities of knowledge and information resources. And they observe that trademark and publicity rights can stifle expression while promoting a culture of consumerism. As legal

---

[67] *See* http://web.wmitchell.edu/intellectual-property/ (accessed 14 October 2014).
[68] *See* ibid; *see also* http://www.mipla.net/ricofiles/pdf/LegalCORPSIAPfor MIPLA.pdf (accessed 14 October 2014).
[69] *See* Institute of Intellectual Property and Social Justice at Howard Law School webpages, accessed 14 October 2014 at http://www.iipsj.org/.
[70] *See also* Jamar and Mtima, note 48 above.

service providers assist marginalized individuals and communities with IP acquisition and commercial deals, they should be mindful of sound policy arguments leveled at the broader legal doctrines and ways in which IPRs can harm the disenfranchised and powerless.

Legal service providers working with entrepreneurs must also avoid exaggerating the value of IPRs and an individual's potential for commercial success. Patent applications can cost several thousand dollars to prepare. Most inventions disclosed to patent attorneys do not merit the expense of preparing and filing a patent application, and many patent applications never mature into issued patents. Litigation to enforce patents, moreover, is among the most expensive type of commercial litigation.[71] Indeed, all intellectual property litigation can be expensive. The ease with which IPRs can be acquired through low-cost legal services may mislead an entrepreneur into under-valuing the costs of managing and enforcing IP. This requires legal service providers to ensure that entrepreneurial clients appreciate the ongoing maintenance expense associated with owning IP.

IV. CONCLUSION

Economic opportunity is empowering. It allows individuals and communities freedom to achieve wealth, which in turn provides them the capacity to lead the "kind of lives we value". This chapter makes the case that lawyers are a crucial component to a society arranged to provide people of limited financial means the opportunity to achieve wealth and therefore freedom.

The United States already has a strong intellectual property rights regime, sound contract laws, and a well-developed judicial system for enforcing property and contract rights. It also has a vast number of law schools as well as attorneys skilled in intellectual property acquisition, IP enforcement, and sophisticated business transactions. Lawyers can make a difference in closing the gaping inequality gap in America.

---

[71] According to a study conducted by the American Intellectual Property Lawyers Association, the median litigation costs were $650,000 for claims under $1 million and $5 million for claims over $25 million. Jim Kerstetter, "How much is that patent lawsuit going to cost you?", CNET News (5 April 2012) accessed 14 October 2014 at http://news.cnet.com/8301-32973_3-57409792-296/how-much-is-that-patent-lawsuit-going-to-cost-you/. In this regard it is critical that communal IP education initiatives avoid a "top-down" perspective and are structured to be pragmatically responsive to the specific needs of the target community. *See* Chapter 9 herein.

First, local and state governments should create and support programs that assist low-income and marginalized entrepreneurs with intellectual property and business legal assistance. These programs should be neutral to technology sectors and should not attempt to pick winners, eliminating cultural bias and providing opportunities for innovation. They should also require recipients of government support to show commitment through matching funds, in-kind contributions, or other personal investment that encourages self-help, "skin in the game", and long-term success.

Second, law firms should expand their definition of pro bono-worthy matters to include offering public education on intellectual property, business formation and finance. These educational programs should be offered in places that are comfortable, nearby, and familiar to people who might not otherwise visit a government building, law firm conference room, or university class room. Law firms should make their best intellectual property and deal lawyers available to help entrepreneurs establish and grow their companies. And they should look for ways to give economic opportunities – freedom – to those who do not come from established wealth and privilege but have the personal desire to create it for themselves and their families.

Finally, law schools must infuse law students with a sense of obligation to serve people who are seeking economic opportunity and self-improvement, as well as those who need defense and legal counseling through a crisis. Law schools should develop and support clinics that help underprivileged persons with IP acquisition, licensing and enforcement, along with business formation and financing. They should also accept lower-income applicants and persons from traditionally excluded racial, ethnic and economic groups to provide them with professional opportunity as well as to populate more diverse communities with skilled attorneys.

Lawyers are privileged to have the educational foundation and bar license to earn a fine living. Among their duties is to help their fellow Americans gain economic advantages previously out of reach. These efforts can create a just society that promotes capabilities and freedom for all.

7. Intellectual property training and education for social justice
Peter K. Yu*

INTRODUCTION

Social justice issues have been present in the intellectual property debate for as long as intellectual property rights have existed. Their longstanding presence is unsurprising considering that intellectual property rights have always been designed with authors, inventors and other rights holders in mind. What is different today, however, is the increased public attention devoted to the protection and enforcement of intellectual property rights. Although this subject was once considered arcane, obscure, specialized and highly technical,[1] the mass media, consumer advocates, user communities and civil liberty groups have now actively participated in the intellectual property debate.

The past decade alone has seen a large and ever-growing number of public protests against the use of intellectual property rights to protect medicines, textbooks, seeds and computer software.[2] Only three years ago, the signing of the secretly-negotiated Anti-Counterfeiting Trade

---

* This chapter draws on research from the author's earlier article in the *American University International Law Review* and a study he conducted for the World Intellectual Property Organization (WIPO) in his role as the rapporteur for the International Roundtable on WIPO Development Agenda for Academics, held for the English-speaking countries in Singapore in November 2011. The views expressed herein are strictly personal and should not be considered or interpreted as those of WIPO. The author would like to thank Erin Cassidy and Lindsey Purdy for excellent research and editorial assistance.

[1] Andrew Gowers, *Gowers Review of Intellectual Property* (Norwich: HMSO 2006), 1; Susan K. Sell, *Private Power, Public Law: The Globalization of Intellectual Property Rights* (Cambridge: Cambridge University Press 2003), 99; Peter K. Yu, "Currents and Crosscurrents in the International Intellectual Property Regime", 38 Loy. L.A. L. Rev. 323, 419 (2004).

[2] Amy Kapczynski, "The Access to Knowledge Mobilization and the New Politics of Intellectual Property", 117 Yale L.J. Pocket Part 262, 263 (2008).

Agreement (ACTA) brought hundreds of thousands of people into the streets in major European cities in the middle of winter.[3] Across the Atlantic, individuals were equally concerned about the introduction of highly controversial copyright legislation, such as the PROTECT IP Act (PIPA) and the Stop Online Piracy Act (SOPA). These concerns eventually led to an unprecedented, massive service blackout launched by Wikipedia, Reddit, WordPress and other Internet companies in the run-up to the US presidential election.[4] If social justice issues rarely came up in the intellectual property debate a decade ago, these issues have now been heard loud and clear.

To a large extent, the emergent and increasingly robust micro-level debate parallels a longstanding and largely similar macro-level debate in the international arena. For several decades, developing countries, most notably Brazil and India, have voiced concerns about the imbalance in the international intellectual property system.[5] Since entering into force in January 1995, the Agreement on Trade-Related Aspects of Intellectual Property Rights (TRIPS Agreement) of the World Trade Organization (WTO) has imposed on these poor countries high international minimum standards that ignore their local needs, national interests, technological capabilities, institutional capacities and public health conditions. Even worse, despite the developing countries' considerable struggle with problems posed by these unsuitable standards, developed countries continue to push aggressively for higher standards through TRIPS-plus bilateral, plurilateral and regional trade agreements.

Frustrated by these developments, Brazil and Argentina advanced a proposal to establish a Development Agenda at the World Intellectual Property Organization (WIPO) in October 2004.[6] After three years of deliberation and compromise, the Agenda and its 45 recommendations were finally adopted. Recommendation 1 specifically required the technical assistance provided by WIPO be "development-oriented, demand-driven and transparent, taking into account the priorities and the special needs of developing countries . . . as well as the different levels of development of Member States". That recommendation further stated that "design, delivery mechanisms and evaluation processes of technical assistance programs

---

[3] Monica Horten, *Copyright Masquerade: How Corporate Lobbying Threatens Online Freedoms* (London: Zed Books 2013), 107–14.

[4] Peter K. Yu, "The Alphabet Soup of Transborder Intellectual Property Enforcement", 60 Drake L. Rev. Discourse 16, 29 (2012).

[5] Peter K. Yu, "A Tale of Two Development Agendas", 35 Ohio N.U. L. Rev. 465, 505–7 (2009).

[6] Ibid, 515–16.

should be country specific". Underscoring the need for these initiatives, the Development Agenda formally announced WIPO's shift away from the simplistic "one size fits all" – or, more precisely, "super size fits all"[7] – approach that has dominated intellectual property law and policy in the past few decades.[8]

The establishment of the WIPO Development Agenda is highly important from the standpoints of both development and social justice. Issues targeted by its recommendations ranged from transfer of technology to response to the digital divide and from preservation of the public domain to protection of genetic resources, traditional knowledge and traditional cultural expressions. More importantly for our purposes, the Development Agenda has provided a rare opportunity for us to rethink and redesign intellectual property training and educational programs.[9] Such redesign is badly needed if we are to reorient intellectual property law and policy toward the goals and principles of social justice. The improvements provided by this redesign would also foster better responses to the needs, interests and concerns of the weak, the vulnerable, the marginalized and the otherwise disadvantaged in both developed and developing countries.

Commentators have widely documented the injustice found in the currently out-of-balance intellectual property system at both the domestic and international levels. However, few have focused on the need to revamp training and educational programs. A rare exception is a study entitled *Intellectual Property Training and Education: A Development Perspective*, conducted by Jeremy de Beer and Chidi Oguamanam and commissioned by the International Centre for Trade and Sustainable Development, a Geneva-based non-governmental organization.[10]

---

[7] Shamnad Basheer and Annalisa Primi, "The WIPO Development Agenda: Factoring in the 'Technologically Proficient' Developing Countries", in Jeremy de Beer (ed.), *Implementing the World Intellectual Property Organization's Development Agenda* (Waterloo: Wilfred Laurier University Press 2009), 110; James Boyle, "A Manifesto on WIPO and the Future of Intellectual Property", 2004 Duke L. & Tech. Rev. 9, 4; Peter K. Yu, "The Global Intellectual Property Order and Its Undetermined Future", 1 WIPO J. 1, 9 (2009).

[8] Jeremy de Beer and Chidi Oguamanam, "Intellectual Property Training and Education: A Development Perspective" (2010) ICTSD Programme on IPRs and Sustainable Development, Issue Paper No. 31, 4; Ricardo Melendez-Ortiz, *Foreword* to de Beer and Oguamanam, above, vi, vi.

[9] On teaching of individual intellectual property subjects, see Yo Takagi, Larry Allman and Mpazi Sinjela (eds), *Teaching of Intellectual Property: Principles and Methods* (Cambridge: Cambridge University Press 2008); "Teaching Intellectual Property Law", 52 St. Louis U. L.J. 715 (2008).

[10] De Beer and Oguamanam, note 8 above.

In 2011, WIPO also conducted two International Roundtables on WIPO Development Agenda for Academics. The first one was held for English-speaking countries in Singapore, while the second was held for French-speaking countries in Beirut, Lebanon shortly after. Drawing on the insights and experiences provided by the English roundtable and a WIPO-commissioned study, this chapter discusses how intellectual property training and educational programs can be revamped to promote a "social justice" dimension of intellectual property policy and research.

This chapter begins by calling for an expansion of coverage in intellectual property training and educational programs. It further offers five sets of guidelines on efforts to redesign these programs. This chapter then calls for the programs to facilitate the development of a more diverse set of skills and perspectives. It reminds us that such development is especially needed in light of the rapid expansion of intellectual property rights and the growing inter- and multi-disciplinary nature of the intellectual property debate.

Although this chapter focuses primarily on the macro-level debate concerning developing countries, it complements other chapters in the volume that discuss the micro-level debate and the plight of historically marginalized communities in the developed world. Like developing countries, these communities face similar challenges posed by a lack of resources, expertise, leadership, negotiation sophistication and bargaining power.[11] Owing to inequitable rules and standards, many members of these communities also fail to benefit, or fully benefit, from their own creations and inventions. Because the needs and interests of the marginalized communities in the micro-level debate often align with those in the macro-level debate, what we learn from one debate could easily illuminate the other.

REDESIGNING TRAINING AND EDUCATIONAL PROGRAMS

Adopted at the 2007 WIPO General Assembly, the Development Agenda brought to the fore a new set of issues that can be incorporated into training and educational programs. These issues range from the use of flexibilities in international intellectual property agreements to the development of laws and policies to address the specific needs of developing countries. These specific needs include the access to essential medicines, educational materials, computer software and information technology; the transfer

---

[11] See Chapters 4 and 5, for example.

of technology, the preservation of culture and the public domain, the promotion of biological diversity; and the protection of genetic resources, traditional knowledge and traditional cultural expressions.

While incorporating these issues into the existing training and educational programs is both important and beneficial, such incorporation alone will not be sufficient. *Instead, the existing programs need to be redesigned to strengthen the focus on intellectual property, development and social justice.* To help achieve this goal, this section outlines five areas that will be important in any program seeking to develop that particular focus. Because issues concerning developing countries tend to be ignored or get short shrift, this section will provide illustrations relating to these countries, even though the promotion of development and social justice is important to both the developed and developing worlds.

The Bottom

The Development Agenda states explicitly that technical-assistance programs have to be "development-oriented, demand-driven . . . and country specific". Drawing its cue from this Agenda, this chapter refrains from a top-down approach that tries to determine what intellectual property issues will be important to promote development objectives. Instead, the chapter embraces a bottom-up approach using local needs, interests, conditions and priorities as the starting point.

To date, many of the existing programs cover the fundamentals of the intellectual property system, which range from copyrights to trademarks and from patents to trade secrets. If international treaties are included, the programs tend to focus on key intellectual property conventions and agreements, such as the Paris Convention, the Berne Convention, the Madrid Agreement and Protocol, the Hague Agreement, the Lisbon Agreement, the Rome Convention, the Patent Cooperation Treaty, the TRIPS Agreement and the WIPO Internet Treaties.[12]

With respect to developing countries, however, it is worth questioning whether such an approach is ideal. For example, many of these countries are likely to receive substantial benefits from the protection of utility models, industrial designs, geographical indications, genetic resources, traditional knowledge and traditional cultural expressions.[13] Indeed, the development of sub-patentable inventions has been historically

---

[12] Peter K. Yu, "Teaching International Intellectual Property Law", 52 St. Louis U. L.J. 923, 926–7 (2008).

[13] Peter K. Yu, "Intellectual Property and Asian Values", 16 Marq. Intell. Prop. L. Rev. 329, 380–3, 389–92 (2012).

demonstrated to be a successful tool for developing countries to catch up with their more developed counterparts – Japan being a very good example.[14] Developing countries have also been quite successful in exploiting traditional medicines and practices[15] and sequential and cumulative innovation (as opposed to path-breaking innovation enshrined in the existing international intellectual property system).[16] Thus, it is important to ask not only what type of intellectual property rights training and educational programs should cover, but also what type of rights the participants of these programs would find the most useful.

Moreover, some important topical issues and problem areas warrant extended treatment. For example, given the widespread HIV/AIDS, tuberculosis and malaria pandemics in sub-Saharan Africa,[17] instructors for training and educational programs in the region likely will have to spend a tremendous amount of time covering issues concerning the relationship between the patent system and access to essential medicines.[18] At times, it may also be useful to consider the special needs of local industries and policymakers – for example, which sectors are fast-growing in the country,[19] and which issues are likely to be raised in bilateral, plurilateral and regional negotiations?

---

[14] Hiroyuki Odagiri, Akira Goto and Atsushi Sunami, "IPR and the Catch-Up Process in Japan", in Hiroyuki Odagiri, Akira Goto, Atsushi Sunami and Richard R. Nelson (eds), *Intellectual Property Rights, Development, and Catch-Up: An International Comparative Study* (Oxford: Oxford University Press 2010), 95.

[15] Nitya Nanda and Ritu Lodha, "Making Essential Medicines Affordable to the Poor", 20 Wis. Int'l L.J. 581, 586 (2002).

[16] Odagiri, Goto and Sunami, note 14 above, 126; Jerome H. Reichman, "Intellectual Property in the Twenty-First Century: Will the Developing Countries Lead or Follow?", 46 Hous. L. Rev. 1115, 1124 (2009); Yu, note 13 above, 389–92.

[17] On access-to-medicines problems relating to HIV/AIDS, see Obijiofor Aginam, John Harrington and Peter K. Yu (eds), *The Global Governance of HIV/AIDS: Intellectual Property and Access to Essential Medicines* (Cheltenham: Edward Elgar Publishing 2013); Benjamin Coriat (ed.), *The Political Economy of HIV/AIDS in Developing Countries: TRIPS, Public Health Systems and Free Access* (Cheltenham: Edward Elgar Publishing 2008).

[18] On the widespread access-to-medicines problems precipitated by the TRIPS Agreement, see Pedro Roffe, Geoff Tansey and David Vivas-Eugui (eds), *Negotiating Health: Intellectual Property and Access to Medicines* (London: Earthscan 2005); Frederick M. Abbott, "The WTO Medicines Decision: World Pharmaceutical Trade and the Protection of Public Health", 99 Am. J. Int'l L. 317 (2005); Peter K. Yu, "The International Enclosure Movement", 82 Ind. L.J. 827 (2007).

[19] UNCTAD-ICTSD Project on Intellectual Property Rights and Sustainable Development, *Resource Book on TRIPS and Development* (Cambridge: Cambridge University Press 2005), 127; Peter K. Yu, "International Enclosure, the Regime Complex, and Intellectual Property Schizophrenia", 2007 Mich. St. L. Rev. 1, 25–7.

In addition, it may be important to discuss issues concerning the establishment of intellectual property or technology transfer offices, especially under a constrained budget and when capacities are limited.[20] It is also worth discussing the strengths and weaknesses of developing specialized courts in the intellectual property area.[21] Although commentators and economists have rightly noted the high costs of building infrastructure and establishing institutions, it is worth noting that low-cost, streamlined models exist for the development and operation of intellectual property offices.[22] These offices, for example, can be funded by user fees or supported through outsourcing arrangements.[23]

Thus, it is important for training and educational programs to identify the different institutional options available to the participants. The more affordable the acquisition of intellectual property rights is, the larger is the number of local beneficiaries of the intellectual property system, and the more developing countries can harness that system to promote development objectives. A reduced operating budget will also help developing countries retain scarce economic and human resources for other competing public needs.[24]

The Flip Side

Traditional intellectual property training and educational programs tend to focus on the rights recognized by international treaties and national laws. Limitations and exceptions, however, are not always emphasized. Equally ignored are the obligations of rights holders[25] – for example,

---

[20] Anatole Krattiger et al. (eds), *Intellectual Property Management in Health and Agricultural Innovation: A Handbook of Best Practices* (Oxford and Davis: Centre for the Management of Intellectual Property in Health Research and Development and Public Intellectual Property Resource for Agriculture 2007), 537–672.

[21] John T. Cross, Amy Landers, Michael Mireles and Peter Yu, *Global Issues in Intellectual Property Law* (St. Paul: West/Thomson 2010), 40–6.

[22] Commission on Intellectual Property Rights, *Integrating Intellectual Property Rights and Development Policy* (London: Commission on Intellectual Property Rights 2002), 145–6; Robert M. Sherwood, *Intellectual Property and Economic Development* (Boulder: Westview Press 1990), 181–5; Sean A. Pager, "Patents on a Shoestring: Making Patent Protection Work for Developing Countries", 23 Ga. St. U. L. Rev. 755 (2007).

[23] Peter K. Yu, "Enforcement, Economics and Estimates", 2 WIPO J. 1, 2 (2010).

[24] Ibid, 3–4.

[25] Peter K. Yu, "The Objectives and Principles of the TRIPS Agreement", 46 Hous. L. Rev. 979, 1035–7 (2009).

obligations in relation to anti-competitive practices. The omission of these two sets of issues is particularly disturbing. In the intellectual property system, limitations and exceptions are just as important as rights.[26] If the system is to function properly, rights should also be balanced by obligations.

Thus, development-friendly training and educational programs should not only focus on the justifications for and the nature and extent of the rights; they should also detail the available flexibilities within the intellectual property system as well as the policy options that take advantage of these flexibilities. In addition, these programs should provide a critical analysis of the strengths and weaknesses of the available policy options as well as an objective assessment of their costs and benefits. In determining these costs, it is important not to emphasize only economic costs but also social and cultural costs. For many developing countries, the negative social and cultural impacts of an out-of-balance intellectual property system are likely to be quite substantial.[27]

For instance, for training and educational programs conducted in developing countries, it will be useful to

> emphasize the eligibility requirements for the different forms of intellectual property rights; the non-protection of ideas, procedures, methods of operation, and mathematical concepts in copyright law; the availability of compulsory licensing of patented pharmaceuticals; unrestricted use of generic terms notwithstanding the protection of trademarks; the importance of technical and functional considerations in laws involving trade dresses and industrial designs; permissive limitations and exceptions under the three-step test; remedies for anticompetitive practices, abuse of rights and restraints on trade; and special exemptions that seek to respond to national exigencies.[28]

More specifically in the area concerning public health exigencies, it will be useful to discuss not only the justifications for and the nature and extent of patent rights, but also compulsory licenses; parallel importation; government use provisions;[29] and the introduction of exceptions for research,

---

[26] James Boyle, *Shamans, Software and Spleens: Law and the Construction of the Information Society* (Cambridge, MA: Harvard University Press 1996), 138.
[27] Commission on Intellectual Property Rights, note 22 above, 4; Yu, note 18 above, 890.
[28] Yu, note 12 above, 932–3.
[29] James Love, "Access to Medicine and Compliance with the WTO TRIPS Accord: Models for State Practice in Developing Countries", in Peter Drahos and Ruth Mayne (eds), *Global Intellectual Property Rights: Knowledge, Access and Development* (New York: Palgrave Macmillan 2002), 81–3.

early working and the development of diagnostics.[30] It is also worthwhile to explore the anti-competitive effects of the patent system, an issue that has received longstanding attention from developing countries.[31]

The Neighbors

Today, the discussion of intellectual property law and policy is no longer limited only to developments within the international intellectual property regime. Increasingly, the participants of training and educational programs need to learn about developments in other international regimes, such as those governing public health, human rights, biological diversity, food and agriculture, and information and communications.[32]

To a great extent, the study of intellectual property requires an "intellectual property and ..." approach that covers neighboring issues that lie outside the intellectual property area.[33] Such a cross-cutting approach is particularly important in light of the continued forum-manipulative activities conducted by both developed and developing countries.[34] These efforts seek to move international discussions to fora that traditionally do not cover intellectual property.

Consider, for example, the protection of genetic resources, traditional knowledge and traditional cultural expressions. Such protection is as much about intellectual property as it is about biological diversity. As a result of this overlap, the protection of these materials has implicated not only international intellectual property treaties, but also the Convention on Biological Diversity and the International Treaty on Plant Genetic Resources for Food and Agriculture (which was negotiated under the auspices of the UN Food and Agriculture Organization).

---

[30] Commission on Intellectual Property Rights, note 22 above, 49–51; Ellen F.M. 't Hoen, *The Global Politics of Pharmaceutical Monopoly Power: Drug Patents, Access, Innovation and the Application of the WTO Doha Declaration on TRIPS and Public Health* (Netherlands: AMB Publishers 2009), 39–59; Edson Beas Rodrigues Jr., *The General Exception Clauses of the TRIPS Agreement: Promoting Sustainable Development* (Cambridge: Cambridge University Press 2012), 159–236.

[31] Peter K. Yu, "TRIPS and Its Achilles' Heel", 18 J. Intell. Prop. L. 479, 520–1 (2011).

[32] Yu, note 5 above, at 522–40.

[33] Yu, note 12 above, at 940.

[34] On these activities, see John Braithwaite and Peter Drahos, *Global Business Regulation* (Cambridge: Cambridge University Press 2000), 564–71; Laurence R. Helfer, "Regime Shifting: The TRIPs Agreement and New Dynamics of International Intellectual Property Lawmaking", 29 Yale J. Int'l L. 1 (2004).

Even more complicated, because the protection has a close relationship with the protection of indigenous rights, one has to pay special attention to rights articulated in the Declaration on the Rights of Indigenous Peoples, the UNESCO Convention on the Safeguarding of Intangible Cultural Heritage and the UNESCO Convention on the Protection and Promotion of the Diversity of Cultural Expressions. One also has to pay attention to the fact that indigenous peoples often do not have sufficient representation in the negotiation of many of the existing international treaties.[35]

In addition, one needs to be mindful of the human rights interests protected under the Universal Declaration of Human Rights, the International Covenant on Civil and Political Rights and the International Covenant on Economic, Social and Cultural Rights. General Comment Nos. 17 and 21, the two interpretive comments authored by the Committee on Economic, Social and Cultural Rights, also provide important normative guidance on the development of intellectual property rights and the protection of genetic resources, traditional knowledge and traditional cultural expressions.

Within the larger picture of intellectual property and development, it may even be useful to examine intellectual property issues in light of the UN Millennium Development Goals. These eight development goals are: (1) eradicate extreme poverty and hunger; (2) achieve universal primary education; (3) promote gender equality and empower women; (4) reduce child mortality; (5) improve maternal health; (6) combat HIV/AIDS, malaria and other diseases; (7) ensure environmental sustainability; and (8) develop a global partnership for development.

Finally, because of the ever-expanding scope of intellectual property rights and the ability for these rights to spill over into other areas of international regulation, intellectual property training and educational programs should feature inter- and multi-disciplinary perspectives.[36] Many of the existing programs focus primarily on the legal aspects of intellectual property. However, it is increasingly important to consider other aspects of intellectual property, such as political, economic, social and cultural. It is therefore no surprise that Recommendation 45 of the

---

[35] Rosemary J. Coombe, "The Recognition of Indigenous Peoples' and Community Traditional Knowledge in International Law", 14 St. Thomas L. Rev. 275, 284–5 (2001); Tom Greaves, "IPR, A Current Survey", in Tom Greaves (ed.), *Intellectual Property Rights for Indigenous Peoples, A Sourcebook* (Oklahoma City: Society for Applied Anthropology 1994), 14; Dean B. Suagee, "The Cultural Heritage of American Indian Tribes and the Preservation of Biological Diversity", 31 Ariz. St. L.J. 483, 488 (1999).

[36] De Beer and Oguamanam, note 8 above, 38; Yu, note 12 above, 940.

WIPO Development Agenda explicitly recognized "the context of broader societal interests and especially development-oriented concerns".

If intellectual property is to become a catalyst for development, understanding how to exploit intellectual property rights – for example, through licensing models and business strategies – will be as important as understanding how to comply with laws and treaty obligations. Indeed, the more interdisciplinary the perspectives that participants can acquire from training and educational programs, the more likely they will be able to come up with strategies and solutions that are tailored to local needs, interests, conditions and priorities.

Developing countries and commentators sympathetic to these countries have widely criticized the existing intellectual property system for its bias toward developed countries, which created this system more than a century ago. Unlike these standards, however, licensing models and business strategies can benefit any country that has valuable intellectual property assets. Thus, by developing a better and more sophisticated understanding of these models and strategies, participants from developing countries will be able to derive greater benefits from what Michael Finger and Philip Schuler described as "poor people's knowledge".[37] These countries will also be better prepared to take advantage of any future beneficial adjustments to existing intellectual property standards.

The Elephants

Because of the significant power asymmetry between developed and developing countries, the weaker countries often have to take into consideration the policies and approaches adopted by more powerful countries. It is therefore important to identify the models practiced by developed and emerging countries and assess their strengths and weaknesses in light of specific local conditions.

In doing so, the participants of training and educational programs will be able to obtain information about what policy measures could help them catch up with countries in the developed world. The participants will also be able to better anticipate future changes in the international intellectual property regime, which are often fostered through norm-setting activities in the multilateral forum or through the establishment of bilateral, plurilateral or regional trade agreements.

---

[37] J. Michael Finger and Philip Schuler (eds), *Poor People's Knowledge: Promoting Intellectual Property in Developing Countries* (Washington, DC and New York: World Bank and Oxford University Press 2004).

For participants from the developing world, it is important to understand not only the positions taken by the United States and the European Union, but also large developing countries, such as Brazil, China and India.[38] The latter, especially China, have been increasingly active in Africa and Latin America. In the near future, their models will likely be quite influential in these continents.[39]

Moreover, a better understanding of the different positions taken by powerful, developed countries and large developing countries may help increase the policy options available to participants from smaller developing countries. To begin with, the participants of training and educational programs can draw on lessons from developed and large developing countries to determine for themselves which model best suits their local conditions.

Although commentators tend to analyze intellectual property issues along the North-South divide, it is worth remembering that developed countries have significant disagreements among themselves. Consider the United States and the European Union, for example. Thus far, commentators have reported wide disagreements between these two trading powers over the treatment of moral rights and geographical indications. As shown by the recent ACTA negotiations, these two powers also strongly disagree over whether criminal measures should be extended to patent infringement.[40]

As if those differences were not enough, the United States has embraced a broad fair-use privilege in its copyright law, leading to the emergence of a large number of innovative technology start-ups. Meanwhile, European policymakers and commentators continue to question whether such a broad interpretation of exceptions to copyright would satisfy the three-step test in the Berne Convention, the TRIPS Agreement and the WIPO Internet Treaties.[41]

More importantly for developing countries, identifying the divergent approaches that powerful, developed countries take and the tension

---

[38] Peter K. Yu, "The Middle Intellectual Property Powers", in Tom Ginsburg and Randall Peerenboom (eds), *Law and Development in Middle-Income Countries: Avoiding the Middle-Income Trap* (New York: Cambridge University Press 2014), 84.

[39] Peter K. Yu, "Sinic Trade Agreements", 44 U.C. Davis L. Rev. 953, 1020–2 (2011).

[40] Peter K. Yu, "ACTA and Its Complex Politics", 3 WIPO J. 1, 11 (2011); Peter K. Yu, "Six Secret (and Now Open) Fears of ACTA", 64 SMU L. Rev. 975, 984 (2011) (Yu, "Six Secret Fears").

[41] Ruth Okediji, "Toward an International Fair Use Doctrine", 39 Colum. J. Transnat'l L. 75, 115 (2000).

resulting from such divergence will help them fight off foreign pressure. After all, it is much easier to reject standards that are still contested in the developed world than those that have already been harmonized among the major trading powers.

Understanding the differences among developed countries will therefore help the participants of training and educational programs avoid transplanting foreign models that are unsuitable to local conditions.[42] Even better, such knowledge will help prevent developing countries from committing to conflicting obligations demanded by their more powerful trading partners through bilateral, plurilateral or regional trade agreements.[43]

The Visionary

Different countries have different historical traditions, political arrangements, social and economic priorities, cultural values and legal philosophies. It is therefore no surprise that countries also have very different intellectual property systems. Although the international intellectual property regime is built upon harmonized international minimum standards, these standards do not work well for every developing country. Nor do they reflect all the available policy options. As a result, it is important for the participants of training and educational programs to learn more about the different standards, policy options and innovation models that are suitable to local conditions.

While the WIPO Development Agenda has repeatedly emphasized the need for country-specific, context-sensitive models, developing those models is not always easy.[44] Indeed, it can be rather difficult and costly to come up with new alternative models that differ significantly from those practiced in developed and large developing countries.[45] Thus, training and educational programs should use best efforts to provide information about these alternative models, with additional assessments on both the models' strengths and weaknesses.

In the area of access to essential medicines, for example, it is insufficient for training and educational programs to identify only exceptions and limitations (although such identification remains very important). These

---

[42] Yu, "Six Secret Fears", note 40 above, 1035–8.
[43] Peter K. Yu, "TRIPS and Its Discontents", 10 Marq. Intell. Prop. L. Rev. 369, 407 (2006).
[44] Melendez-Ortiz, note 8 above, vi.
[45] Peter K. Yu, "Intellectual Property Training and Education for Development", 28 Am. U. Int'l L. Rev. 311, 332 and fn. 92 (2012).

programs should also highlight the different non-property based models that can help promote creativity and innovation. Examples of these models are those relying on grants, subsidies, prizes, advance market commitments, reputation gains, open and collaborative models, patent pools, public-private partnerships and equity-based systems built upon liability rules.[46]

In addition, training and educational programs should inform the participants about the different ways of interpreting the standards laid down in international agreements. Because norms are usually political compromises struck by negotiating parties, they are often open to widely different interpretations. Notwithstanding these flexibilities, many developing countries unfortunately do not have the needed resources, capacity and political clout to come up with alternative interpretations.[47] Training and educational programs should therefore provide this much-needed assistance.

A case in point is the international obligations concerning the enforcement of intellectual property rights. It is important to learn how to comply with these obligations, including the minimum standards, optional requirements and best practices among developed countries. The programs should also cover alternative ways to conceptualize the existing enforcement obligations.[48] For example, how should the participants re-conceptualize intellectual property enforcement? Should they take account of both rights and responsibilities? Should they focus on anticompetitive practices, abuse of rights, and restraints on trade? Are there other internationally acceptable enforcement measures not practiced by developed countries and major intellectual property exporting countries?

Finally, if the intellectual property system is to promote development objectives, it needs to be viewed as a component of a larger innovation system.[49] The participants of training and educational programs need to understand the interplay between intellectual property rights and other complementary factors.

---

[46] Peter K. Yu, "Intellectual Property and Human Rights in the Nonmultilateral Era", 64 Fla. L. Rev. 1045, 1078 (2012).
[47] Peter K. Yu, "Access to Medicines, BRICS Alliances, and Collective Action", 34 Am. J.L. & Med. 345, 386 (2008).
[48] Yu, note 23 above, at 17.
[49] Daniel J. Gervais, "TRIPS and Development", in Daniel J. Gervais (ed.), *Intellectual Property, Trade and Development: Strategies to Optimize Economic Development in a TRIPS Plus Era*, 1st edn (New York: Oxford University Press 2007), 4; Peter K. Yu, "Intellectual Property and the Information Ecosystem", 2005 Mich. St. L. Rev. 1, 15.

For instance, Keith Maskus identified several non-intellectual property factors that could play significant roles in attracting foreign direct investment: public and private investments in education and training; the removal of impediments to the acquisition of human capital; the development of national innovation systems that promote dynamic competition; support for basic research capabilities; the removal of disincentives for applied research, development and commercialization; the institution of incentive structures to stimulate local innovation; and efforts to take greater advantage of access to scientific and technical information existing online or elsewhere.[50]

In the area of technology transfer, Professor Maskus further identified a wide variety of complementary factors: the movement of newly trained labor among enterprises; the laying out of patents; product innovation through the legitimate "inventing around" of patents and copyrights; the adoption of newer and more efficient specialized inputs to reduce production costs; the introduction of efficient and competitive international enterprises; increasing competition and rising demands for sub-contracting; access to a wider variety of specialized products, inputs and technologies; a deeper and better-trained skilled labor pool; and rising real wages.[51]

In my earlier works, I have also noted the importance of creating an enabling environment for effective intellectual property enforcement.[52] Among the key preconditions for successful intellectual property law reforms are "a consciousness of legal rights, respect for the rule of law, an effective and independent judiciary, a well-functioning innovation and competition system, sufficiently-developed basic infrastructure, a critical mass of local stakeholders, and established business practices".[53]

Thus, successful training and educational programs should identify the role the intellectual property system will play in promoting creativity and innovation while fostering development. They should also provide knowledge about how the system interacts with other complementary factors, thereby allowing the participants to understand the full spectrum of policy options available for promoting development objectives.

---

[50] Keith E. Maskus, "The Role of Intellectual Property Rights in Encouraging Foreign Direct Investment and Technology Transfer", 9 Duke J. Comp. & Int'l L. 109, 151 (1998).
[51] Ibid, 146.
[52] *E.g.* Peter K. Yu, "Intellectual Property, Economic Development, and the China Puzzle", in Gervais, note 49 above, 213–6.
[53] Yu, note 31 above, 500.

SKILLS AND PERSPECTIVES

In addition to imparting knowledge, values and perspectives, a key goal of training and educational programs is to inculcate in the participants a set of specialized skills and analytical perspectives. The adoption of the WIPO Development Agenda requires us to rethink not only the contents delivered through these programs, but also the specialized skills and perspectives the programs seek to develop. This section focuses on five broadly defined sets of skills and perspectives, which will be useful for promoting a "social justice" dimension of intellectual property policy and research.

Negotiation Skills

Negotiation skills are of paramount importance whether one is a policymaker, a business executive, a patent attorney, a licensing officer, a technology transfer manager or an owner of valuable intellectual property assets. At the macro level, government officials constantly have to negotiate with their foreign counterparts over what intellectual property standards their countries need to adopt. While the multilateral process allows developing countries to enhance bargaining power by building coalitions, these countries can become highly vulnerable in bilateral, plurilateral and regional negotiations. The development of strong negotiation skills is therefore badly needed to overcome their lack of bargaining leverage in non-multilateral discussions.

At the micro level, negotiation skills are also very important. In the area of protection for genetic resources, traditional knowledge and traditional cultural expressions, for instance, informed consent and benefit-sharing obligations are often fulfilled through the establishment of material transfer agreements.[54] As important as these agreements are, they are likely to be of limited effectiveness if the relevant parties from developing countries do not have the requisite skills to negotiate for suitable arrangements.

Moreover, although litigation remains an important part of intellectual property law practice, most disputes are settled in courts and resolved through negotiations. Oftentimes, the negotiation of these settlements entails not only intellectual property lawyers but also non-law practitioners. These practitioners tend to have a deep understanding of the industry as well as the various competitive advantages, constraints and challenges confronting the affected parties. It is therefore important for training and

---

[54] Alan B. Bennett, Wendy D. Streitz and Rafael A. Gacel, "Specific Issues with Material Transfer Agreements", in Krattiger et al., note 20 above, 697.

educational programs to help the participants develop strong negotiation skills.

Economic Analysis

Empirical research is one of the key focuses of the WIPO Development Agenda. One of the six "clusters" of recommendations, for example, focuses on assessment, evaluation and impact studies. Impact assessments have indeed been widely embraced in the areas of human rights, public health and biological diversity.[55] In addition, in August 2009, WIPO brought in Carsten Fink, an established expert in international economics, to serve as its first Chief Economist. Since its establishment, the Economics and Statistics Division has put together a wide variety of seminars and publications, including most notably the *World Intellectual Property Report*.

Thus far, developing countries have a very limited pool of homegrown economists who can provide the needed assessment on the intellectual property system.[56] This assessment becomes even more complicated when it has to take account of such factors as trade flows, foreign direct investment and diffusion of technology. Oftentimes, policymakers from developing countries have to rely on assistance from the outside or data supplied by industries or nongovernmental organizations.

Even if we ignore the widely documented flaws regarding industry data, data supplied by self-interested parties – whether industry or nongovernmental organizations – are hardly impartial.[57] As a result, it is important for training and educational programs to help facilitate independent economic research in the intellectual property area. At the very least, the programs should equip the participants with better analytical skills to judge for themselves the accuracy, relevance and implications of the data supplied by third parties.

The ability to engage in economic analysis is equally important at the micro level. How well a business or licensing model will perform will ultimately depend on the economics within the relevant sector. Indeed, with the increasing roles intellectual property rights play in today's knowledge-based economy, it is no longer sufficient to study laws and policies alone.

---

[55] Yu, note 46 above, at 1096–8.
[56] Keith E. Maskus, Sean M. Dougherty and Andrew Mertha, "Intellectual Property Rights and Economic Development in China", in Carsten Fink and Keith E. Maskus (eds), *Intellectual Property and Development: Lessons from Recent Economic Research* (Washington, DC and New York: World Bank and Oxford University Press 2005), 311.
[57] Yu, note 23 above, 7–8.

It is also important to better understand the economic implications of these laws and policies as well as those of the alternative policy options.

Business Insights

A successful intellectual property system depends on the existence of viable and sustainable business models that help facilitate the acquisition, exploitation, commercialization, management and transfer of intellectual property rights. To a large extent, intellectual property laws can be viewed as business regulations that have significant impacts on competition, market structure and consumer choices.[58]

Thus far, training and educational programs have focused primarily on the compliance aspects of intellectual property protection. There is indeed a great need for programs identifying business models that work well for the unique conditions in developing countries. At the macro level, it would also be helpful to identify models that allow developing countries to pool together limited resources to create economies of scale and scope and to provide a greater aggregate market.[59]

Notwithstanding the importance of locating business models suitable to developing countries, few programs thus far have focused on identifying these models. The lack of such a focus is due in part to the fact that expert instructors for training and educational programs tend to originate from developed countries and multinational corporations. Such a lack can also be attributed to the limited research devoted to the area. It is therefore no surprise that Recommendation 26 of the WIPO Development Agenda "encourages Member States, especially developed countries, to urge their research and scientific institutions to enhance cooperation and exchange with research and development institutions in developing countries".

Finally, as intellectual property rights continue to expand and diversify, it is important that the participants of training and educational programs better understand the different models that can be built upon existing rights. The more successfully local creators, inventors and businesses use the intellectual property system to promote their interests, the more likely the system can be harnessed to promote the interests of developing

---

[58] Michael A. Gollin, *Driving Innovation: Intellectual Property Strategies for a Dynamic World* (Cambridge: Cambridge University Press 2008), 23; Frederick M. Abbott, "The Cycle of Action and Reaction: Developments and Trends in Intellectual Property and Health", in Roffe, Tansey and Vivas-Eugui, note 18 above, 36; Keith E. Maskus, "Teaching the Economics of Intellectual Property Rights in the Global Economy", in Takagi, Allman and Sinjela, note 9 above, 166.

[59] Yu, note 18 above, at 882.

countries. A greater stake in the system on the part of these countries would also generate benefits for developed countries and their supportive rights holders.[60]

Historical Appreciation

History is important, not only because it tells us what happened in the past, but also because it provides important lessons and directions for the future. As the philosopher George Santayana wrote, "Those who cannot remember the past are condemned to repeat it".[61] Given the recurrence of intellectual property developments, including past efforts made by developing countries to recalibrate international intellectual property standards, it is particularly important for training and educational programs to help the participants understand past developments.

In fact, the establishment of the WIPO Development Agenda has demonstrated how important the past has been. In the 1960s, for instance, countries already pushed for the establishment of a development agenda. This "Old Development Agenda" eventually included the drafting of the Stockholm Protocol Regarding Developing Countries, the formation of WIPO as a UN specialized agency, the development of the draft International Code of Conduct on the Transfer of Technology under the auspices of the United Nations Conference on Trade and Development (UNCTAD), and negotiations concerning the revision of the Paris Convention.[62] There are also remarkable similarities between the "common heritage of humankind" concept advanced at that time and the commons concept widely used today in the free software, open source, free culture and access to knowledge movements.[63]

While developing countries and their supporters have achieved only limited success in the Old Development Agenda, the existence of that Agenda has shown that the recent pro-development efforts are not entirely new. An important question for us therefore is: How different is the present Agenda from the old Agenda? After all, if the Agenda merely repeats its failed predecessor without making significant adjustments, how likely is it to succeed the second time?[64]

---

[60] Yu, note 31 above, at 523–4; Peter K. Yu, "The Copyright Divide", 25 Cardozo L. Rev. 331, 431–3 (2003).
[61] George Santayana, *The Life of Reason: Or the Phases of Human Progress* (New York: C. Scribner's Sons 1932), 232.
[62] Yu, note 5 above, at 468–511.
[63] Ibid, 541–2.
[64] Ibid, 543.

In addition to studying past efforts developing countries have made, training and educational programs can make use of case studies on how a select group of countries successfully caught up with their more developed counterparts in terms of both economic and technological developments. For example, the United States, Japan, South Korea and Singapore have all been developing countries, yet they are highly economically developed and technologically proficient today.[65] Following this trend, commentators have already begun studying the economic and technological transformation of the so-called BRICS countries (Brazil, Russia, India, China and South Africa).[66]

In *Intellectual Property Rights, Development, and Catch-up: An International Comparative Study*, for example, Hiroyuki Odagiri, Akira Goto, Atsushi Sunami and Richard Nelson provided an important collection of studies on the catch-up processes that developed, emerging and large developing countries have experienced.[67] Training and educational programs that provide a deeper understanding of these case studies are likely to be useful for policymakers from developing countries. These case studies will also be useful to authors, inventors and businesses, most of whom rely on intellectual property rights to succeed.

Global Awareness

Global perspectives are particularly important to policymakers and industry leaders from developing countries. Without a doubt, international politics plays a rather important role in determining how countries negotiate at the international level and what intellectual property standards countries ultimately adopt. Indeed, a growing number of intellectual property scholars have emphasized the importance of studying trade geography, international relations and global politics.

With the rapidly changing geopolitics and the arrival of new and emerging players in the international intellectual property regime,[68] it is no longer sufficient to have the simplistic view that the international intellectual property debate reflects a North-South divide. Today, there are many important and intriguing developments among developed countries,

---

[65] Peter K. Yu, "The Rise and Decline of the Intellectual Property Powers", 34 Campbell L. Rev. 525, 528–43 (2012).

[66] *E.g.* Jim O'Neill, *The Growth Map: Economic Opportunity in the BRICs and Beyond* (New York: Portfolio 2011), 69–79.

[67] Odagiri et al., note 14 above.

[68] Yu, note 5 above, at 546–54; Peter K. Yu, "Virotech Patents, Viropiracy, and Viral Sovereignty", 45 Ariz. St. L.J. 1563, 1645–54 (2013).

between developed and large developing countries and between developed and developing countries. While developed and large developing countries have stood side by side on certain issues, they are bitter opponents concerning others.[69]

At the global level, as opposed to the international level, there are also many interesting developments featuring non-state and sub-state actors.[70] The widely cited example of non-state arrangements concerns ICANN (Internet Corporation for Assigned Names and Numbers), which is a private not-for-profit US corporation in California that is charged with coordinating the Internet domain name system.[71] Although ICANN is not a governmental agency, it has contractual obligations with the US Department of Commerce.[72]

There are also important developments concerning a wide variety of non-state actors. These players include multinational corporations, political activists, consumer advocates, civil liberties groups, academics, media and individual citizens. A better understanding of global developments therefore will provide not only a more complete picture of the ongoing development of the international intellectual property system, but also insights into where opportunities and challenges will lie for developing countries.

Inevitably, concerns will arise over whether a focus on geopolitical developments would politicize the materials for training and educational programs. However, it is fair to state that the omission of such an important set of issues will be a disservice to the participants of these programs. Indeed, given the contentious and polarized nature of the existing international intellectual property debate,[73] it is virtually impossible to ignore the complex political dynamics in the international intellectual property system. Moreover, as Jeremy de Beer and Chidi Oguamanam observed, "That the topic is controversial and generates a wide array of differing perspectives should be a reason to engage it, not to shy away from it".[74]

To avoid politicizing training and educational programs, it will be

---

[69] Yu, *ACTA and Its Complex Politics*, note 40 above, at 13.
[70] Ibid, 15; Yu, note 47 above, at 375.
[71] Yu, note 1 above, at 427.
[72] Milton L. Mueller, *Ruling the Root: Internet Governance and the Taming of Cyberspace* (Cambridge, MA: MIT Press 2002); A. Michael Froomkin, "Wrong Turn in Cyberspace: Using ICANN to Route around the APA and the Constitution", 50 Duke L.J. 17 (2000).
[73] Yu, note 7 above, at 7–10.
[74] De Beer and Oguamanam, note 8 above, at 31.

helpful to focus these programs on identifying the various positions the different players have taken and explaining their concerns and strategies. It will also be useful to document the state of play in the larger international intellectual property regime. Such documentation would provide the participants with important information about available opportunities in the international intellectual property arena as well as those potential allies that can help them achieve their development objectives.

By being balanced, transparent and inclusive, the programs will better equip the participants with the needed information concerning the complex politics within the international intellectual property system while avoiding further polarizing the debate. Such transparency and inclusiveness are indeed strongly supported by the WIPO Development Agenda, whose recommendations specifically mention the need for openness and transparency. Having balanced and transparent programs is also important because "even seemingly 'technical' training has embedded in it ideological views about the role of [intellectual property] in society".[75]

CONCLUSION

Redesigning intellectual property training and educational programs is important from the standpoints of both development and social justice. If we are to successfully reorient intellectual property law and policy toward the goals and principles of social justice, we need to go beyond discussion and analysis to think more about how intellectual property rights are taught in training and educational programs. After all, how these rights are exploited, protected, enforced, managed, interpreted or even perceived could affect the overall fairness of the existing intellectual property system – domestic and international alike.

Although this chapter draws on experiences and insights from a WIPO-commissioned study that focused primarily on policy issues and macro-level developments, much of the discussion in the chapter informs the debate on intellectual property, development and social justice. For example, a large part of this debate concerns developing countries – the marginalized community in the international intellectual property regime. Issues such as development, inclusion, access, empowerment, equality, fairness and justice are also important to both the micro- and macro-level debates. Challenges confronting the weak, the vulnerable, the marginalized and the otherwise disadvantaged also abound in both debates,

---

[75] Ibid, 9.

even though direct counterparts to developed, emerging and developing countries do not exist in the former debate.

Moreover, many of the developments brought about by the WIPO Development Agenda will benefit the marginalized communities in both debates. The recently-adopted Marrakesh Treaty to Facilitate Access to Published Works for Persons Who Are Blind, Visually Impaired, or Otherwise Print Disabled, for instance, responds to the needs, interests and concerns of both developing countries and the visually impaired in both developed and developing countries. Likewise, the marginalized communities in either debate remain highly alarmed by the over-enforcement, and at times abuse, of intellectual property rights.

Ultimately, different communities will need different training and educational programs. There is simply no universally effective approach to promoting development and social justice. What works well for one community may not work well for another. Thus, instead of using a top-down approach, trying to determine what intellectual property issues will be important to promote development and social justice, this chapter uses a bottom-up approach to identify options that can be used to redesign intellectual property training and educational programs. It is my hope that the provided discussion will not only make these programs more relevant and meaningful to marginalized communities, but will also provide a useful starting point for promoting a "social justice" dimension of intellectual property policy and research.

8. Intellectual property social justice in action: Public Interest Intellectual Property Advisors

Michael Gollin, Pacyinz Lyfoung, Lateef Mtima and Connor McNulty

INTRODUCTION

The 21st century is witnessing a transition from tangible goods to intangible assets having the highest economic value[1] and this has naturally pushed intellectual property (IP) laws and systems to the forefront of social change debates. The discussion has historically been polarized, between developed countries and big business interests positioned on one side, against developing countries, small business and social justice advocates for the poor. The former are depicted as seeking to maintain their economic dominance through the establishment of strong global IP law regimes, while the latter are typically portrayed as seeking to resist such efforts, following the rationale that IP tends to impede poor countries' development and keep their populations in poverty. But such binary thinking obscures the potential of intellectual property law and frameworks as social change mechanisms under a simplistic prejudice that IP necessarily serves only big business' purposes and helps the expansion of monopolistic powers.

A better view is that intellectual property law can serve as a powerful tool for social change, as part of the evolutionary shift of human activity and national economic output from tangible property to intangible property production and exchange. Furthermore, technological advances have accelerated those processes, pushing unknown boundaries in the domain of IP, making it harder for legal frameworks to catch up with, let alone

---

[1] *See* "Measuring the full impact of digital capital", accessed 14 October 2014 at http://www.mckinsey.com/insights/high_tech_telecoms_internet/measuring_the_full_impact_of_digital_capital.

anticipate, what IP's next form and appropriate management might be.[2] Within that context, empowering the disenfranchised to benefit from IP can help them participate in the growing creative and innovation economies, which is simultaneously a goal of social activism and a practical strategy for economic development.

This chapter goes beyond a critique of IP-related social deficiencies or injustices to articulate how IP law and practice can serve as an instrument for social change, focusing on the work of a leading NGO working for the global public interest in the IP context: Public Interest Intellectual Property Advisors (PIIPA). PIIPA's practical IP direct pro bono services can serve as a model for socially conscious interpretation, application, and adaptation of IP law, all necessary steps on the road toward IP Empowerment. To promote fairer and more equitable IP laws and practices, historically marginalized and underserved groups, as well as communities and nations from the developing world need assistance in critically assessing when to utilize the IP system for their best interests, or to seek changes to the system.

Empowering IP social entrepreneurs can help combat the problem of income inequality and disparate access to resources. We can look at the world as including IP "haves" and "have-nots" and reframe how IP practices from the IP haves can serve as an engine to bring benefits to the IP have-nots. One benefit is access to advanced technologies. For example, with life-saving medicines invented in wealthy countries, such as antiretroviral drugs for HIV/AIDS, national measures, public-private licensing and other sophisticated IP practices can accelerate access for poor people in developing countries. Similarly, advanced crops with desirable traits can become more widely available in poorer countries in collaborations under the terms of international treaties on plant protection. A second benefit that IP practices can achieve is support for creative enterprises in developing countries. For example, in the Nollywood case described below, use of copyright protections for Nigerian movies has led to increased revenue for the producers, and therefore higher incomes for directors, actors and crews, with higher investment and a growing creative sector. Thus, IP social entrepreneurial efforts can bring into a developing country more access to foreign modern advances, and more wealth to support local creative and innovation economies.

---

[2] Michael Gollin, *Driving Innovation: Intellectual Property Strategies for a Dynamic World* (Cambridge University Press, New York 2006), 25.

Balancing the Public Interest and Private Ownership in IP

To better appreciate the nature of IP law, it might be helpful to recall that law and legal constructs, if not from natural law genesis, are intended to reflect social values and establish rules of engagement among society's members.[3] Two generally accepted rationales for IP law have been that it provides a mechanism to trade/exchange intangible property of the mind and it protects the moral rights of creators/inventors over their creations/inventions.

Different types of IP protection apply to different types of intangible property and can have various public goods implications, with various mechanisms of private or public enforcement. Copyrights are important as they impact access to knowledge and information. Whereas copyrights do not cover names, trademarks and publicity rights do. Publicity rights are a very personal form of intellectual property, which does not protect a person's intellectual output but rather, provides for property rights *in attributes of the person itself*. Trademarks identify the origin of goods and services, which helps the producer control quality and which helps the consumer rely on that producer's quality of goods or services. Trademarks are vital in commercial contexts for most types of products and services.

In contrast, Geographical Indicators (GIs) also serve similar purposes of guaranteeing quality based on origin, but they are tied to geographic locations and instead of being private property rights owned and enforced by private individuals or companies, they are communal rights enforced by national governments. GIs tend to be used for food and craft products, and are discussed in relation to international food trade and indigenous or traditional cultural expressions.

Patents represent an intense level of protection, granting exclusivity to inventors to incentivize innovation. However, that exclusivity is balanced with several safeguards, such as publication of the invention, which enables others to use the information for their own research and efforts at innovation, and a 20 year time-limit, so that eventually, the invention will become part of the public domain. Furthermore, where there is a high-level public interest, exceptions and flexibilities are available: for example, in the field of global health, in the TRIPS agreement, compulsory licensing can be used to produce medicines necessary to address public health crises.

In contrast, trade secret protection relies on the fact that the knowledge is known to have commercial value but is intentionally kept secret by its

---

[3] *See* http://plato.stanford.edu/entries/law-ideology/ (accessed 14 October 2014).

owner's "non-competition" agreements. Unlike, patents, trademarks and copyrights, generally no government registration process is available or required.

Traditional or indigenous knowledge refers to the cultural heritage that is identified with many communities, generally passed down through generations, orally. Traditional knowledge (TK), especially as it relates to genetic resources (GR), has become particularly important with the advent of the Convention on Biological Diversity (CBD), which specifically references its protection and mandates prior informed consent from countries where TK/GR is obtained, with the requirement of a material transfer agreement, and equitable access and sharing of benefits. The World Intellectual Property Organization (WIPO) has formed a standing committee on Genetic Resources, Traditional Knowledge and Folklore to explore ways to apply principles of intellectual property protection to traditional knowledge.

IP related to plants falls under an assortment of legal frameworks. The TRIPS agreement requires that plants be patented unless a sui generis system is established. The Convention for the Protection of New Varieties of Plants (UPOV) provides such an alternative; however, its focus on plant breeders and industrial agriculture has raised controversy over farmers' rights and poorer countries' food security and livelihoods.[4] The CBD also comes into play with regards to obtaining biological materials from plants. Finally, the International Treaty for Plant Genetic Resources for Food and Agriculture (ITPGRFA) facilitates the transfer of genetic resources for 64 essential crops and forage species, with benefit sharing provisions.

Dynamic Nature of Intellectual Property Legal Frameworks

Probably more so than any other field of law, the IP legal framework is a very dynamic system where the law provides clarity to facilitate exchanges between parties who want such certainty in order to interact productively with each other, such as between inventors and employers and commercialization partners, while at the same time, the law also allows exceptions and flexibilities that could protect the essential public goods at stake in some situations, such as global health or food crises, as well as access to information and knowledge for human and economic development. When

---

[4] Tzen Wong and Graham Dutfield (eds), *Intellectual Property and Human Development: Current Trends and Future Scenarios, A Publication of Public Interest Intellectual Property Advisors* (Cambridge University Press, New York 2011), 121. *See also* Chapter 9 herein.

designing IP legal frameworks, especially at the national level, critically evaluating the types of public or private rights involved and assigning enforcement responsibility to private or public mechanisms is important.

For anyone to successfully navigate the complex IP legal system, expert assistance is required, and to promote a level playing field and the public interest, pro bono services were conceived as a central part of the mission of Public Interest Intellectual Property Advisors (PIIPA).

I. IP SOCIAL ENTREPRENEURSHIP IN ACTION: PUBLIC INTEREST INTELLECTUAL PROPERTY ADVISORS (PIIPA)

The re-organization of global trade in the 1990s mandated minimum international intellectual property standards for any Member State wishing to accede to the multilateral system of international trade embodied by the World Trade Organization, through the adoption of the TRIPS Agreement (Agreement on Trade-Related Intellectual Property Rights). In addition to international trade laws and regulations, other international treaties and agreements have expanded international intellectual property rights, such as the United Nations Convention on Biological Diversity (CBD), and the International Convention for the Protection of New Varieties of Plants. As these treaties have multiplied, their Secretariats have dealt continuously with issues involving the impact of intellectual property on developing countries and other public organizations. In addition, international organizations, such as WIPO, have examined in-depth the role of intellectual property in issues of particular concern for developing nations, such as traditional knowledge, cultural heritage and communal rights.[5]

Despite these rapid changes and their effects on developing countries, most developing countries do not have access to sufficient qualified intellectual property professionals who are willing and able to help them address the myriad issues they now face. Rather, most of the participants on the global and national stage were economists, academics, anthropologists, scientists and policy specialists, but not intellectual property professionals. In response to this need, in 2002, an international association of concerned individuals decided to establish a new public interest organization. The new organization was named Public Interest Intellectual Property Advisors (PIIPA), and was incorporated as a non-profit, tax-exempt

---

[5] *See* http://www.wipo.int/tk/en/ (accessed 14 October 2014). *See also* Chapter 8 herein.

global pro bono initiative to provide intellectual-property-related services for governments, agencies and research institutions in developing countries, other public interest organizations, local communities and even individual inventors.

Since its founding, PIIPA's service model has focused on more practical and less policy-oriented actions. PIIPA's goal is to demonstrate through direct services to concrete problems that IP does work for development, to provide balance and information from a neutral NGO perspective that may help harness the power of informed debate to solve problems, and combat the fear and ignorance that make solutions impossible and lead to protracted disputes. PIIPA's beneficiaries are finding new ways to solve problems in such contentious and difficult fields as traditional knowledge, biodiversity, health, and agriculture.

The rest of this chapter reviews the global public interest IP context in which PIIPA's approach serves a unique niche responding to the growing need for intellectual-property-related legal and professional assistance for developing countries, and in the public interest. It also reflects upon PIIPA's decade-long experiences via case studies and educational activity highlights.

II. GLOBAL PUBLIC INTEREST IP SECTORS.

The following section discusses specific examples of intellectual property-related issues that affect developing nations and the need for professional legal assistance to address such issues.

A. Agricultural Technology

The protection of agricultural technology, and biotechnology in particular, is an important and contentious area of intellectual property. Agricultural biotechnology, in its broadest interpretation, refers to the application of biotechnology to agricultural problems in order to increase crop yields, open up new growing environments, use fewer chemical pesticides, improve nutritional content and decrease energy consumption in growing and processing.[6] The highly-touted benefits of agricultural biotechnology are not readily accepted by everyone, and many have concerns

---

[6] *See* Michael A. Gollin, "At the Crossroads: Intellectual Property Rights and Agricultural Biotechnology 1", Third Asia-Pacific Conference on Agricultural Biotechnology: Issues and Choices, Thailand (1996) (on file with author).

ranging from possible increased use of herbicides to unintended effects stemming from the planting, use and consumption of genetically modified organisms. Along with the rapid pace of technology innovation, a host of legal mechanisms for protecting the intellectual property rights in these agricultural biotechnology advances have developed.[7]

Major changes in the legal regime surrounding agricultural biotechnology have occurred in recent decades, ranging from a requirement of the International Union for the Protection of New Varieties of Plants (UPOV) that "[e]ach Contracting Party shall grant and protect breeders' rights",[8] to the United States Supreme Court's decision in *Diamond v. Chakrabarty* that genetically modified bacteria are "compositions of matter" or "manufacture" subject to patenting.[9] This legal regime continues to evolve.[10] In 2013, the US Supreme Court's Myriad decision restricted gene patenting to sequencing with high frequency of human intervention,[11] to the alarm of many in the biotechnology sector and to the continued scrutiny of the rest of the world, which refers to US patent law as guidance on international gene patenting standards.[12]

Also, the enforcement of intellectual property licensing strategies by agricultural biotechnology companies has led to high-profile court challenges against farmers, for example in the Canadian case of *Monsanto v. Percy Schmeiser*.[13] Intellectual property concerns pervade even technical, non-legal measures to prevent farmers from re-using seeds from past growing

---

[7] For a discussion of these various mechanisms in the United States and elsewhere in the world, see Neil D. Hamilton, "Who Owns Dinner: Evolving Legal Mechanisms for Ownership of Plant Genetic Resources", 28 Tulsa L.J. 587, 594 (1993).

[8] UPOV, note 3 above, art. 2.

[9] 447 U.S. 303, 310 (1980).

[10] See discussion of Harvard Mouse in Michael A. Gollin, "Answering the Call: Public Interest Intellectual Property Advisors" 17 Wash. U. J. L. & Pol'y 187 (2005).

[11] *Association for Molecular Pathology v. Myriad Genetics*, 569 U.S. 12-398 (2013).

[12] PIIPA's IP Audit of CIAT, Staff Interview, January 2014. The patentability of genes, whether human or from any biological source, remains an issue with a wide diversity of opinions and with the US taking the lead of on a certain approach .

[13] [2004] 1 S.C.R. 209, 2004 SCC 34, accessed 14 October 2014 at http://scc-csc.lexum.com/scc-csc/scc-csc/en/item/2147/index.do. This landmark case brought issues of biotechnology patenting at the forefront. It did not address the issue of accidental growing of patented seeds, however, it ruled that intentional planting of second generation patented seeds (even if first generation is uncertain) constituted "use" as prohibited under patent law.

seasons, such as the so-called genetic-use restriction ("Terminator") technology. Multilateral organizations such as WIPO and WTO have been involved in extensive reviews and discussions to mitigate detriments to small farmers and develop new legal mechanisms to cope with such restrictions.[14] Other IP management strategies also evolved from NGOs' and private foundations' engagement in the issues, such as complex licenses to preserve research for humanitarian purposes for golden rice[15] or grant making requiring grantees to adopt intellectual property terms facilitating technology transfer to poor countries.[16]

The rapid changes in agricultural biotechnology in recent years are likely to continue as genetic manipulation techniques open up new avenues for scientific research and new corporate business strategies confront farmers with the need to understand intellectual property rights. Developing countries and farmers, therefore, have a need to understand how these new technologies will impact them and how the decisions regarding the management of intellectual property rights in these new technologies will affect them.

B. Biodiversity

In 1992, the United Nations Conference on Environment and Development convened in Rio de Janeiro and created two international agreements – the UN Framework Convention on Climate Change and the CBD.[17] Generally, the CBD "established sovereign national rights over biological resources and committed member countries to conserve them, develop them sustainably, and share the benefits resulting from their use".[18] Although the CBD has now 193 parties and has been signed by at least 168 countries,[19]

---

[14] Gollin, "Answering the Call", note 10 above.

[15] Rice was engineered to include genetic material from daffodils causing vitamin A production. The resulting varieties have been as heavily praised by the biotechnology industry, see http://www.isaaa.org/kc (accessed 14 October 2014), as they have been criticized by the anti-genetic engineering movement, see http://www.grain.org/article/entries/4777-golden-rice-is-no-solution-to-malnutrition (accessed 27 October 2014).

[16] See http://www.mcknight.org/grant-programs/international/collaborative-crop-research (accessed 27 October 2014).

[17] United Nations Conference on Environment and Development: Rio Declaration on Environment and Development, Principle 22, 14 June 1992, 31 I.L.M. 874, 880 (hereinafter Rio Declaration)].

[18] See Gollin, "Answering the Call", note 10 above.

[19] See Parties to the Convention on Biological Diversity/Catagona Protocol on Biosafety, accessed 14 October 2014 at http://www.cbd.int/information/parties.shtml.

significant debate surrounded its passage and still plagues the implementation of the CBD today.[20] The 2010 Nagoya Protocol on Access to Genetic Resources and the Fair and Equitable Sharing of Benefits Arising from their Utilization supplements the CBD and provides for a more transparent legal framework on the CBD's objective to promote those issues.[21]

Many unique biological resources, which are concentrated in developing countries of high biodiversity, remain in demand as sources of leads for new products, or for scientific collections.[22] This demand has led many biodiversity-rich developing countries to exercise their rights over biological resources established by the CBD by enacting national laws and rules to protect their resources.[23] Requirements for informed consent and benefit-sharing as preconditions to access to biological resources have resulted in contractual arrangements between biodiversity source countries and biotechnology and pharmaceutical corporations seeking access to the biological resources, typically in the form of biodiversity prospecting agreements or access and benefit sharing agreements.[24]

Developing countries have a need for professional legal advice regarding the passage and implementation of effective laws, the formation and execution of appropriate biodiversity prospecting agreements, enforcement in the event of a breach, and in some instances, to defend against biopiracy. Source countries may place a high value on these contracts in monetary, environmental, and political terms. Thus, legal representation to adequately and appropriately handle the intellectual property issues that arise in the context of biodiversity prospecting agreements is crucial.

C. Traditional Knowledge

For several years, WIPO's Intergovernmental Committee on Intellectual Property and Genetic Resources, Traditional Knowledge and Folklore (WIPO IGC Committee) has been both examining the existing intellectual property mechanisms that could be used to protect traditional knowledge and debating the development of a sui generis system for protection of

---

[20] *See* Sarah A. Laird and Kerry ten Kate, "Biodiversity Prospecting: The Commercial Use of Genetic Resources and Best Practice in Benefit Sharing", in Sarah A. Laird (ed.), *Biodiversity and Traditional Knowledge* (Routledge, London and New York 2002), 241, 243.
[21] Nagoya Protocol, accessed 27 October 2014 at http://www.cbd.int/abs/text/.
[22] Laird and ten Kate, note 20 above, 241–2.
[23] *See* Gollin, note 4 above.
[24] *See* Gollin, "Answering the Call", above note 10, for more discussion on details of those agreements.

traditional knowledge.[25] WIPO Members have indicated that, depending on the country involved, a wide range of intellectual property laws may be available to protect traditional knowledge, ranging from patent to trademark to copyright to trade secret.[26] By 2013–2014, the IGC has been in the process of negotiating a WIPO Treaty on Traditional Knowledge, which is generating much debate, especially around the issue of the extent to which protecting TK would take away from the public domain.[27]

Regardless of an international treaty on TK, IP professionals can still provide critical expertise that could also be of great assistance in applying existing laws to particular situations, and in shaping existing or developing new laws to protect traditional knowledge. This need may be particularly great, for example, in developing countries that export crafts and natural products, and those where tourism plays a significant role in the country's economy.

D. Health Care

Access to essential medicines spurred much debate and action over the past decade. Ten years ago, developing countries of sub-Saharan Africa struggled with AIDS,[28] which went well beyond the scientific problem of devising a treatment to the formidable task of obtaining affordable versions of any treatments.[29] TRIPS requires its members to award "patents ... for any inventions, whether products or processes, in all fields of

---

[25] *See* WIPO Secretariat, *Review*, note 5 above; WIPO Secretariat, *Elements*, note 5 above; *see also* Chapter 9 herein.

[26] *See* WIPO Secretariat, *Review*, note 5 above, 3–6; WIPO Secretariat, *Report of Existing Intellectual Property Protection of Traditional Knowledge*, WIPO Doc. WIPO/GRTKF/IC/4/7 (5 November 2002) (reporting further responses to questionnaire on existing protection for traditional knowledge from the Fourth Session of the Committee).

[27] "New WIPO Text on Traditional Knowledge Protection Cleaner but Issues Remain", 28 April 2013, IP-Watch, accessed 14 October 2014 at http://www.ip-watch.org/2013/04/28/new-wipo-text-on-traditional-knowledge-protection-cleaner-but-issues-remain/.

[28] In 2000, it was estimated that since the AIDS epidemic began, over 15 million Africans have died from AIDS and almost 25 million sub-Saharan Africans are infected with HIV/AIDS. Press Release, The World Bank Group, World Bank Steps Up Fight Against AIDS in Africa (14 September 2000).

[29] *See* World Health Organization Essential Drugs and Medicines Policy (noting that 50% of the population in developing countries lack access to essential drugs and that 50 to 90% of drugs in developing countries are paid for out-of-pocket, which places the heaviest burden on the poor), accessed 27 October 2014 at http://www.who.int/medicines/en/.

technology, provided that they are new, involve an inventive step and are capable of industrial application".[30] Article 70(8) of TRIPS sets forth procedures for establishing "patent protection for pharmaceutical and agricultural chemical products".[31] Developing countries have attempted to avoid the drug-restrictive effects of patents in developed countries and their own by relying on the TRIPS parallel importation and compulsory licensing measures,[32] but these strategies have met with only limited success. The 2001 Doha Development Agenda (Doha Declaration), an agreement between WTO Members did not fully resolve the issue of lack of inequitable access to medicines.[33]

Despite significant advances in addressing the global HIV/AIDS crisis thanks to a plethora of public-private partnerships such as the Global Fund for AIDS, Malaria and Tuberculosis,[34] and the emergence of innovative R&D models, such as the Medicine Patent Pool,[35] nations are still engaged in long multilateral negotiations on global solutions for R&D on Neglected Diseases.[36] The practical use of intellectual property strategies on a case-by-case basis[37] can help leverage public health exceptions and flexibilities, such as compulsory licensing, to negotiate greater access to medicines with large pharmaceutical companies.

The 2003 WHO Framework Convention on Tobacco Control spurred recent challenges by tobacco companies claiming infringement of their trademarks in response to national efforts to regulate plain packaging of tobacco products.[38] In the past few years, both the WHO[39] and the

---

[30] TRIPS, note 1 above, art. 27(1), 332.
[31] TRIPS, note 1 above, art. 70(8), 351.
[32] *See* Carlos M. Correa, *Intellectual Property Rights, the WTO and Developing Countries: the TRIPS Agreement and Policy Options* (Zed Books, New York 2000), 42–4.
[33] For an overview and access to the relevant legal documents involved in the debate over TRIPS and the provision of pharmaceuticals to developing countries, including the latest materials relating to the Doha Declaration, see http://www.wto.org/english/tratop_e/trips_e/pharmpatent_e.htm (accessed 14 October 2014).
[34] http://www.theglobalfund.org/en/ (accessed 14 October 2014).
[35] http://www.medicinespatentpool.org/ (accessed 14 October 2014).
[36] http://www.who.int/phi/en/ (accessed 14 October 2014).
[37] Michael A. Gollin, *Sustainable Innovation for Public Health,* FDLI UPDATE MAG., Jan. 2002, accessed 14 October 2014 at http://www.venable.com/files/Publication/831fd999-70ae-402a-9a75-331d1eed437e/Presentation/PublicationAttachment/b93411a8-3713-4689-9e32-0dd0a1b6e1d4/816.pdf.
[38] http://www.nytimes.com/2013/12/13/health/tobacco-industry-tactics-limit-poorer-nations-smoking-laws.html?_r=0 (accessed 14 October 2014).
[39] http://www.who.int/nmh/events/2013/revised_draft_ncd_action_plan.pdf (accessed 14 October 2014).

174   *Intellectual property, entrepreneurship and social justice*

UN[40] adopted multilateral agreements on Non-Communicable Diseases, which opened the doors for a whole range of other global health activities, from more emphasis on nutritional quality of foods to new pushes for greater access to medicines for chronic diseases. Furthermore, in 2013, the WHO and the World Bank officially collaborated on joint indicators for universal healthcare, concretely pushing forward that agenda, in which greater access to generic medicines and preventative food security and quality priorities carry IP implications.[41] Those more recent global public health issues are broadening the range of global health public interest IP needs and expanding the scope of public interest IP impact on innovation in public health, as global society seeks to find an equitable balance between the public health needs of today and of tomorrow.[42]

E. Technology Transfer and the Environment

Developing countries are essential players in environmental conservation. Transfer of environmentally sound technologies is an integral, albeit still controversial and still to be fully realized, strategy of climate change efforts, as per Article 4.5 of the UN Framework Convention on Climate Change and Article 10c of the Kyoto Protocol.[43] Transfer of renewable energy sources and low greenhouse gas emitting engines and generators are initiatives promoted by the Global Environment Facility under the auspices of the IPCC.[44] As efforts to ensure environmentally sound technology transfer continue to grow, developing countries will increasingly be called upon to navigate thickets of intellectual property rights in order to license and access the relevant technologies.

Recently, the Global Environment Facility, the implementation fund for the CBD, funded the Asian Development Bank to design and pilot a marketplace broker bringing together low-carbon technology owners, buyers and financing.[45] Furthermore, WIPO started WIPO-Green, an online global network and marketplace for green technology exchanges,

---

[40] http://www.who.int/nmh/events/un_ncd_summit2011/en/ (accessed 14 October 2014).
[41] http://www.who.int/healthinfo/country_monitoring_evaluation/UHC_WBG_DiscussionPaper_Dec2013.pdf (accessed 14 October 2014).
[42] *See* Gollin, note 37 above.
[43] https://unfccc.int/cooperation_and_support/technology/items/1126.php (accessed 14 October 2014).
[44] Global Environment Facility (2004), *at* http://gefweb.org (accessed 14 October 2014).
[45] http://www.adb.org/projects/documents/establishment-market-place-transfer-low-carbon-technologies-asia-and-pacific-tcr (accessed 14 October 2014).

with the goal of facilitating and making progress on concrete green technology transfers.⁴⁶ IP with public interest dimensions remain a key feature of such climate change/green technology transfers.

F. Open-Source, Internet Access, and Information Technologies

The increasing need for access to, and reliance on Internet resources worldwide, including in developing countries, raises similarly pressing concerns about fair and equal access to these resources. Organizations such as Open Source,⁴⁷ IP Justice,⁴⁸ the Electronic Frontier Foundation,⁴⁹ the Global Internet Liberty Campaign,⁵⁰ and The Digital Divide Network⁵¹ have highlighted the public interest need for legal advice and representation in this evolving arena. Current concerns include building a global public domain of open source materials, the importance of copyright law and protecting individual privacy, to name just a few. As access to the Internet becomes more globalized, so do concerns about access and fair use. Professionals experienced in these intellectual property issues can help address the public interest needs for information access.

Recognizing that technology enables greater transfer and exchange of knowledge that can accelerate development, in 2011, WIPO's Committee on Development and Intellectual Property (CDIP) started implementing Recommendation 36 of WIPO's Development Agenda, focusing on exchanging experiences on open collaborative projects and IP-Based Models.⁵² In recent years, in the US, federal agencies have been looking into making available the "white space" in radio frequencies that would make access to the Internet free and easy, both providing more equitable access and possibly accelerating innovation,⁵³ thus maximizing the greater economic benefits of a "wifi future".⁵⁴

---

[46] https://www3.wipo.int/wipogreen/en/about/ (accessed 14 October 2014).
[47] *See* Open Source Initiative (2005), accessed 14 October 2014 at http://opensource.org.
[48] *See* http://ipjustice.org (2003) (accessed 14 October 2014).
[49] *See* http://eff.org (accessed 14 October 2014).
[50] *See* http://gilc.org (accessed 14 October 2014).
[51] *See* http://www.digitaldividenetwork.org (accessed 14 October 2014).
[52] *See* http://www.wipo.int/meetings/en/doc_details.jsp?doc_id=159417 (accessed 14 October 2014).
[53] *See* http://www.forbes.com/sites/parmyolson/2013/02/05/what-happens-if-america-gets-free-nationwide-wifi-google-wins-carriers-lose/ (accessed 14 October 2014).
[54] http://wirelessfuture.newamerica.net/ (accessed 14 October 2014).

III. THE PIIPA EXPERIENCE

For over more than a decade, PIIPA has brought together IP professional volunteers from its IP Corps to represent developing country clients and provide capacity building in more than a hundred international public interest IP projects in thirty developing countries. The following case studies illustrate the vast range and reach of PIIPA's direct assistance and educational activities.

A. PIIPA Case Studies

African Agricultural Technology Foundation[55] – Kenya – Biotechnology
Members of PIIPA's IP Corps assisted the African Agricultural Technology Foundation in bringing necessary technology to small, resource-poor farmers in sub-Saharan Africa. The IP Corps helped arrange negotiations between the International Maize and Wheat Improvement Centre (CIMMYT) and a private company for the development of herbicide-resistant maize varieties. Coated with the herbicide imazapyr, these varieties are effective against Striga, a witchweed that damages the welfare and livelihood of over 100 million people in sub-Saharan Africa. The Foundation stated that with sustained use of the maize, Striga could be ultimately eradicated in the long term.

Ibis Reproductive Health[56] – Zimbabwe and South Africa – HIV/AIDS Technology
PIIPA worked with Ibis Reproductive Health to bring anti-HIV/AIDS technology to vulnerable women in Zimbabwe and South Africa. In collaboration with several research partners in the US and Africa, Ibis is conducting a clinical trial in "Methods for Improving Reproductive Health in Africa" (MIRA). PIIPA's IP Corps members assisted the project by conducting a patent landscape analysis to ensure that the products studied and used in the trial were not protected by third-party patents. With PIIPA's further assistance, Ibis has explored ways to provide access to the study products (when they are proven to have effectiveness against HIV) to research participants, the local trial community of over 5,000 women, and to populations on a larger scale. In their opinion, PIIPA's assistance in addressing these access issues could secure a better chance for these products to end up more rapidly in the hands of women who need them most.

---

[55] *See* Gollin, "Answering the Call", note 10 above.
[56] Ibid.

Mycoguild[57] – International – Biotechnology

PIIPA helped develop mycotechnologies, fungi that may have enormous environmental benefits. Mycoguild is an international non-profit corporation founded to unite the scientific community, patent holders, governments, corporations and the legal community to further the use of mycology for environmental restoration. With the help of PIIPA, Mycoguild acquired legal advice in relation to a patent pool it is developing to enable the further commercial study and use of mycotechnologies (fungi and their ability to degrade pollutants). The patent pool was to benefit projects in water conservation, agriculture, salmon habitats and any entity or community with a contamination or pest issue. Mycoguild maintained that any country with an environmental issue was a stakeholder in the project, and that the long-term impacts of the project would include opening access to scientific research and ensuring a cleaner planet able to put "previously-contaminated land back to work". Mycoguild said that PIIPA had been an indispensable resource in the project, and presents a catalyst for social and environmental change.

International Alpaca Association (IAA) – Peru – Trademark

Alpaca farming provides an income for some of the poorest communities in isolated areas of the Andes. The International Alpaca Association (IAA), a Peruvian private-sector NGO, represents many of the area's independent breeders and fiber processors. An American farm applied to register the certification mark "Alpacamark" in the US. If the farm registered the mark, it could prevent the IAA in using its certification mark in the US, making it more difficult to export alpaca products. PIIPA's IP Corps members assisted the association in actions to oppose the US application. In its impact assessment, the IAA said that it would not have been possible for them as a NGO to undertake this project without the pro-bono assistance of PIIPA. In the long term, successful opposition would also help promote socially responsible business dealings with developing countries.

Kenya Wildlife Service (KWS) – Kenya – Biopiracy

PIIPA helped Kenya Wildlife Service (KWS) challenge alleged biopiracy. During a research mission, Genencor International took samples from a lake in Kenya without the authorization of the KWS. The samples were then found to contain a valuable enzyme that was used by Procter & Gamble in Tide detergent and stonewashed denim. No profits or benefits went to the country from which the resource was extracted. The KWS

---

[57] Ibid.

approached PIIPA to help them with legal assistance in the US, England, and Africa against the two multinational corporations. Negotiation between parties was intense and long-lasting.[58] Results were not publicly disclosed.

Datadyne – Sub-Saharan Africa – Open-Source Technology
The lack of public health information in sub-Saharan Africa has allowed the spread of disease. PIIPA helped Datadyne, a US-based consultancy, reverse this trend by creating inexpensive, open-source tools for data collection, analysis and utilization. The "EpiSurveyor" project targeted the entire population of sub-Saharan Africa – approximately 600 million people, of whom approximately 25 million were HIV-infected and in need of consistent and reliable healthcare. Working from the fact that people in the region relied on cell phones and rarely had Internet access, it let anyone collect and send data on a mobile device. It is now the World Health Organization's standard for data collection in sub-Saharan Africa. In their impact assessment, Datadyne stated that PIIPA's assistance through the IP Corps was essential in developing a workable open-source license that would otherwise have incurred a huge financial burden to the project.

Ibero American Science and Technology Education Consortium (ISTEC) – Americas and Iberian Peninsula – Digital Technology
The Ibero American Science and Technology Education Consortium (ISTEC) is an NGO comprised of educational, research, industrial, and multilateral organizations throughout the Americas and the Iberian Peninsula. Personnel at the University of New Mexico visited countries in Latin America and found a serious need for better technology in Latin America, as well as a lack of international cooperation in the field of information technology. They established ISTEC to foster scientific, engineering, and technology education; joint international research and development efforts among its members; and to provide a cost-effective vehicle for the application and transfer of technology. PIIPA provided pro bono assistance for ISTEC on IP matters relating to the International Symposium on Digital Libraries, an international conference created and supported by ISTEC. The symposium has been held annually in venues in Latin America and Spain since 2003. It provides a forum where the

---

[58] Mark Lacey, 'An Age-Old Salt Lake May Yield a Washday Miracle', *NY Times*, 21 February 2006, accessed 14 October 2014 at http://www.nytimes.com/2006/02/21/international/africa/21lake.html?pagewanted=print&_r=0.

most recent technologies and trends in digital libraries are presented and debated with emphasis on academic libraries and their supportive role for research and education in their institutions, as well as their contribution to the development of society. In addition, PIIPA assisted ISTEC to obtain trademark protection for the Symposium name and logos with the US Patent and Trademark office.

Harvest Plus – International – Biotechnology
Poor nutrition in developing countries causes anemia, blindness, mental retardation and other devastating health problems. PIIPA helped Harvest Plus make biofortified crops available in these countries to provide people with more of the nutrients they need. These crops had enhanced-ability to store iron and zinc, and could also be enriched in Vitamin A and other nutrients. This effort was divided into two phases, each of which focused on a group of crops of importance to developing countries. Harvest Plus is a "challenge program" of the Consultative Group on International Agricultural Research (CGIAR). PIIPA provided specific assistance on IP issues for Harvest Plus in the area of plant molecular biology, plant breeding and plant intellectual property and expertise on IP issues related to their strategic planning. PIIPA staff traveled to Cali, Columbia, to assist a Harvest Plus board meeting in better understanding the need for careful consideration of IP issues in their strategic planning. Through this project, healthier crops were brought to developing countries and malnutrition and disease were being fought.

National Institute for the Defense of Competition and Intellectual Property (INDECOPI) – Peru – Patents
Two US companies obtained US patents on extracts from maca plants, claiming to have discovered its medicinal properties – particularly its ability to boost libido. In fact, people in the Andes had been using the maca root in this way for centuries. The Peruvian Working Group (headed by the National Institute for the Defense of Competition and Intellectual Property, or INDECOPI) (the Peruvian Patent Office) requested PIIPA's pro bono assistance in challenging the validity of the patents, so that Peruvian farmers would not be prevented from preparing maca extracts for import to the US. PIIPA helped INDECOPI assemble evidence that the patents were invalid because of prior traditional knowledge – the patent owners were attempting to profit from knowledge they did not create. "The maca case has been used to raise awareness of the need to prevent misappropriation of biological resources and traditional knowledge through the grant of patents", said Begoña Venero of INDECOPI. "Assistance from PIIPA has been priceless".

National Institute for the Defense of Competition and Intellectual Property (INDECOPI) – Peru – Bilateral trade negotiations and disclosure of origin requirement

Peru's National Institute for the Defense of Competition and Intellectual Property (INDECOPI) asked PIIPA for pro bono assistance in preparing a legal analysis for bilateral trade negotiations between Peru and the United States. The US argued that international intellectual property treaties blocked Peru from having "disclosure of origin" requirements in its patent applications, where applicants are required to state where they obtained biological materials. PIIPA commissioned a pro-bono legal report on the subject from the IP clinic at American University's Washington College of Law. The report supported Peru's position that international treaties were compatible with Peru's initiative to enact disclosure of origin requirements. PIIPA published the report on the PIIPA website to assist other developing countries in bilateral and multilateral trade negotiations.

Amazonlink, Brazil and Peru – Trademark

Cupuacu is an Amazonian fruit, which serves as a primary food source for indigenous people in Brazil and Peru. It became a valuable export product because of its similarity to chocolate. A Japanese company tried to register the name "Cupuacu" as a trademark, to block Amazonian exports of the product. Amazonlink.org, a Brazilian NGO, approached PIIPA to assist with opposing the trademark "Cupuacu" filed in the US Founded in September 2001 in Rio Branco, Brazil, Amazonlink.org's mission was to "overcome political, cultural, ideological and linguistic boundaries in favor of collaboration in the pursuit of preservation of the Amazon and improvement of living conditions of its inhabitants". PIIPA secured counsel for the applicant, the Japanese company withdrew its trademark, and the matter was ultimately resolved without legal action.

Nollywood – Nigeria/US – International Nigerian Artists' Copyrights Protection

With an 85 per cent level of piracy, Nollywood, the emerging Nigerian film industry, needed measures to be immediately put in place to safeguard the continuity of its industry. The African Artists Collaborative (AAC) with PIIPA's support created a Copyright Registration Initiative and Online Infringement Removal Strategy. After copyrights registration and publication of the works in the United States, AAC identified infringing websites that illegally streamed the artists' films. PIIPA assisted AAC in utilizing the Digital Millennium Copyright Act to persuade Internet Service Providers (ISPs) that the unauthorized streaming violated the US copyright laws and infringed the artists' copyrights; PIIPA also helped in issuing Cease and Desist letters to infringers. Next, a "Copyrighted in the US" Logo Initiative was initiated in collaboration with the FAN-USA and PIIPA representing attorneys. The cost of the implementation of this Copyright logo campaign was born by the US-based African film distributors, even though it increased the product price. The success of these efforts sent an encouraging message to the African filmmakers, who were often skeptical about the practical application of Intellectual Property Rights to their works, that the AAC/PIIPA Copyright Registration Initiative could directly impact their revenue stream. Furthermore, with regards to US benefits, as a direct result of AAC's efforts, on 4 November 2010 in Brooklyn, New York, the Kings County District Attorney announced an investigation into the counterfeiting and illegal sale of movies from the Nigerian film industry. The DA noted that: "The sale of bootleg and counterfeit goods deprives the city and state of New York of millions of dollars in sales tax revenue, at a time when we all need it most, and it deprives the artists who made the movies of their well-deserved proceeds."

Fogarty Center of the US National Institutes of Health – International – IP Training Materials

The Fogarty Center of the US National Institutes of Health provides grants to International Cooperative Biodiversity Groups (ICBGs), which are teams of developing country researchers. The Fogarty Center arranged for PIIPA to help the grantees, with sample agreements, templates, lists of frequently asked questions, "do's and don'ts" and links to other relevant sources, and by arranging representation in negotiations. PIIPA provided a training session, and prepared the Bioprospecting Resource Manual and related training materials, all of which are posted on the PIIPA website.

World Intellectual Property Organization (WIPO) – Patent landscape report on avian flu

WIPO and the WHO commissioned PIIPA to produce a report on patent issues related to avian flu viruses and their genes. A team of PIIPA IP Corps members completed an initial patent landscape analysis, which was the basis for expert review and discussion in late 2007. The factual, neutral work of PIIPA's volunteers helped to untangle an international controversy, exemplified by Indonesia's refusal to provide avian flu specimens. PIIPA helped to remove obstacles to avian flu research, while protecting the ability of developing countries to share in the benefits of innovation.

PIIPA's Human Development and IP Book

In November 2010, PIIPA released a book "Intellectual Property and Human Development: Current Trends and Future Scenarios". Funded by the Ford Foundation, and prepared by PIIPA's global team of IP professionals and partners in human development, this book examines the social impact of intellectual property laws as they relate to health, food security, education, new technologies, preservation of bio-cultural heritage and contemporary challenges in promoting the arts. It explores how intellectual property frameworks could be better calibrated to meet socioeconomic needs in countries at different stages of development, with local contexts and culture in mind. Scenarios for the future are discussed. A resource for policy-makers, stakeholders, non-profits and students, this volume highlights alternative modes of innovation that are emerging to address such diverse challenges as neglected or resurgent diseases in developing countries or the harnessing of creative possibilities on the Internet. The chapters emphasize not only fair access by individuals and communities to intellectual property – protected material, whether a cure, a crop variety, clean technology, a textbook or a tune – but also the enhancement of their own capabilities in cultural participation and innovation.

IP, Research and Agricultural Development in Latin America and the Caribbean (LAC)

In November 2010, the International Center for Tropical Agriculture (CIAT),[59] PIIPA, and a core team of organizations organized a workshop in Cali, Colombia on *Intellectual Property, Research and Agricultural Development in Latin America and the Caribbean (LAC)*. More than 65 participants attended the workshop from eight countries, and represented the private sector, agricultural ministries, universities and research institutions in the LAC region. The workshop enabled an identification of the following key emerging demands for IP expertise within the region: (1) exchanging experiences of successful public-private partnerships and developing tools to help institutions monetize their IP assets; (2) connecting the IP Platform to a larger network of IP practitioners through institutions like CIAT and PIIPA; (3) creating capacity building tools aimed at university and regional research centers to equip them with basic IP management systems; (4) facilitating discussion and access to expertise related to the International Treaty on Plant, Genetic Resources for Food and Agriculture; (5) organizing workshops on open access and management of traditional knowledge; and (6) capacity building for plant variety protection, including protection under the International Union for the Protection of New Varieties of Plants (UPOV).

---

[59] International Center for Tropical Agriculture (CIAT) www.ciat.cgiar.org (accessed 14 October 2014).

Navajo Language Digital Preservation Project – US, Najavo Community

This project sought to promote the use of Navajo language related materials and the revitalization of the language. The material to be transcribed was a Navajo-only periodical that was printed in the 40s and 50s, Adahooniłigii. Since the publication of this newsletter there had been no other periodicals in only Navajo. The current availability of this periodical to the Navajo community was sparse. Krytle Seschillie, a young Navajo woman, could only make a digital copy of the periodical via her access to an Inter Library Loan as a university student. The Navajo public had no access to these materials, especially the Navajo language learner, or instructor in some cases. To make these available to everyone, Krytle needed to first verify that these articles were the work of a government office, The Department of Interior and Bureau of Indian Affairs, and as such were in the public domain. PIIPA assistance allowed the project to go forward.

IP Audit of Four Selected Colombian Agricultural Businesses – Colombia – Global Food Security and Farmers' Livelihoods

In the third phase of PIIPA's year-long project to enhance export opportunities for innovative high-value Colombian agricultural products, PIIPA IP Corps members conducted an IP Audit of four selected Colombian agricultural businesses. The project focused on identifying intangible assets, and examining and evaluating the strengths and weaknesses in the procedures used to protect each intangible asset and secure appropriate intellectual property rights. Where necessary, the audit provided tools to develop additional processes, make improvements to existing processes, and take correcting measures to help ensure capture of future intellectual property rights. According to Fruexcol, one of those four companies: "PIIPA's assistance has been an important support for our company because it helped us with accessing financial resources to participate in an international fair, which permitted us to reach new markets and realize the importance of the US and Canadian trademark processes. In addition, PIIPA provided ongoing legal assistance throughout those processes." PIIPA's involvement had a long-lasting impact, as it created a new awareness about the great importance of intellectual property at the company, which would help it ensure a good future for its people and their communities.

Ganga Library, Inc. – Global Digital Library for Public Access to Nobel Prize Winners' Materials

Ganga Library, Inc. is a non-profit organization seeking to establish a library holding media pertaining to Alfred Nobel and laureates, which is digital, global, multilingual, interactive and not-for-profit. Originally, they sought PIIPA's help to obtain permission from copyright holders to include their works in Ganga's library. Notwithstanding Ganga's lack of financial resources, PIIPA provided legal assistance to help the Ganga Library advance towards its goal at several steps of the way, including assistance with its organizational incorporation, which resulted in the ability to recruit community volunteers; with securing copyrights permission for a biography of Sir John Gurdon, Nobel laureate in Physiology or Medicine, 2012, that he had generously sent to the Library; with a trademark application at the USPTO, which is still pending; with drafting a letter requesting publishers to grant permission to include their media in the Library; and later, with negotiating fees. According to one of the Library founders: "PIIPA's assistance is enabling our Ganga Library to commence its mission of globally meeting the needs of people to access great ideas to solve scientific, social and planetary problems. Reading materials from brilliant minds is inspirational. Ganga Library kindles a fire in our patrons revealing to them their hidden aspirations, abilities and skills. We would like to express our gratitude to PIIPA for the immense help they are providing our library."

Device to Safely Mix Liquids in the Global Health Sector – Morocco
In 2008, Salah Aouads, a Moroccan inventor, came up with an idea to increase the safety of mixing liquids and decided to patent it. The director of the US National Institutes of Health's Office of Technology Transfer connected him to PIIPA for pro bono IP assistance. A private law firm took on his case, with several of their attorneys performing a prior art search, drafting and filing a patent at the USPTO, first as a provisional patent in 2011 and then as a non-provisional patent in 2012. Thanks to that experience, Mr. Aouads self-filed a PCT at WIPO from Morocco. This resulted in a favorable written opinion from the international search authority (ISA). In the meantime, Mr. Aouads started working on creating a structure capable of raising the necessary funds to extend the patent to the rest of the world, with the national phase starting in 2013, and to support the possible development of the device, without success. That setback forced him to switch his plans from a complex business that would cover the whole distribution process from conception to protection/patenting to development and then, commercialization, to a simple business based on conception, patenting, and then licensing/technology transfer. Mr. Aouads came back to PIIPA to solicit additional pro bono assistance with this next phase of his innovation journey, which would eventually increase safety in the global health sector.

B. Conclusion Highlights from PIIPA's Body of Work on Global Public Interest IP

The added-value of a global public interest IP network and clearinghouse
PIIPA's body of work focusing on global public goods for over a decade demonstrates the utility of public interest IP in leveling the playing field of IP, whether working with individuals, communities, developing countries or developed world entities benefiting developing countries. Furthermore, PIIPA's business model of direct services focusing on concrete action and concrete needs achieves real local impact, despite polarization in global IP policy and advocacy. PIIPA has helped create international standards that were adopted by multilateral organizations, such as the WHO's use of Datadyne's open source data collection and transmission via mobile phones, which is now a standard practice for data collection in sub-Saharan Africa. PIIPA's neutral positioning as a pro bono organization gives it an advantage in helping resolve IP stalemates between polarized IP opponents, such as between the government of Indonesia and the WHO, during the avian flu crisis, through the collection and analysis of a flu patent landscape report providing objective information that can facilitate negotiations. PIIPA's work with the CGIAR's Harvest Plus program helped provide critical IP guidance and expertise in the development and distribution of fortified food that can contribute to global food security. PIIPA's interventions have led to the establishment of long-lasting public institutions further promoting technological innovation in a broad range of areas, from a patent pool to fully develop the potential of mycotechnologies' ability to degrade pollutants to the creation of a digital library sharing the works of Nobel Prize winners to inspire other innovators.

The foregoing are only a few examples from over 100 projects PIIPA completed in the past ten years. PIIPA's approach to effectuating intellectual property social justice empowers people via IP tools and mechanisms, and stands out as a uniquely pragmatic way to find practical solutions despite polarized views. In essence, PIIPA's work evidences that socially responsible IP development and exploitation is not only a real and viable option, it is also an integral part of promoting social justice and sustainable economic development around the world.

PIIPA's creation of a global community of public interest IP lifelong volunteers and its impact on the legal profession
One of PIIPA's most remarkable achievements has been its ability to foster a community of talented and dedicated IP attorneys who have developed long-term commitments to public interest IP, in addition to their own busy

professional careers. The list is extensive, but the two following examples illustrate the types of impact PIIPA has had on the profession.

Venable LLP, a US law firm, supported the establishment of PIIPA in Washington, DC, as an outgrowth of Venable's pro bono program, with contributions of time by PIIPA founder and Venable partner Michael Gollin and other attorneys and staff. The firm has provided steady in-kind contributions of time and space throughout PIIPA's existence, and firm attorneys have handled numerous pro bono matters. This support has been a crucial component in PIIPA's success.

Jorge Goldstein first volunteered for the Maca case in the mid-2000s, which led him to take human rights classes, and inspired him to create a pro bono program on IP and Human Rights at the law firm where he is a partner. Pro bono service is part of his legal practice, and he speaks at global IP public good events and advises on specific projects. His continued support of global public interest IP led him to serve as a member of PIIPA's Board of Directors.

Donna Perdue first assisted with a small project for a statement paper on the topic question, "How Have Technological Developments and Structural Changes Affected the Competitive Dynamics of the Seed Industry?", for the "Agriculture and Antitrust Enforcement Issues in Our 21st Century Economy" meeting in Ankeny, Iowa in 2010.[60] After starting her own law firm, she volunteered for a bisphenol A (BPA) alternatives project for The Center for International Environmental Law (CIEL), conducting a patent landscape partly about BPA. The project specifically examined whether legislation restricting BPA drove patenting of alternatives, looking at activity over time. Next, she worked with other PIIPA IP Corps members on a WIPO Plant Salinity tolerance patent landscape project, investigating developments for increase plant tolerance to soil salinity, in light of anticipated increased salinity of soils. Later, she joined the PIIPA pro bono team conducting an inventory of intellectual assets for a global agriculture R&D center. Over the years, Donna Perdue's contribution to public interest IP in the global agriculture sector as a repeat PIIPA volunteer has been exemplary.

---

[60] USDA report at http://www.justice.gov/atr/public/workshops/ag2010/ (accessed 14 October 2014).

CONCLUSION

At the systemic level, PIIPA's IP pro bono activities have provided an avenue for private law firms to promote pro bono responsibility among their IP attorneys while giving them unique international IP experience that they might not have found in their regular practices. Firms like DLA Piper, Venable and Steptoe and Johnson have recruited full teams of attorneys to complete innovative public interest IP projects, such as the IP audit of the agricultural sector for a whole country like Colombia, the groundbreaking clarification of global innovation on plant-resistance to climate change factors, or the concrete articulation of the role of IP in including women and girls in global human and economic development. Such public-private collaborations between PIIPA and private law firms, harnessing the excellence of private IP sector resources for public interest IP and fostering knowledge exchanges between public and private IP attorneys as well as between North and South IP attorneys, have resulted in invaluable contributions to global public goods.

PART III

Engagement and activism

9. Worth more dead than alive: Join the NoCopyright Party and start killing copyrights for their own good
Ann McGeehan

INTRODUCTION – WHAT WOULD THOMAS JEFFERSON DO?

We should have listened to Thomas Jefferson. Ever-suspicious of both monopolies and legislators, he wanted the Constitution to say:

> Monopolies may be allowed to persons for their own productions in literature and their own inventions in the arts for a term not exceeding __ years but for no longer term and for no other purpose.[1]

In other words, no monopolies would be allowed except for patents and copyrights, and even those rights could not extend beyond a constitutionally-set maximum term. Apparently, Jefferson felt that legislators could not be trusted when it came time to setting – or extending – the terms of patents and copyrights, and was hoping for something stronger than the Constitution's "limited times" language.[2] True to form, legislators soon proved him right, by extending copyright terms from the original

---

[1] Letter from Thomas Jefferson to James Madison (28 August 1789). It is regrettable that Jefferson's commitment to the freedom of ideas did not extend to the freedom of the human beings under his personal dominion. *See* Lucia C. Stanton, *"Those Who Labor for My Happiness": Slavery at Thomas Jefferson's Monticello* (University of Virginia Press, Charlottesville 2012). Nevertheless, as shown below, his ideas regarding the importance of the public domain can be used to provide social justice for historically marginalized groups today.

[2] U.S. Const. Art. 1, § 8, cl. 8 (empowering Congress to "To promote the Progress of Science and useful Arts, by securing for *limited Times* to Authors and Inventors the exclusive Right to their respective Writings and Discoveries") (emphasis added).

maximum of 28 years to 42 years in 1831, to 56 years in 1909, to life plus 50 years in 1976, and to the current term of life plus 70 years – life plus three generations – in 1998. In a cruel twist that Jefferson might nonetheless have approved of (at least in principle),[3] the Supreme Court has refused to get involved, and (adding insult to injury) has even pointed to Congress's repeated extensions as evidence that the practice must be constitutional.[4] The only thing we know for sure about the meaning of "limited times" is that some members of our Congress have believed – and others can presumably be persuaded to believe – that it means anything up to and including forever minus a day.[5]

Jefferson didn't actually say what his preferred maximum term would be; he left a blank. It's doubtful, however, that he would have tolerated more than 28 years. After all, he lumped copyrights with patents, and the maximum patent term in the 1790 Act was 14 years, which may well have seemed generous in view of the fact that most countries did not grant patent rights at all.[6] Let's assume he would have filled the blank with 28 years – the maximum possible term for a copyright under most generous pre-constitutional state statutes,[7] and the maximum possible term

---

[3] *See* Letter from Thomas Jefferson to Abigail Adams, 11 September 1804 ("The Constitution . . . meant that its coordinate branches should be checks on each other. But the opinion which gives to the judges the right to decide what laws are constitutional and what not, not only for themselves in their own sphere of action but for the Legislature and Executive also in their spheres, would make the Judiciary a despotic branch.").

[4] *See Eldred v. Ashcroft*, 537 U.S. 186, 201-04 (2003); ibid, 204 ("The [Copyright Term Extension Act] follows this historical practice [of retrospectively extending existing copyright terms] by keeping the duration provisions of the 1976 Act largely in place and simply adding 20 years to each of them. Guided by text, history, and precedent, we cannot agree with petitioners' submission that extending the duration of existing copyrights is categorically beyond Congress' authority under the Copyright Clause.").

[5] 1998 Congressional Record, Vol. 144, Page H9951 (7 October 1998) (remarks of Congresswoman Mary Bono).

[6] Letter from Thomas Jefferson to Isaac McPherson, 13 August 1813 ("Accordingly, it is a fact, as far as I am informed, that England was, until we copied her, the only country on earth which ever, by a general law, gave a legal right to the exclusive use of an idea. In some other countries it is sometimes done, in a great case, and by a special and personal act, but, generally speaking, other nations have thought that these monopolies produce more embarrassment than advantage to society; and it may be observed that the nations which refuse monopolies of invention, are as fruitful as England in new and useful devices.").

[7] *See* Francine Crawford, "Pre-Constitutional Copyright Statutes", 47 J. Copyright Soc'y U.S.A. 167, 177–8 (2000) (setting forth durations of copyrights in the states prior to the Constitution).

under the Copyright Act of 1790. If we make that assumption, that means that in 1790, Jefferson considered 28 years to be more than sufficient to "Encourage Learned Men to Compose and Write useful Books" – which, to Jefferson, would have been the main point of copyright law.[8]

In other words, under a social contract theory, while Jefferson understood that the public must suffer "the embarrassment of a monopoly" for some period of time in order to get people to create copyrighted works, he would not have wanted the public to suffer that embarrassment any longer than necessary. The fact is, for copyrighted works to do their best work to "promote progress" and "encourage learning",[9] they should come into the public domain at a time when they are still relevant to that endeavor.

The folly of copyright term extension (as opposed to contraction) has been pointed out again and again. Given the huge increases in population, affluence, and access to markets domestic and foreign, copyrightholders today stand to make more money than ever before from their copyrighted works. And the potential benefits to the public of putting works into the public domain are far greater than ever before – public domain works are instantly accessible for free by anyone with an Internet connection, and, with the advent of the Internet and huge, searchable databases, the value of having non-obsolete materials in the public domain cannot be overestimated.[10] All relevant factors – including the copyright system's implicit promise of social justice[11] – should have pushed the "social contract" in the direction of shorter terms, not longer.

Sadly, the chief beneficiaries of copyright term extensions are not up-and-coming creators; instead it's typically soul-less corporations or the heirs of long-dead creators, seeking to prolong the income streams from

---

[8] The Statute of Anne (1709), from which our copyright laws derive, gave as a primary purpose "the Encouragement of Learned Men to Compose and Write useful Books".

[9] Remember, the initial purpose of copyright law was to "Promote the progress of Science" for the "encouragement of learning", and the subject matter of the 1790 Copyright Act was limited to "maps, charts, and books". Copyright Act of 1790, 1 Stat. 124. Although the subject matter of copyright now includes subject matter that is designed more to entertain than educate, that does not provide any reason to think copyright terms should be longer. Any entertainer whose works still entertain 28 years after creation has already made a pile of money.

[10] The only works that we know for sure are in the public domain are those that were created in 1923 or earlier. There is a wealth of interesting work there, but it is almost only of historical interest. It is not fulfilling the Constitutional directive of "promoting progress in science".

[11] Lateef Mtima and Steven D. Jamar, "Fulfilling the Copyright Social Justice Promise: Digitizing Textual Information", 55 N.Y.L. Sch. L. Rev. 77 (2010/11).

their already-too-long monopolies. And in many cases, these monopolists are not even U.S. monopolists,[12] so the whole argument that "helping" copyrightholders this way somehow benefits the U.S. economy is both laughable and specious. In operation, and absent a "moral rights justification", the extreme length of copyright terms, and the repeated extensions for the benefit of the few is akin to using the tax system to get the rest of us – including the marginalized groups that have the most to gain from a vibrant public domain – to pitch in to build Bill Gates a yacht.

But enough has been written about all of that. It's time for us to do something about it. Below, we demonstrate, as a theoretical matter, that a copyright is "worth more dead than alive"[13] – specifically, that the social value of a work in the public domain is far greater than the social value of the same work under copyright. That being the case, game theory and economics-101 tell us that the public and the copyright holder should agree upon terms for euthanizing the copyright: the public should be willing to pay, and the copyright holder willing to accept, any amount over the amount the copyrightholder would have earned over the life of the copyright. Killing copyrights in this way would release the deadweight loss caused by the copyright monopoly, with a net gain to society. We then propose to demonstrate, with your help, the value-generating effect of killing copyrights, by simply doing it, en masse. When people have become comfortable with this use of disruptive technology[14] to maximize social value and attain social justice, we will move on, by expanding the reach of the program beyond the borders of the United States, and beyond copyrights to patents.

---

[12] Jonathan Band and Jonathan Gerafi, "Foreign Ownership Of Firms in IP-Intensive Industries", (March 2013), accessed 14 October 2014 at infojustice.org/wp-content/uploads/2013/03/foreignownrep.pdf.

[13] Mr. Potter to George Bailey, *It's a Wonderful Life* (Liberty Films 1946). Part of the reason that quote is so familiar is that the movie, *It's a Wonderful Life*, was considered to be in the public domain from 1974 (when the film company failed to renew its copyright in the film) to 1993 (when the successor-in-interest to the film company began asserting its rights based on the fact that the film was a derivative work of a copyrighted story, to which the successor-in-interest held the film rights). *See* http://en.wikipedia.org/wiki/It's_a_Wonderful_Life (accessed 14 October 2014). There can be little doubt that the movie created more social value while copyright-free than under copyright, proving the point that copyrights are almost always worth more dead than alive.

[14] Joseph L. Bower and Clayton M. Christensen, "Disruptive Technologies: Catching the Wave", 73 Harv. Bus. Rev. 43–53 (1995); *see also* "The Rewards of Risk, What You Can Learn from Mavericks, Daredevils, and Troublemakers", *Outside Magazine* (December 2013) (special "Disrupters" issue).

A CALL TO ACTION

Consider this chapter a call to collective action to restore copyright terms to Jefferson's original vision. Cap them at a total of 28 years – ideally less.[15] Think about it – if copyright terms had been constitutionally capped at 28 years, everything published before 1986 would simply be in the public domain, no questions asked. Instead, where are those works today? Well, a vanishingly small fraction of them – like Martin Luther King's "I have a Dream" speech,[16] like Disney's *Snow White*,[17] and like the Happy Birthday Song[18] – are still making money for the copyright holders, and are thus available to us, the public, at monopoly pricing. For most of the rest – literally millions upon millions of works – the copyrightholders – who are often dead or impossible to identify – have almost zero expectation of making any money from the works, and the public nevertheless has almost zero access to them. It does not take a rocket scientist to realize that the lack of access to this information is suboptimal. Useful information contained in millions of books is simply hidden from view, at the very moment that technology has handed us the tools to easily search, access and learn from these works.

---

[15] Jefferson would doubtless see even a 28-year term under today's conditions as vastly excessive. Five years would be more like it – if copyright terms were limited to five years, then (as of this writing) everything written before 2009 would be in the public domain, and available for all to use, at no cost. A five-year term would provide a more-than-sufficient reward to creators, and would make for a vibrant, up-to-date public domain that would extend new opportunities for learning, creativity, and social advancement to marginalized groups. But instead of reducing copyright terms to keep the copyright reward at a constant value, our legislators have expanded them again and again, and thereby made a mockery out of the idea of using the public domain to promote the progress of anything.

[16] *Estate of Martin Luther King, Jr., Inc. v. CBS, Inc.* (194 F.3d 1211 (11th Cir. 1999). Iro-ny *noun* \ī-rə-nē also |ī(-ə)r-nē\: The fact that this clarion call for social justice has remained shackled as "private property" for the last half-century.

[17] *Snow White* was released in 1937 (http://en.wikipedia.org/wiki/Snow_White_and_the_Seven_Dwarfs_(1937_film), accessed 14 October 2014), while the 1909 Act, with its 56-year term (including renewal) was in effect. Its copyright would have expired in 1983, but for the fact that the 1976 Act increased its term (as a work for hire) to 75 years. It would have expired "again" in 2012, but for the fact that the 1998 CTEA extended its term to 95 years. Absent further extensions, it will fall into the public domain in 2032.

[18] While there are legitimate questions about whether the Happy Birthday Song is actually under copyright, that has not stopped Warner Brothers from attempting to enforce a copyright in it. Robert Brauneis, "Copyright and the World's Most Popular Song", GWU Legal Studies Research Paper No. 1111624 (2010).

Will early public release of these works ever happen through legislation? Not likely. Treaty obligations prevent it. Based on our accession to the Berne Convention, the United States is obligated to provide at least a life-plus-50 term for most kinds of works,[19] and our own trade representatives are hard at work trying to up this to life-plus-70.[20] The chances that the U.S. will repudiate these positions and enact shorter terms are nil.

HOW TO CONVERT $100 INTO $3 MILLION

So here's what we do. Initially, let's consider copyrighted books. Everyone who owns or thinks they own a copyright in a non-fiction book that was published before 1986, raise your hand. Yes, you. Now, consider how much money that copyright has made you in the last 10 years. If the answer is zero, you're in luck. The NoCopyright Party will give you $100 for the copyright right now, and will take the copyright back behind the barn and put a bullet in its head.[21] That will put the book in the public domain and make sure the world gets easy access to the book. We will also let the world know what a great and selfless individual you are, for agreeing to let us kill your copyright.[22]

Why are we willing to pay that money? Because we are 100 per cent confident that your book, once in the public domain, will create much more than $100 of value for the public. And we're willing to give away $1,000 of our own money to prove it. If we donate it to the public domain, we will feel that we are donating not just $1,000, but a value many times

---

[19] Berne Convention Art. 7(1).
[20] Article 4.3 of the current draft of the Trans-Pacific Partnership Free Trade Agreement provides that copyright terms shall be "not less than the life of the author and 70 years after the author's death". *See* http://en.wikipedia.org/wiki/Trans-Pacific_Partnership_intellectual_property_provisions#Article_4:_Copyright_and_Related_Rights (accessed 14 October 2014. Mexico, which has a copyright duration of life plus 100, has apparently proposed that other members of the partnership adopt that term as a norm. *See* https://wikileaks.org/tpp/static/pdf/Wikileaks-secret-TPP-treaty-IP-chapter.pdf (accessed 14 October 2014), at 51.
[21] Email us at party@nocopyright.com (subject line: "kill it off").
[22] The first ten takers will get the $100 right off the bat. For everybody else, we will do everything we can – as explained below – to make sure you get your $100. Fine print: We reserve the right to not pay if we genuinely think you are trying to take advantage of us. But if your book was published by a major publishing house, and is over 100 text-filled pages long, we cannot conceive of a reason not to pay you the $100. We're limiting this unconditional offer to non-fiction books right now, but if you have a copyright in anything else that you'd like to sell us for $100, just let us know.

that. Consider: A book that has been published has gone through a significant acceptance process, and represents countless hours of sustained effort by the author, not to mention reviewers, editors, fact-checkers, and proofreaders. Conservatively speaking, it seems reasonable to assume that the value to each member of the United States public of having such a worked-over work in the public domain is at least one cent. We honestly believe that the welfare of every single person in the United States would be increased by at least that much, by the mere possibility of having free access to *your* book. If that's right, our $100 investment creates $3 million in value for the U.S. public.[23] That's a pretty good return on a charitable investment.

And, for only a limited time,[24] we'll extend this unconditional offer to non-fiction books copyrighted *after* 1985 as well. So anybody who's got a deadweight copyright on your hands: here's your chance to make $100 and be a hero.

IF YOU'VE GOT $100, YOU CAN DO IT TOO

While we currently have to limit ourselves to giving our own money to the first ten takers of this offer, we're pretty sure that we can help the rest of you get your $100 too. The case for creating $3 million of social value for a mere $100 sells itself; in fact, if you are reading this article, and agree that $100 is a good price for getting a copyright in a relatively-recently published book into the public domain, please send us an email. We'll match you to an author willing to part with his or her copyright at that price, and the world will be a better place – you will have done your part to advance the cause of social justice via release of intellectual property.

What if you don't agree that getting a single work into the public domain is worth a penny-per-person? Maybe you would discount entirely the "potential" access of millions of citizens who we know darn well won't actually access and use the book. While we question that assumption – it seems to us that the potential to access a book has real value, even if the book is never accessed – we can still prove the net social value of a work in the public domain is many times greater than its net social value when under copyright, even if we focus only on the people

---

[23] Since the population of the United States exceeds 300 million, a penny-per-person comes out to more than $3 million.

[24] That's a joke – we mean "limited time" in the infinity-minus-one-day sense. Of course we are interested in more recent copyrights. In fact, we're more interested in them.

who actually would access the book. It's a simple matter of releasing deadweight loss.

The proof is as follows. Copyright law facilitates monopoly pricing. Under a monopoly, the monopolist maximizes profits at a point where supply is restricted. The loss to society as a result of the monopolist's artificially high price structure (and the reduced supply it entails) is called "deadweight loss".[25] The size of the deadweight loss is particularly great where the monopoly price far exceeds the "perfect competition" price. For IP-dependent products – like copyrighted works – the IP-protected price is often a significant multiple of the perfect competition price.[26]

Let's put it in concrete terms, and talk about physical books for a moment. Assume that under copyright, a book that costs $1 to print will sell for $15. People who think they might get anywhere from $1.01–$14.99 of value out of the book won't buy it – it's a losing proposition; they are priced out of the market. That's an inefficiency – the copyright-holder would love to sell the book to these people (since they'd be willing to pay him more than his cost of production), but he can't do so without losing money. Sure, if the monopolist lowers his price to $1.01, then the $1.01–$14.99 crowd will buy the book. When the price goes down, demand increases and supply rises to meet demand. But under monopoly conditions, the monopolist won't lower his price, since he would lose out on the big profits he was making on the people who were willing to pay $15 for the book. When the monopolist does the math, he realizes that he maximizes profits by keeping prices high. That results in a suboptimal

---

[25] *See, e.g.,* http://en.wikipedia.org/wiki/Deadweight_loss (accessed 14 October 2014).

[26] "Deadweight loss" is one of the greatest tragedies of using patent protection for incentivizing the creation of medically-important pharmaceuticals. The term "*dead*weight" has particular significance for historically marginalized groups, as the "need" for high on-patent prices can mean the death of marginalized patients who cannot afford the drugs that their bodies need to survive. *See Fire In the Blood* (2013 documentary) (documenting death of millions of Africans from AIDS stemming from big pharma's blockage of generic drugs). In an ideal world, there would be a way to compensate the inventor/patentholder up front for the value of the invention/patent, and then release the needed pharmaceutical into the public domain, thereby releasing the deadweight loss. If our legislators do not wake up and realize this one day soon, the crowd will have to take matter into its own hands, much as we are proposing for copyrighted works. To this end, we encourage interested readers to keep their eyes on www.patentbreak.com, a site under construction to break patent monopolies for global gain, and to watch for our forthcoming article, in which we explore ways of addressing the toxic deadweight loss in the pharmaceutical industry in the context of industry shenanigans that amplify that loss.

distribution – many people who would have been willing to buy the book for a dollar or more won't do so. Absent the ability to price discriminate, those are sales lost by the monopolist, and benefits lost to society.

By placing the book into the public domain, all of the people who were willing to pay $1–$14 for the book will be able to access and use the book and realize that value. The deadweight loss is released, and society benefits. The people who were willing to pay $15 or more for the book still get that value out of the book. But now, the masses of people who would have bought and benefited from the book at a lower price also get to enjoy it. With the $14 markup for the physical book, the amount of deadweight loss released will be a multiple of the social value of the book under monopoly.

In a world of physical books – and for that matter, other physical products – there is therefore always a net social benefit to breaking a monopoly. If it can be done with the monopolist's consent – by, for example, paying the monopolist one dollar more than the exact amount he would have made under monopoly conditions – everybody benefits, without disturbing the incentives for others to follow the path of the monopolist.

With the Internet and digital book readers, the model changes dramatically. Now the marginal cost of production (that is, another digital copy) is nearly zero, and the perfect competition price is, in fact, "free". But the monopolist still doesn't lower the price, even for a digital book, for the same reasons as above. Expressed as a multiple of cost, the profit margin for a copyrighted e-book is essentially infinite. Accordingly, for copyrighted works that can be digitized, the "deadweight loss" – and the social value realized from breaking the monopoly – can be enormous, since it encompasses the aggregate value of the work to every single member of society. With the advent of searchable electronic databases, great good can be done if reasonably current publications are available as search hits, and then available, without restriction, for further reproduction and study.[27] Even if we assume that a significant proportion of society will get zero value out of a given book, they may well benefit from the work of others that builds upon the copyrighted work. And in any event, we have to acknowledge that there are members of society that would get 10, 20, 40 cents worth of value out of having free access to and use of that book. Those nickels and dimes add up, quite possibly to millions of dollars. Accordingly, no matter how you look at it, paying $100 to put a published book into the public domain unlocks a social value worth many times that much.

---

[27] The current life-plus-70-year copyright term prevents this. The public domain is therefore virtually useless as a research tool, at least for conducting anything other than historical research.

With our $100 offer, we are aiming at low hanging fruit, and we believe that others will see the merit of investing $100 in this way. If you're the copyright holder and haven't been making money from the book, then you'll take the $100, and earn the gratitude of an adoring public, which will now have completely free access to your book. To sweeten the pot, for anyone who "buys" a copyright for the public domain this way, we will – at the donor's option – give the donor credit in several ways: we can embed some text of the donor's choosing on a page of the book, and we can give the donor (and other donors) recognition on the www.NoCopyright.com website. Any copy of the work downloaded from NoCopyright.com will have the embedded information.[28]

Of course, if you are a business, the embedded information can be an advertisement, your business will get philanthropic credit on NoCopyright.com, and you'll get a lot of good publicity for making such a civic-minded contribution. You'll want to consult a tax professional, but it seems to us that donating to the public domain for advertising purposes would be a tax deductible business expense.[29]

IF YOU'VE GOT $1, YOU CAN CREATE $30,000 VALUE

Under the above analysis, and as shown with more math below, the multiplier effect applies even when the copyright holder is making some money from the book. In that case, too, as a matter of simple mathematics, the public at large should be willing to pay the copyrightholder his expected income from the book up front, as a lump sum payment, in order to realize the multiplier effect that comes from unlocking the monopoly and getting the book into the public domain.

The easiest way to see this is to recognize that the money a copyright-holder makes from a book over the term of the copyright is money that is paid to the copyright-holder, by the public, one way or another, for access to and use of the book. In other words, for every copyrighted book, there is a value – let's call it V – that the public will, over time, give the copyright-holder. All we're proposing is that the public and the copyright-holder agree that the payment be made up front. If that can be arranged,

---

[28] Of course, since the work will be in the public domain, we will not be able to prevent downloaders from stripping the text out of the work in future copies that they distribute.

[29] 26 U.S.C. 162(a). Treas. Regs. §§ 1.162-1(a), 1.162-20(a)(2).

then there would be no real cost to either the public or the copyrightholder to getting the book into the public domain immediately. And the benefits to both sides would be enormous – the copyrightholder would get his money up front and guaranteed, and the public would immediately realize the value of unlocking the copyright.

To put an economics-101 spin on it all, consider that the social value of the book ("SV") is actually somewhat greater than V, because of "consumer surplus" – customers who buy the book for $15 might be getting $20 out of value out of the book. So:

$$SV_{copyright} = V_{c1} + V_{c2} + V_{c3} + \ldots + V_{cn}$$

Where V_{cx} is the actual value to the xth customer of the book, and "n" is the total number of customers who are willing to buy at the copyrighted price. But:

$$SV_{NoCopyright} = V_{c1} + V_{c2} + V_{c3} + \ldots + V_{cn} + V_{cn+1} + V_{cn+2} + \ldots + V_{cn+300,000,000}.$$

In other words:

$$SV_{NoCopyright} = SV_{copyright} + V_{cn+1} + V_{cn+2} + \ldots + V_{cn+300,000,000}.$$

Even if you don't think that free access to the work is worth a penny to the 300,000,000th person, you will have to admit that there is a lot of fat in $V_{cn+1} + V_{cn+2}$, and so on – these are the people who would buy the copyrighted work if it were priced just slightly lower than the copyrighted price. All of that value is released when the bonds of copyright are broken.

But even this equation doesn't capture the full social value of killing off the copyright. To be complete, the equation should take into account additional benefits to the author and the public. The author will benefit from wider distribution of one of her books, which should drive up demand for her other works, which she is free to leave under copyright, for the time being. The public also will realize additional benefits as other authors step in and create derivative works based on the unlocked book. Various intangible social benefits accrue – society as a whole may benefit from the free accessibility of the book, as that access might give rise to insights and creativity that will in turn benefit society. The following equation captures some of those benefits as well.

$$SV_{NoCopyright} = SV_{copyright} + V_{cn+1} + V_{cn+2} + \ldots + V_{cn+300,000,000} + V_{author} + V_{derivative\ works} + V_{intangible}$$

In other words, by unlocking any copyrighted work, a net social value of $V_{cn+1} + V_{cn+2} + \ldots + V_{cn+300,000,000} + V_{author} + V_{derivative\ works} + V_{intangible}$ is realized. While reasonable minds can differ as to what this value is for any given work, there is no dispute that it is there, for every copyrighted work, waiting to be released.

Thus, all that is needed is a mechanism to get civic-minded people and civic minded copyrightholders to work together to release this value. To facilitate this, the NoCopyright website will also have an important additional feature. It will allow copyrightholders to set their own price, and for bidders – the rest of you – to work cooperatively to meet the price, and to kill the copyright.

That way, the rest of you will get the same good, multiplier-effect-based feeling that we will get from buying up $100 copyrights and donating them to the public domain.[30] And you only have to put up as much as you feel comfortable putting up, all with the knowledge that your charitable dollars are experiencing the multiplier effect that comes from killing copyrights.

The implementation is simple, and is described in more detail in US Patent No. 8,484,120, under which www.NoCopyright.com is licensed. In short, if you are a copyrightholder, you provide us a copy of your work – preferably although not necessarily digitized – and prove to our satisfaction that you are, indeed, the copyrightholder. You then set a price, and enter a binding commitment such that, upon receipt of that price, your work is released to the public domain under a CC0 license. We then list your work, along with any description of the work that you care to provide, on www.NoCopyright.com, along with your asking price. Members of the public – subscribers to the NoCopyright Party newsletter, Facebook friends, and so on – then have the opportunity to bid on the work, with the goal of meeting your price before the deadline. Anyone who bids will have an incentive to persuade friends and family to bid as well, so that they too can experience the multiplier effect and benefit from any pot-sweeteners that we offer. Bidders can offer various kinds of matching bids, for example, agreeing to match a given dollar amount, or agreeing to pay a certain percentage of the remaining bid-price differential if others do the same. If your price is met, the work falls into the public domain, and everyone is happy. If your bid is not met, you have the option of accepting whatever the total bids are, or simply walking away from the

---

[30] In order to get works into the "public domain" – or as close as possible to being in the "public domain" – we would use the Creative Commons CC0 license (*see* http://wiki.creativecommons.org/CC0_FAQ), and apply the public domain mark to them (http://creativecommons.org/about/pdm) (both accessed 14 October 2014).

playground, taking your copyright with you. Disappointed bidders are either refunded their money, or are given the option of rolling it over into a subsequent "auction".

EVERYONE CAN PLAY – THE SKY IS THE LIMIT

We understand that some authors feel an attachment to their works, and might never want to let them go, even if they can get more money from NoCopyright than copyright. That's fine. But given that the terms of copyright are so long, many copyrights are held by the heirs of original authors. If you have inherited a copyright and don't know what to do with it, come to us. You'll certainly be able to get $100, and if you can persuade the crowd that it's worth more than that, the sky may well be the limit.

And of course, the NoCopyright Party is inclusive – we seek to get all useful works into the public domain. That means not just books, but anything else that might be subject to copyright, including pictures, photographs, computer programs, songs, sound recordings, architecture and videorecordings.[31] Indeed, certain creators, like photographers or graphic artists, might find that they can publicize and monetize their works instantly by putting them up for "auction" on NoCopyright.com. If enough graphic artists and photographers participate, we will build a library of high quality works that are guaranteed to be royalty-free, for use in PowerPoint® presentations and other designwork. Songwriters and recording artists can use www.NoCopyright.com not only to instantly monetize their works, but also to maximize their distribution, so as to showcase the creators' talents.

A WORD ABOUT TERMINATION RIGHTS

We anticipate that NoCopyright.com will be particularly attractive to creators and heirs who exercise their termination rights[32] to recover their copyrights, as it will provide an instant return on the termination endeavor. But there is also an altruistic point to be made here, in favor of simply exercising termination rights and putting the work into the public

---

[31] Of course, other copyrighted aspects of songs, music, movies, etc., such as performance rights, etc. might create complications to this analysis, but these can be addressed if all parties cooperate.

[32] *See* 17 U.S.C. §§ 203, 304(c), 304(d); 37 CFR § 201.10.

domain. Many of us grew up in the 1970s and 1980s, and doubtless some of our parents were writing books during that period, during the primes of their lives. Our parents are now either gone or in their 80s or 90s, and their books are forgotten. The copyrights are owned by publishers – possibly just the last in a long chain of mergers and acquisitions – and if things stay that way, the work won't see the light of day until 70 years after our hypothetical parent (i.e. the author) has died.

But the law provides a way for authors (or their heirs) to wrest their copyrights back from oblivion. The "termination rights" window is open for only five years, 35 to 40 years after the grant of a transfer or license for works created on or after 1 January 1978, 56 to 61 years after the copyright date for works published between 1955 and 1977, and 75 to 80 years from the date of copyright for certain works published before that. To exercise the right, you have to specify a date within the applicable 5-year window that you want the right back, and you have to provide notice to the current owner of the copyright two years before that date.[33] Roughly speaking, for a post-1977 work you need to provide the notice no later than 38 years from grant of the license or transfer (which will often be 38 years from the the copyright date); for a 1955–1977 work, you need to provide the notice no later than 59 years from the copyright date; and for a qualifying work that is over 75 years old, you'll need to provide notice before the 78-year point.[34] In other words, if you're reading this in 2014, the window for exercising your rights is open for works created and licensed or transferred in 1978 and 1979, and it will start to close soon – in 2016. Windows are also open for works copyrighted in 1936–1939 and 1955–1958, but they are closing fast.

So even if you miss out on the $100, we are calling on YOU to figure out if there are any termination rights in your family to be exercised. If so, you should exercise them, and then decide whether you want to kill off the copyright. Many aging academic authors would be delighted to know that their work has not died out – that it still comes up, in its entirety, on Google searches, even if there's no money to be made. Those books were labors of love to begin with; most authors feel a pang of remorse when they think that their work – with all of its hard-won wisdom and painfully polished prose – will never be read again. And remember, there is not a minute to lose. The window for providing notice is closing every day on dozens if not hundreds of works published in 1936 and 1955, and next year (2015) 1937 and 1956 will be on the block. Needless to say, if you do exercise termination rights

---

[33] 17 U.S.C. § 304(c)(4)(A); *see also* 17 U.S.C. § 203(a)(4)(A).
[34] 17 U.S.C. § 304(d)(2).

and euthanize your regained copyright, the NoCopyright Party would be proud to host the work on www.nocopyright.com.[35]

WHY BOTHER?

We've already explained how killing copyrights creates social value, promotes social justice, and makes everyone feel better all around. But you might think that it won't change your life. You can already get books you want from the library, and, even though much of what's available on the Internet is copyrighted, you can access most of it for free. YouTube is free, Netflix, Hulu and digital music are cheap, and reasonably rights-free digital art is relatively easy to find. Books are not all that expensive, and used books are downright cheap. And people are increasingly releasing things under Creative Commons licenses. If anything, you're concerned about information overload.

The difference is that the public domain is pure. Something that's in the public domain is free for everybody to use, in whatever manner they want. You might think you "own" a song you bought on iTunes, but just see what happens if you try playing it on a street corner.[36] And just because you checked an Arthur Miller play out of the library doesn't mean you're allowed to perform it, or adapt it for children. You might be able to read something online, but can you legally save a copy of it for later viewing? The NoCopyright movement will show the world the awesomeness of having modern works truly[37] in the public domain. And it will not stop

---

[35] Unless we deem the content inappropriate. A "beta version" of a tool for determining whether you can exercise termination rights is available from Creative Commons at: http://labs.creativecommons.org/demos/termination (accessed 21 November 2014), and useful tables of important dates are available at http://alterandkendrick.com/protecting-your-musical-copyrights/statutory-termination-of-transfers-recapturing-copyrights (accessed 21 November 2014). You can also contact the NoCopyright Party directly (party@nocopyright.com) if you need help exercising your rights. It's the least we can do.

[36] You would be violating the public performance right. *See* 17 USC § 106(4) & USC § 100.

[37] Getty's recent decision to allow "free access" to large numbers of photos, *see* Tom Risen, *Getty Images Allows Free Access to Photos*, US News & World Report (6 March 2014), is a case in point. Those photographs remain under copyright, and thus are not truly free – people still cannot make derivative works or otherwise use them commercially. And freelance photographers suffer, as people will have a large body of free works to choose from. The NoCopyright model allows freelance photographers to sell their works directly to the public, once and for all, and then gives the public complete access to those works, no strings attached.

there. While the social energy released by breaking the bonds of copyright will clearly make the world a better place, www.NoCopyright.com is only the first stage in demonstrating the power of the public domain to enhance social welfare and promote social justice. The NoCopyright demonstration will raise consciousness of the simple fact that *after* the intellectual property reward has caused a creator or inventor to create or invent, society need not simply submit to the inefficiencies of a monopoly, and instead can proactively work with the creator or inventor to get the work into the public domain, where it can benefit all of humankind. Nowhere is this idea more important than in the pharmaceutical context, where the patent price is a huge multiple of the cost of production, with the result that pharmaceutical companies engage in all kinds of perfectly legal but anti-social practices[38] designed to maintain the monopoly profits. The inefficiencies caused by these practices represent social value just waiting to be unlocked, by the next phase of the demonstration started by www.NoCopyright.com. Because making the patent-side version of www.NoCopyright.com work has an international dimension, and will require cooperation of state and federal politicians, insurance companies, and the public – not to mention pharmaceutical companies – we start with

---

[38] Such practices – all of which can be done legally, if the drug company is careful – include (i) campaign contributions to federal legislators in exchange for patent term extensions, (ii) campaign contributions to politicians not to enact price controls (which are present in every other industrialized Western country); (iii) campaign contributions to state legislators to enact laws against use of generic drugs; (iv) biased studies in favor of patented drug versus off-patent drugs; (v) evergreening of patents through follow-on patents and Orange Book tricks; (vi) "pay-for-delay" reverse settlements with generics; (vii) providing doctors with lucrative consulting contracts, in exchange for the doctors' goodwill; (viii) encouraging doctors to prescribe particular medications (e.g. through use of kickbacks plus good-looking pharma reps); and (ix) direct marketing to consumers – advertising that tells consumers to ask their doctors for drugs that they do not truly need. *See generally* Marcia Angell, *The Truth About Drug Companies, How They Deceive Us and What to Do About It* (Random House, New York 2004); Ben Goldacre, *Bad Pharma, How Drug Companies Mislead Doctors and Harm Patients* (Faber & Faber, New York 2012); Katherine Greider, *The Big Fix: How the Pharmaceutical Industry Rips off American Consumers* (PublicAffairs, New York 2003). Unfortunately, the dollar amounts at stake also lead some pharmaceutical companies, on occasion, to engage in illegal activities in order to keep patent profits high. *See, e.g.*, Katie Thomas, "J.&J. to Pay $2.2 Billion in Risperdal Settlement", *New York Times*, 2 November 2014; Katie Thomas and Michael S. Schmidt, "Glaxo Agrees to Pay $3 Billion in Fraud Settlement", *New York Times*, 2 July 2012; Gardiner Harris, "Pfizer Pays $2.3 Billion to Settle Marketing Case", *New York Times*, 2 September 2009. *See also* note 27 above (explaining the deadly consequences of *dead*weight loss in the pharmaceutical context).

the demonstration on the copyright side. But we will not lose sight of the patent-side goal.

GETTING IT OFF THE GROUND – NOCOPYRIGHT AND BEYOND

As we hope you agree by now, the economics of all of this are unassailable. Creators should be able to use the system to extract exactly as much or more money out of their works as they would have been able to if the work remained under copyright. The public benefits for obvious reasons. Donors benefit because their donated money is so well-spent, due to the multiplier effect. And corporate donors can benefit even more, since donating works to the public domain provides both advertising opportunities and positive publicity.

Celebrities, special interest groups, and others who have their own networks and fan bases can play a big role in freeing copyrights, by getting the word out. Book clubs such as Double Day, The Literary Guild, Scholastic, and Oprah 2.0 could be great laboratories for this kind of disruption. Back in the day, being selected by Oprah could make millions for an author. If book clubs were to join together and condition selection on an agreement that the book would go into the public domain after say, five more years of copyright, what author would refuse? www.NoCopyright.com can facilitate getting works into the public domain in this way.

But we don't have to wait for Oprah. We – all of us – can "prime" the NoCopyright pump by putting up our own works for "auction", and letting our friends know about it. Start with photographs and videos. Numerous successful businesses have already tapped into the deeply-ingrained human need to share photographs and videos with friends and strangers.[39] But it can be mind-numbingly difficult to tell if any of this

---

[39] Even Maslow would classify this kind of sharing as a form of "self-actualization". Abraham Maslow, "A theory of human motivation", 50 *Psychological Review* 370, 382–4 (1943) (accessed 14 October 2014 at http://psychclassics.yorku.ca/Maslow/motivation.htm). Recent evidence, however, suggests that the drive to share videos and pictures is even more fundamental than that. *See e.g.*, http://en.wikipedia.org/wiki/Anthony_Weiner_sexting_scandals (accessed 14 October 2014).

The history of Mazlow's later book, *Eupsychian Management* (1965), could be a case study for the NoCopyright approach. The book had long been out of print in 1987, when Sam Cannon received permission from the publisher to post a laboriously-typed-out copy of it to an electronic bulletin board. When the copy later migrated to the World Wide Web – and started generating buzz for the

treasure trove of shared content is truly in the public domain. If each of your facebook friends is willing to put up $1 to get one of your photographs into the public domain, then voilà, you've made $500. And perhaps you'd be willing to put up a dollar or two to get your friends' photos and videos into the public domain as well.

* * *

Although we are the "NoCopyright Party" and our mission is to kill copyrights, that doesn't mean we are against all copyright laws. To the contrary, the copyright system has served this country quite well – it has incentivized the creation and distribution of millions and millions of entertaining, instructive, creative and innovative works. In fact, as should be clear from our explanation, our own system for getting works into the public domain operates hand-in-hand with the copyright system. We encourage authors to stick with the copyright system for the early years of the life of their works – during those years, the market provides a great return, as the very people who will benefit most from the work are willing to pay the copyrighted price. As a work loses currency, and the market contracts, that is when, as a matter of simple common sense, creators should change course. We can thus use the copyright reward to provide the incentive to create, and then – when the time is right – use the power of the crowd and the profit motive of the author to put the copyright out of its misery and release all of its pent-up social value in one blinding flash.

In declaring our independence from England, Jefferson noted that sometimes it "becomes necessary for one people to dissolve the political bands which have connected them with another". We believe that Jefferson would view today's excessively-long copyright terms the same way, and would urge people to come together to dissolve those bands as well, much as this chapter has proposed. Join the NoCopyright Party now!

---

original book – Maslow's heirs had it taken down. *See* Tom Petzinger, "Copyright Imbroglio Entangles a Work That Web Gave Away", *Wall Street Journal* (10 October 1997) (available, as annotated by Sam Cannon, at http://www.maslow.org/sub/petz.php (accessed 14 October 2014)). It then enjoyed a brief print run, and now is essentially unavailable again – as of this writing, new copies on Amazon start at $186.85 (6 offers) and used copies start at $62.23 (13 offers). Using www.NoCopyright.com, books like this – which have demonstrated value, and yet provide little real income for the heirs – can be brought into the public domain through crowdfunding. Readers who know of other such books – any out-of-print copyrighted book that sells on Amazon for over $100 – are encouraged to send their titles to us at party@nocopyright.com, and we will start campaigns to have their copyrights killed.

10. I am my brother's keeper: How the crossroads of entrepreneurship, intellectual property and entertainment can be used to affect social justice
Loren E. Mulraine

> An individual has not started living until he can rise above the narrow confines of his individualistic concerns to the broader concerns of all humanity.
> Martin Luther King, Jr.

INTRODUCTION

Growing up in the Bronx, New York, our neighborhoods served as the fulcrum for the world we knew. Like many in my neighborhood, we were immigrants. My family had come to New York from the West Indies, for higher education, to make a better life and to contribute to a growing, energetic society. In many ways, the ultimate goal was to have a transformative effect upon our family tree. Many children, my sisters and I included, grew up in homes where we welcomed our parents' siblings and their families – our aunts, uncles and cousins – to live with us for a transitional period as they adjusted to life in "the States". My aunt and uncle in Brooklyn had done the same for us, several years earlier. This pattern served to cement the bonds of family, ease the transition to a new country, and unbeknownst to me, plant the first seeds in my mind of what it meant to be my brother's keeper. It was also a primer on what it means to be an entrepreneur and how it fuels upward mobility.

Unlike my children, who today are driven by car or ride school buses to elementary, middle and high school, virtually all school kids in New York's five boroughs[1] walked to their elementary

---

[1] New York City's five boroughs are The Bronx, Brooklyn, Manhattan, Staten Island, and Queens. While almost all elementary school kids in the city walk to

schools.² I attended P.S. 78 (officially named Anne Hutchinson Elementary School), which sat on Needham Avenue in the Bronx in the Eastchester District. The journey to school generally encompassed the Boston Road neighborhood flanked by Gun Hill Road to the south and Eastchester Road to the north. It was a middle class neighborhood with an assortment of multi-family homes, apartments and townhomes. Our journey would take us past a host of corner stores and family businesses including Pete's West Indian Bakery, which sat on the west side of Boston Road, just south of Eastchester, where we could satisfy our hunger with a beef patty and cocoa bread. If we had a taste for New York's most enduring staple food, we would visit Tony's or Sal's Pizzeria where the often imitated, but never duplicated New York-style Pizza would be devoured for 50 cents a slice. For that same 50 cents, we could purchase the latest record, a "45" of course, at the RecordRama, which sat on the east side of Boston Road between Fenton and Corsa Avenues. An album could be purchased for $3.99 or $4.99 at that same neighborhood record store. My first album purchase was the 1976 Earth, Wind & Fire album entitled "Spirit".³ For a few bucks, we could get a haircut at one of several barbershops on Boston Road. If you needed clothing items, any number of stores between Gun Hill and Eastchester could fit the bill. Not to mention my Mom's friend Marilyn who essentially ran her own mobile clothing store. I'm convinced that Marilyn would have had a nationwide, or potentially global enterprise if the Internet had existed at that time.

It never occurred to me during my elementary and middle school years, but we were surrounded by entrepreneurs. All of those establishments were family businesses or sole proprietorships, created by entrepreneurs, many of whom were immigrants or first generation U.S. citizens who were pursuing the American dream. The area was quite diverse, with West Indians, Puerto Ricans, Italians, Jews, multi-generational African-Americans, and just about every other ethnic group owning a piece of the neighborhood and serving to educate us in the ultimate melting pot. It was New York, it was the 1970s, and it was the very best place to get a 360-degree view

---

school, they are more likely to take the city bus or train to their assigned middle or high schools.

² This may partially explain why from 5th grade through my high school graduation, schools were only closed due to weather on one occasion, the nasty blizzard of 1979. In contrast, the schools my children attend are often closed based on a prediction of snow as little as 1–2 inches.

³ I actually still have the original shrink wrap as proof that it was on sale that first month for $3.99.

of small business in its most fertile ground, a multicultural, middle class neighborhood.

Growing up in a neighborhood where I was surrounded by entrepreneurs, it is no surprise that business has always excited me. I had my first job at the age of 13, when I took over my friend Mark Steven Mayfield's paper route and began delivering the *New York Daily News* and *New York Times* throughout my neighborhood. It was a great training ground for developing a strong and consistent work ethic – papers had to be delivered by 6:00 a.m. daily and 7:00 a.m. on Sundays – rain, snow, or shine. I even had my first experience as "management" when I hired a friend to make deliveries on my behalf on Saturdays. I was soon loaning money to my sister and other family members whenever they were in need.

I didn't understand it when I was 13, but entrepreneurship has always been the fuel that ignites financial growth and creates generational wealth. In this chapter, I will first look at how this fuel has historically been a powerful accelerant when combined with media, intellectual property, and entertainment. I will then give examples of how artists, specifically in the African American community, have used it to ignite the fires of social justice, and close by revisiting how these tools and energies can be directed to promote communal economic empowerment, that is, how I can be my brother's keeper.

ENTREPRENEURSHIP, SOCIAL JUSTICE AND SOCIAL ENTREPRENEURSHIP: CONTEMPORARY DEFINITIONS

> The ends you serve that are selfish will take you no further than yourself but the ends you serve that are for all, in common, will take you into eternity.
> Marcus Garvey

The tools of entrepreneurship can be used to effectuate social change and social justice, and to that end, thereby stimulate and achieve social entrepreneurship. Moreover, entrepreneurs are the visionaries behind the small businesses that drive economic development. In turn, this economic development has the potential to serve as my brother's keeper in at least two regards: (1) there is the aphorism that a rising tide lifts all boats.[4]

---

[4] Senator John F. Kennedy coined this phrase during a campaign speech in Canton, Ohio in September 1960. It has since become a common axiom utilized to describe the belief that improvements in the general economy will benefit all participants in that economy.

(2) if entrepreneurs themselves are committed to changing their communities for the good of everyone, and stimulating opportunities for those who are traditionally excluded from economic abundance, there will be a social justice impact that changes the lives of "the least of these".[5]

In a broad sense, entrepreneurship is simply "enterprise", or the pursuit of enterprise. The classic dictionary definition of an entrepreneur is "one who organizes, manages, and assumes the risks of a business or enterprise".[6] Howard University's Entrepreneurship, Leadership, and Innovation Institute defines entrepreneurship and the entrepreneurial mindset as "the process of opportunity discovery, risk evaluation and adding value to situations, projects, activities and organizations".[7] *The Economist* magazine defines entrepreneurship as the modern-day philosopher's stone: a mysterious something that supposedly holds the secret to boosting growth and creating jobs. All of these definitions anticipate the creation of something from nothing, or at least the creation of something tangible in the form of a business, from something intangible – the germination of an idea.

"Entrepreneurship is a way of life that offers unlimited possibilities to those who truly believe in it and live by it. But at the same time, entrepreneurship is a way of life that can totally alter the course of your life if misunderstood".[8] It is the unlimited possibilities that we must unleash by showing entrepreneurs how serving as their brother's keepers can allow them to change their lives and the lives of others simultaneously. At the same time, it is the misunderstanding of entrepreneurship as an egocentric endeavor that we need to minimize.

Among the many descriptors of social justice are the following: using your passions and talents to meet the needs of those around you; giving a voice to the voiceless; providing access to education for everyone; making a conscious decision to live one's life for the betterment of humanity; using what you have been given to bless others around you; seeing a need in the community and coming together to meet it.[9] The solutions offered

---

[5] The King will reply, "Truly I tell you, whatever you did for one of the least of these brothers and sisters of mine, you did for me." Matthew 25:40, New International Version.

[6] The Merriam-Webster online dictionary, www.merriam-webster.com.

[7] W. Sherman Rogers, *The African American Entrepreneur – Then and Now* (Praeger Publishing, New York (2010)), 155.

[8] Tito Phillips, Jr., *7 Reasons Why Most Entrepreneurs Fail In Business* (2011), accessed 15 October at http://www.naijapreneur.com/why-entrepreneurs-fail/. Chapter 2 of this book offers a thorough exposition on the topic of entrepreneurship.

[9] The website www.whatissocialjustice.com (accessed 15 October 2014),

at the end of this chapter are designed to be a catalysts for much many of these descriptors.

THE USE OF ENTREPRENEURSHIP TO ACHIEVE ECONOMIC JUSTICE ECONOMIC EMPOWERMENT AND CIVIL RIGHTS

> The cause of economic justice is the cause of social justice.
> Dr. Martin Luther King, Jr.

There is a close relationship between social justice and economic justice. The Center for Economic and Social Justice defines the two as follows:

> Social justice encompasses economic justice. Social justice is the virtue, which guides us in creating those organized human interactions we call institutions. In turn, social institutions, when justly organized, provide us with access to what is good for the person, both individually and in our associations with others. Social justice also imposes on each of us a personal responsibility to work with others to design and continually perfect our institutions as tools for personal and social development.[10]

> Economic justice, which touches the individual person as well as the social order, encompasses the moral principles which guide us in designing our economic institutions. These institutions determine how each person earns a living, enters into contracts, exchanges goods and services with others and otherwise produces an independent material foundation for his or her economic sustenance. The ultimate purpose of economic justice is to free each person to engage creatively in the unlimited work beyond economics, that of the mind and the spirit.[11]

Throughout the 20th and into the 21st century, there has often been a direct relationship between entrepreneurship and economic justice. More than a century ago, the likes of W.E.B. Du Bois, Booker T. Washington and Marcus Garvey were among the leaders of the Black economic empowerment movement. Martin Luther King, Jr. and Malcolm X were also among the most important voices for economic justice in the latter half of the 20th century.

---

conducted an international campaign where they interviewed scores of individuals to come up with a comprehensive definition of social justice.

[10] Center for Economic and Social Justice, "Defining Economic Justice and Social Justice", accessed 15 October 2014 at http://www.cesj.org/learn/definitions/defining-economic-justice-and-social-justice/.

[11] Ibid.

Booker T. Washington's "self help" philosophy took root during the last two decades of the 19th century. In addition to founding Tuskeegee Institute (now Tuskeegee University) in 1880, Washington founded the Negro Business League with the intent of creating a Black capitalist class. Washington famously called upon league members to teach the masses to acquire property, to be more thrifty and economical, and he resolved to establish an industrial enterprise wherever the opportunity presented itself.[12]

Marcus Garvey was a great admirer of Booker T. Washington, even being stimulated by Washington's book "Up From Slavery", which played a foundational role in the development of Garvey's program of black economic empowerment.[13] Garvey was a staunch proponent of economic empowerment as a means to freedom and prosperity. His program of economic self-reliance included the Black Star Line, the Negro Factories Corporation and the Black Cross and Navigation Corporation.[14] Garvey's message was one of pride, self-help and the absolute necessity for black entrepreneurship and black economic empowerment.[15]

Even before Booker T. Washington, Marcus Garvey and W.E.B. Du Bois, there was Frederick Douglass, who embraced the rhetoric of market capitalism. The rhetoric of market capitalism in the antebellum period and its association with the concept of political freedom meant one thing to the African American slave and quite another to white slaveholders.[16] To Douglass, the ideological linkage between capitalism and liberty quickened his resolve to escape by enabling him for the first time to envisage what it might mean to lay claim to the rights of his own labor.[17] While he was consistently critical of the state of capitalism, particularly its injustices for laborers, Douglass was not anti-capitalist. In fact, he was a strong proponent of capitalism, or private enterprise.[18] Douglass believed that in

---

[12] Lance Selfa, "Booker T. Washington and Black capitalism", The Socialist Worker, accessed 14 October 2014 at http://socialistworker.org/2012/05/11/booker-washington-and-black-capitalism.

[13] Muhammad Ali Salaam, *A Black Man's Journey in America: Glimpses of Islam, Conversations and Travels* (Xlibris Corporation, Bloomington 2011), 77.

[14] Robert Trent Vinson, *The Americans are Coming! Dreams of African American Liberation in Segregationist South Africa* (Ohio University Press, Athens, OH 2012), 93.

[15] Gilbert R. Mason, *Beaches, Blood, and Ballots: A Black Doctor's Civil Rights Struggle* (University Press of Mississippi, Jackson 2000), 27.

[16] Robert S. Levine, *Martin Delany, Frederick Douglass and the Politics of Representative Identity* (University of North Caroline Press, Chapel Hill 1997).

[17] Ibid, 134.

[18] Waldo E. Martin, *The Mind of Frederick Douglass* (University of North Carolina Press, Chapel Hill 1984), 129.

the midst of the failings of capitalism, there was much to praise as well. One of the praise-worthy characteristics was individual socioeconomic betterment and national economic progress.[19] In fact, Douglass believed the best way to create employment opportunities in the private sector was through small-business development.[20] In 1869, Douglass formulated a land reform proposal that encouraged the federal government to become a purchaser and seller of land in order to counteract the collusion schemes of southern landowners. The words and actions of Douglass epitomize what we would consider the entrepreneurial spirit. Being able to claim the rights to one's own labor is the essence of entrepreneurship. Once those rights have been realized, a myriad of possibilities are available to allow the entrepreneur to participate in socioeconomic betterment, and contribute to the growth of economic justice.

Martin Luther King, Jr., was also an advocate of the highest order for social justice and economic empowerment. He empathized with those who suffered economic exploitation. In fact, he lost his life during a visit to Memphis, Tennessee where he was advocating for economic empowerment for the Memphis sanitation workers. He was an advocate for radical economic reform at a societal level and at the level of individual behavior.[21] He believed in and had a tireless work ethic. King also believed that individually we should see our financial responsibility as a sacred responsibility.[22] Economic reform, hard work, financial and sacred responsibility are signposts at the intersection of entrepreneurship and social justice, and the formula for economic justice.

LAW AND ECONOMICS VS. SOCIAL JUSTICE

Laws and policies intended to promote the development, use, and exploitation of intellectual property are most typically associated with theories of law and economics, and until recently, were generally not analyzed or applied from a social justice perspective. What is the law and economics model and how does it actually apply to intellectual property and entertainment law? How does this model compare with

---

[19] Ibid.
[20] K. Carl Smith, *Frederick Douglass Republicans: The Movement to Reignite America's Passion for Liberty* (AuthorHouse, Bloomington 2011), 33.
[21] Wright L. Lassiter, Jr., *The Power of Thought: A Series of Messages Celebrating the Life of Dr. Martin Luther King, Jr.* (Trafford Publishing, Bloomington 2011), 56.
[22] Lassiter, note 21 above, 56.

the social justice model for intellectual property and entertainment law?

While scholarship on law and economics model for intellectual property is a relatively recent phenomenon which began in the 1970s, the economic analysis of intellectual property can be dated to classical economists such as Adam Smith,[23] Jeremy Bentham[24] and John Stuart Mill,[25] as well as other early 20th century economists such as Arthur Cecil Pigou,[26] Frank William Taussig[27] and Sir Arnold Plant.[28] The law and economics model places an emphasis on incentives and people's responses to these incentives. The theory is that people will act, not act, or change their actions, based on the knowledge of how, under the law, these actions may affect them financially. When penalties for an action increase, people will undertake less of that action.

As Landes and Posner state in their text, *The Economic Structure of Intellectual Property Law*, the dynamic benefit of a property right is the incentive that possession of such a right imparts to invest in the creation or improvement of a resource in period 1 (for example, planting a crop), given that no one else can appropriate the resource in period 2 (harvest time). It enables people to reap where they have sown. Without that prospect, the incentive to sow is diminished.[29] From this perspective, a songwriter would be less likely to write songs, a sculptor less likely to create a

---

[23] Adam Smith, best known for his seminal work *The Wealth of Nations* is often referred to as the "father of modern economics" and remains one of the most influential thinkers in the field of economics.

[24] Jeremy Bentham was a British economist most often associated with his theory of utilitarianism and the idea that "it is the greatest happiness of the greatest number that is the measure of right and wrong".

[25] Mill was a prolific scholar and educator who was heavily influenced by Jeremy Bentham and his theories of utilitarianism. Mill's extensive scholarship on economic theory included the book *Mill's Principles*, one of the most widely read economic books of his era.

[26] Arthur Pigou was a British welfare economist who focused his economic theories on maximizing the well-being of society. Pigou was greatly concerned with how to use economic theory to promote social well-being.

[27] Frank William Taussig, a renowned economist and educator was perhaps best known for creating the foundations of modern trade theory. Among his many works dealing with trade and tariff issues, he also published in the area of intellectual property with *Inventors and Money Makers*, Brown University lectures (1915).

[28] Sir Arnold Plant published the groundbreaking articles "The Economic Theory Concerning Patents for Inventions" and "The Economic Aspects of Copyright in Books" in 1934.

[29] William M. Landes and Richard A. Posner, *The Economic Structure of Intellectual Property Law* (Harvard University Press, Cambridge, MA 2003).

work of art and an inventor less likely to invent if competing songwriters, sculptors and inventors can utilize their works without remuneration. At the very least, these creators would be hard pressed to commit their fulltime efforts to their art.

Law and economics has been the most common way of looking at intellectual property rights, but what about IP's effects on social and cultural life? What if we could stimulate creation for reasons beyond the economic incentives? In other words, what is the social justice or global justice model and how can we apply this to IP and entertainment law?

The social justice and global justice perspective is that intellectual property does more than incentivize the production of more goods. It fundamentally affects the ability of citizens to live a good life. In her book *From Goods to A Good Life*, Madhavi Sunder says "The dominant law-and-economic theory of intellectual property law is premised on a thin theory of culture as commodities. But culture is not just a set of goods; it is a fundamental component of a good life."[30] Why should intellectual property be only viewed as a means to promote and protect property? Sunder argues that we must consider the possibility of intellectual property being a means to promote and circulate culture.

The comparison of the law and economics approach and the social justice approach leads to an inevitable question: why can't these two theories coexist? Perhaps the epiphanic moment occurs when we recognize that intellectual property can move beyond the traditional walls of law and economics into a world where doing well is on equal footing with doing good. Sunder invites us to look at these possibilities as she challenges us to a richer understanding of intellectual property law's effects on social and cultural life.

When elements of each theory are strategically used, these theories may not even be competitors. In fact, one need only look at the colors of the spectrum to recognize that no single hue exists in a vacuum. Likewise, the social justice approach to intellectual property has a more comprehensive function when it is considered within the law and economics framework and vice versa. Fusing these theoretical approaches allows us to utilize the best of each framework. An example of this fusion would be the creation of an artistic work (for example, a film, song or work of fine art) that generates economic value for the creator while creating social value for the intended audience (for example, educating the audience on a topic or academic area).

---

[30] Madhavi Sunder, *From Goods to a Good Life* (Yale University Press, New Haven 2012).

ENTERTAINMENT, IP AND MEDIA MEETS SOCIAL JUSTICE

One of the most effective paths to social and global justice is through entrepreneurship. A plethora of examples supports this assertion. Entrepreneurship is not just a means to personal wealth, but it is a means to changing your family tree and providing greater freedom to affect meaningful change in your community. One needs to look no further than the world of hip hop music, which has permeated not only music, but art, clothing, television and culture as a whole. This permeation, along with the street smarts and business acumen of its creators has served to change many a family tree. But the power of entrepreneurship in music is not limited to the hip-hop world, it is equally at home other genres of music, in filmmaking, television, and other forms of media, intellectual property and entertainment.

So, how does an entrepreneur or creator of intellectual property affect social justice? Let's take a close look at two approaches: (1) Entrepreneurs and creators can use the financial gain from their intellectual property to sow into their communities (or other communities) and thereby change the lives of the residents of those communities; or (2) they can use their art to change the narrative for their communities, that is, tell stories that have socio-political impact on their communities.

The Music Business

First we review two case studies of the music industry which provide a road map for how an entrepreneur can leverage IP assets and business savvy, and create joint ventures and business partnerships to affect culture and write an unprecedented history not only for their companies, but for their communities as well.

Kenny Gamble and Leon Huff: Philadelphia International Records, Mighty Three Music

Kenny Gamble and Leon Huff started their company, Philadelphia International Records (a/k/a Philly International or PIR) in 1971. Along with their songwriting partner, Thom Bell (who often also wrote with Linda Creed), they formed Mighty Three Music to house their publishing interests. They established "The Sound of Philadelphia" with their songwriting and production for the likes of The O'Jays,[31] The

---

[31] O'Jays hits included "Back Stabbers", "Love Train", "Now That We Found

Intruders,[32] Jerry Butler,[33] Harold Melvin & The Bluenotes,[34] Teddy Pendergrass,[35] The Three Degrees,[36] Billy Paul,[37] Archie Bell & The Drells,[38] MFSB,[39] Lou Rawls,[40] The Jacksons,[41] Patti LaBelle[42] and The Jones Girls,[43] among others.

Even as accomplished songwriters and producers, Gamble and Huff found it hard to collect on the money they had earned as writers and producers for other record labels. Kenny Gamble speaking on the business climate when he and Leon Huff founded Philadelphia International Records confirmed that it had been the norm for African-Americans to be cheated out of a lot of their music and their royalties. The industry had closed so many doors on them that "in order for us to make it, we had to

---

Love", "For The Love Of Money", "I Love Music", "Stairway to Heaven" and many others.

[32] Intruders hits included "Cowboys to Girls", "We'll Be United" and the classic "I'll Always Love My Mama".

[33] Jerry Butler's hits included "Only The Strong Survive".

[34] Along with the O'Jays, Gamble & Huff had their greatest success with Harold Melvin & The Bluenotes, whose hits included the classic "If You Don't Know Me By Now", as well as "I Miss You", "The Love I Lost", "Yesterday I Had The Blues", "Bad Luck", "Wake Up Everybody", "Hope That We Can Be Together Soon" and others.

[35] Teddy Pendergrass, after leaving his post as lead singer of Harold Melvin & The Bluenotes had continued success with the sound of Philadelphia including his gold and platinum albums "Teddy Pendergrass", "Life Is A Song Worth Singing", "Teddy", "Live! Coast to Coast" and "TP", all of which were released between 1977 and 1980.

[36] The Three Degrees topped the charts with "When Will I See You Again", and also provided the vocals on TSOP's Soul Train Theme Song.

[37] Billy Paul's "Me and Mrs. Jones" is a soul classic.

[38] Archie Bell & the Drells hits on PIR included "Can't Stop Dancing" and "Could Dance All Night".

[39] MFSB (Mother, Father, Sister, Brother) hit the charts on PIR with "Zach's Fanfare (I Hear Music)", "Love Is The Message" and "My One and Only Love".

[40] Lou Rawls revitalized his career on PIR with the 1976 release "All Things in Time" which included "You'll Never Find" and the subsequent album releases "Unmistakably Lou", "When You Hear Lou, You've Heard It All", "Let Me Be Good To You" and "Sit Down and Talk To Me".

[41] The Jacksons, after leaving Motown, found success on PIR with the hits "Enjoy Yourself" and "Show You the Way to Go".

[42] After splitting from her trio, LaBelle, Patti LaBelle released her early solo projects "The Spirit's In It" and "I'm In Love Again" on PIR.

[43] Widely recognized as one of the most talented female vocal groups of the 1970s and 1980s, The Jones Girls had moderate chart success but were "Quiet Storm" favorites with their PIR albums "The Jones Girls", "At Peace With Woman", "Get As Much Love as You Can" and "Keep It Coming".

do it on our own".⁴⁴ And did they ever do it! Philly International produced music that was the soundtrack of the 1970s and early 1980s. As songwriters and producers, they had their fingers on the pulse of the culture of the black community writing songs like "If You Don't Know Me By Now", "The Love I Lost", "Backstabbers", "Don't Leave Me This Way", "You'll Never Find", "When Will I See You Again" and dozens of other huge hits.

Their music also had a cultural awareness and called for change and activism, for example, "Wake Up Everybody", which was a call for the collective culture to actively engage in making the world a better place: "Wake up everybody, no more sleeping in bed, no more backward thinking time for thinking ahead . . . The world won't get no better, if we just let it be, the world won't get no better, we gotta change it yeah, just you and me." "Love Train" became an anthem calling for unity and breaking down the walls of racism and nationalism. When discussing the lyric to "Love Train" Gamble says: "that song came around 1972–73…when the Vietnam War was still happening. It was just unbelievable, the sentiment in the country and around the world. People were just so hostile to each other. Huff and I were talking, and we were saying, "People all over this world need to be together". "Love Train" was a way to say that without it being dogmatic or like you were beating somebody over the head with a message. But it was fun; it was light and it was happy. We were talking about people sharing and caring about each other, and that's a good thing. That message is still out there today.⁴⁵ "Message In Our Music" admonished the listener to "open your ears and listen here . . . we're gonna talk about the situation of our nations all over the world, try and make you see, things ain't like they're supposed to be".

Gamble & Huff sold their song catalog to Warner-Chappell in 1991 (for multi-millions), and they continue to reap benefits from the catalog, with licensing deals that include Coors Light ("Love Train"), The Apprentice ("For The Love of Money"), Verizon ("Ain't No Stoppin' Us Now," written by McFadden and Whitehead but part of the Philly International catalog), and numerous other TV shows, films, and public performances.

It is one thing to gain economic success and to be content with a mindset of "to the victor goes the spoils". But Gamble and Huff put their money

---

⁴⁴ On their own did not mean without partners. Gamble and Huff started the company with the assistance of CBS Records after EMI had turned them down. This is an important point when considering the importance of taking advantage of strategic partnerships, joint ventures, and the like, in building our entrepreneurial ventures.

⁴⁵ Ken Sharp, "Gamble & Huff: Soul Deep", *American Songwriter Magazine*, (Feb. 2009).

where their mouths were and leveraged their economic clout and community visibility to make meaningful changes to their beloved city of Philadelphia. Their humanitarian work includes numerous projects to clean up the inner city and help African American youth; Leukemia and Cancer research; neighborhood development, including a bookstore, restaurants, a mosque, low-income housing, several charter schools and their "Clean Up The Ghetto Project". Most of these projects have been built by locally hired labor.

One of their current projects involves branding Philadelphia as the city of R&B, which includes spearheading the development of the Rhythm & Blues Foundation. As a blueprint, they are using Nashville, which has successfully branded itself as "Music City USA".[46] More than 40 years after they launched their company, Gamble and Huff are still affecting the culture of their Philadelphia community and the world. Looking back at our definition of social justice: Gamble and Huff have clearly used their passions and talents to meet the needs of those around them; they have given a voice to the voiceless; provided access to education through their charter schools; and they have provided affordable housing for their community. There is no question that they have seen a need in their community and they have come together to meet that need. Although Philadelphia International has had an enormous impact on social justice and economic justice, the company from its inception was an example of classic entrepreneurship. As evidenced by their history, however, this classic entrepreneurship eventually spawned philanthropy and triggered social entrepreneurship offshoots. The business model of Philly International was built around the classic entrepreneurship model, that is, Gamble and Huff had a product and service, they recognized a gap in the marketplace, and they took affirmative steps to fill the gaps of the market's deficiencies through their products and services. The end result was a hugely successful economic engine that took its place among the leaders of commerce in urban America. Only then did they have the means to look at expanding their brand to philanthropy leading to social and economic justice. The ultimate impact on social and economic justice was overwhelming, as the entrepreneurs utilized the spoils of their success to have a massive impact on society. Gamble and Huff have eagerly taken on the responsibility to be their brother's keeper.

---

[46] Nashville, Tennessee actually was first nicknamed the music city after the Fisk Jubilee Singers toured Great Britain and Europe in 1873. When the group performed "Steal Away to Jesus" and "Go Down, Moses" for Queen Victoria, she was so impressed by the Singers that she commented that with such beautiful voices, they had to be from the Music City of the United States. It was then that the nickname for Nashville, Tennessee – Music City USA – was born.

Russell Simmons: Def Jam Recordings, Rush Productions

Russell Simmons launched his entertainment and management company, Rush Productions and Rush Management with rapper Kurtis Blow as his first client. When he co-founded Def-Jam Recordings it was because the major labels did not see commercial value in the rap and hip-hop genre.[47] Simmons felt strongly that there would be a huge market for this genre so he and his partner Rick Rubin started Def Jam. Their early signings were T La Rock & Jazzy Jay, LL Cool J and the Beastie Boys.[48] The rest is history. Simmons had no doubt that this music would change the culture of young urban America. This vision has actually had a lasting effect on urban culture all over the world.

Known as the Godfather of hip-hop, Simmons was one of the first to recognize the cultural value and economic potential of this music genre to spawn not only music, but also lifestyle items such as clothing, jewelry, food and beverage, financial products, and so on. Entrepreneurs such as Sean Combs, Jay-Z, 50 Cent, and others have followed his path to multimedia success. Simmons has also been his brother's keeper – literally, as he has served as a mentor and role model for his brother Joseph "Rev Run" Simmons (of Run DMC) and Run's daughters, Angela and Vanessa, who have become successful entrepreneurs in their own rights with their very successful Pastry line of women's and girls' athletic shoes and accessories. Simmons says that while race still poses disadvantages in business, it can also be an advantage for the savvy entrepreneur. For example, there is a perception of authenticity that comes with minority entrepreneurs serving their own communities. Likewise, there is an inherent trust when minority entrepreneurs have business models that are designed to serve the needs of their communities. There is growing support for the belief that "while social group identities may impose unequal, if not discriminatory, starting positions, membership in these same social groups can provide opportunities to mobilize resources together".[49] This is not an

---

[47] It is notable that the corporate music industry has historically struggled with recognizing the commercial viability of black music forms. This was true in the 1950s when the labels released Pat Boone's sanitized versions of music by Little Richard and other black artists, the 1960s and 1970s when black artists were first relegated to "black divisions" of record labels, which carried with it lower budgets, fewer promotion dollars, and the like; the late 1970s and early 1980s when the likes of Luther Vandross were not signed to major labels because they believed that R&B and soul music by adult artists could not sell; and the 1980s when the major labels said rap and hip hop would never sell and would be a fad.

[48] The first two singles carrying the Def Jam logo were LL Cool J's "I Need A Beat" and the Beastie Boys "Rock Hard", both of which were released in 1984.

[49] Zulema Valdez, *The New Entrepreneurs, How Race, Class and Gender*

insignificant statement and it should be digested and reflected upon by all up and coming entrepreneurs who fall within an underrepresented class.

Following his departure from Def Jam, in 1999, Russell created a fashion empire in Phat Farm and its progeny – Baby Phat (run by his then-wife Kimora Lee Simmons) – and Run Athletics (run by his brother Rev Run). Simmons' success in developing a genre of urban streetwear helped open the door for a generation of new designers including FUBU, Roc-A-Wear, Sean John, Derion, Enyce, Ecko and many others. His film and television production company with partner Stan Lathan, Simmons Lathan Media Group, created the enormously successful HBO series, "Def Comedy Jam" and "Russell Simmons Presents Def Poetry", the Hollywood box office hit "The Nutty Professor" and the Tony Award-winning stage production "Russell Simmons Presents Def Poetry Jam on Broadway", as well as the international MTV hit "Run's House", and "Running Russell Simmons".

In addition to his commercial enterprises, Simmons gives back to the community through his Rush Philanthropic Arts Foundation, as well as the Foundation for Ethnic Understanding. The Rush Philanthropic Arts Foundation (RPAF), which Simmons founded with his brothers Joseph (Rev Run) and Danny, provides New York City's inner city youth with exposure to the arts. By providing this cultural opportunity that would otherwise not be available, RPAF is allowing inner city youth to expand their cultural horizons while they bring their own culture to an area of the arts that is often bereft of urban influences. RPAF focuses primarily on education programs for children and exhibits featuring emerging artists. The foundation serves nearly 3,000 students and exhibits the work of 40–50 emerging artists each year. RPAF also operates two art galleries, one in Manhattan and the other in Brooklyn.

Simmons is also Chairman of the Board of Directors of the Foundation for Ethnic Understanding (FFEU), an organization that describes itself as being dedicated to ethnic understanding, reconciliation and peace. It promotes racial harmony and strengthens inter-group relations. FFEU has gained respect on an international level and was among the leading organizations speaking on behalf of peace following the 2013 Boston Marathon bombing and other ethnically or racially charged events.

In 2003, in a clear example of social entrepreneurship, Simmons

---

Shape American Enterprise, (Stanford University Press, Redwood, CA 2011). Valdez notes that the long history of collective capital accumulation and mutual aid among Black entrepreneurs dates back to before the Civil War. This is one example of how these marginalized groups transform their perceived weaknesses into strengths.

co-founded Unirush Financial Services with consumer debt investor David Rosenberg. Initially built to provide access to the 60 million Americans rejected by or under-served by the consumer banking industry, it was one of the pioneers of the now rapidly growing "general purpose reloadable" (GPR) debit card business – a $300 billion industry.

In 2008, Simmons founded GlobalGrind.com, the leading online destination for celebrity entertainment, music, culture and politics for the new, post-racial America. This company now reaches over 2.6 million monthly unique visitors. In its first year of sales operations, Global Grind generated $1.2 million in sales and has surpassed all hip-hop sites to be in a category of its own.

Following the historic Hip-Hop Summit organized in June of 2001, Simmons co-founded the Hip-Hop Summit Action Network (HSAN) with civil rights activist Dr. Benjamin Chavis, a former head of the NAACP. HSAN's mission is to harness the cultural relevance of hip-hop music as a catalyst for education advocacy and other societal concerns fundamental to the well-being of at-risk youth throughout the United States. Among HSAN's major initiatives were helping to spearhead the first changes in 30 years to the repressive Rockefeller Drug Laws, which were repealed through Simmons' activism in 2008, and a successful First Amendment challenge to the NY State lobbying regulations that sought to prevent raising public awareness about state legislative issues.

Simmons' activism has grown out of his many years of traveling and advocating nationally and internationally on behalf of his brands. His platforms have consistently revolved around social justice, education, inclusion and financial empowerment. His passion is rooted in giving a powerful voice to emergent new creative and social movements, and integrating them into the American psyche.

Russell Simmons has clearly manifested the embodiment of meeting the needs of those around him, giving a voice to the voiceless, providing access to education through his arts foundation, and seeing a need in his community and coming forward to meet that need. Mirroring the transition made by Gamble and Huff, Simmons' early enterprises were examples of classic entrepreneurship. The success that was realized through these ventures lead to philanthropy and eventually economic and social justice ventures, such as RPAF and FFEU, both of which are clear examples of social entrepreneurship.[50]

---

[50] Much has changed in the recording industry over the past 15 years. The industry is very different from the one that existed when Gamble and Huff started PIR or when Russell Simmons launched Def Jam. On the one hand, artists have

These case studies demonstrate how intellectual property social justice can be attained by black creative artists and entrepreneurs in the music business, and how they can in turn further utilize entrepreneurial mechanisms to achieve economic enrichment and empowerment for their communities. Unfortunately, however, these success stories remain the exception and not the rule. There are still many past wrongs and ongoing inequitable practices in the industry which continue to frustrate the mandates of intellectual property social justice, and which might be redressed through application of the remedial IP social justice and the mechanisms of social entrepreneurship.

Case Study: Barrett Strong and the Motown Contradiction

Motown. The name evokes a bygone era of classic songs, dynamic performers, crisp choreography, classy outfits and the elevation of black musicians, songwriters and performers into the nation's pop culture. The term "the Motown sound" is symbolic of a once marginalized genre of music – R&B was once called "race music" – taking its place at the very top of the musical food chain during the heyday of Motown Records, from the early 1960s to the mid 1970s. But amidst the glamour and glory of the Motown machine lived a less celebratory reality. The unfortunate truth is that many of the artists, musicians and songwriters who were a part of "Hitsville, USA" were exalted musically while at the same time being pillaged financially. The list of artists whose relationships with Motown eventually turned sour reads like an abridged version of the Motown roster. Florence Ballard, Martha Reeves (Martha and the Vandellas), Marvin Gaye, The Funk Brothers, The Isley Brothers, Gladys Knight & The Pips, Teena Marie, Michael Jackson and Holland-Dosier-Holland, to name a few. At best, the treatment they received from the label was unethical – at worst it was systematic piracy. Motown's questionable financial practices stood in stark contrast to what the company stood for as a recording label. On the

---

become better educated about the business and have flexed their entrepreneurial muscles to start their own recording, production, and management companies. The availability of the Internet and its unlimited platform for distribution and direct marketing, along with the shift to digital music forms standing side-by-side with physical product, has empowered small business enterprises who no longer need to spend tens of thousands of dollars on manufacturing and inventory. Unfortunately, there has also been a major change in recording contracts that has been quite detrimental to the legal and business rights of recording artists. I will be exploring in great detail the phenomena of the multiple rights deal (aka, the 360 deal), the controlled composition clause, and the economic justice and potential anti-trust issues therein, in a law journal article that is nearing completion.

one hand they elevated young talented African Americans, many from the projects of Detroit, and gave them an opportunity to share their immense talents with the world. On the other hand, these same artists were given no creative control, had their production ideas marginalized, and most of all were systematically denied the true value of their contributions to this ultra-successful corporation. One of the earliest examples of this mistreatment has recently reared its ugly head as a Motown songwriting legend recently discovered a gross travesty perpetrated on him by Motown many years ago.

Barrett Strong, is one of the most successful songwriters of the Motown era. His hits include "I Heard It Through The Grapevine", "Just My Imagination (Running Away With Me)", "War", "Papa Was A Rollin' Stone", "Smiling Faces", "Ball of Confusion" and "I Can't Get Next To You" just to name a few. Barret's first hit, "Money (That's What I Want)", written in 1959 was copyrighted under the names Barrett Strong, Janie Bradford and Berry Gordy and assigned to Jobete Publishing (Motown's publishing entity). Barrett had actually come up with the musical riff and melody by himself, after which he collaborated with Janie Bradford who co-authored the lyrics with him. In 1962, unbeknownst to Barrett, Jobete Publishing sent a letter to the U.S. Copyright Office informing them that there was a mistake on the copyright registration and that Mr. Strong's name should be removed.[51] Barrett did not become aware of this sleight of hand (and of contract) until 2012 during a review of his copyrighted works. There are a number of issues involved in this situation, not the least of which is why the copyright office allows substantive changes to be made to copyright registrations without the approval and signature of all interested parties.[52]

What can be done to help Barrett Strong? Moreover, what can be done to keep this situation from happening to other songwriters? Certainly, the most important goal is to have Mr. Strong's name restored to the copyright registration. This would be valuable not just in regaining Barrett's rightful place as a recipient of the royalty stream and a possible retrospective royalty settlement, but also the incalculable value of correcting the historical narrative. As an additional matter, Berry Gordy, at that time the sole owner of Jobete Music, was also simultaneously serving as Barrett Strong's personal manager. At the very least these facts present the specter

---

[51] Larry Rohter, "For a Classic Motown Song About Money, Credit Is What He Wants", *New York Times*, 21 August 2013.

[52] This is an issue we are currently pursuing with the Copyright Office in an attempt to stimulate a change in policy.

of blatant conflict of interest and breach of fiduciary duty with Gordy's self-serving decision to remove Strong's name from the copyright without his knowledge, at the very same time that Gordy was Strong's personal manager.

The legal challenges that must be overcome from Barrett Strong's perspective, include statutes of limitations, as well the equitable defense of laches. In copyright infringement cases, the statute of limitations is three years from the date of the infringement or three years from the date that the plaintiff should have reasonably known of the infringement.[53] It is generally held that the statute of limitations starts from the date of the last infringement act. In other words, if an infringement begins in 1970 but is still continuing in 2014, at the very least the copyright owner would be able to receive damages for the infringement that has occurred over the last three years. It is possible that the damages could extend back to the beginning of the infringement if the copyright owner did not know and could not have reasonably known about the infringement until the last three years. The argument on behalf of Strong would first be that his knowledge of the infringement did not occur until 2012, thus the three-year statute of limitations has yet to expire. Alternatively, the infringement is still occurring, so even if he were not able to recapture lost royalties due to an unreasonable failure to be aware of the infringement, he would still be able to secure royalties prospectively since the infringement is still taking place.[54]

With regard to the defense of laches, the actual definition of laches is an unreasonable delay in pursuing a right or claim, in a way that prejudices an opposing party. Failure to assert one's rights in a timely manner can result in a claim being barred by laches. A key policy reason for laches is to prevent a party from sleeping on their rights and failing to mitigate damages in an effort to artificially build up the amount of damages. The argument on Strong's behalf is that he believed, and was reasonable in his belief that his name was still on the copyright registration. As such, he did not unreasonably delay in pursuing his cause of action. After all, he was on the registration when the song was originally filed with the copyright office and as an original claimant he had no reason to believe that he had been removed from the copyright registration. Moreover, Gordy's action of willful subterfuge in surreptitiously changing the names on the copyright registration negates laches.

---

[53] 17 U.S.C. § 507(b) – No civil action shall be maintained under the provisions of this title unless it is commenced within three years after the claim accrued.

[54] *Money (That's What I Want)* continues to generate money for Jobete Publishing and is also the first song performed in the current Broadway play celebrating the music of Motown.

The equitable defense of laches took center stage – or center "ring" in a recent dispute over the screenplay, book and film *Raging Bull*. The case, *Petrella v Metro-Goldwyn-Mayer*, was recently decided by the U.S. Supreme Court. In 1991, petitioner Paula Petrella renewed the copyright to her father's 1963 screenplay, *The Raging Bull*, which later became the basis for the critically and commercially acclaimed film *Raging Bull*. Despite intermittent correspondence between legal representatives for both parties, respondents MGM continued to market the film during the ensuing years. Believing there was no agreement without pursuing litigation, Petrella sued for copyright infringement in 2009. The three-year statute of limitations barred her from recovery for infringement that occurred prior to 2006. Although the statute did not bar recovery of damages and injunctive relief for acts of infringement that occurred in 2006 or later, the district court granted summary judgment for respondents, holding that the non-statutory defense of laches entirely barred Petrella's suit. The Ninth Circuit affirmed, based on binding circuit precedent, and denied hearing en banc.

The federal courts of appeals were divided 3-2-1 over whether the non-statutory defense of laches can bar a civil copyright suit brought within the express three-year statute of limitations. Three circuits, the Fourth, Eleventh, and Second had held that laches cannot completely bar relief for acts of infringement that occur within the statutory period. Two circuits, the Sixth and Tenth, strongly disfavored laches and restricted it to exceptional circumstances. The Ninth Circuit liberally allowed a laches defense in copyright cases, and had also adopted a presumption in favor of applying laches to continuing copyright infringements. The issue before the Supreme Court was: Whether the non-statutory defense of laches is available without restriction to bar all remedies for civil copyright claims filed within the three-year statute of limitations prescribed by Congress, 17 U.S.C. § 507(b).

The argument against laches in the Barrett Strong case would benefit most from the state of the law in the Fourth Circuit. In *Lyons Partnership, LP v Morris Costumes, Inc.*,[55] the plaintiff was the sole copyright owner of the Barney character, a green and purple dinosaur used in children's entertainment. Lyons sued to enjoin the defendants from using and renting out costumes that resembled Barney and violated Lyons' interests in the character. Morris Costumes argued that Lyons' claims were barred by laches because of a delay between Lyons' initial contact with Morris and the actual filing of the lawsuit. The plaintiffs argued that they were not barred

---

[55] 243 F.3d 789 (2001).

from asserting claims based on sales occurring within three years of filing suit. The court agreed, and determined that laches could never bar a claim that was brought within the statutorily mandated time frame.

Even if the Supreme Court were to adopt a stance based on the middle ground approach of the Sixth Circuit, Mr. Strong would still be able to pursue a copyright infringement action. The Sixth Circuit set forth its approach to laches in *Chirco v Crosswinds Communities, Inc.*[56] Avoiding the extremes of the Ninth and Fourth Circuits, the Sixth Circuit requires "rare circumstances" must be shown in order for laches to bar a copyright infringement case. The *Chirco* case involved a copyright owner of architectural plans who brought suit against a defendant when he learned the defendant was planning to use the designs for a condominium complex. While this suit was brought within weeks of learning of the alleged infringement, the plaintiff learned of another planned infringement but did not bring suit until 18 months later. By this time, the defendant had begun the building process and had incurred great expense in developing the property. The Sixth Circuit held that the plaintiff's delay in the second instance constituted "rare circumstances" and laches applied. There are no analogous "rare circumstances" in Mr. Strong's case.

Ultimate, *in Petrella*, the Supreme Court, in a 6-3 decision, ruled that laches cannot be invoked as a bar to pursuing a claim of damages brought within §507(b)'s three year window.[57] However, in extraordinary circumstances, laches may, at the very outset of litigation, curtail equitable relief. The 6-3 majority in *Petrella* was not along the typical ideology of the Justices, as conservative Justices Antonin Scalia, Clarence Thomas and Samuel Alito joined in the opinion by liberal Ruth Bader Ginsburg, while Chief Justice John Roberts and Anthony Kennedy joined a dissent by liberal Justice Stephen Breyer. It is important to note that Justice Ginsburg's opinion pointed out that copyright owners must still be mindful to avoid the judicial doctrine of estoppel, which would deny all damages if it can be shown that the plaintiff engaged in deception. Moreover, laches is still a viable defense for actions in equity. The Court's decision will put more onus on movie studios and other copyright users to be more vigilant in searching their titles and communicating with copyright holders.

Principles of intellectual property social justice support the middle ground approach. Once infringement has been established, there is no legal or policy basis to preclude actions brought within the limitations

---

[56] 474 F.3d 227 (2007).
[57] *Paula Petrella v. MGM, Inc.*, et al., Docket No. 12-1315, Supreme Court of The United States. 10 January 2014.

period, unless there has been some inequitable conduct on the part of the plaintiff prejudicial to the defendant or other circumstances antagonistic to copyright social utility or justice. In the Strong case, not only is there no evidence of misconduct on plaintiff's part, but the application of laches would promote intellectual property injustice and concomitant inequitable practices and policies.

Intellectual property social justice is not restricted to remedial action. In this context, "remedial action" refers to attorneys pursuing, and judges and triers of fact providing, remedies through the court system. While this will inevitably be part of the solution, the glaring problem is that it can only occur after creators such as Barrett Strong have already experienced harm. In contrast to remedial action, a proactive measure is one that would attempt to create or control a situation by causing something to happen rather than responding to it after it has happened. Proactive measures in this instance include legislative and social justice mechanisms that can and should be put in place to minimize the need for remedial action. The Barrett Strong case, while it may have unique facts, is not unique in its overall effect. There are scores of artists, both from earlier eras, and in the current marketplace, who are taken advantage of on a daily basis. How do we prevent this from happening in the future? Education, advocacy, and of course the vigilant pursuit of justice under law . . . then more education and more advocacy.

There are also potential entrepreneurial solutions – some classic entrepreneurship and others social entrepreneurship – for providing this education and advocacy, including the following: (1) Group or online basic IP educational programs offered at low fees to community and civil rights groups and individuals; (2) IP litigation support to individuals on a structure contingency basis; (3) individual IP transactional support in exchange for an irrevocable assignment of a small percentage of royalties (for example, 5–10 per cent); and (4) for "successful" artists, tax shelter/trust and estate advice in order to structure long-term donations, trusts, and foundations to the benefit of non-profit community IP Empowerment/ Social Entrepreneurship entities – here the non-profit recipient offers the tax shelter opportunities. A brief overview of each of these solutions follows:

(1) *Basic IP education* The model for online or web-based education has been created and has developed to a highly sophisticated level. Universities and state bar organizations have embraced the technology that allows for online and web-based training. In fact, brick and mortar institutions of higher education are essentially in an arms race to develop as many online, web-based, and hybrid course offerings

as possible in order to compete with online institutions. Technology allows this type of venture to be undertaken at a minimal capital outlay. The wheel has already been invented allowing IP social justice practitioners to build platforms that serve the same purpose. Courses could be taught in a variety of styles, e.g., the Khan Academy strictly academic model that is perpetually available on a website or server, or alternatively the webinar model or live audience model that is available for a limited time. This entity would be designed to teach important skills to intellectual property creators, which would allow the creators to sustain themselves. This would also solve an on-going educational deficiency that has not been solved by government (statutes and court holdings) or the private sector, but can be solved by a social entrepreneurship venture of this type.

(2) *IP litigation support exchange* One of the greatest challenges faced by the individual artist battling against a well-heeled corporation is overcoming the expense of litigation. This poses a difficult hurdle to overcome. Moreover, it is made more problematic because the amount of hours that must be invested in litigation tends to discourage private attorneys from undertaking these time-intensive cases with no possibility of remuneration. One possible solution is creating a hybrid pro bono/contingency fee arrangement where the attorneys do not charge up front fees but share in the settlement either after a certain threshold, or with some sliding scale based upon the recovery. An additional feature would be the requirement that the client agree to either accept a reasonable settlement offer if made or pay reasonable fees and expenses if such settlement offer is declined. The benefit for the client is evident. Instead of neglecting to protect their legal rights, the IP creators would be able to stand up to the corporate machine with some muscle of their own.

(3) *Individual IP transactional support exchange* Individual IP transactional support could also be offered in exchange for an irrevocable assignment of a small beneficial interest in the royalty stream (e.g., 5–10%). This would allow the client to receive the immediate benefit of high-end legal counsel, while providing a beneficial interest to the attorney. The effect of this type of transactional support would be similar to the artist having a transactional attorney as a part of their business entity, placing them on a level playing field with their corporate counterparts. Many entertainment attorneys routinely enter into fee agreements with their clients, which instead of being based on an hourly rate or flat fee/retainer are based on a percentage of the deal (e.g. the first fund for a record deal, the performance fee for an actor, the advance paid to an entertainer by the party procuring their

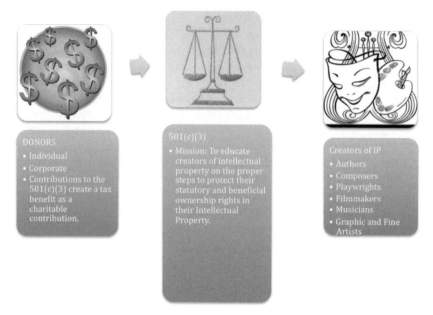

Figure 10.1 Tax shelter/trust advice model

services).[58] Likewise, most plaintiff's attorneys often enter into fee arrangements based upon the amount of the recovery in the litigation, i.e., contingency fee agreements.[59] Accordingly, there is some precedent for this type of arrangement. If managed effectively, this could certainly be a win/win for all parties.

(4) *Tax shelter/trust advice* This model provides a clear social justice entrepreneurship model that is essentially a joint venture between the donor and the IP social justice provider. This organization would resemble Figure 10.1.

The 501(c)(3) can schedule tours that would take the organization to key artistic hot spots in the U.S. where live seminars could be held at universities or the headquarters of arts organizations. Cities such as New

---

[58] Percentage deals for entertainment attorneys are often in the range of 5–10% of the deal, wish some being higher based on the complexity of the work or other factors.

[59] Most contingency fee agreements for personal injury and other plaintiff's cases are paid at 33% of the total recover plus expenses, with some being as high as 40%.

York, Los Angeles, Nashville, Atlanta, San Francisco, Austin, Chicago, Washington, D.C. and Seattle would be ideal landing spots for the tour. The 501(c)(3) itself could secure the expertise of practitioners and academicians in the various regions to reduce overhead costs. And for those cities that are not designated as tour stops, the course material could be made available via podcast, online streaming, or digital download, as well as written transcript. Each tour stop would focus on a different IP topic, for example, the legal essentials of music publishing, recording contracts, screenwriting, independent film production and the like. The courses can be designed to have a level of simplicity that is accessible for the IP creators who have no business or legal backgrounds but can perhaps also have sufficient complexity to satisfy general CLE requirements for attorneys who are not experienced in these areas. There are a number of arts-centered organizations that could be used as blueprints for this organization including the Health Alliance for Austin Musicians (HAAM) based in Austin, Texas that provides healthcare for self-employed musicians in Austin; several organizations throughout the U.S. that provide music lessons for free (or close to free) for underprivileged children, such as the W.O. Smith Music School in Nashville, Tennessee; and organizations in many major cities that provide opportunities for exposing underprivileged students to the arts, such as the previously mentioned Rush Philanthropic Arts Foundation (RPAF).

CONCLUSION

Whatever the eventual solution may be, there can be no argument that an answer is desperately needed. What the world needs is more songwriters like Barrett Strong who can enrich the lives of millions through their talents. What the world doesn't need is more stories of the despair experienced by these creators.

One of the leading theories behind the justification of copyright law is the theory of Natural Law or the Labor Model. "Natural rights" or "inherent entitlement" is based on the rights of authors to reap the fruits of their creations.[60] John Locke based the Labor Model on the belief that in owning their bodies, people also own the labor of their bodies and, by extension, the fruits of their labor.[61] Under the Utilitarian or Economic

---

[60] Robert Brauneis and Roger Schechter, *Copyright Law, A Contemporary Approach* (West Publishing, Eagan, MN 2011).
[61] John Locke, *Second Treatise on Civil Government* (1690).

Rational for copyright law, authors are granted limited monopoly through copyright law, a private property right over the author's creation, with the market ultimately determining its value.[62]

> The United States Constitution, Article 1, Section 8, Clause 8, grants Congress the right "To promote the Progress of Science and the useful Arts, by securing for limited Times to Authors and Inventors, the exclusive right of their respective Writings and Discoveries.[63]

Writers like Barrett Strong who devote their lives to creativity are classic examples of authors being failed by the very system that has been put in place to protect them – not because of a flaw in the statute, but because of a lack of understanding of their rights. Today's entertainment and IP lawyers have a rich opportunity to be at the forefront of providing a solution to these economic justice and social justice issues.

By using intellectual property and entrepreneurship to break down the walls of social injustice, I can indeed be my brother's keeper.

---

[62] Brauneis and Schechter, note 59 above.
[63] The United States Constitution, Article 1, Section 8, Clause 8.

11. Accentuate the positive, eliminate the negative: Intellectual property social justice and best practices for entrepreneurial economic development

Llewellyn Joseph Gibbons[1]

Whether the modern-international intellectual property regime promotes innovation and economic progress in developing countries is passionately contested from differing perspectives of the ideological divide. It is relatively uncontroversial that every country that has achieved a developed industrial economy did so by free riding on the intellectual property of citizens of more developed countries.[2] Lamentably, these same acts, by currently developing nations, are now castigated as intellectual property piracy because global norms of intellectual property have shifted dramatically in the past 50 years.[3] One of the effects of the World Trade Organization (WTO) and the Agreement on Trade Related Aspects of Intellectual Property (TRIPS) on developing economies was to effectively close off the legal unlicensed uses of technology as one possible avenue to economic development.

Most recently, an equally important, if not more important factor has been the increased use of bilateral free-trade agreements, so-called TRIPS plus agreements, between developed and developing countries which further

---

[1] This chapter is based in part on a prior law review article: "Do as I Say (Not as I Did): Putative Intellectual Property Lessons for Emerging Economies from the Not So Long Past of the Developed Nations", 64 SMU Law Rev. 923 (2011).

[2] Adrian Johns, *Piracy: The Intellectual Property Wars from Gutenberg to Gates* (Chicago University Press, Chicago 2009), 6–7.

[3] *See* Sanjaya Lall, "Indicators of the Relative Importance of IPRs in Developing Countries" (2003), 9–10, accessed 15 October 2014 at http://www.iprsonline.org/resources/docs/Lall%20-%20Indicators%20of%20relative%20importance%20of%20IPRs%20in%20DC%20-%20Blue%203.pdf.

limit a developing country's discretion in creating domestic pro-development intellectual property policies and in balancing competing national interests in fiscal and other public policies. At best, it is debatable whether developing countries, especially the least developed countries (LDCs), received any benefit from the Faustian bargain of trading enforceable domestic intellectual property law and policies for a vague, unenforceable promise of technology transfer from the most developed countries.

This chapter contends that if pre-WTO uncompensated transfers of knowledge and know-how were considered a type of developmental subsidy, then as the global intellectual property rights regime tightened its requirements for domestic enforcement of international norms of the intellectual property rights foreign owners, these then-legal (now illegal) leaks of technology transfer should be replaced with some other subsidy – if only to restore the status quo and to place developing countries in no worse a position post-WTO than they enjoyed pre-WTO or in bilateral trade agreements.

The most recent development of so-called TRIPS-plus agreements further supports the chapter's thesis that as one moves from the 18th century codification of domestic intellectual property law in Europe and the United States; to the late 19th century Berne and Paris Conventions which began the internationalization of intellectual property rights norms; to the global WTO–TRIPS regime which provided for the first time the effective domestic enforcement of the rights of foreign intellectual property owners; and now, to the more recent development of bilateral free-trade agreements, a developing country's ability to use intellectual property without the consent of foreign rights holders has increasingly decreased. Consequently, the identified structural problems are aggravated because each new TRIPS-plus (or similar bilateral) agreement creates a higher floor on which subsequent bilateral and international agreements are built, thus constituting a continuous one-way ratcheting of intellectual property rights and obligations, which are then codified into a developing country's domestic law regardless of the LDC actual development needs.

History may provide a solution to these structural problems. Uncompensated intellectual property transfers to developing countries promote economic efficiency, further development goals, and constitute a type of foreign aid subsidy. To a developing country, the economic effect is similar whether a developed country transfers $1 million in foreign aid, purchases a $1 million intellectual property license for the benefit of the developing country, or tacitly permits $1 million worth of unlicensed intellectual property use in a developing country. The first two examples, a transfer payment of $1 million or a purchase of a $1 million intellectual property license, represent an expense borne by the overburdened taxpayers of the developed country. Further, the economic value-received or economic development effect of such payments or licenses are often confounded with accusations of fraud, waste, and inefficiency. However, willful blindness or tacit consent to the use of unlicensed intellectual property may promote development goals more efficiently – often without any measurable cost to the "donor country" or "rights-holder".

The first two examples are top-down, may have significant transaction costs, and are not necessarily responsive to market forces in the developing country. Acquiescence to unlicensed intellectual property transfers, however, ameliorates most of these costs. Absent strong domestic intellectual property enforcement, the developing country will not pay higher prices for imported goods and technologies if these goods and technologies could be produced locally or imported from another developing country (one with a slightly higher level of industrialization) without paying an intellectual property premium. Industries in developing countries that produce "pirated" products for their own marketplace, or for that of other developing countries, may continue or even thrive by catering to the demands of other developing countries – thus expanding domestic manufacturing capability, increasing domestic research and development capability, promoting local economic development and jobs, and in the long run creating a sound basis for a developed economy which ultimately will respect foreign intellectual property rights in its own self-interest.

In contrast, an externally imposed effective domestic intellectual property rights enforcement regime imposes significant actual and opportunity costs on a developing country without *necessarily* conveying any corresponding benefits promoting domestic development.[4] The World Bank estimated that costs of TRIPS compliance to be at least $150 million for a developing country.[5] TRIPS enforcement could be thought of as a policy choice balancing the intellectual property rights of some foreign entities against the costs of providing public health services to 1.5 million people in some of the poorest countries in the world. The trade-off costs between the delivery of public goods or services and the enforcement of private intellectual property rights is arguably an unconscionable burden for any government of any developing country to assume without the assurance of off-setting domestic benefits.

---

[4] William Kingston, *Beyond Intellectual Property: Matching Information Protection to Innovation* (Edward Elgar, Cheltenham, UK and Northampton, MA, USA 2010), 171–72.

[5] Charles W. Schmidt, "Drugs as Intellectual Property", 4 *Modern Drug Discovery*, June 2001, 25–26, 28, accessed 15 October 2014 at http://pubs.acs.org/subscribe/journals/mdd/v04/i06/html/06rules.html.

In addition to the LDC government's enforcement costs, an effective domestic intellectual property rights enforcement regime will also result in higher prices for imported goods and increased fees for technology licenses. As a waggish judge once quipped, "copyright is a tax on reading"; therefore, patents should be considered a tax on innovation; and collectively effective intellectual property enforcement is a de facto tax on a developing country's economy. A less obvious cost, but perhaps a more important one, will be the closure of imitative activities (production of pirated goods). Closing off these opportunities to learn will result in a corresponding loss of economic activity through factory closures, loss of employment, informal domestic research and development, etc. An accidental side effect of strong domestic intellectual property rights is that legitimate domestic production may be hindered by developed country rights holders' threats that misuse intellectual property rights to discourage lawful but unlicensed uses of intellectual property. In the long run, indigenous industries with their own research and development capacity, and their own intellectual property rights will become the driving force for stronger domestic protection of intellectual property rights.

Local market conditions, stage of economic development, access to natural and human resources, and the access to capital will efficiently determine the demand for access to intellectual property. Developing countries are assuming additional burdens to enforce all forms of intellectual property, but not all forms of intellectual property are equally important in the social and economic context of each developing nation. This chapter, however, treats intellectual property as an integral whole and does not engage in a more nuanced debate as to relative degrees of protection for different forms of intellectual property in different sectors in the context of development.[6] This approach focuses the enforcement assessment from the development perspective. For example, in light of the more recent debates regarding genetically modified corps and access to pharmaceuticals in the developing countries, one might instinctively view this as primarily an issue involving patent rights. However, as recent scholarship demonstrates, the key to German industrial growth in the 19th century, and its ability to catch up with the United Kingdom, was not as a result of its robust patent laws, but rather because of Germany's lack of strong copyright protection for foreign works that resulted in wide

---

[6] With one minor exception, because trademark laws are designed to protect consumers from deception, it is hard to posit an economic-development-based justification for a developing country not to enforce trademark or similar unfair competition laws.

dissemination of scientific literature and practical instruction manuals.[7] So superficially, it may appear that the use of patent protected intellectual property is the key to economic development; the reality is that in some developing countries, it may be that cheap reproduction and dissemination of copyrighted works is more significant to economic development than the ability to reproduce patented innovation.

It may be strange to think of black-markets and activities commonly called "piracy" as economically efficient solutions to the question of economic development. But, the classic hallmark of an efficient market is one that responds to producer supply, consumer demand, and has few, if any transaction costs, including those transaction costs imposed by government regulation and of course a respect for property rights. Although highly contested by some scholars, this chapter assumes that the limited legal rights of exclusion granted to rights holders under the rubric of intellectual property are in fact *property*. If these rights are in fact "property" then it would appear that one of the canons of an efficient market is violated by a black-market in intellectual property. However, this dilemma is avoided by defining the efficient market solely in reference to the developing country or more narrowly by specific forms of intellectual property or technologies. This conceit is further in keeping with the 19th and 20th century understanding that intellectual property rights were territorial and that each sovereign solely granted these rights and in the early understanding of copyright, patent, and trademark as a *sui generis* and at best were a limited grant of a right that had some of the characteristics of a property right.

The United States, the original members states of what is now the European Union, and in more recent times, "newly developed" Asian nations such as Japan, Korea and Singapore are models that the best method of promoting long-term, sustained, indigenously lead, and culturally appropriate, economic development is a brief period of no enforcement, followed by a period of lax or selective enforcement, culminating in compliance with strong international intellectual property norms. However, the period of non-compensated uses is not only more efficient at promoting economic development, but in both the short-run, and more importantly in the long run, it would be cheaper for the developed nations rather than their current policies of direct foreign aid or

---

[7] *See* Frank Thadeusz, "No Copyright Law: The Real Reason for Germany's Industrial Expansion?", *Der Spiegel* (Germany), 18 August 2010, accessed 15 October 2014 at http:/www.spiegel.de/international/zeitgeist/0,1518,710976,00.html.

policies that support technology transfer to developing countries. In the short run, this respite from strong intellectual property rights enforcement substitutes in part for direct foreign aid paid for by the taxpayers of developed nations, and in the long run, it promotes the economic growth of developing nations who in time will support strong intellectual property rights enforcement, but more importantly for the developed nations intellectual property rights holders, the LDC will become new markets for their goods and services.

I. THE TRADITION – UNCOMPENSATED TRANSFERS – NOW KNOWN AS PIRACY

While it has not been conclusively proven that the piracy stage of economic development is a *necessary prerequisite* to industrialization (development), it is generally accepted that all of today's developed nations, including the so-called newly industrialized nations passed through at least one uncompensated transfer phase. A careful analysis of the modern experience of Brazil, Russia, India and China – the so-called BRIC countries – shows that they are merely the most recent examples that a critical ingredient to economic success is uncompensated transfers. From this historical record, this chapter concludes that uncompensated use is quite common in the process of maturing into a developed economy.

A. Stages of Development and Piracy

The economic evolution of a nation from developing to developed can be simplified into in a three-stage model. In stage one, arguably the earliest stage or lowest level of economic development, foreign direct investment is rare and usually limited to specialized sectors – often relating to the exploitation of natural resources or developing franchise service industries like a major international brand bottling company. Often, developing countries at stage one have only natural resources or unskilled, cheap labor to offer foreign direct investors. Foreign businesses must create the necessary infrastructure and establish a solid foundation on which to build the eventual capacity to absorb technology. Developing countries must invest in the training of workers and educating junior managers so that these countries eventually have the skills to develop an independent, productive workforce. However, even in this stage, any foreign direct investment will spur local entrepreneurial activity as indigenous small businesses are created to support the foreign investor or to its employees. At this stage, a developing nation's "ex-pats" may return home anticipating growth opportunities and bring with them the skills and capital they have earned while studying and working in more developed nations.

Successfully developing a skilled workforce is a prerequisite to entering stage two. A skilled workforce requires the socialization of a modern economy so that the workers meet the expectations of their employer. In addition to the social skills, such as punctuality by the clock, rather than by a social norm that defines functionality in a more flexible manner, a skilled work force requires a series of competencies that are readily transferable from one position to another in the company, industry, or national economy. This is a period of deskilling skilled labor into a commodity workforce and skilling unskilled labor in to the norms of commodity production. These skills have externalities. A highly skilled local worker will seek entrepreneurial and other opportunities for personal and economic growth either within an employer or see gaps in the economy where there is room for greater efficiencies, new products or services, and then begin to meet these demands.

Enforcement of foreign intellectual property rights may hinder development in stage two; because the local worker may either need to use intellectual property rights that are not exploited in the developing countries; or be unable to obtain the necessary permissions because of transactions costs; or unable to obtain the capital necessary to purchase the necessary rights. Thus possibilities for local growth are denied without conveying any corresponding advantage on the rights holders of more developed nations.

In stage two, the developing nation's economy is now able to absorb technology, to imitate technology at some level, and to contribute minor improvements to the transferred technology or intellectual property used in the domestic economy.[8] Absorptive capacity is "the ability to identify, assimilate, and exploit knowledge from the environment".[9] There are two methods of measuring absorptive capacity. Some scholars use "investment in R&D, provision of formal training and workforce education" while other scholars use "the total factor productivity gap" method to measure absorptive capacity. Critical to the absorptive stage is human capital. Some studies demonstrate that a 1 per cent increase in the average level

---

[8] Ibid, 45.
[9] Richard Kneller et al., "Does absorptive capacity affect who benefits from international technology transfer?" (8 August 2010) (unpublished manuscript), accessed 16 October 2014 at http://www.etsg.org/ETSG2010/papers/Pantea.pdf (emphasis removed) (quoting Wesley M. Cohen and Daniel A. Levinthal, "Innovation and Learning: The Two Faces of R & D", 99 Econ. J. 569, 569 (Sept. 1989)).

of human capital results in up to 17 per cent growth of the GDP over a generation.

In stage two, domestic research efforts are primarily facilitative or associated with technology transfer.[10] As a developing country moves towards the more developed-nation stage, it gradually focuses its research and development efforts on more innovative projects. Unfortunately, at this stage developing countries are not encouraged on their path to economic development. In fact, they are increasingly viewed as an economic threat by rights holders and the governments of some developed countries. The truth is that: "[t]he capacity of [developing] countries to copy advanced technologies is in fact very weak, but is subjectively over-estimated. People . . . may think that all that is stopping them is western-owned intellectual property. In fact, successful imitation requires much more in terms of human and social capital than simply freedom to imitate".[11]

In stage two, foreign direct investment has the maximum economic impact on the national economy. Stage two economies possess the predicate of a skilled workforce and economic infrastructure has been created. Also, there is now a critical mass of local companies that can provide support for the foreign direct investor. The foreign direct investor can focus on its natural advantages in the marketplace rather than focusing on creating a local supply chain or importing everything. At this stage, foreign direct investment is made for rational economic reasons rather than because of tax or other policies of the more developed nations.

Finally, in stage two developing nations now have a national self-interest to begin protecting intellectual property either because they are supporting their own indigenous intellectual property rights holders or because it is in their national interest to be more proactive in protecting the foreign right holders and direct investors, national intellectual property rights policies are now driven by national interest and domestic development rather than the whims of foreign governments.

In stage three, the developing nation is now newly industrialized and is producing its own intellectual property. Innovation-friendly (pro-intellectual property rights) countries tend to be more industrialized, or at least have a higher material standard of living, than countries that are less friendly

---

[10] *See* John H. Dunning and Rajneesh Narula, *Multinationals and Industrial Competitiveness: A New Agenda* (Edward Elgar, Cheltenham UK and Northampton, MA, USA 2004), 45.

[11] *See* William Kingston, "Removing Some Harm from the World Trade Organization", 32 Oxford Dev. Studies 309, 319 (2004), accessed 16 October 2014 at http://www.tara.tcd.ie/bitstream/2262/8696/1/Removing%20some%20harm.pdf.

towards innovation.¹² During this stage, developing nations are very selective as to which intellectual property rights they zealously protect and which rights they encourage misappropriation of.¹³ As developing countries create intellectual property, the amount of intellectual property to zealously protect continually grows – until these countries reach a tipping point and intellectual property protection becomes the new dominant mantra.¹⁴ This is the tipping point where a country moves from developing or newly industrialized to a mature, developed economy and assumes its role as a "mature" or "responsible" player in the global intellectual property regime.

B. Developing Countries as New Strident Voices Defending Intellectual Property

Between stages two and three in the three stage model, developing countries begin to realize that their continued development may require strong intellectual property rights.¹⁵ As one commentator observed:

> In less advanced economies, technology absorption can drive economic growth because countries at the forefront of technology act as a driver for growth by expanding the stock of scientific and technological knowledge, pulling other countries through a 'catch-up' effect. However, the strength of this 'catch-up' effect at the technology frontier decreases with the level of technological development, to the benefit of technology creation. Indeed, technology creation by domestic firms becomes progressively more important as a country moves closer to the technology frontier, because catching up with the frontier translates into increasingly smaller technological improvement.¹⁶

To put it more bluntly, countries protect intellectual property when they are more likely to be the victims of intellectual property theft domestically

---

[12] *See* Bruce Einhorn, "The World's Most Innovative Countries: The 30 Most Innovative-Friendly Countries", *Bus. Week*, accessed 16 October 2014 at http://images.businessweek.com/ss/09/03/0312_innovative_countries/1.htm.

[13] *Cf.* Christoph Antons, "Harmonization and selective adaptation as intellectual property policies in Asia", in Christopher Antons et al. (eds), *Intellectual Property Harmonisation Within ASEAN and APEC* (Kluwer Law International, Alphen aan den Rijn 2004), 109–18, 121.

[14] *See World Bank, Global Economic Prospects and the Developing Countries 2002* (2001), 130–32.

[15] *See generally* Ha-Joon Chang, *Kicking Away the Ladder: Development Strategy in Historical Perspective* (2002).

[16] *See* Emmanuel Hassan, Ohid Yaqub and Stephanie Diepeveen, "Intellectual Property and Developing Countries: A Review of the Literature" (2010), xv, available 3 November 2014 at http://www.rand.org/pubs/technical_reports/2010/RAND_TR804.pdf.

rather than the beneficiaries of the violation of intellectual property rights owned by foreigners. Often these changes in policies are a result of local political forces. For example, local innovative industries will demand domestic strong intellectual property protection – for use as a sword to protect their own innovation against domestic pirates unfairly competing against them in the marketplace, and as local industries compete globally, they do not wish to compete in foreign markets against their own intellectual property assets being exploited by foreign competitors.

Imagine a small, local manufacturer. It must pay for its own research and development and brand development and thus, it cannot compete in terms of price in the marketplace with counterfeit adhesive strips bearing internationally-known brand labels. If the local company is to succeed, it will have to drive the pirates out of the marketplace. Local innovative companies will also use intellectual property rights as a shield against the claims of foreign intellectual property rights holders and to prevent foreign competitors from misappropriating locally-developed innovation. Over time, countries will move from intellectual property scofflaws to reputable members of the intellectual property community. As a result, the quantity or quality of the uncompensated intellectual property technology transfers will decrease, and as these countries develop a vibrant middle class, they will be converted into new markets for developed countries.

C. Brazil, Russia, India, and China (BRIC) Countries as a *Sui Generis* Model of Development

Brazil, Russia, India and China ("BRIC" countries) may be used as an exemplar to test the principle that recently, the WTO and the TRIPS Agreement have barred uncompensated transfers as a route to development. BRIC countries are outside the trade-intellectual property subsidy paradigm discussed in this chapter for several reasons. First, they were pre-WTO, newly industrialized countries rather than economically developing countries. The BRIC countries had already moved beyond the diffusion phase and were at the absorptive or innovative phase of economic development. The BRIC countries became newly industrialized nations during the pre-WTO era. Both China (in 2001) and Russia (in 2012) had a significant industrial base prior to their entry into the capitalist marketplace. The BRIC countries were already on a trajectory to economic development when they entered into the WTO-TRIPs trade regime. Recent events, changes in the economic valuation of and access to natural resources, and better domestic policies merely increased the rate at which they were achieving their already well-established developmental goals.

Even if the BRIC countries were either first or very early second stage "developing countries" at their point of entry into the WTO-TRIPs regime, the BRIC countries are *sui generis*. They are geographically large, control significant natural resources, have large populations, play a unique strategic geopolitical role in their respective spheres of interest, and three of the four are members of the world's most exclusive club: countries with nuclear weapons. Russia and China are also permanent members of the United Nations Security Council, giving them the power to veto any action by the U.N. Security Council. Therefore, trade and intellectual property relationships with these countries are confounded with other factors, such as geopolitical considerations, rather than pure considerations of intellectual property enforcement and proper trade practices. Because of the BRIC countries' size, relative wealth and strategic considerations (including those related to trade as well as to national security concerns) developed countries are loath to use the WTO dispute resolution mechanism or the other levers of soft power, such as foreign aid. Accordingly the BRIC countries currently enjoy development status and access to uncompensated intellectual property transfers that is akin to that historically enjoyed by all countries pre-WTO. Consequently, BRIC countries are examples that do not disprove the uncompensated use as a phase of economic development model.

II. BIRTH OF THE MODERN INTELLECTUAL PROPERTY REGIME

The global intellectual property regime that was ultimately enshrined into TRIPS was largely finalized in the 19th century. The 19th century intellectual property rights treaties were largely Eurocentric, with occasional participation by the United States. And to the degree that the needs of many of the countries that are now part of the developing world were considered, their participation was as colonies or dependencies of the European powers.[17]

The needs and role of the colonies, if and when considered, were considered as part of the historical legacy of mercantilism. Under mercantilism, the role of the colonies was to provide raw materials and to

---

[17] Peter Drahos, "Developing Countries and International Intellectual Property Standard-Setting", Commission on Intellectual Property Rights, accessed 29 October 2014 at http://www.iprcommission.org/papers/pdfs/study_papers/sp8_drahos_study.pdf.

be a marketplace for manufactured goods. Under an economic policy of neo-mercantilism, the role of intellectual property or technology transfer to the then-colonies (now developing nations) as an engine of economic development was marginalized or rejected by the European powers for fear of creating competitors. This legal legacy continued. As colonies became independent, the colonial power's intellectual property laws were often retained as the laws of the newly-independent country with little, if any, consideration as to whether these laws were appropriate for the unique economic-development challenges facing each newly-independent country.

As discussed in Part II, while the dominant body of intellectual property law was developed in the late 19th and early 20th centuries, these intellectual property treaty regimes lacked an effective enforcement mechanism.[18] Nations that had the infrastructure or the human and fiscal capital to move from agricultural economies to industrial economies continued to enjoy an unsanctioned respite from domestic intellectual property enforcement obligations. As one historian observed,

> Without an international intellectual property regime, abiding by these notions was left to the voluntary actions of states. The United States merely paid lip service to the principle of international intellectual property. Ignoring intellectual property entitlements across national lines enabled Americans to build an industrial powerhouse founded upon the intellectual labor of Europeans.[19]

The experience of other now-developed nations supports this conclusion. A German economic historian, Eckhard Höffner, concluded that Germany's lack of copyright law was at the foundation of Germany's

---

[18] *See* Berne Convention for the Protection of Literary and Artistic Works [hereinafter Berne Convention] (available 29 October 2014 at http://www.wipo.int/treaties/en/ip/berne/trtdocs_wo001.html), art. 33 ("(1) Any dispute ... may ... be brought before the International Court of Justice ... unless the countries concerned agree on some other method of settlement. ... (2) Each country may ... declare that it does not consider itself bound by the provisions of paragraph (1). With regard to any dispute between such country and any other country of the Union, the provisions of paragraph (1) shall not apply."); Paris Convention for the Protection of Industrial Property [hereinafter Paris Convention (available 29 October 2014 at http:// www.wipo.int/treaties/en/ip/paris/trtdocs_wo020.html], art. 28(1) ("Any dispute between two or more countries of the Union concerning the interpretation or application of this Convention ... may ... be brought before the International Court of Justice ... unless the countries concerned agree on some other method of settlement.").

[19] Doron S. Ben-Atar, *Trade Secrets: Intellectual Piracy and the Origins of American Industrial Power* (Yale University Press, New Haven 2004).

industrial development in the 19th century.[20] In order to protect its domestic industries from foreign competition, Germany did not join the Paris Convention until 1903, 20 years after the Convention was first opened to signatories.[21]

The ability of countries to ignore either the intellectual property rights of foreigners or to interpret flexibly their treaty obligations changed with the creation of the WTO and the TRIPS Agreement. For the first time, international intellectual property treaties provided a carrot by offering tariff concessions to encourage countries to adopt a minimum level of domestic intellectual property protection and a stick through the WTO dispute resolution mechanisms to encourage effective intellectual property rights enforcement at the national level.[22]

The creation of the WTO required that developed countries make certain vacuous commitments that are integrally related to intellectual property, primarily in the area of technology transfer. The quid pro quo for developing nations entering into the WTO, especially the TRIPS Agreement, and for providing effective intellectual property rights enforcement for foreign rights holders was the largely unfulfilled promise by the developed countries to promote technology transfer to developing countries.

Surrendering the uncompensated transfers of intellectual property subsidy was not necessarily a rational bargain. Appropriate technology transfer provides numerous benefits: "[provides] more and better competition, upgrade[s] domestic innovative capacity, increase[s] R&D employment, give[s] better training and support[s] to education, and reverse[s] 'brain drain' effects."[23] However, while the WTO and the TRIPS Agreement promoted increased intellectual property protection in the developing nations,

---

[20] *See* Frank Thadeusz, "No Copyright Law: The Real Reason for Germany's Industrial Expansion?", *Der Spiegel*, 18 August 2010, accessed 16 October 2014 at http://www.spiegel.de/international/zeitgeist/0,1518,710976,00.html.

[21] *See* Kingston, note 11 above, at 67.

[22] Christine Thelen, Comment, "Carrots And Sticks: Evaluating the Tools for Securing Successful TRIPs Implementation", 24 Temp. J. Sci. Tech. & Envtl. L. 519, 520–24 (2005).

[23] Hassan, Yaqub and Diepeveen, note 12 above, 3. This article contends that the global Realpolitik makes exercising these rights under TRIPS or the WTO problematic at best, and at worse, it threatens a developing country with unilateral sanctions and/or proceedings before a WTO panel. As a practical matter, these flexibilities, except in the BRIC countries or perhaps the Republic of South Africa, are not really available options. The failure of the United States to abide by WTO rulings in connection with the ongoing U.S.-Antigua IP dispute is one example. See Dispute Settlement: Dispute DS285, *United States — Measures Affecting the Cross-Border Supply of Gambling and Betting Services*, accessed 3 November 2014 at http://www.wto.org/english/tratop_e/dispu_e/cases_e/ds285_e.htm.

the WTO and developed nations failed to deliver on their moral obligation to provide technology transfer that would at least equal the uncompensated use subsidy or even necessarily their promises of increased technology transfer at any level greater than it was during the pre-WTO phase.

While foreign direct investment and the export trade are significant factors in economic development and improving the material well-being in developing countries, the conclusions of the academic and non-governmental organization studies on whether the WTO, TRIPS and domestic-strong intellectual property rights law are good for the economic development of developing countries is, to be charitable, at best mixed. Strong intellectual property rights do not necessarily encourage foreign direct investment. Consequently, the theory that piracy is a necessary stage on the road to economic development may be tested in the future.

III. EFFICIENT PIRACY AND THE INEFFICIENT FOREIGN AID

There are two well-established models for foreign supported economic development. The first model is that of direct foreign aid. Developed countries provide economic or in-kind assistance to developing countries. The second model is technology transfer and is based on the voluntary technology transfer or direct foreign investment by the private sector. Both of these development models may fail because often they are more responsive to the domestic political and economic agenda of the private business entity or the donor-developed country than to the actual or self-perceived needs of the recipient-developing country. This chapter suggests rejecting economic development options narrowly limited to these two development models as a false choice. Instead it recommends a third development model: one that acquiesces to, or at least tolerates, uncompensated intellectual property transfers as long as the core economic incentives that promote the future production of intellectual property in developed (and developing) countries are adequately protected.

A. Foreign Aid

Direct foreign aid is often caricatured or stereotyped as being a species of waste, fraud, abuse, inefficiencies and political pork – often hurting more than it helps developing countries. The reality is that direct foreign aid or in-kind aid plays a significant role in alleviating poverty and suffering in the developing world and a critical role in the provision of public health services. However while, foreign humanitarian aid, education aid and infrastructure development aid may create the infrastructure ultimately to support economic development in moving from stage one to stage two of economic development, foreign aid *may* be less efficient than uncompensated intellectual property transfers as a developmental subsidy to promote industrialization in an LDC.

Under the existing direct foreign aid regime, a developed country provides economic support for programs in developing countries that the developed country finds "worthy", or are at least in the developed country's self-interest to support. Foreign aid administered through an international or multi-national organization often suffers from the same problems as purely bilateral aid. Foreign aid projects are often motivated more by donor country domestic politics rather than a desire to meet the actual needs of the recipient-developing country.

Foreign aid is also often provided to developing countries for strategic-geopolitical aims rather than to meet the actual needs of developing countries or as part of a strategic-economic-efficient development program. Over the past few decades, U.S. foreign aid has been directed by perennial strategic and peace concerns in the Middle East, the Cold War, or the Clinton Administration's "environmental, population, and democracy-building concerns" rather than by a pro-economic growth policy or by local needs in developing nations. And under the Bush and Obama Administrations, national security and fighting terrorism were the primary factors in the allocation of U.S. foreign aid rather than actual needs or development goals of the recipient countries. Sadly, the U.S. is not alone in using foreign aid as an instrument of national political policy.

> Other donor [countries] have their own objectives. For many years Sweden targeted aid toward "progressive" societies. In France, governments since De Gaulle have sought to promote the maintenance and spread of French culture and the French language as well as the preservation of French influence, particularly in West Africa. French aid has also often been disproportionately concentrated among nations with which France has extensive commercial ties. In Japan, aid has historically flowed disproportionately to neighboring Asian nations in which Japan has the greatest commercial interests, and Japan has in the past often tied aid to purchases of Japanese products.

In general, pressure groups such as trade associations and, in the United States, ethnic political blocs "have also proven quite adept at steering aid to their favored recipients."[24] This is a ubiquitous structural failure in the delivery and use of foreign aid, and as a structural problem, it prevents the

---

[24] Evan Osborne, "Rethinking Foreign Aid", 22 Cato J. 297, 307 (2002).

efficient use of foreign aid to promote an indigenously constructed and economically efficient development agenda.

Further, there are often explicit requirements or implicit understandings that the recipient country uses the foreign aid to purchase goods and services from the donor country that are not necessarily the optimal goods or services or the goods even detrimental, to economic development. As one commentator found, "[i]f aid is not particularly given with the intention to foster economic growth, it is perhaps not surprising that it does not achieve it".[25]

Even if developed countries could disregard their domestic politics and foreign policy predilections, it is a sad truism that most foreign aid programs are rife with waste, fraud, and inefficiency. So that even when foreign aid is targeted wisely and dedicated to economic development, foreign aid is still an inefficient means through which to achieve development, and the actual delivery of that aid is problematic. The potential for waste, fraud, and inefficiency exists in both the donor country's ability to deliver the foreign aid and the recipient country's ability to administer aid wisely. If either party fails at these tasks then foreign aid is at best wasted, and at worst further weakens a developing country by promoting a culture of corruption or dependency. Sadly, providing direct foreign aid, rather than increasing the funds available for development or humanitarian relief, often results in a mere substitution of local funding by foreign funding without any actual increase in the relevant services.

Finally, the law of unintended consequences may come into play because foreign aid oftentimes exacerbates local needs and adds to local misery in other areas, even while achieving the donor country's intended goal.[26] Even targeted development aid may also result in failure.

> American foreign aid has often harmed the Third World poor. In Indonesia, the government confiscated subsistence farmers' meager plots for AID-financed irrigation canals. In Mali, farmers were forced to sell their crops at giveaway prices to a joint project of AID and the Mali government. In Egypt, Haiti, and elsewhere, farmers have seen the prices for their own crops nose-dive when U.S. free food has been given to their countries.[27]

---

[25] Ibid.

[26] Sajal Lahiri, *Theory and Practice of Foreign Aid* (Elsevier, 2007), 422 (foreign aid harms exports and results in price increases developing countries); Paul Collier and Anke Hoeffler, "Unintended Consequences: Does Aid Promote Arms Races?", 69 Oxford Bull. Econ. & Stat. 2, 11–12 (2007). *See also* Chapter 2 herein.

[27] James Bovard, "The Continuing Failure of Foreign Aid", Cato Pol'y Analysis No. 65 (Jan. 1986), accessed 16 October 2014 at at http://www.cato.org/pubs/pas/pa065.html.

Therefore, even when foreign aid targeted for economic development is delivered and spent properly, there is no assurance that the aid will actually improve the quality of life for the people in the developing country or even promote economic development. In sum, foreign aid is often designated for the political and economic benefit of the donor country. This means that waste, fraud and inefficiency in either or both the donor or recipient countries (and the iron law of unexpected consequences) make the question of whether foreign aid efficiently promotes or inefficiently hinders economic development *at best* an open question.

B. International Technology Transfer Incentives

If one gives the post-WTO/TRIPs regime the benefit of the doubt as to whether the benefits of the technology transfer provisions of the WTO/TRIPS regime exceed the development loss from eliminating the pre-WTO/TRIPS uncompensated intellectual property transfers is still unclear. International technology transfer (ITT) is based on a mixed model of incentives ranging from governmental to pure market incentives. The fact that technology transfer is often to some degree market driven is a factor to commend it; however, technology transfers does not appear to be a better tool than foreign aid to promote development. Under the existing technology transfer model, either a developed country creates incentives for its domestic industries to invest in favored developing nations (and regions) – thus reinforcing the biases built into domestic politics as a factor in direct foreign aid; or private companies, for strategic market reasons (or altruistic motives), decide to invest in a developing country – usually, the sounder option if the goal is true sustained economic development.[28]

Companies seeking to invest in developing countries face a host of problems, including distance from markets; poor infrastructure; lack of human capital (skilled labor); lack of local companies to provide necessary ancillary goods and services; weak or no enforcement of contracts, property and other laws; recipient country or donor country licensing, regulatory and other policies that discourage or complicate investment; corruption; and political instability. "Technology transfer is neither simple nor cost free".[29]

---

[28] *See* Keith E. Maskus, "Encouraging International Technology Transfer", 33–35 (2004), accessed 16 October 2014 at http://www.iprsonline.org/unctadictsd/docs/CS_Maskus.pdf.

[29] *See* Maskus, note 28 above, at 19 ("The bulk of econometric studies that incorporate measures of investment costs find that they significantly reduce FDI and MNE activity at all levels of development.").

There are significant costs in adapting first world technology into an economically, technically, and culturally appropriate form so that it is suitable for use in a developing country. For example, the technology may require a steady electrical power supply in a country where power outages or spikes are the norm, access to clean potable water, or even that the resulting products may need to be redesigned so that they do not need special handling, such as refrigeration, in the marketplace or when used by consumers. The resources are so common as to be unnoticed in developed countries but critically lacking in many developing countries.

Coupling voluntary foreign investment with a donor country's incentive to support foreign direct investment does not substantially change the picture. As one prominent professor found:

> First, few new initiatives have been reported; virtually all are continued from prior policy decisions. Second, there are virtually no programs aimed specifically at the LDCs, rather their benefits are available to all developing countries (or even developed countries). Third, the programs are largely in the form of technical assistance and capacity building, with payments typically made to source-country consultants for this purpose. Fourth, where assistance payments are made to developing countries for the purpose of technology acquisition, it is generally for recognized regional development purposes, such as within the EU or NAFTA. Fifth, measurement of the extent of technology transfer is typically restricted to the dollar value of the assistance provided rather than some meaningful measure of effectiveness or results in transferring information. Of course, it must be acknowledged that precise measurements of technology transfer are extremely difficult to make without revealing proprietary information. Sixth, some countries make available for transfer the results of certain public research programs, though the extent of active efforts to shape that information varies widely.[30]

There are technology transfer policies that developed countries could adopt that would make foreign direct investment or technology transfer more attractive to private industry, such as granting preferential access to their domestic markets; structuring the tax code to encourage investment in developing countries; providing suitable financing for these investment projects; assisting in developing a skilled, healthy workforce in developing countries; and promoting education in the recipient country.[31] All of these

---

[30] Maskus, note 28 above, 35.
[31] *See generally* Dirk Willem te Velde, "Understanding Developed Country Efforts to Promote Foreign Direct Investment to Developing Countries: The Example of the United Kingdom Transnational Corporations", December 2007, accessed 16 October 2014 at http://unctad.org/en/docs/iteiit20074a4_en.pdf; United Nations Conference on Trade and Development, 15 October 2010, *Developing*

policies should result in reducing regulatory and tax barriers, transaction costs, including informational transactions costs, without attempting to distort the developing country's natural advantages or forcing domestic development policy to be consistent with the source nation's internal political or economic norms.

C. Piracy as Market Efficiency

Both direct foreign aid and technology transfer are inefficient modalities to support efficient economic development. Heretofore, all successfully developed nations free rode on the intellectual property of more developed nations. Consequently, the current international trade regime presents a false dilemma – either direct foreign aid or technology transfers. There are alternatives. One solution is to return to the pre-WTO model of permitting uncompensated and unlicensed uses of foreign intellectual property in developing countries instead of the current *de facto* policy of limiting uncompensated transfers to those developing nations that are politically or economically powerful to flout international trade rules. Unlicensed uses may not have the unintended consequences of foreign aid. The individualized decisions of free market participants and the ability of developing nations governments to regulate private economic activity should assure that the negative externalities of uncompensated use are minimized. Moreover, unlike government programs, once the negative externalities are noted, the free market may act more quickly to ameliorate the inadvertent effects of transferred technology.

A policy of permitting uncompensated uses of intellectual property leads to at least two questions whether uncompensated transfers or unlicensed uses of intellectual property promote development and what are the putative effects of uncompensated transfers on the utilitarian incentives behind the existing intellectual property regime. Since intellectual property rights are granted to innovators and creators in order to spur further innovation and creative works, which benefit the public – essentially the second question is whether the supply, demand, and price structures of developing nations can be segregated from those of the developed world.

Start with the unremarkable proposition that free markets are more efficient than regulated markets in allocating scarce resources and promoting economic growth.[32] One could extrapolate from this proposition a

---

Productive Capacities in Least Developed Countries: Issues for Discussion, accessed 16 October 2014 at http://www.unctad.org/en/docs/aldc20101en.pdf.

[32] Warwick E. Murray, *Geographies of Globalization*, 137–38 (Routledge, London and New York 2006).

more highly speculative assumption that a free marketplace in unlicensed intellectual property is more likely to promote economic development in developing countries than either direct foreign aid or incentivized technology transfer as they are analogous to a command economy or to use the roughly accurate but rather rhetorically loaded term "socialism". Further, one lesson that may be drawn from history is that those countries that have successfully transitioned from developing or agricultural economies to developed or industrial economies all did so during periods of lax or no transnational enforcement of intellectual property rights. The development norm in history was not the enforcement of intellectual property rights but, instead, the positive and proud flouting of the intellectual property rights of non-citizens as an aid to national development. In contrast to today's view of intellectual property as a pro-free trade ideal, for many years, intellectual property rights were excluded from free trade agreements because they were viewed as a barrier to trade.

1. Utilitarian intellectual property rights

One may suppose that the first axiom of any policy change is "do no harm". So, the first question is whether lax enforcement of foreign intellectual property rights would cause any signficant harm. Both developed and developing nations have a strong shared interest in the continued production of new innovation and creative works originating in the more developed countries. There are many theories that justify the periods of legal exclusivity granted to intellectual property rights holders. The utilitarian justification for intellectual property rights is that absent a period of time in which only the creator or inventor of intellectual property may exploit their work there would be no economic incentive to create new works of authorship or to create new inventions. This presupposes that, while intellectual property works require some investment to create, once works are created they are easily copied so that a competitor not bearing the costs of creation could undercut the price charged by the creator-investor and readily flood the market with cheaper reproductions of the protected work.

Governments, rather than calibrating the intellectual property rights incentives necessary to create new intellectual property with the costs and returns on investment, choose instead the longest period of time and the most robust degree of exclusivity necessary to provide an incentive to develop the most costly copyrighted work or patented innovation. These policies then become the floor for intellectual property protection. Thus, modern intellectual property law provides ever increasing protection for rights holders with no corresponding benefit to the public (including increased incentives to innovate or to create) and creates artificial barriers to further innovation and to the creation of new works during the statutory period of exclusivity.

Consequently, for many industries and types of works, the term and scope of existing intellectual property protection is well in excess of the level of protection necessary to provide an adequate or reasonable incentive to create new intellectual property. Over time, the scope of intellectual property rights has been expanding. Subject matters such as genetics, business methods and software are now patentable, and works created long ago, by authors who are long dead, are enjoying enlargement of copyright protection as their works are exploited in new mediums and the copyright term is constantly extended. Therefore, because most forms of intellectual property are overprotected, intellectual property holders are capturing a significant part the consumer surplus and simultaneously imposing a signficant deadweight loss on the economy. As a result, some minor slippage or leakage of the intellectual property rights holders' claim to a "global zone" of exclusivity should have no effect on a necessary reasonable utilitarian incentive structure to create or innovate. In economic terms, these unauthorized and uncompensated uses proposed in this Chapter decrease the deadweight loss on the economy and increase the consumer surplus without affecting the monopoly profits that the intellectual property rights holder enjoys as a utilitarian reward for her creativity and industry.

2. Piracy is an efficient development modality
If a policy change of lax enforcement of foreign intellectual property rights results in no harm being done to the utilitarian incentives to create and to innovation in developed nations, which under the *utilitarian model* behind intellectual property is their sole legitimate interest, then the question to be asked is whether unlicensed uses are more efficient in promoting developmental goals than direct foreign aid or incentives for technology transfer. A market-driven policy for intellectual property or technology transfer that permits access to and use of intellectual property in response to market demand for technology or information in a local developing country's markets will promote development efficiently. Uncompensated intellectual property transfers as a developmental policy may have much to commend it because uncompensated transfers may mark an attempt to return to the well-worn paths that led to past successful economic development.

This historic fact does not suggest that developed country intellectual property rights holders should grant developing countries an indefinite period or a blank check on intellectual property enforcement. It recognizes an internalized limit that at some stage of economic development, nations start noticing that the economic development of *other* nations is free-riding on the intellectual property rights belonging to their citizens, and only then do these nations begin to develop strong domestic laws protecting intellectual property rights. National self-interest and long-term *sustained* economic development is ultimately the best limitation on uncompensated uses of foreign intellectual property and not outside pressure on the weakest nations.

Most individuals living in a market economy take it as a given that free markets are better than governments in allocating scarce resources. Free market piracy lacks the inefficiency of what is essentially a command economy of intellectual property or technology demand created by government policies. Unlicensed use is not responsive to the political vagaries of the domestic or foreign policies of the donor or recipient countries. Further, the direct and indirect transaction costs that are related to licensing intellectual property rights are avoided: direct costs (such as royalty fees and negotiating the scope of the license) and indirect costs (such as locating the owner of the intellectual property and administering the license or insuring that unlicensed uses do not infringe foreign intellectual property rights).

There is less inefficiency in a "market" based on unlicensed uses in the delivery of the intellectual property; each market player receives the unit of intellectual property or technology that the market participant demands at a price that is responsive to its individualized needs and the marginal costs of production. Of course the marginal cost to the pirate does not include the very economically significant fixed costs of research, development, marketing, licensing, regulatory compliance, and so on that were paid by the intellectual property rights holder or investor.

In other words, the market effect of foreign intellectual property rights is marginalized as a domestic market factor, and the prices for tangible embodiments of goods protected by foreign intellectual property may remain low because intellectual property rights will not serve as a barrier to market entry and the production of these goods. This would result in a market characterized by increased competition and lower prices. Potentially, there will be numerous entities competing to sell goods in the marketplace and thus, creating something that approximates a free market for these products – one that is largely unconstrained by an artificial intellectual property monopoly.

Technology or intellectual property may be modified to suit local conditions without the transaction costs of negotiating a licensee agreement or seeking permissions. Adaptation, or even imitative use, of technology to meet local needs is often the foundation of an independent local research and development sector.[33] If local industry has to understand a product

---

[33] *See* Paz Estrella E. Tolentino, *Technological Innovation and Third World Multinationals* (Routledge, London 1993), 46–47.

in order to replicate it and then build, buy, or modify the technology to produce the product. These efforts will, then, result in truly effective technology transfer. Think of the proverb that points out the salient difference between giving a fish and teaching a person to fish. An industry in a developing country, which is developed from independently reverse-engineering a product and the associated, manufacturing process, has gained more than one that merely received an instruction manual, foreign advisors and a prefabricated factory and is only asked to provide an unskilled and undifferentiated workforce. And at least in theory, the very least developed (stage one) countries may lack any significant imitative industrial capacity. These countries may benefit greatly from unlicensed access to copyrighted scientific articles, educational materials, practical training manuals or other materials that improve that country's human capital rather than the ability to produce goods or render services that are protected by foreign patent rights.

3. Marginal costs, marginal losses, and foreign aid as marginal compensation

Academic and industry leaders approach the battle of high versus low barriers of intellectual property protection, in both the arena of public opinion and before legislative bodies, as an all-or-nothing, zero-sum game. But, there is academic research that suggests that some policies governing spillovers and externalities may approach a Pareto optimal solution – benefiting both innovators and society at large in both developed countries and developing countries. Intellectual property and technology transfers are not zero-sum games; properly administered, they may actually change the size of the pie. Intellectual property is characterized by high costs of creation compared with the relatively low costs of subsequent reproduction. While the cost of producing the first and subsequent units of intellectual property is relatively easy to calculate, calculating the losses caused by piracy of intellectual property is often problematic.

Accurately valuing the economic losses to intellectual property owners in developed countries is significant because the basis of the utilitarian model is the highly contested *assumption* that an intellectual property holder is entitled to a period of market exclusivity (or monetary damages when that exclusivity is breached) as an incentive to produce new innovation and creative works. In the absence of evidence to the contrary, this chapter assumes that the marginal cost per unit of unlicensed use (actual losses) in developing nations is relatively small. While tacitly accepting unlicensed uses in developing countries is the preferred model, and contending that the economically less efficient solution (but the more politically expedient one) may be for some developed nations to compensate their citizens at their *actual* market price in developing country damages (foregone sales) caused by unlicensed use in developing countries for the uncompensated uses, rather than to use these resources to provide further incentives (either direct subsidies or tax credits) for authorized technology transfer programs. Basically, foreign aid funds will purchase "licenses" for developing countries rather than forcing compliance with existing, inefficient international intellectual property norms and inefficiently indirectly purchasing the same rights at higher costs through foreign aid programs.

CONCLUSION

The thesis of this chapter is that developing countries need access to intellectual property at little or no cost to facilitate their economic development in an efficient manner. This does not require an affirmative change in the current, *de jure* international legal regime. The TRIPS Agreement, the WTO, the Paris Convention and the Berne Convention all have sufficient flexibilities to permit developing countries to engage in unlicensed uses that do not threaten the core incentives that arguably drive investment, innovation and the production of new works, especially for developed country rights holders. Developed countries may strategically weigh the costs of infringement to their rights holders against the benefits conferred on the developing country and refrain from using the levers of power at their disposal to force compliance with the broadest possible interpretation of the scope of intellectual property rights.

This chapter offers its advice with one significant caveat that developed countries may not look to the pricing structure of the pirated economy to determine developed countries prices. This caveat is based on experiences regarding the global debate on pharmaceutical and medical device prices. Demagogues should not be credibly able to point to the lower developing country "pirated" price to contend those prices should be charged in the developed world nor make arguments that intellectual property rights holders are gouging consumers in the developed world, or complaints regarding developing countries free riding on the research investments of the developed world. Further, "[m]ost of the clamor that pharmaceutical prices are unfairly low in foreign countries is based solely on anecdotal evidence".[34]

---

[34] Patricia Danzon, "The Price of Pharmaceuticals: International Comparisons and the Effects of Controls", Am. Enterprise Inst. For Pub. Pol'y Res. (12 December 2003).

Pharmaceutical price differentials across countries roughly reflect differences in income. Adjusting the price indices by per capita income suggests that drug price levels are actually slightly higher in other major markets. For the basket used in this study, drug prices in Canada are 4 percent higher than in the United States and are 25 percent higher in the United Kingdom. In Chile and Mexico, prices are nearly 430 percent higher than found in the U.S. when normalized for income. While the American public protests that drug prices abroad are too low, the data suggest that we in fact are asking low-income countries to contribute more for pharmaceuticals than they can reasonably afford.[35]

Pharmaceutical R&D is a large, globally-joint fixed cost, where optimal pricing is a function of demand elasticities. Using income as a proxy for elasticity, we conclude that higher drug prices for high-income countries are both efficient and equitable. For the United States to artificially dampen prices through re-importation or price controls would create inappropriate price uniformity and lower social welfare.[36]

Unfortunately, policymakers in developed nations will face the politically unpalatable reality that intellectual property rights holders will shrilly complain that they are losing money, that workers in United States or the European Union are losing jobs and that future research and innovation are being hindered. However, even the shrill claims are unclear as to whether the claimed damages are caused by pirate sales in the developed world or uncompensated uses in the developing world. The practical effect of tolerated, uncompensated uses in developing countries on the market price, profits and revenues in the developed nations would be nominal. Even if all the demand in all the developing countries by consumers who can afford a licensed product is aggregated, it would still represent a miniscule and insignificant portion of the potential global market, with the sole exception of the narrow classes of products that are only designed for, or especially cater to, the needs of the developing world.[37]

The proposed model of a nuanced enforcement of intellectual property rights in developing countries is not unconstrained, and if properly

---

[35] Ibid.
[36] Ibid.
[37] There are a variety of measures for defining the global middle class. Some experts define it as those individuals with between $2 and $4 per day per person in purchasing power. Others have used ranges from $10 to $100 per day per person depending on the country. *See* Homi Kharas, "The Emerging Middle Class in Developing Countries" (OECD Dev. Ctr., Working Paper No. 285, 2010), 8–9, accessed 16 October 2014 at http://www.oecd.org/dataoecd/12/52/44457738.pdf. It is clear that the global middle class outside of the developed countries are, at this point in time, marginal as factors driving actual demand for most licensed products.

applied, it will have no effect on the utilitarian incentives that justify intellectual property rights law. Developed countries should stop turning a blind eye to unlicensed uses in developing countries only at the point where there is sufficient injury to their rights holders so that continued uncompensated use may result in under-investment in the production of new intellectual property. This might occur if the product is one that is developed for developing country markets. Undeniably, this is not an objective test but rather a nuanced, individualized multifactor test with indeterminate factors that should be carefully weighed and applied industry-by-industry, product-by-product, firm-by-firm and, most importantly, individual-*developed* country by individual-*developing* country. This would not require a change in the global intellectual property regime; rather, it would merely require the selective enforcement and management of intellectual property rights through a judicious use of existing instrumentalities.

A modicum of moral suasion may be applied by governments or consumers in the developed world to encourage rights holders to grant licenses or to provide their products in the developing world at a price approaching the marginal cost of production. The political process has already commenced to reframe these issues in the context of patented, life-saving pharmaceutical products from a focus on property rights and free-riding to a view that balances the patent incentives for innovation and the actual costs imposed on patent owners through compulsory licenses, with the social impact on providing these medicines in developing countries. Alternatively, developed countries may purchase licenses from domestic intellectual property rights holders that permit developing countries, on reasonable terms, to exploit intellectual property. If one accepts the market value for these products as the fair market price in a developing country, then the costs of these licenses will be nominal at best and licenses will be more readily affordable. The strategic value of licensing rather than piracy is that rights holders may use license terms to protect critical markets and uses while permitting developing countries to use the intellectual property in a manner that has a minimal effect on the owner's profits. Uncompensated transfers are a one-size-fits-all solution, while licensing is a customizable solution that often benefits both parties. Further, a liberal or low price licensing regime reinforces international norms of intellectual property and reinforces the expectation that at some point developing countries become developed and will have to pay for continued uses of intellectual property. This avoids the slide into intellectual property anarchy.

Moreover, each of these scenarios present opportunities for indigenous, development oriented entrepreneurial endeavor. One reason "black market" distribution networks thrive is that they address various unmet needs, such as making essential products available at prices that citizens in developing countries can afford. Unauthorized dealers in IP products can typically service such markets at a profit, given that they do not have research and development costs or many of the other overhead expenses associated with innovative or original product development. However, rights holders and/or their emissaries can compete and indeed control these sub-markets if they would permit their products to be sold at or near marginal production cost and instead rely solely upon the markets in developed countries to recoup their indirect costs. Depending upon the structure of such "blind-eye" (or at least IP myopic) arrangements or policies, rights holders could derive a variety of benefits from such relaxed enforcement strategies. Rights holders could thereby support the development of and exert some influence over the resulting distribution lines for their products, and thus in some respects "recapture" local sales that would otherwise go to wholly unauthorized dealers. They could obtain important information about indigenous consumer needs and interests, which could prove highly valuable as the community develops a middle class and otherwise continues its economic development. Further, the resulting entrepreneurial vehicles should help to identify and stabilize indigenous consumer markets, expand the pertinent semi-skilled and skilled labor force, and otherwise enhance the local commercial infrastructure, to the ultimate benefit of both the rights holder and the developing community.

The old adage of teaching a person to fish versus giving a person a fish remains true today. Intellectual property policy must return to first principles and remain grounded in historical experience unless there is a good reason to depart from the successful historical model of uncompensated transfers as a subsidy for economic development. So far, there is no such reason other than providing the possibility, and sometimes the reality, of additional income from developing countries. While in the short run, this may be of some benefit to the rights holders of developed countries, it then makes intellectual property rights one more pillar supporting global poverty rather than a liberating international force for economic growth and in time providing new or more profitable markets for rights holders. If tacit acceptance of unlicensed uses in developing countries can co-exist with the utilitarian incentives underlying the existing intellectual property regime then it is socially wrong and economically irrational to force this system on unwilling participants who are unable to comply with the demands for increased enforcement and simultaneously support pro-development and growth national priorities. Intellectual property policy recognizes short-term social losses in market exclusivity for the long-term social benefit of innovation and creativity. Today, this may change to require an acceptance of short-term economic losses for the future benefits of a new markets and a politically stable economic environment.

PART IV

Commencement

12. From swords to ploughshares: Towards a unified theory of intellectual property social justice
Lateef Mtima

Intellectual property social justice provides a context through which to consider the role of intellectual property protection in the total political economy.[1] Like all other social ordering mechanisms, intellectual property protection is but one function within a complex and organic social system designed to promote the well-being of the societal body as a whole. As intellectual property has moved to the forefront of daily life, however, scholars, activists, and policy makers have called for a greater harmonization of intellectual property protection with other important social mechanisms and objectives. Toward this end, leading "IP social reformists" have argued that prevailing intellectual property norms can and should be socially rehabilitated by resorting to appropriate extrinsic disciplines, such as human rights jurisprudence and critical legal theory,[2]

---

[1] *See e.g.* John C. Reitz, "Centennial World Congress on Comparative Law: Political Economy as a Major Architectural Principle of Public Law", 75 Tul. L. Rev. 1121, 1125, 1127–8 (2001) ("Each country's principle of political economy . . . is a normative statement reflecting the conception that predominates within that country of what the appropriate relationship between the individual and the state should be . . . [T]he United States has an especially market-oriented political economy . . . The social welfare states of western Europe have more state-centered political economies . . . though less so than socialist states like the People's Republic of China . . . Like France, Germany has a long intellectual tradition that posits a strong role for the state to play in assuring basic welfare for everyone in society."); Vincent Mosco, *The Political Economy of Communication* 24 (2nd edn, Sage Publications, London 2009) ("One can think about political economy as the study of the social relations, particularly the power relations, that mutually constitute the production, distribution, and consumption of resources.")

[2] *See e.g.* http://www.law.cornell.edu/wex/critical_legal_theory (accessed 16 October 2014) ("Critical legal studies . . . is a theory that challenges and overturns accepted norms and standards in legal theory and practice. Proponents of this theory believe that logic and structure attributed to the law grow out of the power

so as to infuse the intellectual property regime with a progressive social consciousness.

Intellectual property social justice occupies a unique space in the IP social reform discourse. Whereas the predominating reformist rhetoric confronts the challenge as one of importing pertinent social values *into* the IP regime, intellectual property social justice eschews any implicit conceptualization of intellectual property protection as inherently devoid of non-economic/socially benign objectives. Whether as an implement of positive social law or an acknowledgement of natural rights and the "social contract",[3] the ultimate function of intellectual property protection is to cultivate human development and advancement: the intellectual property regime is structured to encourage, access and apply human creativity and innovation because it is socially useful to do so. While economic incentives and commoditization mechanisms are certainly elements of intellectual property protection, they are not its only features or concerns. Intellectual property social justice regards the values of equitable access, inclusion and empowerment as essential and indeed *intrinsic* to the enterprise. From this perspective, intellectual property social justice confronts "IP law and economics"[4] extremes as promoting and perpetuating socially wasteful inefficiencies in the contemporary intellectual property protection apparatus. Through IP Empowerment, intellectual property social justice realigns the mechanism so as to recoup the resulting social losses and maximize the overall efficiency and productive impact/output of the intellectual property system.[5]

---

relationships of the society. The law exists to support the interests of the party or class that forms it and is merely a collection of beliefs and prejudices that legitimize the injustices of society. The wealthy and the powerful use the law as an instrument for oppression in order to maintain their place in hierarchy. The basic idea of CLS is that the law is politics and it is not neutral or value free."); Betsy B. Baker, "Constructing Justice: Theories of the Subject in Law and Literature", 75 Minn. L. Rev. 581–2 (1991) ("Critics of the legal system have long observed its tendency to distort or ignore connections between its human subjects and the empirical world of their experience . . . In opposition to law's antisubjective tendencies . . . several legal theorists . . . argue . . . that the legal system needs to admit more subjective concerns to legal discourse and to recognize more the humanity of the subject in law.")

[3] John Locke, *Two Treatises of Government, Second Treatise* § §26–9, 127–8.

[4] *See generally* William M. Landes and Richard A. Posner, "An Economic Analysis of Copyright Law", 18 J. Legal Stud. 325 (1989).

[5] Lateef Mtima, "Copyright Social Utility and Social Justice Interdependence: A Paradigm for Intellectual Property Empowerment and Digital Entrepreneurship", 112 W. Va. L. Rev. 97, 126–7 (2009); Bill Ivey, *Arts, Inc.: How Greed and Neglect Have Destroyed Our Cultural Rights* (University of California Press, Berkeley 2008), 23–5, 50–56.

INTELLECTUAL PROPERTY AND THE SOCIO-POLITICAL ECONOMY

The technological innovations and breakthroughs of the latter half of the 20th century inspired many social activists, scholars and policy makers to question how famine, pandemic disease, poverty, and illiteracy could still persist throughout much of the world.[6] Although unprecedented achievements in pharmacology and bio-farming, together with the advent of digital information technology and the Internet, presaged new standards of global health, education and knowledge and information exchange, the fruits of innovative and creative advance did not reach many of those who needed them most. For many considering the problem, the mandates of civilized culture demanded that a solution to this social paradox be found.

Although by no means the only impediment to the pervasive uplift of the global social welfare, certain perceived requirements of the intellectual property regime were often cited as a critical stumbling block. For many intellectual property experts, this presented an incongruous state of affairs; it was simply incomprehensible that the very social ordering mechanism designed to promote human intellectual endeavor could also serve as a major obstacle to the socially responsible dissemination of its beneficial outcomes.[7]

For some intellectual property scholars and theorists, resort to human rights discourse, particularly with respect to addressing social conditions in the developing world, seemed the most viable course. They argued that fundamental human needs must be assessed in conjunction with contemporary human accomplishment in the calibration of human rights. Put differently, once the means to address critical social deficiencies become manifest, the recognition of basic human rights requires that such advances be deployed as necessary to alleviate human suffering, degradation, and social inhibition.[8]

---

[6] *See e.g.* Amartya Sen, *Development as Freedom* (Anchor Books, New York 1999), 3.

[7] *See e.g.* Joseph E. Stiglitz, "Economic Foundations of Intellectual Property Rights", 57 Duke L. J. 1693, 1701, 1716–19 (2008).

[8] *See, e.g.* Margaret Chon, "Intellectual Property and the Development Divide", 27 Cardozo L. Rev. 2821, 2912 (2006) ("If the instrumental mandate of intellectual property law is truly to increase knowledge for positive purposes, then there must be fuller consideration of the provision of basic needs and other global public goods such as food security, education, and health care. Undernourished, diseased, dying, undereducated, or extremely impoverished populations are viewed by many as negative externalities both qualitatively and quantitatively more serious than the danger of under-incentivizing authors

While conditions in the developing world spurred "IP as human rights" ratiocination, a few intellectual property scholars directed their attention toward IP-related social deficiencies in the developed world. A principal concern was the lack of equitable participation in the intellectual property system on the part of historically marginalized groups and communities. The central focus of these analyses was the failure of the intellectual property regime to account for the realities of racism, sexism, and other systemic social inequities in the interpretation and enforcement of the intellectual property law. Consequently, many of these scholars advocated

---

and inventors. The latter is the externality to which intellectual property law devotes its exclusive attention. This disjuncture over priorities has highlighted an increasingly untenable intellectual solipsism of the intellectual property policymaking framework, as intellectual property globalization encounters ethical concerns associated with development.") Mary W.S. Wong, "Toward an Alternative Normative Framework for Copyright: From Private Property to Human Rights", 26 Cardozo Arts & Ent. L.J. 775, 830 (2009) ("Many ... scholars share the belief that the current international IP regime does not adequately accommodate concerns of distributive social justice, and the relatively simplistic utilitarian balancing act it currently espouses tends to favor IP producers (who are located primarily in developed, mostly Western, countries). It does not easily allow for non-economic developmental considerations that are emphasized by human rights jurisprudence and norms, and that are socially beneficial objectives that IP regimes ought to incorporate. Alongside specific proposals for addressing these inadequacies, [these] scholars ... support (either explicitly or implicitly) a broader approach that incorporates social and cultural theory, and that more clearly maps to less utilitarian objectives such as self-actualization, freedom of choice, and human development.") Steven D. Jamar, "Symposium: The Global Impact and Implementation of Human Rights Norm: A Social Justice Perspective on the Role of Copyright in Realizing International Human Rights", 25 Pac. McGeorge Global Bus. & Dev. L.J. 289–90 (2012) ("A cornerstone of the human rights movement is access to information. Civil and political rights – like freedom of expression, free exercise of religion, meaningful participation in government – require an educated citizenry with access to information. Economic, social, and cultural rights – such as the right to an education, to health care, to economic development, to a clean environment, and more generally to participate in the social and cultural life of a nation – also depend upon access to information in a general way, for education, as well as in a more particular way for each of the domains listed; i.e., information about health, disease, medicines, and treatments; information about business methods, the economy, and know-how including intellectual property; information about the environmental consequences of various actions; and information about, and in some sense even constituting, the arts and culture. Thus the right to access information is not only an important right in and of itself, but it is important for how it supports other human rights.") *See generally* Johanna Gibson, *Creating Selves: Intellectual Property and the Narration of Culture* (Ashgate Publishing, Farnham 2006), 1–9.

for the importation of critical legal theory principles into intellectual property jurisprudence, in order to assure a more socially equitable and efficacious system.⁹

A flaw in, or perhaps more accurately a limitation of these disparate efforts to import extrinsic analytic disciplines into the intellectual property protection schema is that thus far, they have not been especially permeable to interdisciplinary cross-fertilization.¹⁰ This is none too surprising, however, in that the evaluation of a discreet subject matter through an extrinsic disciplinary lens tends to lead to analytical theories and methodologies endemic to that extrinsic discipline. Thus for example, where IP-based impediments to access to medicines are assessed as an alienation of human rights, the validity of IP commoditization policies are likely to come under scrutiny.¹¹ On the other hand, where inequitable IP enforcement is assessed as institutionalized bias, systemic mechanisms for corrective justice naturally come to mind.¹²

Intellectual property social justice departs from IP-*extrinsic* reform theories in that its core premise is that the principles of equitable access, inclusion, and empowerment are *intrinsic* to intellectual property protection as a social ordering mechanism. A particular benefit of this approach is that the instances in which intellectual property protection is permitted to obstruct critical social welfare imperatives are not addressed as independent IP social maladies, but rather as symptoms of an IP-systemic malaise, engendered and perpetuated by a misconstruction of and consequential imbalance in the intellectual property regime. Intellectual property social justice therefore prioritizes holistic revitalization of the intellectual property infrastructure over localized responses to its symptomatic ills. In this sense, intellectual property social justice is perhaps

---

⁹ *See e.g.* K.J. Greene, "Intellectual Property at the Intersection of Race and Gender: Or Lady Sings the Blues", 16 Am U. J. Gender Soc. Pol'y & L. 365, 367–70, 378–82 (2008).

¹⁰ For two notable exceptions *see* "Symposium, Intellectual Property and Social Justice" 48 How. L.J. 571, et seq. (2005); "Symposium: Intellectual Property and Social Justice", 40 U.C. Davis L. Rev. 559, et seq. (2007).

¹¹ *See e.g.* Madahavi Sunder, *From Goods to A Good Life: Intellectual Property and Global Justice* (Yale University Press, New Haven 2012), 1–3. "[I]ntellectual property laws have profound effects on human capabilities . . . Intellectual property incentivizes pharmaceutical companies to innovate drugs that sell – hence we are flooded with cures for erectile dysfunction and baldness, but still have no cure for the diseases that afflict millions of the poor, from malaria to tuberculosis, because these people are too poor to save their lives".

¹² *See e.g.* K.J. Greene, "Copyright, Culture & Black Music: A Legacy of Unequal Protection", 21 Hastings Comm. & Ent. L.J. 339, 356–60, 383–91 (1999).

more aptly described as a theory of IP social *restoration*, as opposed to IP social *reform*.[13]

Its distinctive rationale notwithstanding, intellectual property social justice should not be viewed as antagonistic to theories which transfuse human rights edicts, critical legal theory tenets, or similar socio-legal principles in to the intellectual property regime. Without question, intellectual property protection must achieve and maintain a measure of "social interoperability" with other important social ordering mechanisms and goals.[14] Intellectual property social justice merely rejects as false any implicit dichotomization of intellectual property social objectives from egalitarian social values. Intellectual property social justice therefore establishes a common analytical foundation for IP social reform ideologies and aggregates them within a unified theory of socially cognizant, and socially just, intellectual property protection.

APPLYING THE UNIFIED THEORY OF INTELLECTUAL PROPERTY SOCIAL JUSTICE

Intellectual property social justice contemplates intellectual property protection as an essential and propitious part of a healthy and well-balanced socio-economic diet. As a corollary proposition, intellectual property social justice accommodates the ecumenical tenets of intellectual property social utility.

Intellectual property social justice is an indisputably essential feature of a positive social utility IP regime. For example, in the United States, the express positive social utility function of its intellectual property regime is to promote the progress of the arts and sciences. To fulfill their role in this social enterprise, individuals must enjoy meaningful and equitable access to and participation in the intellectual property system and its outputs.[15]

---

[13] Compare Mtima, note 5 above, 135 ("This approach ... acknowledges that certain social deficiencies gnaw at the very foundations of [intellectual property] protection.") with Sunder, note 11 above, 3 (Calling for "intellectual property law and legal decision makers to expressly recognize and contend with the plural values at stake in cultural production and exchange").

[14] Anupam Chander and Madhavi Sunder, "Is Nozick kicking Rawls's Ass? Intellectual Property and Social Justice", 40 U.C. Davis L. Rev. 563, 564–78 (2007) ("No human domain should be immune from the claims of social justice. Intellectual property ... structures social relations and has profound social effects"). Lateef Mtima, "Symposium: Intellectual Property and Social Justice", 48 How. L.J. 571, 575–6 (2005).

[15] William Patry, *How to Fix Copyright* (Oxford University Press, New York

Intellectual property social justice is also consonant with natural rights intellectual property regimes. Institutionalized misappropriation of the intellectual property product of marginalized members of society is an intellectual property social injustice which directly contravenes natural rights edicts.[16] Similar reasoning supports the socially beneficent dissemination of intellectual property to address critical social needs. Under natural rights theory, society provides intellectual property producers with protection for their "divine" property rights, which protection the remaining populace enables, in exchange for society's assurance that their own intellectual property rights and interests (including equitable access to intellectual property output) will receive reciprocal respect and consideration. Unless that promise is fulfilled, the social bargain is one-sided and illusory; non-rights holders acknowledge and sustain rights holders' property interests, but their own natural rights are compromised as they receive nothing in return.[17]

2011), 91: "All works exist only in context with past and present authors and culture: readers can only understand contextually; that is within shared communal understanding. . . . Creativity requires the breathing space necessary to permit all authors to draw on the whole of culture". Patricia Aufderheide and Peter Jaszi, *Reclaiming Fair Use* (University of Chicago Press, Chicago 2011), xi (discussing "the consequences of a deformed and shrunken understanding of copyright policy and its purpose" and observing that "when people . . . are constantly afraid that they might get caught for referring to copyrighted culture . . . they can't do their best work. Their work as well as their imaginations shrink down to what they think might be possible . . . [T]his misunderstanding cripples creativity at its base and deforms the growth and development of our own culture"). Of course, the invocation of positive social utility as the basis for intellectual property protection is not unique to the American IP regime. *See e.g.* Article 1 of the Copyright Law of Japan ("The purpose of this Law is, by providing for the rights of authors and the rights neighboring thereon…to secure the protection of the rights of authors, etc., having regard to a just and fair exploitation of these cultural products, and thereby to contribute to the development of culture").

[16] John Locke, *Second Treatise* § §26–9.
[17] *See e.g.* Jamar, note 8 above, 296–7 ("Natural rights . . . are subject to limitations for the overall public good – indeed, serving the public good is an obligation under the social contract between a society and its citizens. Individual human civil and political rights are subject to various limitations, such as protecting the rights of others and protecting morals and national security. With respect to real property, the power of eminent domain, zoning, nuisance, and other limitations for the public good are commonplace. Intellectual property – even if founded on natural law – is properly subject to similar limitations for the public good. As with core human rights like freedom of expression, intellectual property rights cannot be so absolute that they unduly impinge on other rights . . . or undermine the public good . . . Thus, a natural rights perspective is not necessarily antithetical to crafting intellectual property law, policy, and administration to encourage

In addition to serving the theoretical social objectives of the predominating IP regimes, intellectual property social justice also delineates how these systems can address imperative developed and developing world IP social problems. While intellectual property social justice can be framed and articulated in the strategic activist lexicon of the American Civil Rights Movement, the remedial purview of intellectual property social justice is not restricted to the IP social deficiencies which arise in the developed world.[18]

For example, a critical challenge in the developing world is addressing IP-based impediments, including producer pecuniary perquisites, to affordable access to drugs and medicines. Intellectual property social justice theory mollifies producer-user tensions key to this issue by dispelling the economic incentive premise which characterizes producer compensation options as binary extremes of monetary reward or nothing.[19] Once intellectual property is made manifest, creator/inventor secular reward can only be attained through dissemination; even the most ardent profiteer understands that there is no profit to be had in hoarding or discarding commercially unmarketable inventory. Where monetary reward is simply not available or practical, intellectual property social justice mandates the pursuit and acknowledgement of alternative compensation, whether it be artistic exposure, scholarly/professional affirmation, critical/

---

innovation and entrepreneurship; balancing interests is the key."); Adam Mossoff, "Who cares what Thomas Jefferson thought about patents? Reevaluating the patent 'privilege' in historical context", 92 Cornell L. Rev. 953, 971–3 (2007); Ante Wessels, "Copyright Law and the International Covenant on Economic, Social and Cultural Rights", accessed 16 October 2014 at http://infojustice.org/archives/author/ante-wessels; International Covenant on Economic, Social and Cultural Rights, Article 15(1).

[18] See Chapter 1. Indeed, the Civil Rights Movement itself benefited greatly from developing world influences such as the non-violent protest teachings of Mahatma Gandhi, and in turn helped to spark the colonial independence movement in Africa. *See e.g.* Nirupama Rao, http://www.politico.com/story/2013/03/mahatma-gandhis-lightguided-martin-luther-king-jr-88581.html (accessed 16 October 2014); Gadadhara Pandit Dasa, http://www.huffingtonpost.com/gadadhara-pandit-dasa/martin-luther-king-jr-and_3_b_4631610.html (accessed 16 October 2014).

[19] *See generally* Margaret Jane Radin, "Property and Personhood", 34 Stan. L. Rev. 957 (1982); Joseph E. Stiglitz, note 7 above, 1696–8; Rebecca Tushnet, "Economies of Desire: Fair Use and Marketplace Assumptions", 51 Wm. & Mary L. Rev. 513, 515 (2009) ("Psychological and sociological concepts can do more to explain creative impulses than classical economics. As a result, a copyright law that treats creativity as a product of economic incentives can miss the mark and harm what it aims to promote").

public acclaim, or simply inspiration for further artistic exploration and/or information useful to further research and development, as being in the best interests of *all* intellectual property stakeholders, as well as society as a whole.[20]

Another important intellectual property challenge which persists throughout much of the developing world is the question of protection for traditional or indigenous knowledge and expression (TKE).[21] Intellectual property social justice precludes unauthorized use and exploitation of such material not only as a matter of fairness but of international comity. Affording primacy to Western intellectual property definitional and eligibility criteria merely perpetuates IP Imperialism and calcifies developing world antagonism toward and disregard for Western IP regimes.[22] By extending respect and legal parity to developing world TKE, intellectual property social justice reinforces global IP integrity and promotes more socially efficacious and beneficial exploration and exploitation of this invaluable human heritage.[23]

---

[20] Indeed, rationales that restrict incentive/reward status to economic compensation invite a corollary assessment that intellectual property endeavor which does not generate monetary revenue itself lacks value. *See e.g.* Johanna Gibson, note 8 above, 21 ("[T]he narrative of intellectual property objectifies the creative process. . . . Creativity outside the intellectual property paradigm is seemingly delegitimated, unimaginable, and valueless". Cristian Timmermann, "Life Sciences, Intellectual Property Regimes and Global Justice" (2013), accessed 16 October 2014 at http://www.academia.edu/4963224/_2013_Life_Sciences_Intellectual_Property_Regimes_and_Global_Justice (arguing that such perspectives discourage "non-commercial" scientific research).

[21] *See e.g.* Christine Haight Farley, "Protecting Folklore of Indigenous Peoples: Is Intellectual Property the Answer?", 30 Conn. L. Rev. 1, 1 (1997) (discussing unauthorized exploitation of Native American and Australia Aboriginal TKE); *see generally* Doris Estelle Long, "*Traditional Knowledge and the Fight for the Public Domain*", 5 J. Marshall Rev. Intell. Prop. L. 617, 620 (2006).

[22] Joseph E. Stiglitz, note 7 above, 1709, 1716; Peter K. Yu, "The Copyright Divide", 25 Cardozo L. Rev. 331, 402–3 (2003); Jo Recht, "Intellectual Property in Indigenous Societies: Culture, Context, Politics, and Law", 6 Dartmouth L.J. 277, 282–3 (2008); Lateef Mtima, "What's Mine is Mine but What's Yours is Ours: IP Imperialism, the Right of Publicity, and Intellectual Property Social Justice in the Digital Information Age", 15 SMU Sci. & Tech. L. Rev. 323, 332–6 (2012); Xuan-Thao Nguyen, "Trademark Apologetic Justice: China's Trademark Jurisprudence on Reputational Harm", 15 U. Penn. J. Bus. L. 131 (2012).

[23] *See* J. Michael Finger and Philip Schuler, *Poor People's Knowledge: Promoting Intellectual Property in Developing Countries* (World Bank Publications 2004); *WIPO Methodology and Tools for the Development of National IP Strategies*, accessed 16 October 2014 at http://www.wipo.int/ipstrategies/en/methodology/.

FROM ENLIGHTENING THEORY TO EMPOWERING ACTION

Intellectual property social justice theory provides an elucidative lens through which policy makers, jurists, and attorneys can re-envision intellectual property protection. Moreover, as a mechanism for inclusive advancement, intellectual property social justice further contemplates the collaborative participation of social activists and laypersons, together with experts from other professional and scholarly fields, in restoring the intellectual property social equilibrium.

The analyses in this book collectively distill IP Empowerment into three principal restorative functions: ensuring IP social justice; promoting IP social empowerment; and facilitating IP social interoperability:

Ensuring IP Social Justice – Institutionalized misappropriation of intellectual property/TKE and systemic indifference to IP-related social deficiencies are anathema to the intellectual property social function. In Chapters 9–11 we have seen how IP social activists can collaborate in Equality through Entrepreneurship ("ETE") endeavor to address these and other IP social inefficiencies and restore the intellectual property protection apparatus to optimum performance.

Promoting IP Social Empowerment – Beyond eschewing outright injustice, intellectual property protection should promote development and advancement for all groups and nations – the IP system is not a "zero-sum" game. In Chapters 6–8 we have seen how affirmative IP Empowerment necessarily begins with communal IP education, and in Chapters 2–5 we have seen how IP Empowerment ETE strategies and ventures can be devised and implemented.

Among the avenues for IP socio-economic empowerment that warrant particular attention are those that have been opened by the advent of digital information technology. The ongoing Western shift from goods-based to information-based economies, together with the evolution of the global marketplace, provides historically marginalized groups and developing nations new and relatively inexpensive channels through which to exploit their intellectual property output.[24] Such groups and nations can also more easily collaborate with

---

[24] *See e.g.* Derek Slater and Patricia Wruuck, *We Are All Content Creators Now: Measuring Creativity and Innovation in the Digital Economy*, The Global Innovation Index 2012, 163 ("Today, artists and entrepreneurs use the Internet to create fantastic new things. Just look at services such as iTunes and YouTube, which have launched careers and created entirely new markets that reach a huge audience. The Internet is democratizing innovation, empowering people to create,

each other, as well as partner with established intellectual property purveyors.[25] Indeed, many previously inaccessible mainstream markets and business opportunities can now be tapped, in as much as "on the Internet, nobody knows you're a minority".[26]

Marginalized groups and developing nations can further employ digital information technology to make use of mainstream intellectual property in the public domain, for a wide range of empowerment purposes.

> This new generation views intellectual property as the raw materials for its own creative acts, blurring the lines that have long separated producers from consumers. Witness a disc jockey named "Dangermouse" who mashes up the Beatles' *White Album* and hip-hop artist Jay-Z *Black Album* to create the award-winning *Grey Album*. Witness girl fans of Harry Potter who post stories at www.fanfiction.net to retell life at Hogwarts from Hermione's perspective. Witness Nintendo's Wii game console, which allows players to personalize their "Mii" avatars – from gender and skin color down to the shape of their eyes – before setting off on their adventures. . . . Our children now have the virtual building blocks to render cultural universes their own.[27]

Whether applied toward re-constructing cultural/historic narratives, pursuing political autonomy, or building economic independence, digital information technology can be a powerful IP Empowerment tool.

Facilitating IP Social Interoperability – Intellectual property social justice and empowerment enhances IP social utility for society as a whole. In Chapter 9, the *NoCopyright Party* explores the ecumenical reach of IP social justice through an entrepreneurial vehicle. An example of IP social justice/utility as a social movement can be seen in the Open Source Software Movement.[28] As discussed in the Prologue, a computer software program is essentially a set of instructions written for computers, much the same as an instruction manual or a recipe book is written for human

---

exchange, and implement new ideas, and to make those ideas available to people all around the world, with minimal barriers to entry").

[25] Andrea L. Johnson, "The Rule of Law, Privatization, and the Promise of Transborder Licensing, Evolving Economies" (Edward Elgar, Cheltenham, UK and Northampton, MA, USA 2012), 221–3.

[26] en.wikipedia.org/wiki/On_the_Internet,_nobody_knows_you%27re_a_dog (accessed 16 October 2014); *The New Yorker*, 5 July 1993, p. 61, Vol. 69, No. 20.

[27] Madhavi Sunder, note 11 above, 13. For scholarly exploration of the intersection of IP and gender, *see e.g. IP/Gender: Gender and the Regulation of Traditional Knowledge*, http://www.pijip.org/events/ipg2014/ (accessed 16 October 2014).

[28] *See e.g.* Christopher M. Kelty, *Two Bits: The Cultural Significance of Free Software* (Duke University Press, Durham, NC 2008), 97–117; Richard M. Stallman, "The GNU Project", in *Free Software, Society: Selected Essays of Richard M. Stallman* (Free Software Foundation, Boston, MA 2002), 15–16. I am indebted to Greg Vetter for his indagative suggestions on this topic.

beings. A software program can be enhanced or improved by revising or adding to lines of its code, thereby making instructions easier for a computer to understand and carry out and/or adding new functions to its capabilities. Different programmers will have different ideas for revising lines of code, and so the more programmers who participate, the better and more effective the ultimate result.

Adherents to Open Source Software promote collaborative enhancement of software programs by waiving copyright protections which preclude third party revisions to their programs, in exchange for similar waivers by programmers who wish to make improvements upon their work. Consequently, extended "generations" of programmers are able to collaborate in enhancing and improving software programs, which are then made available to the public. This use of copyright, sometimes referred to as "copyleft", is a social justice-oriented and paradigm changing example of how copyright can be used to incentivize creative endeavor in the public interest.[29] The rewards participating programmers gain include the satisfaction of enhancing programs, professional acclaim, and similar accolades. Open Source collaboration is thus not dependent upon monetary incentives – rather, it is motivated primarily by the belief that the public's computer capability options should not be restricted to commercial software industry goals and dictates (that is, competitive non-disclosure and limited range of functionality) any more than crayon manufacturers should be allowed to pre-determine the extent to which children will be able to mix and blend their choice of crayon colors.

> The origination of free software by Stallman was cloaked in activism. He perceived that software is inherently of insufficient quality when the source code is not available or shareable, because in these situations one cannot revise the code or have others revise it. He expressed his view . . . tinged . . . by his political perspective that full self-determination with one's computer is a fundamental freedom. In this view, even if one cannot reprogram the software herself, the opportunity to do so, or to pay someone else to reprogram it, is critical.[30]

The intersection of intellectual property social justice/social utility is also evident in a current controversy in the field of patents, that of the patent assertion entity ("PAE"), sometimes pejoratively labeled a "patent troll". In

---

[29] See e.g. Greg R. Vetter, "Exit and Voice in Free and Open Source Software Licensing: Moderating the Rein over Software Users", 85 Oregon L. Rev. 183, 186 (2006) "The free software advocates designed a counterintuitive copyright-based licensing system that demands preservation of the right to share software in a form that promotes functional freedom for computer users".

[30] Greg R. Vetter, note 29 above, 191.

general, a PAE is a person or entity that holds a patent which it has not used to produce a product but who nonetheless asserts its patent rights to preclude use of the invention by others.[31] PAEs have become controversial because some PAEs acquire patents as part of a lie-in-wait "patent troll" business strategy, whereby the PAE's principal objective is to identify products in the marketplace that somehow infringe the patent, and then utilize the threat of patent infringement litigation to extract a royalty or other payments.

Whereas critics properly decry patent troll strategies, many unfairly tarnish all PAEs with this brush. Such critics overlook small and historically marginalized inventors who lack access to the financial capital and other resources needed to turn their patents into actual products – indeed, a fair opportunity to commercialize their inventions would be the answer to their entrepreneurial dreams and aspirations.[32] Many of these inventors cannot afford the expense of obtaining a patent, and the few that surpass this hurdle often discover that this expenditure is but a fraction of the costs involved in bringing their inventions to market. Labeling such inventors (or those willing to undertake the financial risk of acquiring their patent rights) as IP pariahs, simply because they assert the same rights which majority patent holders assert (and sometimes abuse) is a double injustice.

> [C]ase studies show numerous examples of a small startup patent owner—attempting to gain investors or build a product based on intellectual property—being exploited by large already-existing companies that did not respect patent rights. For MercExchange, eBay spent considerable time learning of [the small inventor's] business and patent filing history before making the decision to infringe [his] patents. Similarly, for CSS, large ATM companies...learned of [the small inventor's] Super ATM product capabilities years before introducing their own infringing ATM products. Accordingly, from the case studies, the only evidence of large actors using size or resources to advantage is on the part of the large-company defendant patent infringers.[33]

COMMENCEMENT: CHANGING THIS BUSINESS

In the information society, intellectual property is the coin of the realm. "For centuries, no one much thought about copyright in daily life. Now we

---

[31] *See* Ryan T. Holte, "Patent Trolls or Great American Inventors: Case Studies of Patent Assertion Entities", 59(1) St. Louis U. L. J. (2014), http://ssrn.com/abstract=2426444 (accessed 16 October 2014).

[32] Ryan T. Holte, note 31 above, 3 ("[L]ittle has been done to contextualize the debate by examining the particularized facts concerning the patent holders themselves, the stories behind their inventions, or the entities that represent their interests"). Recall for example, the history of Network Solutions in the opening chapter.

[33] Ryan T. Holte, note 31 above, 35.

don't have a choice."[34] To achieve socio-economic and political parity, historically marginalized communities and developing nations must focus their attentions toward enhanced intellectual property and TKE development, protection, and beneficial exploitation. Most importantly, these nations and communities must take a seat at the global IP law and policy table.[35]

Social entrepreneurship, particularly "Equality through Economics" social entrepreneurship, is an effective means through which to achieve many critical IP Empowerment objectives. Initiative, sacrifice, investment, achievement, and eventually dominance in a trade are the characteristics which define "middleman" entrepreneurial upward mobility. This trail can be blazed in the global information society, beginning with grassroots IP education and aptitude[36] and identification of "low-hanging IP fruit" in copyright, trademark, and patentable business method protection, complemented by investment in low-capital information technology enterprise, such as writing software code, building websites, and servicing IT systems.[37] Moreover, such IP/IT entrepreneurial dexterity could be concomitantly deployed to address imminent intellectual property-related social needs[38] and specialized interests.[39]

---

[34] Patricia Aufderheide and Peter Jaszi, note 15 above, 7.

[35] See e.g. "*Cross Regional Statement by Egypt at the Human Rights Council: Towards a Human Rights Approach to Intellectual Property*", accessed 16 October 2014 at http://infojustice.org/archives/32423; "Letter on Behalf of IIPSJ in Opposition to the Stop Online Piracy Act of 2011", accessed 16 October 2014 at http://iipsj.org/images/stories/pdf/IIPSJ-Letter-to-House-re-SOPA.pdf; "IIPSJ Comments to the United States Copyright Office, Library of Congress, Regarding Orphan Works and Mass Digitization", accessed 16 October 2014 at http://www.copyright.gov/orphan/comments/noi_10222012/Institute-for-Intellectual-Property-and-Social-Justice.pdf.

[36] See e.g. IP Awareness Assessment, accessed 16 October 2014 at http://www.uspto.gov/inventors/assessment/index.html.

[37] See e.g. Harry Bradford, "Jaylen Bledsoe, High School Sophomore, Builds $3.5 Million IT Company in Little over 2 Years", accessed 16 October 2014 at http://www.huffingtonpost.com/2013/09/03/jaylen-bledsoe_n_3860585.html.

[38] Some innovative examples include organizations FabLabDC, accessed 16 October 2014 at http://www.fablabdc.org/about/history/, which provides individuals in historically marginalized and developing communities with technical space and resources to develop solutions to IP-related social deficiencies, and The Detroit Sound Conservancy, accessed 16 October 2014 at http://detroitsoundconservancy.org/about/, an organization dedicated to the preservation and dissemination of "the indigenous music of Detroit", including "pre-Motown" classic R&B music.

[39] See Derek Slater and Patricia Wruuck, note 24 above, 167 ("You may never listen to the ukulele songs of Julia Nunes – or any ukulele songs for that matter – but the economy and society are clearly better off in a world where she can go online, find her fans, and launch a successful career. Ukulele fans cannot

The recognition of the principle of intellectual property social justice as fundamental to intellectual property protection opens a new chapter in the global political economy. Intellectual Property Empowerment invites everyone to become genuine stakeholders in the IP system. And when everyone participates, we make a hearty "IP nail soup" that nourishes all.[40]

---

find music like Julia's at the average record store, but on YouTube some of her videos have received millions of viewings.").

[40] In this European folk tale, a homeless traveler persuades villagers to each contribute to the soup he prepares which initially contains only water and a nail, but through collaboration becomes a hearty repast for the entire village http://www.academia.edu/4963224/_2013_Life_Sciences_Intellectual_Property_Regimes_and_Global_Justice (accessed 16 October 2014).

Index

Abel, Richard L. 14
Abrams, R. 48
ACE inhibitors 82
ACTA (Anti-Counterfeiting Trade Agreement) 140–1, 151
activation, of social entrepreneur 43
Adams, Abigail 192
Advocacy strategy 51
affirmative action policies 76, 88, 89
African Agricultural Technology Foundation (Kenya) 176
African Americans
  African-American business ownership, in 21st century 66–7
  dehumanization 9
  economic progress 23–4, 65
  Emancipation Proclamation, effect 9
  emigration to Pepper Coast of Africa 12
  hypertension in 85
  Jim Crow racial discrimination laws 10, 11, 12, 14, 15, 25, 87
  lack of recognition and support for IP achievements 2, 6
  and legal services 129
  as musicians 219
    see also Motown, case study
  race specific drugs 80
  social equality goal 25
  Talented Tenth see Talented Tenth (educated blacks)
  see also blacks; Jim Crow racial discrimination laws; Kauffman Firm Survey (KFS), start-ups; marginalized groups and communities, historical; slavery
African Artists Collaborative (AAC) 180, 181
Agar, Nicholas 87

Agreement on Trade Aspects of Intellectual Property (TRIPS agreement) 130, 141, 167, 173, 235, 244, 258
agricultural technology 168–70
AIA (Leahy-Smith America Invents Act), 2011 132
Alinsky, Saul D. 33, 54
Allman, Larry 142
Alperovitz, G. 34
Amazonlink.org (Brazilian NGO) 180
American Bar Association 133
American Intellectual Property Lawyers Association 138
Anatomy of Racial Inequality, The (Loury) 91
Anti-Counterfeiting Trade Agreement (ACTA) 140–1, 151
antitrust law 36
Antons, Christoph 243
Aouads, Salah 184
Argentina 141
assimilation 92
Association of Black Cardiologists 80
AT&T 104–5
Attanasio, John B. 87
Aufderheide, Patricia 19, 271, 278
avian flu, patent landscape report on 181

Babson College 47
backward planning, and forward execution 48
Baker, Lewis J. 98
Band, Jonathan 194
Banik, Mark 88
banking system 36
bankruptcy protection 36
Barnett, Jonathan 122
Baumol, W.J. 36–7
Bayh-Dole Act (1980) 106, 107

Bell, Thom 218
Bell Laboratories 104–5
Ben-Atar, Doron S. 246
Bennett, Alan B. 155
Bennett, Lerone 9, 10, 13
Bentham, Jeremy 216
Berne Convention 246, 258
BiDil, case study (colorblindness) 79–86, 89
    FDA rejection of application for marketing 79–80
bigotry, in marketplace 77
biodiversity 170–1
biopiracy 177–8
biotechnology 168–70
    PIIPA case studies 176, 177
black market distribution networks 260–1
blacks 9–13, 10, 13, 23–6, 48, 56
    "black patients" 81, 82, 86, 87, 88
    business ownership in 21st century 66–7
    educated (Talented Tenth) *see* Talented Tenth (educated blacks)
    and intellectual property as essential business asset 64, 65
    see also African Americans; marginalized groups and communities, historical; racial discrimination; slavery
Block, F. 34
Bovard, James 250
Bower, Joseph L. 194
Boyle, James 122, 147
Bradford, Harry 278
Braithwaite, John 148
Branson, Richard 45
Brasco, Christopher J. 105, 114
Brauneis, Robert 233
Brazil 141, 151
BRICS countries (Brazil, Russia, India, China and South Africa) 159, 240
    as *sui generis* development model 244–5
Brooke, Peter 48
Brookfield, Stephen 55
Brown-Nagin, Tomiko 8, 23
Buffington, Kirk W. 95

Bullard, Sara 13, 14
Bureau of Labor Statistics, Business Employment Dynamics 35
Bush, George W. 39
Business Employment Dynamics, Bureau of Labor Statistics 35
business intelligence 111
business ownership
    African-American, in 21st century 66–7
    intellectual property ownership by new business owners 67–9
    Kauffman Firm Survey (KFS)
        African American business owners 70, 72
        background 67
        findings 73–4
        innovators subset 69
        mergers and acquisitions 71
        revenue and licensing activities of new business owners 71–3
        survival rates 70–1, 74
    multiple owners 68
    primary owner 68
business schools 34, 35, 46
Butler, John Sibley 9, 21, 24
Bygrave, William D. 22, 47

Cantillon, Richard 36
Cao, Lan 93
Capacity Building strategy 51
capitalism 34, 55, 214, 215
Carnegie, Andrew 36, 45
Carpenter, Megan M. 17, 64
CBD *see* Convention on Biological Diversity (CBD)
CDIP (Committee on Development and Intellectual Property) 175
Center for Economic and Social Justice 213
Center for International Environmental Law (CIEL) 186
Chander, Anupam 270
Charity strategy 51, 52
China 151, 244
Cho, Albert 44
Chon, Margaret 20, 123, 267
Christensen, Clayton M. 194
Cibinic, John 114

civil disobedience 13
civil rights and empowerment
   case law
      Brown v. *Board of Education* 11, 13, 77
      Missouri ex. rel. Gaines v. *Canada* 11
      Murray v. *Maryland* 11
      Plessy v. *Ferguson* 9–10, 11, 76
   civil rights social action platform 11–14
   economic empowerment 1–29
   economic justice economic empowerment and civil rights 213–15
   historical perspective 22–7
   Intellectual Property Empowerment, achieving 5–8
   social justice centred-law and civil rights activism 5–8
   see also intellectual property empowerment
Civil Rights Era, US 5, 8, 24
Civil Rights Movement, US 21, 272
   civil protest strategy 13, 20
   gains of 26
   Houston as legal architect 10–11
   and Intellectual Property Empowerment 5, 15
      intersections 8, 9–14
   and intellectual property social justice theory 64
   three-pronged strategy (legal action, social activism and individual empowerment) 64
classical entrepreneurship, social entrepreneurship distinguished 25–6, 39–40
clinical trials, inclusion of race and gender in 80, 83
Clinton Administration 249
cloud computing 111
Coady, Moses 55
Codified Change 50
Cogar, Elizabeth 25
Cohn, Jay 79, 80, 85
collaborative action 28–9
collateral policies 98
collective entrepreneurship 39
colorblindness principle 76–94

case law
   Batson v. *Kentucky* 88
   Grutter v. *Bollinger* 88
   KSR v. *Teleflex* 85
   Shelley v. *Kraemer* 88
case studies 79–86, 87, 89, 94
color of money 77
controversy 76
and diversity 76–7, 92, 93–4
inclusive marketplace 94
lessons for social entrepreneurship and market theory 86–94
liberal theories of race 90, 91, 93
pragmatic approach 92
and pragmatism 92
Committee on Economic, Social and Cultural Rights 149
common heritage of mankind 158
Competition in Contracting Act (CICA) 1984 103
competition principle, public procurement 101
confrontation 54
Congress of Racial Equality 13
Constitution, US 15
   Thirteenth Amendment 78
   Fourteenth Amendment 50, 86
   colorblindness principle 76, 77
   patent and copyright laws 122–3
Consultative Group on International Agricultural Research (CGIAR) 179, 185
Convention on Biological Diversity (CBD) 147, 166, 167, 170–1
   Global Environment Facility 174
   Nagoya Protocol on Access to Genetic Resources and the Fair and Equitable Sharing of Benefits Arising from their Utilization 171
Conway, Danielle M. 4, 96, 100, 105, 109, 113
Coombe, Rosemary J. 149
cooperatives 38–9
Cooter, Robert 121, 127, 134
copyright xvii–xviii, 18
   balancing public interest and private ownership 165
   economic rational 233–4

284   *Intellectual property, entrepreneurship and social justice*

fair-use privilege 151
intellectual property rights 121, 122, 124
  'killing' 194, 196, 201
    reasons for 205–7
  making money 196–203
  monopoly pricing 194, 198
  'NoCopyright Party' 196, 200, 202, 203, 205, 206, 207–8, 275
  and public domain 195, 199, 202
  registration 123–4
  termination rights 203–5
  terms 191–208
    beneficiaries of term extensions 193–4
    call to action to restore terms to original 195–6
    capping of 195
    shortcomings of present system 193, 195–6, 199
  'worth more dead than alive' 194
corrective justice 93
Crawford, Francine 192
Creative Class 37
Creative Economy 37
"creator/destroyer" entrepreneurial activity 23, 24
Creed, Linda 218
Cross, John T. 146
Crouch, Robert A. 83

Daly, L. 34
Danzon, Patricia 258
Datadyne (US-based consultancy) 178, 185
de Beer, Jeremy 142, 149, 159
de jure racial discrimination 11
deadweight loss 198, 199
deal lawyers 127, 129
Declaration on the Rights of Indigenous Peoples 149
Dees, Gregory 39, 46
Def-Jam Recordings 222–5
Dell, Michael 45
Department of Defense (DoD) 111
  "rule of two" 108, 109
developing countries
  defense of IP 243–4
  Development Agenda (WIPO) 144–5
  Stockholm Protocol Regarding Developing Countries 158
  training and education 151–2
Development Agenda (WIPO) 150, 152, 155, 161, 162
  empirical research 156
  Old Development Agenda 158
  recommendations 141–2, 157
  see also World Intellectual Property Organization (WIPO)
Development as Freedom (Sen) 38
development policies 128–9
Diana Project 44
Diepeveen, Stephanie 243, 247
Digital Divide Network 175
Digital Millennium Copyright Act 180
digital technology 178–9
Disney, Walt 45, 195
distribution agreements, complexity 127
diversity, value of 76–7, 92, 93–4
DoD *see* Department of Defense (DoD)
domain name registration service system, development for Internet 1
double patenting 81
Dougherty, Sean M. 156
Douglass, Frederick 54
Drahos, Peter 148, 245
Drayton, Bill 39
Du Bois, W.E.B. 12, 13, 23, 25, 213, 214
Dubin, Jon 134
Dunning, John H. 242
Dutfield, Graham 166
duties of care 137–8

economic development, and innovation 120–8
economic empowerment, and civil rights 1–29
economic justice 23, 213
Economic Structure of Intellectual Property Law, The (Landes and Posner) 216
eDiscovery 111
Edison, Thomas 17, 45
education
  IP Educator 42
  legal 135–7

and training *see* training and
    education
Education strategy 51
Edwards, Harry T. 23
effectuation 47
Einhorn, Bruce 243
Electronic Frontier Foundation 175
entertainment and media 218–33
    music business 218–25
entrepreneurial state 34
entrepreneurs
    classification 36
    intellectual property start-up 16
    IP Entrepreneurs 42, 43–4, 45
    opportunities, identifying 42–3
    role and qualities 41–4
entrepreneurship
    applying entrepreneurship approach
        48–56
    best practices for entrepreneurial
        economic development 235–62
    as a business practice 37
    definitions 34, 119, 212
    embracing 20–22
    entrepreneurial exploitation xx
    and equal opportunity 78
    future, considerations for 58–9
    hegemony 54, 55
    history 36, 38
    intellectual property social justice,
        achieving 33–63
    "middleman" 21, 25, 278
    model of social change 50–51
    policies 125–6
    reasons for 34, 37
    refining the roles and qualities of the
        entrepreneur 41–4
    resistance 54
    social *see* social entrepreneurship
    and social justice 128–33, 211–13
    status quo, impulse to change 43,
        44–6
    steps in entrepreneurial process
        46–8
    strategies for social change 51–3
    Theory of Change 53–4
    unintended consequences 55, 56
Entrepreneurship (Bygrave and
    Zacharakis) 47
EpiSurveyor project 178

equal opportunity, and
    entrepreneurship 78
Equal Protection Clause, Fourteenth
    Amendment 86
Equality through Economics
    philosophy *see* ETE (Equality
    through Economics) philosophy
equivalents doctrine 87
ETE (Equality through Economics)
    philosophy 25, 26, 48
    applying to other IP empowerment
        contexts 28
Etheredge, Kim 16

fair use, judicial application 19
Fairlie, Robert W. 68
fair-use privilege 151
Farley, Christine Haight 273
farmers
    court challenges against 169
    global food security and livelihoods
        of 183
Federal Technology Transfer Act
    (1986) 107
Finger, J. Michael 150, 273
Fink, Carsten 156
Florida, Richard 37
Fogarty Center (US), National
    Institutes of Health 181
Food and Drug Administration (FDA)
    denial of approval for marketing of
        BiDil patent 79–80
    Modernization Acct (1997) 80
Ford, Henry 45
foreign aid 248–51, 258
forward execution, and backward
    planning 48
Foundation for Ethnic Understanding
    (FFEU) 223
Framework Convention on Tobacco
    Control (WHO, 2003) 173–4
free trade agreements (FTAs) 97
Frieire, Paolo 55
From Goods to A Good Life (Sunder)
    217
Froomkin, A. Michael 159
Funding strategy, and social change 52

Gacel, Rafael A. 155
Gamble, Kenny 218–21

Ganga Library, Inc (global digital library for public access to Nobel Prize Winners' materials) 183–4
Garvey, Marcus 12, 23, 25, 211, 213, 214
Gates, Bill 45
gender, inclusion in clinical trials 80
Genencor International 177
General Accounting Office 114
genetic modification 169
genetic resources (GR) 166
Geographical Indicators (GIs) 130, 165
geospatial, non-relational database management systems 111
Gerafi, Jonathan 194
Gervais, Daniel J. 153
Gibbons, Llewellyn Joseph 4
GIS 111
GIs (geographical indications) 130
Glivec (cancer drug) 19
Global Environment Facility 174
Global Fund for AIDS, Malaria and Tuberculosis 173
global information society 2
Global Internet Liberty Campaign 175
Goldstein, Jorge 186
Gollin, Michael A. 157, 164, 168, 169, 170, 171, 176
Google Books Project 19
Gordy, Berry 57
Goto, Akira 145
Gouvin, Eric J. 21, 23
Government Accountability Office 114
Government Procurement Agreement (GPA) 97
Gowers, Andrew 140
Grameen Bank, India 28, 39
Gramsci, Antonio 54, 55
Grant, Joanne 9, 23
Grassroots Mobilization strategy 51
Greene, K.J. 6, 269
Grieff, Edward D. 84
Grigsby, Tyrone 2
gross national product (GNP) 95

"hackathons" 75
Hamilton, Neil D. 169
Hammond, Allen S. 14
Happy Birthday song 195
Hart, David M. 125
Harvest Plus (CGIAR program) 179, 185
Hassan, Emmanuel 243, 247
Health Alliance for Austin Musicians (HAAM) 233
health care 172–4
Hefler, Laurence R. 129, 131
Heimes, Rita 17, 124, 130
Helfer, Laurence R. 20, 148
Henderson, Gina 2, 27
Henley, Raymond 84
hierarchy of needs theory 44
Hip-Hop Summit Action Network (HSAN) 224
Hirschman, Albert 77
historically marginalized groups *see* marginalized groups and communities, historical
Historically Underutilized Business Zone (HUBZone) 104
HIV/AIDS pandemic 145, 172, 173, 176
Höffner, Eckhard 246
Holder, Eric 65
Holte, Ryan T. 277
Horten, Monica 141
Horton, Miles 55
Houston, Charles Hamilton 10–11, 13, 15, 18, 23
    as Special Counsel of NAACP 14
Howard Law School, Washington 137
Howell, Aaron D. 95
Huff, Leon 218–21
human capabilities, improving 128–9
human capital 47
human rights, and intellectual property 129–33
hydralazine 79, 81, 82

Ibero American Science and Technology Education Consortium (ISTEC), Americas and Iberian Peninsula 178–9
Ibis Reproductive Health (Zimbabwe and South Africa) 176
Ibrahim, Dariam M. 119
ICANN (Internet Corporation for Assigned Names and Numbers) 2, 159

Imperial Broom company 24–5
impulses 40
inclusive marketplace 94
India
  Grameen Bank 28, 39
  Intellectual Property Appellate Board 19
  training and educational programs 151
inertia 54
information economy 66
information sector 65
information technologies 175
innovation 119–39
  and economic development 120–8
  empowerment and other social justice considerations 114–16
  facilitating entrepreneurship in 110–16
  intellectual property rights 121–5
  and law 120–28
  roles in innovation industry 116
  and social change 52
  of social entrepreneur 43
  social utility objective 5, 18
  targeted support for IP empowerment in 114
innovative entrepreneurs 36
Institute for Intellectual Property Social Justice 59
integrity principle, public procurement 101
intellectual capital 47
intellectual property
  balancing public interest and private ownership in 165–6
  basic education 230–31
  birth of modern regime 245–8
  conventions and agreements 144
  definitions 66
  digital context 3
  dynamic nature of IP legal frameworks 166–7
  as essential 21st century business asset 64–75
  global public interest IP sectors 168–75, 185
  and human rights 129–33
  imperialism 7
  litigation support exchange 231
  reorientation toward principles of social justice 4
  social empowerment, ensuring 274
  social interoperability, facilitating 275
  and socio-political economy 267–70
  transactional support exchange 231–2
  Western perspectives 3, 7
  see also unified theory of IP social justice
Intellectual Property Appellate Board, India 19
Intellectual Property Empowerment
  achieving 5–8, 107
  benefits 4–5
  as civil and human rights in the 21st century 14–15
  and Civil Rights Movement 5, 15
    intersections 8, 9–14
  collaborative action 28–9
  communal socio-economic progress goal 27
  implementing 28–9
  legal theory 15–20
  and procurement 96–7
  realization 7
  social action platform 8, 20–22, 28
  and social entrepreneurship 22–7
  social objective of 107
  see also civil rights and empowerment
Intellectual Property Institute, William Mitchell College of Law 136–7
intellectual property rights (IPRs)
  enforcement 153, 154
  innovation 121–5
  strong 123
  utilitarian 254–5
intellectual property social justice 3, 15–20
  and Civil Rights Movement 64
  ensuring 274
  entrepreneurship approach to achieving 33–63
  social justice gap 43
  theory 5–6, 20
  training and education for 140–62
intellectual property social platform *see* social action platform, intellectual property

Intellectual Property Training and Education: A Development Perspective (de Beer and Ogamanam) 142
International Alpaca Association (IAA), Peru 177
International Center for Tropical Agriculture (CIAT) 182
International Centre for Trade and Sustainable Development 142
International Code of Conduct on the Transfer of Technology 158
International Cooperative Biodiversity Groups (ICBGs) 181
International Covenant on Civil and Political Rights 149
International Covenant on Economic, Social and Cultural Rights 149
International Maize and Wheat Improvement Centre (CIMMYT) 176
International Roundtables on WIPO Development Agenda for Academics 140, 143
International Symposium on Digital Libraries 178, 179
international technology transfer incentives 251–3
International Treaty for Plant Genetic Resources for Food and Agriculture (ITPGRFA) 147, 166, 182
International Union for the Protection of New Varieties of Plants (UPOV) 166, 169, 182
Internet
  access to 3, 175
  domain name registration service system, development 1
Internet Corporation for Assigned Names and Numbers (ICANN) 2, 159
Internet Service Providers (ISPs) 180
inventions, racially tailored 85
investor-owned firm (IOF) 38
IP Business Entrepreneur 41
IP Creators 41, 45, 49, 56, 58
IP Educators 42, 58
IP Entrepreneurs 42, 43–4, 45, 49, 58
IP Innovators 56
IP Lawyers 41, 45, 58
IP Policymakers/Activists 41–2, 45, 58
IPRs *see* intellectual property rights (IPRs)
isosorbide dinitrate 79

Jaffe, Adam B. 131
Jamar, Steven D. 17, 18, 20, 64, 131, 134, 193
Japan 159, 239
Jaszi, Peter 19, 271, 278
Jefferson, Thomas 191–4, 195, 207
Jim Crow racial discrimination laws 10, 11, 12, 14, 15, 25, 87
Jobs, Steve 45
Johns, Adrian 235

Kapczynski, Amy 19, 140
Kappos, David 128, 134
Kauffman Firm Survey (KFS), start-ups
  African American business owners 70, 72
  background 67
  findings 73–4
  innovators subset 69
  mergers and acquisitions 71
  revenue and licensing activities of new business owners 71–3
  survival rates 70–71, 74
Kauffman Foundation 35
Keller, M.R. 34
Kelty, Christopher 275
Kennedy, John F. 211
Kenya Wildlife Service (KWS) 177–8
Kerrigan, Jack E. 105, 114
Kesan, Jay P. 88
Kharas, Homi 259
King, Martin Luther 13–14, 20, 65, 195, 213, 215
Kingston, William 237, 242
Kirton, Raymond Mark 100
Kneller, Richard 241
knowledge
  access to 22
  traditional 171–2
  see also traditional knowledge and cultural expressions (TKE) of

indigenous peoples, Western misappropriation
Kozinski, Alex 90
Krattiger, Anatole 146
Kroc, Ray 45
Kull, Andrew 90
Kymlicka, Will 93
Kyoto Protocol 174

LaBelle, Patti 219
Lacey, Mark 178
laches, equitable defense of 228–9
Lacy, James V. 114
Lahiri, Sajal 250
Laird, Sarah A. 171
Lall, Sanjaya 235
Landers, Amy 146
Landes, William A. 124, 216
Lassiter, Wright L. 215
law
   and innovation 120–8
   legal education 135–7
   legal theory of Intellectual Property Empowerment 15–20
   property 121
   social justice centred-law and civil rights activism 5–8
   social justice vs. law and economics 215–17
law schools 46, 133, 134, 139
Law strategy 51, 52
Lawson, James 13, 20
lawyers 120, 124–5, 139
   deal lawyers 127, 129
   transactional lawyering, US 127
Leahy-Smith America Invents Act (AIA), 2011 132
least developed countries (LDCs) 236, 238
Lerner, Josh 125, 126, 127, 131
Lessig, Lawrence 105, 111
Leval, Pierre 19
Levi, Wendy 16
Levine, Robert S. 214
Levinson, Justin D. 6
liberal theories of race 90, 91, 93
Liberia, founding of Republic 12
licensing agreements 72–3
Lincoln, Abraham 52
Litan, Robert E. 122

litigation 134–5
litigation support exchange 231
Locke, John 233, 266
Lodha, Ritu 145
Logic Model 53
"lone wolf" intellectual property entrepreneurship 24, 27
Lopez, Ian Haney 76
Loury, Glenn 91, 92
Love, James 147

Mackey, John 45
MacLeod, Adam 34
Madison, James 191
Maine School of Law 136
Malcolm X 213
Marable, Manning 12
March on Washington for Jobs and Freedom (1963), 50th anniversary (2013) 64, 65
marginal costs and losses 257–8
marginalized groups and communities, historical 2, 3, 4, 6, 7, 20
   intellectual property rights, protection 16, 18
   see also African Americans; blacks; Jim Crow racial discrimination laws; slavery
market capitalism *see* capitalism
market efficiency, piracy as 253–8
Market Exchange strategy 51, 52
marketplace
   bigotry in 77
   and colorblindness 77–8, 94
   inclusive 94
Marrakesh Treaty to Facilitate Access to Published Works by Visually Impaired Persons and Persons with Print Disabilities (2013) 19, 162
Marshall, Thurgood 10, 11
Martin, Waldo E. 214
Maskus, Keith E. 154, 156, 251
Maslow, Abraham 44, 207
Mason, Gilbert R. 214
Mayfield, Mark Steven 211
McCadney, Jennifer 113
McCrudden, J. Christopher 100
McCue, Clifford P. 95
McHenry, Emmit J. 2

McNeil, Genna Rae 9, 10, 11, 23
McPherson, Isaac 192
Means, Benjamin 24
MedCo Research Inc. 79
Medicine Patent Pool 173
Melendez-Ortiz, Ricardo 142, 152
mergers and acquisitions 71
Mertha, Andrew 156
Mezirow, Jack 55
Mighty Three Music 218
Mill, John Stuart 216
Millennium Development Goals (MDGs) 149
MIRA (Methods for Improving Reproductive Health in Africa) 176
Mireles, Michael 146
MIT Technology Licensing Office, University of Alabama 49
Mixed Chicks, case of 16–17, 24
Model Rules of Professional Conduct 133, 134
monopolies 191, 194
monopoly pricing, copyright 198
Montgomery Bus Boycott 13
motivation, of social entrepreneur 43
Motown, case study 57, 225–33
Movements strategy 51
Mtima, Lateef 3, 7, 17, 18, 20, 64, 131, 134, 193, 266, 270
Mueller, Milton L. 159
Munzer, Stephen R. 4
music business 218–25
  Motown, case study 225–33
  Philadelphia International Records 218–21
Mycoguild (international non-profit corporation) 177
mycotechnology 185

NAACP (National Association for the Advancement of Colored People), US 10, 13, 23, 224
  Houston as Special Counsel 14
Nanda, Nitya 145
Narula, Rajneesh 242
Nash, Ralph C. 114
Nashville, Tennessee 221
National Association for the Advancement of Colored People *see* NAACP (National Association for the Advancement of Colored People), US
National Institute for the Defense of Competition and Intellectual Property (INDECOPI), Peru 179–80
National Institute of Health 83
National Institutes of Health Guidelines on the Inclusion of Women and Minorities in Clinical Research (1994) 83
National Science Foundation 1
Natural Law theory 233
Navajo language digital preservation project 183
negotiation skills 155–6
Negro Business League 214
neo-mercantilism 246
Network Solutions, Inc 1–2
New Venture Creation (Timmons and Spinelli) 47
New World 2, 12
New York City 209
Nexavar (cancer drug) 19
Niagara Movement 13
Nitromed, case study (colorblindness) 79–86, 87, 94
nitrous oxide, medical use in hypertension and heart disease 79
Nollywood (Nigerian film industry) 164, 180–81
Non-Communicable Diseases, multilateral agreements on 174
non-obviousness requirement, modification of inventions 84, 85
non-profit organizations 38
Normative Change 50
normative legal action 6–7
North, Douglass 36, 50
North American Industry Classification System (NAICS) 69

Obama, Barack 34–5, 65
  Cairo speech (2009) 39
O'Connor, Sean 127
Odagiri, Hiroyuki 145, 159
Office of Technology Commercialization, University of Alabama 49

Office of Technology Transfer, US National Institutes of Health 184
Oguamanam, Chidi 142, 149, 159
O'Jays, The 218, 219
Okediji, Ruth 151
One Million Cups (Kauffman Foundation) 35
1207 Program (DoD) 108–9
O'Neill, Jim 159
open and inclusive society, goal of 92
Open-Source technology 175, 178

PAE (patent assertion entity) 276–7
Parenti, Christian 113
Pareto efficiency 257
Paris Convention 158, 258
Parks, Rosa 13
Patent and Trademark Office, US 67, 81
patent assertion entity (PAE) 276–7
patents xvi–xvii, 36, 81, 131
   first-to-file system 132
   first-to-invent rule 132
   free and open access to 106
   intellectual property rights 121, 122
   law 83, 88, 89, 122
   race neutrality 83
   racial categorization 88, 89
   terms 82
   see also BiDil, case study (colorblindness); Nitromed, case study (colorblindness)
Patry, William 18, 270
Paul, Billie 219
Pedagogy of the Oppressed (Freire) 55
Pelosi, Nancy 65
Pendergrass, Teddy 219
Perdue, Donna 186
performance based specification 115
personalized medicine 80, 86, 94
Petrella, Paula 228
pharmaceutical drugs, access to 22, 87
   see also BiDil, case study (colorblindness); Nitromed, case study (colorblindness)
Philadelphia International Records 218–21
Phillips, Tito 212
Phillips, Victoria F. 27
Pigou, Arthur Cecil 216

PIIPA see Public Interest Intellectual Property Advisors (PIIPA)
PIPA (PROTECT IP Act) 141
piracy 239
   BRIC countries, as *sui generis* development model 244–5
   developing countries, defense of IP 243–4
   development stages 240–3
   as efficient development modality 255–7
   as market efficiency 253–8
"pitch competitions" 75
Plant, Sir Arnold 216
pluralism, racial 78, 93, 94
Porter, Eduardo 119
Posner, Richard A. 124, 216
Potoski, Matthew 95
poverty 65, 129, 149, 163, 248, 267
   global 261
   and public procurement 100, 104
Powell, John A. 90
Pozen, David E. 21, 23, 39
preferences 103
private ordering 126–8
pro bono obligations 133–5
Procter & Gamble 177
procurement see public procurement
product development, complexity 127
productive entrepreneurs 36
profit maximization motive 46, 77
property law 121
PST (professional, scientific and technical) services 69, 70, 72, 73, 74
Public Interest Intellectual Property Advisors (PIIPA) 167–87
   background 167–8
   beneficiaries 168
   case studies 176–84
      African Agricultural Technology Foundation (Kenya) 176
      Amazonlink.org (Brazilian NGO) 180
      Datadyne (Sub-Saharan Africa) 178, 185
      Fogarty Center (US), National Institutes of Health 180, 181
      Ganga Library, Inc 183–4
      Harvest Plus (international) 179

Ibero American Science and
    Technology Education
    Consortium (ISTEC),
    Americas and Iberian
    Peninsula 178–9
Ibis Reproductive Health
    (Zimbabwe and South
    Africa) 176
intellectual property audit for
    four selected Colombian
    agricultural businesses 183
International Alpaca Association
    (IAA), Peru 177
Kenya Wildlife Service (KWS)
    177–8
Latin America and the Caribbean
    (LAC), intellectual property
    and R&E in 182
liquids, device to safely mix in
    global health sector 184
Mycoguild (international) 177
National Institute for the
    Defense of Competition
    and Intellectual Property
    (INDECOPI), Peru 179–80
Navajo language digital
    preservation project 183
Nollywood (Nigeria/US) 164,
    180–1
PIIPA human development and
    intellectual property book
    181–2
World Intellectual Property
    Organization 181
dynamic nature of IP legal
    frameworks 166–7
global public interest intellectual
    property sectors
    added value of a global public
        interest IP network and
        clearing house 185
    agricultural technology 168–70
    biodiversity 170–71
    health care 172–4
    information technologies 175
    internet access 175
    open-source 175
    technology transfer and
        environment 174–5
    traditional knowledge 171–2

human development and intellectual
    property book 181–2
pro bono services 164, 168, 185,
    187
work on global public interest
    added value of a global public
        interest IP network and
        clearing house 185
    global community of public
        interest lifelong volunteers
        185–6
public procurement
    achieving intellectual property social
        justice 110–16
    budgets 112
    business development program 108
    case law
        Adams v. *Robertson* 110
        Adarand Constructors, Inc v. *Pena*
            108, 109–10
    empowerment and other social
        justice consideration in
        procurement of innovation
        114–16
    entrepreneurship
        definitions 108
        facilitating in innovation industry
            110–16
        obstacles to 108–10
        promotion of and strategic social
            entrepreneurship 107–10
    Federal government, role 104–7, 111,
        114
    inclusion of small, disadvantaged
        business in procurement
        markets 107–10
    innovation-implementation chasm
        113
    intellectual property illustration
        104–7
    performance based specification 115
    and power of the purse 99–100
    preferences 103–4
    purpose and goals 101–2
    set-asides 103–4
    small disadvantaged business
        certification program,
        controversy 108–10
    and social justice 103–4
    socio-economic impact 97–100

strategic
  expanding role 99
  in furtherance of social justice 101–7
  and promotion of IP social entrepreneurship 107–10
  structural changes to a government's industrial contractor base 104–7
  subcontracting incentives 103–4
  Supreme Court, role in *Adarand* case 109–10
  targeted support for IP empowerment in innovation industry 114
  wealth distribution 108
publicity rights xix–xx, 165
Putnam, Jonathan D. 123

race
  assimilation 92
  civil construction of a nation's shared purpose and racial categories 91
  inclusion in clinical trials 80, 83
  liberal theories 90, 91, 93
  policy evaluation and racial categories 91
  policy implementation and racial categories 91
racial discrimination 11, 12, 65
  and racial categorization in patent law 88, 89
  separate but equal facilities 76, 77
  see also Jim Crow racial discrimination laws
racial equality movement 13–14
"rainbow republicanism" 92
Rawls, Lou 219
redistributive justice 20
Reedy, E. J. 69
Reitz, John C. 265
remedial justice/action 18, 230
rennin-angiotensin system 82
replicative entrepreneurs 36
revenue and licensing activities, new business owners 71–3
Rhythm & Blues Foundation 221
risk assessment 47
Robb, Alicia M. 68
Robinson, David T. 68

Rockefeller, John D. 36, 45
Rodrik, D. 34
Roffe, Pedro 145
Rohter, Larry 57, 226
Rosen, Mark D. 88
Ruel, Michael D. 83
Russia 244

Sally Beauty Supply, LLC 16
Sandel, Michael J. 87
Santayana, George 158
Sarasvathy, S.D. 47
Say, Jean-Baptiste 36
SBA (Small Business Administration) 108, 109
Scafidi, Susan 93
Schechter, Roger 233
Schmidt, Charles W. 237
Schooner, Steven L. 101
Schramm, Carl 33, 41
Schuck, Peter H. 90
Schuler, Philip 150, 273
Schumpeter, J. A. 33, 41
SDBs (small disadvantaged businesses) 108, 110
Selfa, Lance 214
self-empowerment 21
Sell, Susan K. 140
Sen, Amartya 38, 77, 128, 129, 267
separate but equal principle, race 76, 77
service and professionalism
  duties of care 137–8
  legal education 135–7
  pro bono obligations 133–5
Service Oriented Architecture (SOA) 111
service sector 65
Seschillie, Krytle 183
set-asides 103
Shah, Sonali K. 69
Sharp, Ken 220
Sherman Rogers, W. 8, 21, 212
Shirk, W. Bruce 111
Shuchman, Lisa 16
Sidebottom, Diane M. 105
Simmons, Russell 222–5
Singapore 159, 239
Sinjela, Mpazi 142
Sirolli, E. 43

Sisman, Eugene 132
Slater, Derek 3, 274, 278
slavery 78, 103, 104
  chattel 9, 15
  economic empowerment and civil rights 12, 15–16
  and entrepreneurship approach, applying 52, 56
Sluby, Patricia Carter 6, 16
Small Business Act, Section 8(a) 108
Small Business Administration (SBA) 108, 109
small disadvantaged businesses (SDBs) 108, 110
Smart Grid 111
SMEs (small and medium-sized enterprises) 100
Smith, Adam 216
Smith, D. Gordon 119
Smith, K. Carl 215
Smith, Robert J. 6
Smith, Van 16
social action 7–8
social action platform, intellectual property 7, 8
  Intellectual Property Empowerment 8, 20–2
social capital 47
social change 46
  model 50–51
  strategies for 51–3
social contract theory 193
social entrepreneurship
  classical distinguished 25–6, 39–40
  and colorblindness 94
  ETE, applying to other IP empowerment contexts 28
  and Intellectual Property Empowerment 22–7
social justice
  vs. collateral policies 98
  definitions 212–13
  and economic justice 213
  and entrepreneurship 128–33, 211–13
  innovation industry 114–16
  intellectual property social justice, achieving 33–63
  vs. law and economics 215–17
  and public procurement 103–4

social justice centred-law and civil rights activism 5–8
strategic public procurement in furtherance of 101–7
  see also intellectual property social justice; unified theory of IP social justice
Social Network, The (film) 48
social utility objective 5, 18
socio-political economy, and intellectual property 267–70
SOPA (Stop Online Piracy Act) 141
South Korea 159, 239
Southern America, Reconstruction 9
  post-Reconstruction era 12
Spear, Roger 27
Spinelli, S. 47
Springfield, Illinois race riot (1908) 13
Startup America initiative 34–5
status quo, impulse to change 43, 44–6
Statute of Anne (1709) 193
STEM (science, technology, engineering, mathematics) 49, 75
Stevenson-Wydler Technology Innovation Act (1980) 107
Stiglitz, Joseph E. 267, 273
stigmatizing, designation of racial categories as 88, 89
Stockholm Protocol Regarding Developing Countries 158
Stop Online Piracy Act (SOPA) 141
Streitz, Wendy D. 155
Striga (witchweed) 176
Strom, R.J. 36–7
Strong, Barrett 33, 57–8, 225–33
Stuckey, Kent D. 1
subcontracting incentives 103
Sullivan, Otha Richard 22
Sunami, Atsushi 145
Sunder, Madahavi 7, 64, 130, 217, 269, 275
Survey of Business Owners (SBO), Census Bureau 66, 72

Takagi, Yo 142
Talented Tenth (educated blacks) 12, 26
  Talented Tenth Economic Uplift 23, 24, 25
tangible assets, ownership 65

Tansey, Geoff 145
Taussig, Frank William 216
tax shelter/trust advice 232
technology transfer and environment 174–5
ten Kate, Kerry 171
Tepperman, Andrew B. 123
termination rights, copyright 203–5
Thadeusz, Frank 239, 247
Thelen, Christine 247
Theory of Change 53–4
Three Degrees, The 219
Timmermann, Cristian 17
Timmons, J.A. 47
TIPGRFA (International Treaty for Plant Genetic Resources for Food and Agriculture) 166
Tolentino, Paz Estrella E. 256
trade secrets xv–xvi
Trademark Electronic Application System (TEAS) 124
trademarks xviii–xix, 131
  balancing public interest and private ownership 165
  definitions 67–8
  intellectual property rights 121, 122, 124
  PIIPA case studies 177
  purpose of laws 238
traditional knowledge and cultural expressions (TKE) of indigenous peoples, Western misappropriation 6–7, 21, 273
traditional knowledge (TK) 165, 171–2
training and education, IP
  business insights 157–8
  economic analysis 156–7
  global awareness 159–61
  historical appreciation 158–9
  limitations 146–8
  negotiation 155–6
  redesigning of programs 143–54
  skills and perspectives 155–61
transactional lawyering, US 127
transactional support exchange, individual 231–2
Trans-Pacific Partnership Free Trade Agreement 196
transparency principle, public procurement 101

Travis, Hannibal 14, 19
Trinity of Management 43
TRIPS Agreement (Agreement on Trade Aspects of Intellectual Property) 130, 141, 167, 173, 235, 244, 258
Trotter, Monroe 13
Troutt, David Dante 131
Trubek, David M. 14
TSM (teach, suggest, motivate) test 85

UNCTAD (United Nations Conference on Trade and Development) 158
unemployment, African Americans 65
UNESCO Convention on the Protection and Promotion of the Diversity of Cultural Expressions 149
UNESCO Convention on the Safeguarding of Intangible Cultural Heritage 149
unified communications 111
unified theory of IP social justice 265–79
  action, empowering 274–7
  applying 270–3
  changes, making 277–8
  intellectual property and socio-political economy 267–70
  see also intellectual property; social justice
unintended consequences, entrepreneurship 55, 56
United Nations Conference on Environment and Development, Rio (1992) 170
United Nations Conference on Trade and Development (UNCTAD) 158
United Nations Framework Convention on Climate Change 170, 174
United Nations Security Council (UNSC) 245
United States
  Constitution *see* Constitution, US
  as developing country 159
  inequality in 119
  IPR regime 123
  legal system 127

private property rights regimes 121–2
training and educational programs 151
United States Patent and Trademark Office (USPTO) 67, 81, 124, 128, 132, 134
  Law School Clinic Certification Pilot program 136
Universal Declaration of Human Rights 149
unproductive entrepreneurs 36
UPOV (International Union for the Protection of New Varieties of Plants) 166, 169, 182
USPTO *see* United States Patent and Trademark Office (USPTO)
utilitarian intellectual property rights 254–5

Venable LLP (US law firm) 186, 187
venue of change 50
Veteran's Administration (VA) 79
Vetter, Greg R. 276
Viagra 79
Vinson, Robert Trent 214
virtualization 111
vision, of social entrepreneur 43
visual impairment, and copyright laws 18
Vivas-Eugi, David 145

Warner-Chappell 220
Washington, Booker T. 12, 23, 52, 213, 214
  Equality through Economics philosophy 25, 26, 48
wealth maximization 92–3, 123
  see also profit maximization motive
Weijer, Charles 83
Weisbrot, Robert 9, 11
Weiser, Phil 35–6
Welton, Michael 55
Whitman, John 26, 27, 38
Whitney, Eli 56
Wildavsky, Aaron 46
Wilhelm, Anthony G. 3
William Mitchell College of Law, Intellectual Property Institute 136–7

Williams, Juan 11, 13, 14, 20
Wilson, Valerie R. 65
Winston Smith, Sheryl 69
WIPO *see* World Intellectual Property Organization (WIPO)
WIPO-Green 174–5
Wong, Mary W. S. 268
Wong, Tzen 166
Woods, Granville T. 17, 24
worker-owned cooperatives 39
World Health Organization (WHO)
  Essential Drugs and Medicines Policy 172
  Framework Convention on Tobacco Control (2003) 173–4
World Intellectual Property Organization (WIPO) 170
  Committee on Development and and Intellectual Property 175
  Development Agenda *see* Development Agenda (WIPO)
  formation as UN specialized agency 158
  General Assembly (2007) 143
  Intergovernmental Committee on Intellectual Property and Genetic Resources, Traditional Knowledge and Folklore (WIPO IGC Committee) 166, 171
  International Roundtables on WIPO Development Agenda for Academics 140, 143
  Secretariat 172
World Intellectual Property Report 156
World Trade Organization (WTO) 170, 247
  TRIPS Agreement 130, 141, 167, 173, 235, 244, 258
Wozniak, Steve 45
write of certiorari 109, 110
Wruuck, Patricia 3, 274, 278

Yaqub, Ohid 243, 247
Yu, Peter K. 141, 144, 146, 147, 148, 151, 152, 153, 154, 158, 159
Yunus, Muhammad 39

Zacharakis, S. 47
Zuckerberg, Mark 45